OSF/Motif™
Programmer's Guide

Revision 1.1

(For OSF/Motif Release 1.1)

Open Software Foundation

Prentice Hall, Englewood Cliffs, New Jersey 07632

Cover design
and cover illustration: **BETH FAGAN**

This book was formatted with troff

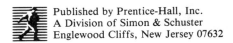 Published by Prentice-Hall, Inc.
A Division of Simon & Schuster
Englewood Cliffs, New Jersey 07632

Printed in the United States of America
10 9 8 7 6 5 4 3

ISBN 0-13-640673-4

Prentice-Hall International (UK) Limited, *London*
Prentice-Hall of Australia PTY. Limited, *Sydney*
Prentice-Hall Canada Inc., *Toronto*
Prentice-Hall Hispanoamericana, S.A., *Mexico*
Prentice-Hall of India Private Limited, *New Delhi*
Prentice-Hall of Japan, Inc., *Tokyo*
Simon & Schuster Asia Pte. Ltd., *Singapore*
Editora Prentice-Hall do Brasil, Ltda., *Rio de Janeiro*

Contents

List of Figures

List of Tables

Preface

This manual is a guide to programming using the various components of the OSF/Motif^{TM} environment; the toolkit, window manager, and user interface language.

Audience

This document is written for programmers who want to create applications in the OSF/Motif environment.

Contents

This document contains 23 chapters and 4 appendixes. Chapters 1 through 9 discuss the Motif^{TM} Toolkit. Chapters 10 through 16 discuss the Motif Window Manager (MWM). Chapters 17 through 23 discuss the User Interface Language (UIL) and Motif Resource Manager (MRM).

Appendix C   provides an alphabetical listing of the UIL arguments, their data type, and their equivalent name in the Motif Toolkit.

Appendix D   lists diagnostic messages issued by the UIL compiler and provides corrective action.

Typographical Conventions

This volume uses the following typographical conventions:

- **Boldfaced** strings represent literals; type them exactly as they appear.

- *Italicized* strings represent variables (for example, function or macro arguments).

- Ellipses (...) indicate that additional arguments are optional.

Chapter 1

Introduction to the OSF/Motif
Toolkit

1.1 The OSF/Motif Toolkit and the X Window System

The OSF/Motif Widget set is based on the Xt Intrinsics, a set of functions and procedures that provide quick and easy access to the lower levels of the X Window system. You can see from Figure 1-1 that the Motif Widget system is layered on top of the Xt Intrinsics, which in turn are layered on top of the X Window System, thus extending the basic abstractions provided by X.

Figure 1-1. User Interface Development Model

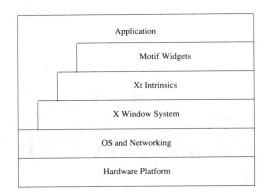

The Motif Widget system supports independent development of new or extended widgets. The Motif Widget system consists of a number of different widgets, each of which can be used independently or in combination to aid in creating complex applications. You can write applications faster and with fewer lines of code using the Motif Widgets; however, Motif Widgets require more memory than similar applications written without them.

This guide explains the individual widgets and shows you how to create and use these widgets in your applications.

1.2 Widget Classes and Hierarchy

Every widget is dynamically allocated and contains state information. Every widget belongs to one class, and each class has a structure that is statically allocated and initialized and contains operations for that class. Figure 1-2 shows the basic widget classes.

Figure 1-2. Basic Widget Class Hierarchy

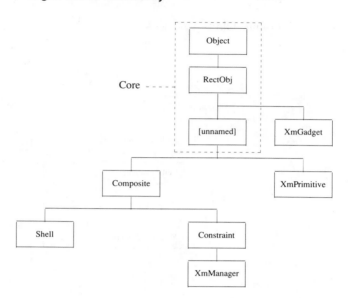

The basic class is the Core class. It contains resources that are inherited by all other classes. Two classes are layered beneath the Core class, the Composite class and the Primitive class. The Primitive class has no other classes beneath it, but the Composite class has two: the Constraint class and the Shell class. Each lower class can inherit some or all of the resources belonging to a higher class. For example, a Manager class widget can inherit some or all of the resources belonging to the Constraint class, the Composite class, and the Core class. You can find exactly what resources a given widget has by examining its manpage in the *OSF/Motif Programmer's Reference*.

This section has a number of hierarchy diagrams to help you understand how the widgets relate to each other. Figure 1-2 shows the highest level of widget classes. You can see that the Core class is composed of Object, RectObj, and an unnamed class. Core is the base class for all other widget classes.

Figure 1-3 shows the subclasses of the Primitive class.

Figure 1-3. Primitive Class Widgets

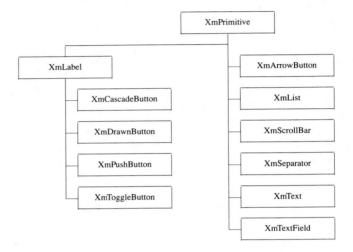

Figure 1-4 shows the Subclasses of the Shell class.

Figure 1-4. Shell Widgets

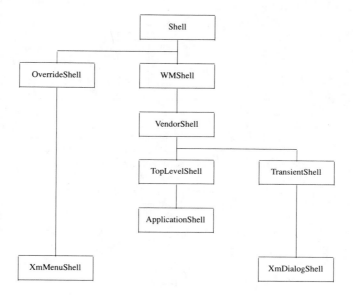

Figure 1-5 shows the Manager class widgets. Note from Figure 1-2 that Manager is a subclass of Composite and Constraint.

Figure 1-5. Manager Widgets

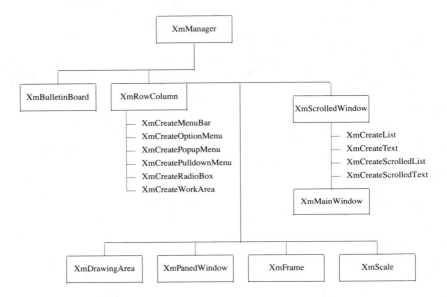

Figure 1-6 shows the Dialog widgets that are a subclass of Manager. Note that all of the Dialog widgets are subclasses of BulletinBoard. Also, note the convenience functions that are present. These are explained in detail in Chapter 5, ''Dialog Widgets and Functions.''

Figure 1-6. Dialog Widgets

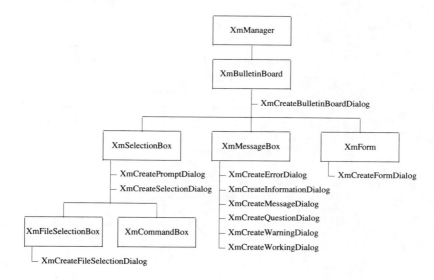

Figure 1-7 shows the gadgets that are an integral part of the Motif toolkit.

Figure 1-7. Gadgets

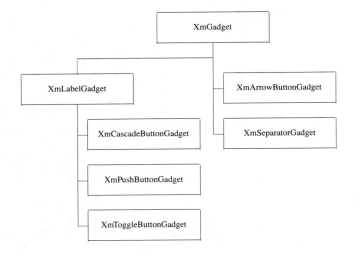

1.3 Compiling Sample Programs

There are a number of sample programs discussed throughout this guide. The source code for most of these programs can be found in the
./demos directory. There is also a Makefile in this directory that you can use to compile and link the programs. Follow this procedure to compile and link a program.

1. Copy the program source code file and the Makefile found in **./demos** to your work directory. Do not attempt to compile the program in the **./demos** directory.

2. Compile the program by executing the following command:

    make *programname*

3. If there is a defaults file commented into the beginning of the source code, move that defaults file to the **/usr/lib/X11/app-defaults** directory before you run the program.

Chapter 2

Widgets, Gadgets, and Convenience Functions

Motif has a variety of widgets and gadgets, each designed to accomplish a specific set of tasks, either individually or in combination with others. Convenience functions create certain widgets or sets of widgets for a specific purpose. This chapter explains widgets, gadgets, and convenience functions.

2.1 Widgets

Widgets are used either individually or in combination to make the creation of complex applications easier and faster. Some widgets display information, others are merely containers for other widgets. Some widgets are restricted to displaying information and do not react to keyboard or mouse input. Others change their display in response to input and can invoke functions when instructed to do so. You can customize some aspects of a widget, such as fonts, foreground and background colors, border widths and colors, and sizes.

An **instance** of a widget class is composed of a data structure containing values and procedures for that particular widget instance. There is also a class structure that contains values and procedures applicable to all widgets of that class.

Widgets are grouped into several classes, depending on the function of the widget. Logically, a widget class consists of the procedures and data associated with all widgets belonging to that class. These procedures and data can be inherited by subclasses. Physically, a widget class is a pointer to a structure. The contents of this structure are constant for all widgets of the widget class. A widget instance is allocated and initialized by **XmCreate***widgetname*, **XtCreateWidget**, or **XtCreateManagedWidget**. See Chapter 3, "Using Motif Widgets in Programs," for specific examples of creating widgets.

This section provides an overview of the available widgets. The manpages in the *OSF/Motif Programmer's Reference* contain detailed information for each of the widgets. The following figure shows how widgets might be combined in an application.

Figure 2-1. Widget Application Screen

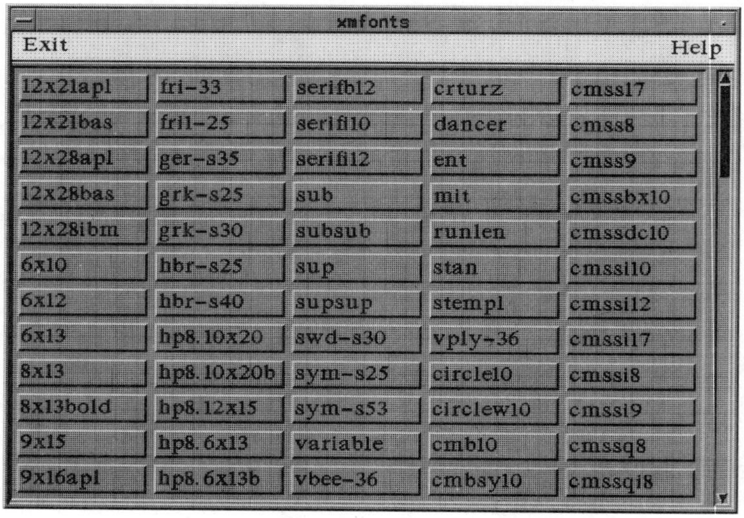

Several types of widgets are shown in Figure 2-1. The large window is a MainWindow widget containing a menu bar and some push buttons, a RowColumn widget with a number of push button gadgets, and a vertical scroll bar. The program that produces this window is called **xmfonts** and is described in Chapter 3.

The sections in this chapter divide the widgets into five categories as shown in the table below.

Table 2-1. Categories of Widgets

Class Name	Widget Class
Shell Widgets	
XmDialogShell	xmDialogShellWidgetClass
XmMenuShell	xmMenuShellWidgetClass
VendorShell	vendorShellWidgetClass
Display Widgets	
Core	widgetClass
XmPrimitive	xmPrimitiveWidgetClass
XmArrowButton	xmArrowButtonWidgetClass
XmDrawnButton	xmDrawnButtonWidgetClass
XmLabel	xmLabelWidgetClass
XmList	xmListWidgetClass
XmPushButton	xmPushButtonWidgetClass
XmScrollBar	xmScrollBarWidgetClass
XmSeparator	xmSeparatorWidgetClass
XmText	xmTextWidgetClass
XmTextField	xmTextFieldWidgetClass
XmToggleButton	xmToggleButtonWidgetClass

Class Name	Widget Class
Container Widgets	
XmManager	xmManagerWidgetClass
XmDrawingArea	xmDrawingAreaWidgetClass
XmFrame	xmFrameWidgetClass
XmMainWindow	xmMainWindowWidgetClass
XmPanedWindow	xmPanedWindowWidgetClass
XmRowColumn	xmRowColumnWidgetClass
XmScale	xmScaleWidgetClass
XmScrolledWindow	xmScrolledWindowWidgetClass
Dialog Widgets	
XmBulletinBoard	xmBulletinBoardWidgetClass
XmCommand	xmCommandWidgetClass
XmFileSelectionBox	xmFileSelectionBoxWidgetClass
XmForm	xmFormWidgetClass
XmMessageBox	xmMessageBoxWidgetClass
XmSelectionBox	xmSelectionBoxWidgetClass
Menu Widgets	
XmCascadeButton	xmCascadeButtonWidgetClass

2.1.1 Shell Widgets

Shell widgets are top-level widgets that provide the necessary interface with the window manager. Different Shell widget classes are provided for the various categories of top-level widgets. The Xt Intrinsics provide some underlying shells and the Motif toolkit provides the remaining shells. The Xt Intrinsics provide the following shell classes:

- **Shell** - This is the base class for shell widgets. It is a subclass of Composite and provides resources for all other types of shells.

- **OverrideShell** - This class is used for shell windows that completely bypass the window manager. It is a subclass of Shell.

- **WMShell** - This class contains resources that are necessary for the common window manager protocol. It is a subclass of Shell.

- **VendorShell** - This class contains resources used by vendor-specific window managers. It is a subclass of WMShell.

- **TransientShell** - This class is used for shell windows that can be manipulated by the window manager but cannot be iconified. It is a subclass of VendorShell.

- **TopLevelShell** - This class is used for normal top-level windows. It is a subclass of VendorShell.

- **ApplicationShell** - This class is used for an application's top-level window. It is a subclass of TopLevelShell.

The classes Shell, WMShell, and VendorShell are internal and cannot be instantiated.

The Motif toolkit provides the following widgets:

XmDialogShell (xmDialogShellWidgetClass)
> The DialogShell widget class is a subclass of TransientShell. Instances of this class are used as the parents of modal and modeless Dialogs associated with other top-level windows. DialogShell provides proper communication with the Motif window manager in accordance with the *Inter-Client Communications Conventions Manual* (ICCCM) for secondary top-level windows, such as Dialogs. See Chapter 5, "Dialog Widgets," for more information about how this widget is used.

XMenuShell (xmMenuShellWidgetClass)
> The MenuShell widget class is a subclass of OverrideShell. Instances of this class are used as the parents of menu panes. See Chapter 6, "Menus," for the specifications of menu widgets and menu shells.

VendorShell (vendorShellWidgetClass)
> The VendorShell widget class is a subclass of WMShell. It provides the common state information and services needed by the window-manager visible shells. See Chapter 4, "Shell Widgets," for more information.

2.1.2 Display Widgets

NOTE: A complete list of resources for each class can be found in the appropriate man page in the *OSF/Motif Programmer's Reference*. Motif provides the following display widgets:

Core (widgetClass)

The Core class is used as a supporting superclass for other widget classes. It provides common resources that are needed by all widgets, including x and y location, height, width, window border width, and so on.

XmPrimitive (xmPrimitiveWidgetClass)

The XmPrimitive class is also used as a supporting superclass for other widget classes. It provides resources for border drawing and highlighting, traversal activation and deactivation, and so on.

XmArrowButton (xmArrowButtonWidgetClass)

The ArrowButton widget consists of a directional arrow surrounded by a border shadow. When the arrow button is selected, the shadow moves to give the appearance that the arrow button has been pressed. When the arrow button is unselected, the shadow moves to give the appearance that the arrow button is released, or out. The arrow button has the same functionality as the push button. The following figure shows four arrow buttons arranged within a RowColumn widget.

Figure 2-2. ArrowButtons

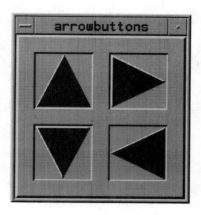

The direction of the arrow is specified by setting the **XmNarrowDirection** resource to the appropriate value. The spacing between the ArrowButtons in Figure 2-2 was obtained by setting the RowColumn resources **XmNmarginWidth**, **XmNmarginHeight**, and **XmNspacing** to 20.

XmDrawnButton (xmDrawnButtonWidgetClass)

The DrawnButton widget consists of an empty widget window surrounded by a shadow border. It provides the application developer with a graphics area that can have the input semantics of push buttons.

Callback types are defined for widget exposure and resize to allow the application to redraw or reposition its graphics. If the DrawnButton widget has a highlight and shadow thickness, the application should take care not to draw in this area. This can be done by creating the graphics context to be used for drawing in the widget with a clipping rectangle. The clipping rectangle should take into account the size of the widget's highlight thickness and shadow.

XmLabel (xmLabelWidgetClass)

A Label widget consists of either text or graphics. It can be instantiated but it is also used as a superclass for button widgets. A label's text is a compound string and can be multidirectional, multiline, multifont, or any combination of these. A label is considered static because it does not accept any button or key input other than the help button on the widget. The help callback is the only callback defined for Label.

XmList (xmListWidgetClass)

The List widget allows you to make a selection from a list of items. The application defines an array of compound strings, each of which becomes an item in the list. You can set the number of items in the list that are to be visible. You can also choose to have the list appear with a scroll bar so that you can scroll through the list of items. Items are selected by moving the pointer to the desired item and pressing the mouse button or key defined as select. The selected item is displayed in inverse colors. The following figure shows the List Widget.

Figure 2-3. List Widget

XmPushButton(xmPushButtonWidgetClass)

The PushButton widget consists of a text label or pixmap surrounded by a border shadow. You select the button by moving the mouse cursor to the button and pressing mouse button 1. When the mouse button is pressed, the widget and shadow colors will invert, giving the appearance that the push button has been pressed. When the mouse button is released, the colors will revert to the original color scheme, giving the appearance that the push button is out. Push buttons are used to invoke actions, such as run, cancel, stop, and so on.

XmScrollBar (xmScrollBarWidgetClass)

The ScrollBar widget allows you to view data that is too large to be viewed in its entirety. Scroll bars are combined with a widget that contains the data to be viewed. When you interact with the scroll bar, the data scrolls. The viewable portion of the data is called the work area.

A scroll bar consists of two arrows pointing in opposite directions at each end of a small rectangle. The rectangle is called the **scroll region**. A smaller rectangle called a slider is positioned within the scroll region. The slider is normally colored to contrast with that of the scroll region. The ratio of the slider size to the scroll region size corresponds to the relationship between the visible data and the total data. For example, if 10 percent of the data is visible in the work area, the slider takes up 10 percent of the scroll region.

You may place the scroll bar horizontally, vertically, or both. Horizontal scroll bars are placed at the bottom edge of the work area and vertical scroll bars are placed on the right edge. The ScrollBar widget is shown in the following figure.

Figure 2-4. ScrollBars

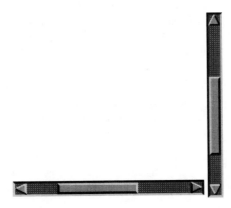

XmSeparator (xmSeparatorWidgetClass)

Separator is a primitive widget to be used as an item separator placed between items in a display. Several different line-drawing styles are provided as well as horizontal or vertical orientation.

The line drawing done within the separator is automatically centered within the height of the widget for a horizontal orientation, and centered within the width of the widget for a vertical orientation.

The XmNseparatorType of XmNO_LINE is provided as an escape to the application programmer who needs a different style of drawing. A pixmap the height of the widget can be created and used as the background pixmap by building an argument list using the XmNbackgroundPixmap argument type as defined by Core. Whenever the widget is redrawn, its background containing the desired separator drawing is displayed.

XmText (xmTextWidgetClass)

The Text widget provides a single-line or multiline text editor that has a user and programmer interface that you can customize. It can be used for single-line string entry, forms entry with verification procedures, multipage document viewing, and full-screen editing. The following figure shows the Text widget.

Figure 2-5. Text Widget

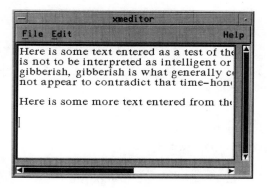

XmTextField (xmTextFieldWidgetClass)

The TextField widget is similar to the Text widget, but is restricted to and optimized for single-line text editing. As with the Text widget, you can customize the user and programmer interface.

XmToggleButton (xmToggleButtonWidgetClass)

This widget consists of a text or graphics button face with an indicator (a square or diamond-shaped box) placed to the left of the text or graphics. Select the toggle button by moving the mouse cursor inside the rectangle and pressing mouse button 1. The indicator is then filled with the selection color, indicating that the toggle button is selected. Toggle buttons are used for setting nontransitory data within an application. The following figure shows Toggle Buttons.

Figure 2-6. ToggleButtons

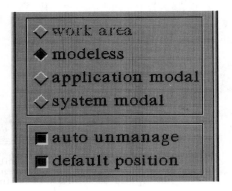

2.1.3 Container Widgets

Container widgets are Composite widgets that provide applications with general layout functionality. Since they are Composite widgets, Container widgets can have children. All of the container widgets are built from the Core, Composite, Constraint, and XmManager widget classes.

Motif provides the following container widgets:

XmManager (xmManagerWidgetClass)

The XmManager class is a Motif widget meta class and is therefore never instantiated as a widget. Its sole purpose is to act as a supporting superclass for other widget classes. It supports the visual resources, graphics contexts, and traversal resources necessary for the graphics and traversal mechanisms. XmManager is built from Core, Composite, and Constraint.

XmDrawingArea (xmDrawingAreaWidgetClass)

The DrawingArea widget is an empty widget that easily adapts to a variety of purposes. DrawingArea does no drawing and defines no behavior except for invoking callbacks. Callbacks notify the application when graphics need to be drawn (exposure events or widget resize), and when the widget receives input from the keyboard or mouse. Applications are responsible for defining appearance and behavior as needed in response to DrawingArea callbacks.

DrawingArea is a Composite widget and is a subclass of XmManager. It supports minimal geometry management for multiple widget or gadget children.

XmFrame (xmFrameWidgetClass)

The XmFrame widget is a manager used to enclose a single child within a border drawn by the XmFrame widget. It is most often used to enclose other Managers when it is desired to have the same border appearance for the XmManager and XmPrimitive widgets it manages.

XmMainWindow (xmMainWindowWidgetClass)

The XmMainWindow widget provides a standard layout for the primary window of an application. This layout includes a menu bar, a command window, a work region, and scroll bars. Any or all of these areas are optional. The work region and scroll bars in the main window behave exactly the same as their counterparts in the ScrolledWindow widget. You can think of the main window as an extended scrolled window with an optional menu bar and an optional command window.

In a fully loaded main window, the menu bar spans the top of the window horizontally. The command window spans the main window horizontally and is placed just below the menu bar. Any space below the command window is managed exactly the same as the scrolled window. To create a fully loaded main window, you create a menu bar, a command window, two scroll bars (one horizontal and one vertical), and a widget to use as the work region. You then call **XmMainWindowSetAreas** with those widget IDs.

XmRowColumn (xmRowColumnWidgetClass)

The RowColumn widget is a general-purpose RowColumn manager capable of containing any widget type as a child. It requires no special knowledge about how its children function and provides nothing above and beyond support for several different layout styles.

The type of layout performed is controlled by how the application has set the various layout resources. It can be configured to lay out its children in either a row or a column fashion. In addition, the application can specify whether the children should be packed tightly together (not into organized rows and columns), or whether each child should be placed in an identically sized box (thus producing a symmetrical look), or whether specific layout should be done (the current x and y positions of the children control their location).

In addition, the application has control over both the spacing that occurs between each row and column, and the margin spacing between the edges of the RowColumn widget and any children that are placed against it.

The RowColumn widget has no 3-dimensional visuals associated with it. If you want an application to have a 3-dimensional shadow placed around the RowColumn widget, then you should create the RowColumn widget as a child of a Frame widget. The following figure shows the RowColumn widget.

Figure 2-7. RowColumn Widget

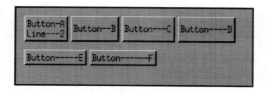

XmScale (xmScaleWidgetClass)

The Scale widget has two basic functions.

- It is used by an application to indicate a value from within a range of values.

- It allows the user to input or modify a value from the same range.

A Scale widget allows you to select a value from a range of displayed values by adjusting an arrow to a position along a line. A scale has an elongated rectangular region similar to that of a scroll bar. Inside this region is a slider that is used to indicate the current value along the scale. You can modify the value of the scale by moving the slider within the rectangular region of the scale. A scale can also include a set of labels and "tick marks" located outside of the scale region. These can be used to indicate the relative value at various positions along the scale.

A scale can be either input and output or output only. An input/output scale is one whose value can be set by the application and also modified by the user by using the slider. An output-only scale is one that is used strictly as an indicator of the current value of something and cannot be modified interactively by the user. The Core resource **XmNsensitive** is used to specify whether the user can interactively modify the value of the scale. Figure 2-8 shows the Scale widget.

Figure 2-8. Scale Widget

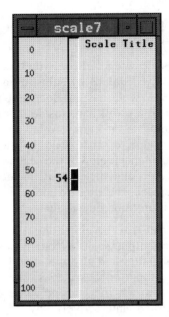

XmScrolledWindow (xmScrolledWindowWidgetClass)

The ScrolledWindow widget combines one or more scroll bar widgets and a viewing area to implement a visible window onto some other (usually larger) data display. The visible part of the window can be scrolled through the larger display by the use of scroll bars.

To use the scrolled window, an application first creates a ScrolledWindow widget, the needed ScrollBar widgets, and a widget capable of displaying any desired data as the work area of the scrolled window. The scrolled window will position the work area widget and display the scroll bars if so requested. When the user performs some action on the scroll bar, the application will be notified through the normal scroll bar callback interface.

The scrolled window can be configured to operate in an automatic manner, so that it performs all scrolling and display actions with no need for application program involvement. It can also be configured to provide a minimal support framework in which the application is responsible for processing all user input and making all visual changes to the displayed data in response to that input.

When the scrolled window is performing automatic scrolling, it will create a clipping window. Conceptually, this window becomes the viewport through which the user examines the larger underlying data area. The application simply creates the desired data, then makes that data the work area of the scrolled window. When the user moves the slider to change the displayed data, the workspace is moved under the viewing area so that a new portion of the data becomes visible.

There are situations where it is impractical for an application to create a large data space and simply display it through a small clipping window. An example of this is a text editor — there would be an undesirable amount of overhead involved with creating a single data area that consisted of a large file. The application should use the concept of a scrolled window (a small viewport onto some larger data), but it should be notified when the user scrolls the viewport so it can bring in more data from storage and update the display area. For this situation, the scrolled window can be configured so that it provides only visual layout support. No clipping window is created and the application must maintain the data displayed in the work area as well as respond to user input on the scroll bars. The following figure shows a scrolled window with some text in it. Note that the scroll bars indicate that scrolling is possible either vertically or horizontally.

Figure 2-9. ScrolledWindow Widget

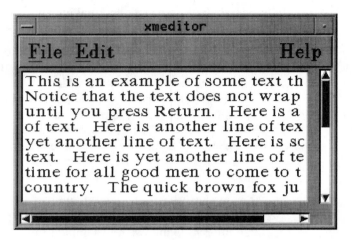

Figure 2-10 shows the same window after partially scrolling down. Compare the positions of the vertical scroll bar and the text with those of Figure 2-9.

Figure 2-10. ScrolledWindow After Scrolling

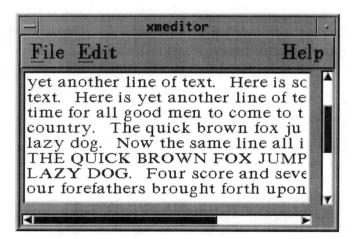

XmPanedWindow (xmPanedWindowWidgetClass)

The PanedWindow manager widget is a Composite widget that lays out children in a vertically tiled format. Children appear from top to bottom, with the first child inserted appearing at the top of the PanedWindow manager and the last child inserted appearing at the bottom. The PanedWindow manager will grow to match the width of its widest child, and all other children are forced to this width. The height of the PanedWindow manager will be equal to the sum of the heights of all its children, the spacing between them, and the size of the top and bottom margins.

The PanedWindow manager widget is also a constraint widget, which means that it creates and manages a set of constraints for each child. You can specify a minimum and maximum size for each pane. The PanedWindow manager will not allow a pane to be resized below its minimum size nor beyond its maximum size. Also, when the minimum size of a pane is equal to its maximum size, then no control sash will be presented for that pane or for the lowest pane. The following figure shows an example of a PanedWindow widget with three arrow buttons as its children.

Figure 2-11. PanedWindow Widget

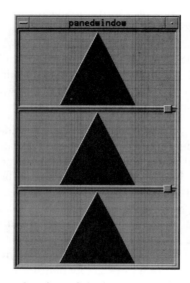

You can adjust the size of the panes. To facilitate this adjustment, a pane control sash is created for most children. The sash appears as a square box positioned on the bottom of the pane that it controls (see Figure 2-11). You can adjust the size of a pane by using the mouse. Position the pointer inside the sash and a crosshair appears. Press and hold mouse button 1 and the pointer changes to an arrow pointing up and down. Continue holding mouse button 1 down while you move the pointer to achieve the desired size of the pane. Release mouse button 1 and the panes will be resized. Figure 2-12 shows the PanedWindow after a pane has been resized.

Figure 2-12. PanedWindow Widget After Pane Resizing

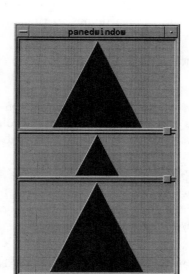

2.1.4 Dialog Widgets

Dialog widgets are container widgets that provide applications with layout functionality typically used for pop-up dialogs. These widgets are used for interaction tasks such as displaying messages, setting properties, and providing selection from a list of items. Dialog widgets are thus used primarily as an interface between the user and the application. A Dialog widget will normally ask a question or present the user with some information that requires a response. In some cases, the application will be suspended until the user provides the response.

A **Dialog** is a collection of widgets, including a dialog shell, a bulletin board (or subclass of BulletinBoard or some other container widget), plus various children of the bulletin board, such as the Label, PushButton, and Text widgets. All of the dialog widgets are built from the Core, Composite, Constraint, and Manager widget classes.

The collection of widgets that compose a Dialog can be built from scratch by building up the necessary argument lists and creating each individual widget in the Dialog. For common interaction tasks, **convenience functions** are defined that create the collection of widgets that comprise a particular dialog. The collections of widgets created by Dialog convenience functions are referred to as **Convenience Dialogs**.

Convenience Dialogs are either modal or modeless. A modal dialog stops the work session and solicits input from the user. A modeless dialog solicits input from the user, but does not interrupt interaction with any application.

Each dialog has one or more convenience functions that create any of the subwidgets in that dialog. For example, a message box has several convenience functions:

- **XmCreateMessageDialog**
- **XmCreateErrorDialog**
- **XmCreateInformationDialog**
- **XmCreateQuestionDialog**
- **XmCreateWarningDialog**
- **XmCreateWorkingDialog**

Each of these convenience functions creates a dialog shell and a message box. Refer to Chapter 5, "Dialog Widgets and Functions," and the individual manpages for more information.

2.1.5 Dialog Widget Descriptions

The following list gives an overview of the Dialog widget set. See the next section for an overview of the convenience dialogs.

XmBulletinBoard (xmBulletinBoardWidgetClass)
> The BulletinBoard widget is a composite widget that provides simple geometry management for children widgets. It does not force positioning on its children, but can be set to reject geometry requests that would result in overlapping children. The bulletin board is the base widget for most dialog widgets, but is also used as a general container widget.

XmCommand (xmCommandWidgetClass)
> The Command widget is a subclass of SelectionBox that includes a command history region and a command input region. The Command widget also provides a command history mechanism.

XmFileSelectionBox (xmFileSelectionBox WidgetClass)
> The FileSelectionBox widget is a subclass of SelectionBox and BulletinBoard used to get a selection from a list of alternatives. FileSelectionBox includes an editable text field for the directory mask, scrolling lists of filenames and directories, and an editable text field for the selected file. Four buttons are available: **OK**, **Filter**, **Cancel**, and **Help** by default.

XmForm (xmFormWidgetClass)
> The Form widget is a constraint-based manager that provides a layout language used to establish spatial relationships between its children. It maintains these relationships when the form is resized, new children are added to the form, or its children are resized, unmanaged, remanaged, or destroyed. Since it is a subclass of BulletinBoard, a form includes the base level of dialog support. Form can also be used as a general container widget.

XmMessageBox (xmMessageBoxWidgetClass)
> The MessageBox widget is a subclass of BulletinBoard used to give information to the user. A message box includes a symbol and a message. Three buttons are available: **OK**, **Cancel**, and **Help** by default.

XmSelectionBox (xmSelectionBoxWidgetClass)
> The SelectionBox widget is a subclass of BulletinBoard used to get a selection from a list of alternatives. A selection box includes a message, an editable text field, and a scrolling list of choices. Four buttons are available: **OK**, **Cancel**, **Apply**, and **Help** by default.

2.1.6 Convenience Dialogs

Convenience dialogs are collections of widgets that can be created by using convenience functions. Each convenience dialog instantiates a dialog widget as a child of a dialog shell. This section lists the convenience dialogs.

BulletinBoardDialog
> The BulletinBoardDialog convenience function instantiates a bulletin board and a dialog shell. The BulletinBoardDialog is used for interactions not supported by the standard dialog set. Necessary dialog components are added as children of the BulletinBoard.

ErrorDialog
> The ErrorDialog convenience function instantiates a message box and a dialog shell. The ErrorDialog is used to warn the user of an invalid or potentially dangerous condition. ErrorDialog includes a symbol and a message. Three buttons are available: **OK**, **Cancel**, and **Help**p by default. The default ErrorDialog symbol is a hexagon with a hand inside.

FileSelectionDialog

The FileSelectionDialog convenience function instantiates a file selection box and a dialog shell. The FileSelectionDialog is used to select a file. FileSelectionDialog includes an editable text field for the directory mask, scrolling lists of filenames and directories, and an editable text field for the selected file. Four buttons are available: **OK**, **Filter**, **Cancel**, and **Help** by default.

FormDialog

The FormDialog convenience function instantiates a form and a dialog shell. The FormDialog is used for interactions not supported by the standard dialog set. Necessary dialog components are added as children of the form.

InformationDialog

The InformationDialog convenience function instantiates a message box and a dialog shell. The InformationDialog is used to give information to the user, such as the status of an action. InformationDialog includes a symbol and a message. Three buttons are available: **OK**, **Cancel**, and **Help** by default. The default InformationDialog symbol is a square icon with an ''i'' in the center.

MessageDialog

The MessageDialog convenience function instantiates a message box and a dialog shell. The MessageDialog is used to give information to the user. MessageDialog may include a symbol and a message. There is no symbol by default. Three buttons are available: **OK**, **Cancel**, and **Help** by default.

PromptDialog

The PromptDialog convenience function instantiates a selection box and a dialog shell. The PromptDialog is used to prompt the user for text input. PromptDialog includes a message and a text input region. Four buttons are available: **OK**, **Apply**, **Cancel**, and **Help** by default.

QuestionDialog

The QuestionDialog convenience function instantiates a message box and a dialog shell. The Question Dialog is used to get the answer to a question from the user. QuestionDialog includes a symbol and a message. Three buttons are available: **OK**, **Cancel**, and **Help** by default. A ''?'' is the default QuestionDialog symbol.

SelectionDialog

The SelectionDialog convenience function instantiates a selection box and a dialog shell. The SelectionDialog is used to get a selection from a list of alternatives. SelectionDialog includes a message, an editable text field, and a scrolling list of choices. Four buttons are available: **OK**, **Apply**, **Cancel**, and **Help** by default.

WarningDialog

The WarningDialog convenience function instantiates a message box and a dialog shell. The WarningDialog is used to warn the user of the consequences of an action, and give the user a choice of resolutions. WarningDialog includes a symbol and a message. Three buttons are available: **OK**, **Cancel**, and **Help** by default. A ''!'' is the default WarningDialog symbol.

WorkingDialog

The WorkingDialog convenience function instantiates a message box and a dialog shell. The WorkingDialog is used to inform users that there is a time-consuming operation in progress and allow them to cancel the operation. WorkingDialog includes a symbol and a message. Three buttons are available: **OK**, **Cancel**, and **Help** by default. The WorkingDialog symbol is a square icon with an hourglass in the center.

2.1.7 Menu Widgets

The RowColumn widget is the basis for most of the menu system components. It has a built-in ability to behave like a RowColumn manager, a radio box, a menu bar, a pull-down menu pane, a pop-up menu pane, and an option menu. Convenience functions have been provided to easily create these special versions of the RowColumn widget.

The Motif menu system is composed of the following widgets and convenience functions:

- XmRowColumn (Widget)

- MenuBar   (Convenience Function)

- OptionMenu (Convenience Function)

- Pulldown Menupane (Convenience Function)

- Popup Menupane (Convenience Function)

- XmMenuShell   (Widget)

- XmCascadeButton (Widget and Gadget)

- XmSeparator   (Widget and Gadget)

- XmLabel   (Widget and Gadget)

- XmToggleButton   (Widget and Gadget)

- XmPushButton (Widget and Gadget)

Applications are not required to use all of these components when using the menu system.

2.2 Gadgets

Gadgets provide essentially the same functionality as the equivalent primitive widgets. The primary motivation behind providing a set of gadgets is to improve performance, both in execution time and data space. This applies to both the application and server processes and minimizes the amount of lost functionality. The performance difference between widgets and gadgets is dramatic, so it is highly recommended that applications use gadgets whenever possible.

Gadgets can be thought of as windowless widgets. This means that they do not have windows, translations, actions, or pop-up children. Also, gadgets do not have any of the visual resources found in the XmPrimitive class for primitive widgets. These visuals are referenced by a gadget from its parent.

Examples of display gadgets include buttons, labels and separators. All of these gadgets are built from the classes of Object, RectObj, and XmGadget. The table below shows the gadgets and their class names.

Table 2-2. Gadgets

Gadget Name	Gadget Class
Object	objectClass
RectObj	rectObjClass
XmGadget	xmGadgetClass
XmArrowButtonGadget	xmArrowButtonGadgetClass
XmSeparatorGadget	xmSeparatorGadgetClass
XmLabelGadget	xmLabelGadgetClass
XmCascadeButtonGadget	xmCascadeButtonGadgetClass
XmPushButtonGadget	xmPushButtonGadgetClass
XmToggleButtonGadget	xmToggleButtonGadgetClass

The following list provides an overview of the set of display gadgets.

Object (objectClass)

> The Object class is an Xt Intrinsics meta class and is therefore never instantiated. It is used as a supporting superclass to provide common resources to other classes.

RectObj (rectObjClass)

> The RectObj class is an Xt Intrinsics meta class and is therefore never instantiated. It is used as a supporting superclass to provide common resources to other classes.

XmGadget (xmGadgetClass)

> XmGadget is a Motif meta class and is therefore never instantiated. It is used as a supporting superclass to provide common resources to other gadget classes.

XmArrowButtonGadget (xmArrowButtonGadgetClass)

> An arrow button gadget has the same functionality as a push button gadget, but displays a directional arrow within itself.

XmSeparatorGadget (xmSeparatorGadgetClass)

> A separator gadget is used to provide a visual separation between groups of widgets. It can draw horizontal and vertical lines in several different styles.

XmLabelGadget (xmLabelGadgetClass)

> A label gadget consists of either text or graphics. It can be instantiated, but it is also used as a superclass for button widgets. The label gadget's text is a compound string and can be multidirectional, multiline, multifont, or any combination of these. The Label gadget is considered static because it does not accept any button or key input other than the Help button on the widget. The help callback is the only callback defined for the Label gadget.

XmCascadeButtonGadget (xmCascadeButtonGadgetClass)

Cascade button gadgets appear in MenuBars or in Popup or Pulldown MenuPanes. A cascade button gadget usually has an associated submenu. When the gadget is armed, by moving the pointer over the gadget and pressing a mouse button, its appearance becomes three dimensional and it displays its submenu. When the gadget is activated, by releasing the mouse button while the pointer is over the gadget or by pressing a mnemonic key, the submenu remains posted. A cascade button gadget has a text or graphical label and, when in a menu, an arrow indicator to the right of the text or graphics that points to the area where the submenu is displayed.

XmPushButtonGadget (xmPushButtonGadgetClass)

Push button gadgets are used to issue commands within an application. A push button gadget displays a label with a border-shadowing graphic. When the push button is selected, the shadow moves to give the appearance that the push button has been pressed. When the push button is unselected, the shadow moves to give the appearance that the push button is out.

XmToggleButtonGadget (xmToggleButtonGadgetClass)

A toggle button gadget consists of a text or graphics button face with an indicator (a square or diamond-shaped box) placed to the left of the text or graphics. You select the toggle button gadget by placing the mouse cursor inside the rectangle and pressing mouse button 1. The indicator is then filled with the selection color, indicating that the toggle button gadget is selected. Toggle button gadgets are used for setting nontransitory data within an application.

2.3 Convenience Functions

Convenience functions are functions that enable you to create certain widgets or gadgets, or groups of widgets or gadgets, by making just one function call. A convenience function creates a predetermined set of widgets and returns the parent widget's ID. Convenience functions are of the form:

XmCreate*WidgetName*

for widgets and gadgets other than Dialog widgets. For dialogs, convenience functions are referred to as **convenience dialogs,** and are of the form:

XmCreate*DialogWidgetName***Dialog**

It is very easy to use a convenience function to create a widget. For example, you can use the following code segment to create a Label widget:

Widget XmCreateLabel *(parent,name,arglist,argcount)*

Widget *parent;*
String *name;*
Arglist *arglist;*
Cardinal *argcount;*

parent	Specifies the parent widget for the Label.
name	Specifies the resource name for the Label. This name is used for retrieving resources, and therefore it should not be the same as any widget that is a child of the same parent, unless identical resource values are to be used for the child widgets.
arglist	Specifies the argument list used to override the default values for the Label's resources.
argcount	Specifies the number of arguments in the arglist.

The **XmCreate***WidgetName* functions create unmanaged widgets. Your application must manage the set of widgets before they will be displayed. You can manage each widget separately or as a group. Use this code segment to create and manage each widget separately:

```
Widget w;

w = XmCreate<widgetname>(parent,  name,
                         arglist,  argcount);
XtManageChild(w);
```

Use this code segment to create and manage widgets with the same parent as a group:

```
int child_count = 0;
Widget w[10];

w[child_count++] = XmCreate<widgetname>(parent,
                       name, arglist, argcount);
w[child_count++] = XmCreate<widgetname>(parent,
                       name, arglist, argcount);
w[child_count++] = XmCreate<widgetname>(parent,
                       name, arglist, argcount);
                                      .
                                      .
                                      .

XtManageChildren(w, child_count);
```

Chapter 3
Using Motif Widgets in Programs

This chapter explains how to write applications that use the Motif Widgets. Writing application programs involves nine steps, as shown in Table 3-1.

Table 3-1. Steps in Writing Widget Programs

Step	Description	Related Functions
1	Include required header files.	**#include <X11/Intrinsic.h>** **#include <Xm/Xm.h>** **#include <Xm/***widget***.h>**
2	Initialize Xt Intrinsics.	**XtAppInitialize()**
3	Add additional top-level windows.	**XtAppCreateShell()**
	Do steps 4 through 6 for each widget.	
4	Set up argument lists for widget.	**XtSetArg()**
5	Create widget.	**XtCreateManagedWidget()** or **XmCreate**<*WidgetName*> followed by **XtManageChild(***widget***)**
6	Add callback routines.	**XtAddCallback()**
7	Realize widgets and loop.	**XtRealizeWidget(***parent***)** **XtAppMainLoop()**
8	Link relevant libraries.	**cc -o***application application.***c ** **-lXm -lXt -lX11 -lPW**
9	Create defaults files.	**/usr/lib/X11/app-defaults/***class* **$HOME/.Xdefaults**

Sections 3.2 through 3.9 of this chapter describe each of the steps shown in the table, except Step 3, which is covered in Section 3.12. The sample code segments of each section build a simple widget program (called **xmbutton**) that implements a PushButton widget. Section 3.1 provides background that introduces the **xmbutton** program.

NOTE: This chapter assumes you have a working knowledge of the C programming language. In particular, you should be familiar with pointers and structures. If you are not, be sure to study a book on programming with C. Books on the topic are widely available in computer bookstores.

3.1 Introduction to the xmbutton Program

This section shows the widget tree diagram, code listing, and defaults file for the **xmbutton** program, as well as the output produced by the program.

3.1.1 Widget Tree Diagram for the xmbutton Program

The following figure shows a widget tree for the **xmbutton** widget.

Figure 3-1. xmbutton Widget Tree

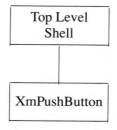

3.1.2 Program Listing for xmbutton.c

The listing shown in this section, **xmbutton.c**, is for the **xmbutton** widget program.

```
/**-------------------------------------------------------------
***
***   file:          xmbutton.c
***
***   project:  Motif Widgets example programs
***
***   description:  This program creates a PushButton widget.
***
***
***        (c) Copyright 1989 by Open Software Foundation, Inc.
***            All Rights Reserved.
***
***        (c) Copyright 1989 by Hewlett-Packard Company.
***
***-------------------------------------------------------------*/


/*   include files   */

#include <X11/Intrinsic.h>
#include <Xm/Xm.h>
#include <Xm/PushB.h>


/*   functions defined in this program   */

void main();
void activateCB(); /* Callback for the PushButton */


/*   global variables   */

char *btn_text;   /* button label pointer for compound string */
```

```
/*----------------------------------------------------------
** main - main logic for demo1 program
*/
void main (argc,argv)
unsigned int argc;
char **argv;
{
  Widget  toplevel; /*  Shell widget  */
  Widget  button;  /*  PushButton widget  */
  XtAppContext app_context; /* application context */
  Arg  args[10]; /*  arg list      */
  register int n;  /*  arg count      */

/*  initialize toolkit  */
  toplevel =
          XtAppInitialize(&app_context, "XMdemos", NULL,
              0, &argc, argv, NULL, NULL, 0);

/*  create compound string for the button text  */
  btn_text =
    XmStringCreateLtoR("Push Here", XmSTRING_DEFAULT_CHARSET);

/*  set up arglist  */
  n = 0;
  XtSetArg (args[n], XmNlabelString, btn_text);  n++;
  XtSetArg (args[n], XmNwidth, 250);  n++;
  XtSetArg (args[n], XmNheight, 150);  n++;
/*  create button  */
  button =
    XtCreateManagedWidget ("button", xmPushButtonWidgetClass,
                                      toplevel, args, n);
/*  add callback  */
  XtAddCallback (button, XmNactivateCallback, activateCB, NULL);
/*  realize widgets  */
  XtRealizeWidget (toplevel);
/*  process events  */
  XtAppMainLoop (app_context);
}
```

```
/*-----------------------------------------------------------
**  activateCB - callback for button
*/
void activateCB (w, client_data, call_data)
Widget  w;    /*  widget id    */
caddr_t  client_data;  /*  data from application   */
caddr_t  call_data;  /*  data from widget class   */
{
/*  print message, free compound string memory,
 *  and terminate program  */
  printf ("PushButton selected.\n");
  XmStringFree(btn_text);
  exit (0);
}
```

3.1.3 Defaults File XMdemos Partial Listing

The **XMdemos** default file, part of which is shown in this section, contains default specifications for general appearance and behavior, plus, in some cases, program-unique specifications. All the example programs in this guide use this defaults file.

```
!
!XMdemos app-defaults file for Motif demo programs
!
!general appearance and behavior defaults
!
*foreground:        white
*allowShellResize:      true
*borderWidth:      0
*highlightThickness:    2
*keyboardFocusPolicy:     explicit
*menuAccelerator:      <Key>KP_F2
```

3.1.4 Output Produced by the xmbutton Program

The following figure shows the resulting screen display for the **xmbutton** program.

Figure 3-2. Sample Program xmbutton Screen Display

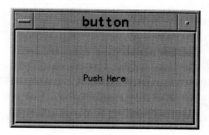

Section 3.10 describes the use of color in screen design, and Section 3.11 introduces some advanced programming techniques. Section 3.12 presents a more involved sample program.

The following sections describe the process for writing widget programs, which was summarized in Table 3-1. Following these steps will help you start writing programs that use the Motif Widgets.

3.2 Including Header Files

Special variables and types of variables used by Motif programs are defined in header files. Include the appropriate files at the beginning of your program. The manpage for each widget specifies the header files that are needed.

Usually this section in your program will look like this:

```
#include <X11/Intrinsic.h>
#include <Xm/Xm.h>
#include <Xm/widget.h>
```

The order in which you place the header files is very important. Generally speaking, you should follow this format:

1. General header files, such as **<stdio.h>**.

2. Intrinsics header files, such as **<X11/Intrinsic.h>**.

3. Motif widget header files, beginning with **<Xm.h>** and including a header file for each widget class you are using in your program. The order of the widget class headers is not critical.

For each widget you are using in your program, replace *widget* with the name of the widget. The manpage for each widget shows the exact spelling of all header files you need. The include files for all widgets are found in the **/usr/include/Xm** directory. For the PushButton widget in the sample program **xmbutton**, the header file name is **PushB.h**. Put a **#include** statement in your program for each type of widget you use. You need to include a header file only once, even if you use a given widget twice in your program. Do not forget to include any other header files (such as **<stdio.h>**) that your program may need.

Intrinsic.h defines the Xt structures and variables. Variables common to all Motif Widgets are defined in **Xm.h**.

3.3 Initializing the Xt Intrinsics

You must initialize the Xt Intrinsics before making any other calls to Xt Intrinsics functions. The function **XtAppInitialize** creates an application context, establishes the connection to the display server, parses the command line that invoked the application, loads the resource database, and creates a shell widget to serve as the parent of your application widgets.

By passing the command line that invoked your application to **XtAppInitialize**, the function can parse the line to allow users to specify certain resources (such as fonts and colors) for your application at run time. **XtAppInitialize** scans the command line and removes those options. The rest of your application sees only the remaining options.

The call to **XtAppInitialize** used by the sample program **xmbutton** is as follows:

```
toplevel = XtAppInitialize(NULL, "XMdemos",
    NULL, 0, &argc, argv, NULL, NULL, 0);
```

This line names the application class **XMdemos**, passes no additional options, and passes the command line that invoked the application. The first parameter is used in setting up defaults files. Defaults files are explained in Section 3.9, ''Creating Defaults Files.''

The syntax of the **XtAppInitialize** function follows. Note that it returns a value of type Widget; therefore, the variable *toplevel* in **xmbutton** must be defined as type Widget.

Widget **XtAppInitialize**(*app_context_return, application_class, options, num_options, argc_in_out, argv_in_out, fallback_resources, args, num_args*)
  XtAppContext **app_context_return*;
  String *application_class*;
  XrmOptionDescList *options*;
  Cardinal *num_options*;
  Cardinal **argc_in_out*;

String **argv_in_out*;
String **fallback_resources*;
ArgList *args*;
Cardinal *num_args*;

app_context_return   Specifies a pointer to the application context. If this is not NULL, **XtAppInitialize** returns the application context created by **XtCreateApplicationContext**.

application_class

    Specifies the class name of this application, which is usually the generic name for all instances of this application. By convention, the class name is formed by reversing the case of the application's first letter. The class name is used to locate the files used to initialize the resource database. For example, the sample program **xmbutton** has a class name of **XMdemos**.

options   Specifies how to parse the command line for any application-speci fic resources. The options argument is passed as a parameter to **XrmParseCommand**.

num_options   Specifies the number of entries in *options*.

argc_in_out   Specifies a pointer to the number of command line parameters.

argv_in_out   Specifies the command line parameters.

fallback_resources   Specifies resources to be used if the application class resource file cannot be read.

args   Specifies resource values to override any other resource specifications for the shell widget created.

num_args   Specifies the number of entries in *args*.

You can use the alternate function, **XtToolkitInitialize**, to just initialize the Xt Intrinsics. It is not as convenient as **XtAppInitialize**, but it is more flexible because it lets you decide the type of shell you want to use. It does not open the display or create an application shell. You must do this yourself using **XtOpenDisplay** and **XtAppCreateShell**. The advanced sample program presented in Section 3.12 initializes the toolkit in this manner.

3.4 Creating Argument Lists for Widgets

The steps in Sections 3.4 through 3.6 must be performed for each widget you wish to create.

Widgets accept argument lists (pairs of resource names and values) that control their appearance and functionality. The list of resources acceptable for a widget comprises not only resources unique to the widget, but also those resources inherited from other widgets. The resources for a given widget are shown in the manpage for the widget.

The simplest way to set an element of an argument list is by using the **XtSetArg** macro. Other methods are described in Section 3.11, ''Advanced Programming Techniques.''

The following program segment declares an array **args** of up to 10 arguments. The size of the array is not important just so long as the number of elements allocated is not less than the number of elements used. The first argument specifies the label for the PushButton. The label is actually a pointer to a compound string that was created by a call to **XmStringCreateLtoR** earlier in the program. See Chapter 8 for more information about compound strings. The last two arguments specify that the widget will have a width of 250 pixels and a height of 150 pixels. The third argument specifies the string to display in the PushButton.

```
Arg args[10];
XtSetArg(args[0], XmNlabelString, btn_text);
XtSetArg(args[1], XmNwidth, 250);
XtSetArg(args[2], XmNheight, 150);
```

An alternate method for **XtSetArg** uses a counter, *n*, rather than a hard-coded index. This method, shown as follows, makes it easier to add and delete argument assignments. It is the method used in the sample program **xmbutton**.

```
Arg args[10];
Cardinal n=0;
XtSetArg(args[0], XmNlabelString, btn_text);
    n++;
XtSetArg(args[n], XmNwidth, 250); n++;
XtSetArg(args[n], XmNheight, 150); n++;
```

The variable *n* contains the number of resources set. It can be passed to the widget create function (explained in Section 3.6) as the argument list count.

CAUTION: Do not increment the counter from inside the call to **XtSetArg**. As currently implemented, **XtSetArg** is a macro that dereferences the first argument twice. This means that if you increment the counter from inside the call, it would actually be incremented twice for the one call.

The syntax for using **XtSetArg** is as follows:

XtSetArg(*arg*, *name*, *value*)
> **Arg** *arg*;
> **String** *name*;
> **XtArgVal** *value*;

arg   Specifies the name-value pair to set.

name   Specifies the name of the resource.

value   Specifies the value of the resource if it will fit in an **XtArgVal**, otherwise the address.

3.5 Adding Callback Procedures

Callbacks are one of the key features of the Motif Widget set. They allow you to write procedures that will be executed when certain events occur within a widget. These events include mouse button presses, keyboard selections, and cursor movements. Callback procedures are the main mechanism your application uses to actually get things done.

You need to complete three steps to add callbacks:

1. Write the callback procedures.

2. Add the appropriate callbacks.

3. Set the widget's callback resources.

Each of these steps is described in the following sections.

3.5.1 Writing a Callback Procedure

Callback procedures return no values, but have three arguments:

- The widget for which the callback is registered.

- Data passed to the callback procedure by the application.

- Data passed to the callback procedure by the widget.

In the sample program **xmbutton**, the callback procedure prints a message to the standard output device (usually the terminal window from which the application was invoked), frees the memory space used by **btn_text** (the PushButton label), and ends the program using the system **exit** call.

```
void activateCB(w, client_data, call_data)
 Widget   w;             /*widget id*/
 caddr_t  client_data;  /*application data*/
 caddr_t  call_data;    /*widget class data*/
{
/*print message and terminate program*/
 fprint("PushButton selected.\n")
 XmStringFree(btn_text);
 exit(0);
}
```

The variable type *caddr_t* is defined by the Xt Intrinsics as a pointer to an area of memory. The **call_data** argument is used only by a few widgets. The manpage for each widget specifies whether it passes any data to its callbacks.

The general syntax of a callback procedure is as follows:

void *CallbackProc*(*w*, *client_data*, *call_data*)
    Widget *w*;
    caddr_t *client_data*;
    caddr_t *call_data*;

w   Specifies the widget for which this callback is invoked.

client_data   Specifies the data that the widget should pass back to the client when the widget invokes the client's callback. This is a way for the client registering the callback to also define client-specific data to be passed to the client: a pointer to additional information about the widget, a reason for invoking the callback, and so on. It is perfectly normal to have *client_data* be NULL if all necessary information is in the widget.

call_data   Specifies any callback-specific data the widget wants to pass to the client. It is widget-specific and is usually set to NULL. It will be defined in the widget's manpage if it is used.

3.5.2 Adding Callbacks

A callback contains information about the callback routine associated with a particular user action.

The sample program **xmbutton** creates a callback by calling the procedure **XtAddCallback**.

```
XtAddCallback (button, XmNactivate,
    activateCB, NULL);
```

The general syntax of **XtAddCallback** is as follows:

void XtAddCallback(*w, callback_name, callback, client_data*)
    Widget   *w*;
    String   *callback_name*;
    XtCallbackProc *callback*;
    caddr_t   *client_data*;

w   Specifies the widget to add the callback to.

callback_name

                Specifies the callback list within the widget to append to.

callback   Specifies the callback procedure to add.

client_data   Specifies the client data to be passed to the callback when it is invoked by **XtCallCallbacks**. The *client_data* parameter is often NULL.

To add more callbacks, just make another call to **XtAddCallback**. In this way you can cause a user event to trigger many callback routines.

You can add a list of callbacks by using the function **XtAddCallbacks**.

The general syntax of **XtAddCallbacks** is as follows:

void XtAddCallbacks(*w, callback_name, callbacks*)
    Widget   *w*;
    String   *callback_name*;
    XtCallbackList *callbacks*;

w   Specifies the widget to add the callbacks to.

callback_name

                Specifies the callback list within the widget to append to.

callbacks   Specifies the null-terminated list of callback procedures and corresponding client data to add.

3.5.3 Setting Widgets' Callback Resources

Many widgets define one or more callback resources. Set the value of the resource to the name of the callback list.

The callback resources for any particular widget are listed in the man page for that widget. The Pushbutton widget used in the sample program **xmbutton** supports three different kinds of callbacks. Each callback could be set up by specifying the callback list as the value of the appropriate resource.

- Callback(s) invoked when the Pushbutton widget is activated (argument **XmNactivateCallback**). This is the callback you use in **xmbutton**.

- Callback(s) invoked when the Pushbutton widget is armed (argument **XmNarmCallback**).

- Callback(s) invoked when the Pushbutton widget is disarmed (argument **XmNdisarmCallback**).

The translation table for this widget has been set so that an activate action occurs whenever the pointer is within the widget and the user presses mouse button 1. An activate action then causes the widget to invoke each of the callback routines on the callback list pointed to by its **XmNactivateCallback** argument. These routines are invoked in the order in which they appear in the callback list. In the case of the sample program **xmbutton**, only the routine **activateCB** is executed.

3.6 Creating the Widget

Now that you have established an argument list for the widget, you can create the widget instance. The following call to **XtCreateManagedWidget** comes from the sample program **xmbutton**.

```
button = XtCreateManagedWidget ("button",
    xmpushButtonWidgetClass, toplevel, args, n);
```

This call names the newly created widget "button" and defines it to be a Pushbutton widget (from the class **xmPushButtonWidgetClass**). The class name **XmPushButton** or the name button can be used in defaults files (discussed in Section 3.9) to refer to this widget. The Pushbutton's parent is "toplevel," the toplevel Shell widget returned by **XtAppInitialize**. The argument list and number of arguments complete the call. This call will create the widget and notify its parent so that the parent can control its specific layout.

There is another way to create widgets, one that does not automatically manage them. Instead, you manage them when you want them to be displayed. Each widget has a create function associated with it. A create function creates the widget it is associated with but does not manage it. You manage the widget with **XtManageChild**. The advanced program in Section 3.12 uses this method of creating widgets.

Widgets form a hierarchical structure called a widget tree. The widget tree for the program **xmbutton** is shown in Figure 3-1. The widget returned by **XtAppInitialize** is the invisible parent for the toplevel application widget, in this case **button**. Usually there are several levels of widgets. Widgets at the higher levels are layout widgets (also called manager widgets) that control and coordinate the primitive widgets located at the leaves of the widget tree. The more advanced sample program later in this chapter illustrates multiple levels of widgets.

The syntax for **XtCreateManagedWidget** is as follows:

Widget XtCreateManagedWidget(*name*, *widget_class*, *parent*, *args*, *num_args*)
    String   *name*;
    WidgetClass *widget_class*;
    Widget   *parent*;
    ArgList   *args*;
    Cardinal   *num_args*;

name   Specifies the resource name for the created widget. This name is used for retrieving resources and should not be the same as any other widget that is a child of the same parent if unique values are necessary.

widget_class Specifies the widget class pointer for the created widget.

parent Specifies the parent widget.

args Specifies the argument list to override the resource defaults.

num_args Specifies the number of arguments in *args*. The number of arguments in an argument list can be automatically computed by using the **XtNumber** macro if the list is statically defined.

3.7 Making the Widget Visible

All widgets are now created and linked together into a widget tree.

XtRealizeWidget displays on the screen the widget that is passed to it and the children of that widget.

The final step in the program is to call the Xt Intrinsics routine that causes the application to enter a loop, awaiting action by the user.

Sample code for this section is as follows:

```
XtRealizeWidget(toplevel);
XtAppMainLoop(app_context);
```

The preceding two statements from the sample program **xmbutton** display the Pushbutton widget and cause the program to enter a loop, waiting for user input. The main role of your application is the setting of widget arguments and the writing of callback procedures. Your application passes control to the Xt Intrinsics and the Motif Widgets once the **XtAppMainLoop** function is called.

The syntax for **XtRealizeWidget** is as follows:

void XtRealizeWidget(*w*)
 Widget *w*;

w Specifies the widget.

3.8 Linking Libraries

When linking the program, be sure to include three libraries, in the following order:

- **libXm.a**, which contains the Motif Widgets
- **libXt.a**, which contains the Xt Intrinsics
- **libX11.a**, which contains the underlying Xlib library

NOTE: The **XmFileSelectionBox** widget requires the **libPW.a** library. This can be included after **libX11.a**.

See Section 1.3 for information about compiling the programs in this chapter. The order in which you place the libraries is very important. The preceding order shown is correct, so be sure that you use the same order when linking in libraries.

3.9 Creating Defaults Files

Up to now, all widget resources have been set by the application using widget argument lists. An additional method for specifying resources is through a set of ASCII files that you can set up for your user. You may also want your user to set up these files to customize the application to individual requirements or preferences.

When writing a program, consider the following factors in deciding whether to specify an argument in a defaults file or in the program itself.

- Using a defaults file provides additional flexibility. Any user can override settings to reflect personal preferences, and a systems administrator can modify the application defaults file for system-wide customization.

- Specifying settings in the program gives the programmer greater control. They cannot be overridden.

- Using defaults files can speed application development. To change a resource value in a defaults file, simply edit the file (using any ASCII editor) and rerun the program. No recompilation or relinking is necessary.

- Using defaults files can simplify your program. Resources in defaults files are specified as strings. When resources are set in your program, they may have to be in some internal format that takes several calls to compute.

- Specifying options in your program may provide more efficient operation for the computer. The process of reading defaults files and interpreting their contents adds processing overhead.

Several files can be used for customization:

- An application-specific file containing system-wide resource defaults for an entire class. This file is usually located in the **/usr/lib/X11/app-defaults** directory, but the location can vary depending on the user's current language environment.

- An application-specific file containing the user's resource defaults for an entire class.

- A file (called **.Xdefaults**) in the user's home directory containing the user's default values for any application.

- An environment-specific file containing the user's default values for applications running on a particular host. This is usually the file **.Xdefaults-**_host_ in the user's home directory.

All files are of the same format. Chapter 13 of this manual, "Managing Windows with MWM," contains a detailed discussion of the format of defaults files.

Defaults files are generally read by the Xt Intrinsics when an application is initialized. For a discussion of the order in which the files are loaded, the location of the files, and the effects of environment variables and the current language environment, see the "Localization" section in Chapter 8.

3.9.1 Application Defaults Files

These files are designed to be created by the applications developer or systems administrator. They are usually located in the **/usr/lib/X11/app-defaults** directory on the machine where the application resides, though there may be a different directory for each of several language environments. Application programs specify the file that contains the application defaults when they call

XtAppInitialize. The *application_class* argument to that function specifies the name of the application defaults file. Several applications can point to the same file.

The following call (taken from the sample program **xmbutton**) causes the Xt Intrinsics to look for an application-specific file (**XMdemos** in this case) for default information.

```
toplevel = XtAppInitialize(NULL, "XMdemos",
    NULL, 0, &argc, argv, NULL, NULL, 0);
```

The following sample defaults file sets the foreground color to white and background color to black.

```
*background: black
*foreground: white
```

3.9.2 User Defaults Files

Each user can create several files to specify resource defaults:

- An application-specific file for an entire class of applications. This file is often in the user's home directory, though there may be a different directory for each of several language environments.

- A **.Xdefaults** file in the user's home directory to specify resource defaults for any application.

- An environment-specific file to specify resource defaults for applications running on a particular host.

- User defaults override application and system defaults and allow different users running the same program to specify personal display preferences, such as color and font selection.

The following sample file changes the background color to blue.

```
*background:  blue
```

3.9.3 Defaults File Example

Here is an example to illustrate the interaction of the defaults files with each other and with arguments specified in programs. Suppose a computer contains the program **xmbutton** as well as the application and user defaults files previously described.

To determine the color of the background, the Xt Intrinsics will do the following:

1. Look for the system defaults and initialize the background color to white. (These defaults are compiled into the widgets.)

2. Look for the application-specific class defaults file and set the color to black.

3. Look for the user's application-class, general, and environment-specific defaults files. In this example, the Xt Intrinsics load the user's **.Xdefaults** file and set the background color to blue.

4. Look for any resource arguments on the command line that started the application. If the command line sets the background resource (**XmNbackground**), this overrides any defaults that have been set by resource files.

3.10 Using Color

The Motif Widgets have been designed to support both color and monochrome systems in a consistent and attractive manner. This is accomplished by incorporating into each widget a variety of visual attributes. Through proper use of these attributes, the widgets will present a dramatic 3-dimensional appearance, giving you the impression that you are directly manipulating the components. This section describes these color attributes and shows you how to use them.

3.10.1 Visual Capabilities and Attributes

The Motif Widgets visual capabilities are based on specialized border and background drawing. The border drawing consists of a band around the widget. The band contains two regions:

- The top and left shadow

- The bottom and right shadow

The background drawing within the widget is referred to as background. The following figure illustrates the drawing areas.

Figure 3-3. Widget Drawing Areas

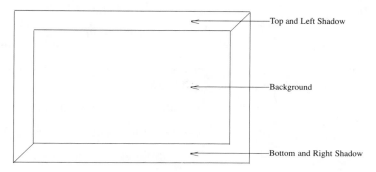

Each area can be drawn from either a color or a pixmap. The top and left shadow is drawn using these Primitive widget resources:

- **XmNtopShadowColor**

- **XmNtopShadowPixmap**

The background is drawn using these Primitive widget resources:

- **XmNbackground**

- **XmNbackgroundPixmap**

The bottom and right shadow is drawn using these Primitive widget resources:

- **XmNbottomShadowColor**

- **XmNbottomShadowPixmap**

All the widgets support the visual attributes for setting the background as described. In general, only Primitive widgets support the border drawing. To use the border drawing for manager widgets, a special manager widget, **XmFrame**, is available. This widget will maintain the geometry of a single child and perform the border and background drawing.

3.10.2 Using the Capabilities

When planning the 3-dimensional appearance of your program's windows, consider the following guidelines:

- Any selectable area should appear to be raised.

- Nonselectable areas should appear to be flat. This can be accomplished by setting **XmNshadowThickness** to 0.

To give the impression that the widget is raised above its parent, set these resources as follows:

- Set **XmNtopShadowColor** to a light color.

- Set **XmNbackground** to a medium color.

- Set the **XmNbottomShadowColor** to a dark color.

The foreground, background, and both top and bottom shadow resources are dynamically defaulted. This means that if you do not specify any color for these resources, colors are automatically generated. A black and white color scheme is generated on a monochrome system, while on a color system a set of four colors is generated that displays the correct shading to achieve the 3-dimensional appearance. If you specify only a background color, the foreground and both shadow colors are generated (based on the background color) to achieve the 3-dimensional appearance. This color generation works best with nonsaturated colors, that is, using pure red, green, or blue will give poor results. Also, colors are generated only at the time of the widget's creation. Changing the background color by using **XtSetValues** will not cause the other colors to be regenerated.

Reversing the top shadow and bottom shadow colors will give the appearance that the widget is set into its parent. Several of the Primitive widgets (buttons, toggles, and arrows, for example) automatically reverse their shadowing when selected to achieve the effect of being pressed. They return to their original shadowing when released.

Use coordinated colors such as light blue for the top shadow color, sky blue for the background color, and navy blue for the bottom shadow color to enhance the 3-dimensional appearance. Using dissimilar colors loses the effect.

The 3-dimensional appearance is more difficult to achieve on monochrome systems. The built-in defaults for all the widgets have been set up for monochrome systems and provide the desired effect. The top shadow is drawn with a 50 percent pixmap, the background is solid white, and the bottom shadow is solid black. This appearance can be further enhanced by setting the background of a manager containing a set of raised children to a pixmap of 25 percent black and 75 percent white.

3.11 Advanced Programming Techniques

The sample program **xmbutton** described in earlier sections of this chapter illustrated the writing of a very simple widget program. The Xt Intrinsics provide additional mechanisms for programmers.

3.11.1 Setting Argument Values

Section 3.4 described the use of **XtSetArg** for setting the values of widget arguments. This section describes three additional methods. The code segments show how the earlier sample program could have been rewritten to use the new methods.

3.11.1.1 Assigning Argument Values

Each element of the type **Arg** structure can be assigned individually.

```
XmString btn_text;
Arg args[10];

btn_text = XmStringCreateLtoR ("Push Here",
   XmSTRING_DEFAULT_CHARSET);
args[0].name = XmNwidth;
args[0].value = (XtArgVal) 250;
args[1].name = XmNheight;
args[1].value = (XtArgVal) 150;
args[2].name = XmNlabelString;
args[2].value = (XtArgVal) btn_text;
```

Be sure to keep name-value pairs synchronized. Note that all argument values have been cast to type **XtArgVal**.

3.11.1.2 Static Initializing

Initializing argument lists at compile time makes it easy to add and delete argument settings in your program. It avoids the need to hard-code the maximum number of arguments when declaring your argument list. These settings are frozen at compile time, however. While the example below shows only a single argument list being created, you can create any number of lists (be sure to declare each list as type **Arg**). Note that you cannot use static initializing to initialize a compound string. You can combine static initializing with run-time assignments to accomplish this, as shown in the next section.

```
static Arg args[] = {
 {XmNwidth, (XtArgVal) 250},
 {XmNheight, (XtArgVal) 150},
 };
```

Note that the values of each argument have been cast to type **XtArgVal**. When the create widget function is invoked, passing it **XtNumber(args)** will compute the number of elements in the argument list.

```
button = XtCreateManagedWidget("button",
  xmPushButtonWidgetClass, toplevel, args,
  XtNumber(args));
```

NOTE: Use the macro **XtNumber** only if you are declaring the argument list of indefinite size as shown previously (**args[]**). **XtNumber** will return the number of elements that have actually been allocated in program memory.

3.11.1.3 Combining Static Initialization with Run-Time Assignments

The final method for creating argument lists initializes a list at compile time (described previously in "Static Initializing") and then modifies the values of the settings using regular assignment statements. The **XtNumber** macro can be used to count the number of arguments, since the argument list is declared with no definite number of arguments. The values can be changed through assignments at run time, but the size of the argument list (the number of arguments that can be specified) is frozen at compile time and cannot be extended.

The following example initializes an argument list of three elements. The last is initialized to **NULL** so it can be given a value later. The value for argument **XmNheight** is changed in the program from its initialized value of 150 to a run-time value of 250.

```
XmString btn_text;

static Arg args[] = {
  {XmNwidth, (XtArgVal) 500},/*item 0*/
  {XmNheight, (XtArgVal) 150},/*item 1*/
  {XmNlabelString, (XtArgVal) NULL},/*item 2*/
};

btn_text = XmStringCreateLtoR ("Push Here",
  XmSTRING_DEFAULT_CHARSET);

args[1].value = (XtArgVal) 250;
args[2].value = (XtArgVal) btn_string;
```

3.11.2 Manipulating Created Widgets

Widget programs to this point have set up argument lists and callbacks for widgets prior to the widgets' creation. You can also modify widgets after they have been created. Such modification usually occurs in callback routines and is illustrated in the sample program **xmfonts** discussed later in this chapter.

3.11.2.1 Retrieving and Modifying Arguments

XtGetValues will return the current value of specified arguments for a created widget. **XtSetValues** will change the value of specified arguments.

3.11.2.2 Adding Callbacks and Translations

XtAddCallback will add a callback routine to a widget's callback list after the widget has been created.

Each widget has a translation table that ties user actions (for example, button presses and keyboard presses) to widget actions. Your application can modify the translation table for any widget. This process is described in any manual on the Xt Intrinsics.

3.11.2.3 Separating Widget Creation and Management

By using **XtCreateManagedWidget**, the sample program automatically adds the newly created widget to its parent's set of managed children. To optimize programs that add a number of widgets to a single parent, you may want to create the widgets using **XtCreateWidget** calls and then add the entire list of children to its parent with a single **XtManageChildren** call. In this way, the parent widget performs its geometry processing of its children only once. This will increase the performance of applications that have a large number of child widgets under a single parent.

Usually, the function **XtRealizeWidget** will display a widget and all of its children. Using the function **XtSetMappedWhenManaged** allows you to turn off automatic mapping (displaying) of particular widgets. Your application can then use **XtMapWidget** to display the widget.

The function **XtDestroyWidget** will destroy a created widget and its children. The destroyed widget is automatically removed from its parent's list of children.

3.12 An Advanced Sample Program

The program presented in this section, **xmfonts**, displays each available font as a Push button. The source code and the application defaults file for this sample program are listed later in this section. They are located on your system in **./demos/xmsamplers/xmfonts.c** and **./demos/xmsamplers/XMdemos.ad**.

You can change the background and foreground colors and other visual attributes by changing the parameters in the **XMdemos** application defaults file. Remember that **XMdemos** is used as a defaults file for all the example programs in this guide. If you change any of the general defaults at the top of the file, other programs will be affected.

When you run the program, you will see the window shown in Figure 3-4.

Figure 3-4. Program xmfonts Main Window

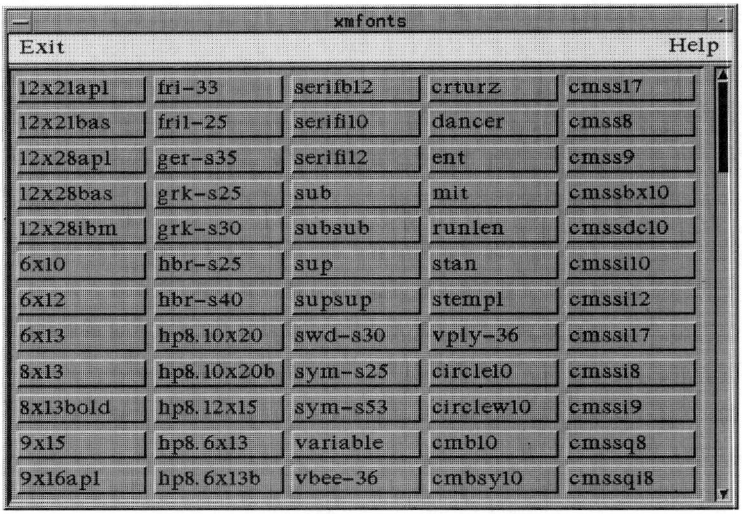

Move the pointer to the push button representing the font you want to see displayed and press mouse button 1. Text in the selected font is displayed in a separate popup window. This window can be removed by pressing the **close** push button or left on the screen to be compared with other text windows that you might select. You can continue this procedure for as long as you desire. Each time the mouse button is pressed, the selected font will be displayed in a separate pop-up window. When you want to exit the program, move the cursor to the **exit** button in the menu bar, then drag the pointer down until the **quit** button appears. Clicking mouse button 1 on the **quit** button will terminate the program.

3.12.1 Windows Used in xmfonts

There are three independent windows displayed in this program (see Figures 3-4, 3-5, and 3-6):

3.12.1.1 Main Window

The main window is the window in which the push buttons are displayed (see Figure 3-4). It is a combination of an application shell, a MainWindow widget, a RowColumn widget, and a number of push button gadgets. The MainWindow widget was chosen because it has the capability of a menu bar and is a convenient envelope for many applications. Although a main window can have three areas (see Chapter 2), only two of the areas are needed here, the menu bar and work region. In this case the menu bar is the parent of a pull-down menu for the exit function and a cascade button for the Help function. The work region consists of a RowColumn widget and possibly a vertical scroll bar. A number of push button gadgets, one for each font, are placed within the RowColumn widget. These are used instead of push buttons to improve program performance. To see the difference for yourself, run the program as it exists. Use the scroll bar to view buttons not displayed. Then change the code in the **xmfonts.c** file (be sure to move this file to your work directory first) so that the line that now reads:

```
button = XmCreatePushButtonGadget(row_column,
     name, args, n);
```

becomes:

```
button = XmCreatePushButton(row_column,  name,
     args, n);
```

Then recompile the program and run it again. You should see considerable difference in the operation of the program, particularly when scrolling through the buttons.

3.12.1.2 Help Window

The Help window is a pop-up window that is a message box (see Figure 3-5).

Figure 3-5. Program xmfonts Help Display Window

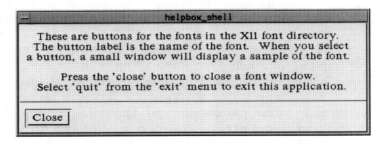

3.12.1.3 Font Display Window

The window that displays the selected font is also a popup window that is a MessageBoxDialog (see Figure 3-6).

Figure 3-6. Program xmfonts Font Display Window

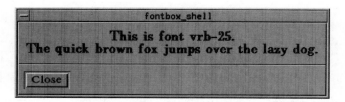

You can have as many text display windows as you want. You can remove them all by simply exiting the program as explained previously, or you can remove each window individually by moving the pointer to the **close** button on the window and pressing mouse button 1.

3.12.2 Widget Hierarchy

This program produces three separate windows. One contains all the push button gadgets and its shell is created using **XtToolkitInitialize**, **XtCreateApplicationContext**, **XtOpenDisplay**, and finally **XtAppCreateshell**. Note the difference between this program and **xmbutton**. Since **XtAppInitialize** opens the display and creates a shell in addition to initializing the toolkit, **xmbutton** did not need to use the functions **XtCreateApplicationContext**, **XtOpenDisplay**, and **XtAppCreateShell**. The other two windows are the Help window and the window that displays text in the selected font. Both of these windows are MessageBoxDialogs created by the function **XmCreateMessageDialog**. This function creates a MessageBox widget and a DialogShell widget.

The widget tree for **xmfonts** is shown in the following figure.

Figure 3-7. xmfonts Widget Tree

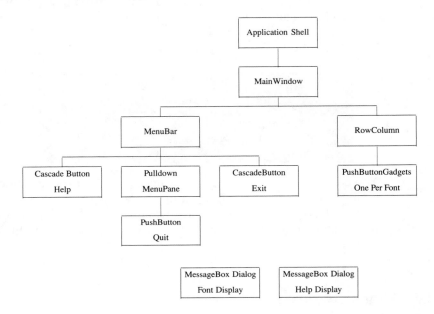

3.12.3 Source Code

The source code for **xmfonts** and the **XMdemos** default file are shown in the following sections.

3.12.3.1 The Program

This section shows the program listing for **xmfonts**.

```
/**-------------------------------------------------------------
***
***   file:     xmfonts.c
***
***   project:  Motif Widgets example programs
***
***   description:  This program creates a button for
***       every font.  When a button is selected,
***       a text sample is displayed using the font.
***
***
***   (c) Copyright 1989, 1990 by Open Software Foundation, Inc.
***       All Rights Reserved.
***
***   (c) Copyright 1989 by Hewlett-Packard Company.
***
***
***   defaults:  xmfonts.c depends on these defaults:
!
*allowShellResize:      true
*borderWidth:        0
*highlightThickness:      2
*traversalOn:        true
*keyboardFocusPolicy:      explicit
*menuAccelerator:      <Key>KP_F2
*fontList:        vr-20
!
xmfonts*XmScrolledWindow.height:    432
xmfonts*XmScrolledWindow.width:      690
xmfonts*menu_bar*background:      #58f
!
***-----------------------------------------------------------*/
```

```
/*----------------------------------------------------------
**   Include Files
*/
#include <stdio.h>
#include <string.h>
#include <sys/types.h>
#ifdef SYS_DIR
#include <sys/dir.h>
#else
#ifdef NDIR
#include <ndir.h>
#else
#include <dirent.h>
#endif
#endif

#include <X11/Intrinsic.h>
#include <X11/IntrinsicP.h>
#include <X11/CoreP.h>
#include <X11/Shell.h>
#include <Xm/Xm.h>
#include <Xm/BulletinB.h>
#include <Xm/CascadeB.h>
#include <Xm/Frame.h>
#include <Xm/Label.h>
#include <Xm/MainW.h>
#include <Xm/MessageB.h>
#include <Xm/PushB.h>
#include <Xm/PushBG.h>
#include <Xm/RowColumn.h>
#include <Xm/ScrollBar.h>
#include <Xm/ScrolledW.h>

/*----------------------------------------------------------
**   Forward Declarations
*/

void main ();          /*  main logic for application  */

Widget CreateApplication (); /*  create main window    */
Widget CreateFontSample (); /*  create font display window  */
Widget CreateHelp ();    /*  create help window    */

void SelectFontCB ();    /*  callback for font buttons  */
void CloseCB ();    /*  callback for close button   */
void HelpCB ();     /*  callback for help button   */
void QuitCB ();     /*  callback for quit button   */
```

```
/*-------------------------------------------------------
**  Global Variables
*/

#define MAX_ARGS 20
#define TITLE_STRING "X Font Sampler"

typedef struct {
  char *fontpath;
} ApplicationData, *ApplicationDataPtr;

ApplicationData AppData;

#define XtNfontPath "fontPath"
#define XtCFontPath "FontPath"
static XtResource resources[] = {
  { XtNfontPath, XtCFontPath, XmRString, sizeof(String),
    XtOffset(ApplicationDataPtr, fontpath),
            XmRString, "/usr/lib/X11/fonts" }
};

static XmStringCharSet  charset =
       (XmStringCharSet) XmSTRING_DEFAULT_CHARSET;

/*-------------------------------------------------------
**  main     - main logic for application
*/
void main (argc,argv)
  unsigned int  argc;
  char        **argv;
{
  Display    *display; /*  Display    */
  Widget     app_shell; /*  ApplicationShell  */
  Widget     main_window; /*  MainWindow    */
  XtAppContext  app_context;

  /*  Initialize toolkit and open the display.
  */
  XtToolkitInitialize();
  app_context = XtCreateApplicationContext();
  display = XtOpenDisplay (app_context, NULL, argv[0],
                          "XMdemos", NULL, 0,
        &argc, argv);
```

```
  if (!display) {
    XtWarning ("xfonts: Can't open display, exiting...");
    exit (0);
  }

  /*  Create application shell.
  */
  app_shell = XtAppCreateShell (argv[0], "XMdemos",
        applicationShellWidgetClass, display, NULL, 0);

  XtGetApplicationResources(app_shell,
            &AppData,
            resources,
            XtNumber(resources),
            NULL,
            0);

  /*  Create and realize main application window.
  */
  main_window = CreateApplication (app_shell);
  XtRealizeWidget (app_shell);

  /*  Get and dispatch events.
  */
  XtAppMainLoop (app_context);
}

/*----------------------------------------------------------
** CreateApplication  - create main window
*/
Widget CreateApplication (parent)
Widget    parent;   /*  parent widget  */
{
  Widget    main_window; /*  MainWindow     */
  Widget    menu_bar; /*  MenuBar      */
  Widget    menu_pane; /*  MenuPane      */
  Widget    cascade;  /*  CascadeButton   */
  Widget    frame;   /*  Frame     */
  Widget    swindow; /*  ScrolledWindow   */
  Widget    row_column; /*  RowColumn     */
  Widget    button;   /*  PushButtonGadget  */
  Widget    hsb, vsb; /*  ScrollBars     */

  Arg    args[MAX_ARGS]; /*  arg list    */
  register int  n;   /*  arg count     */
```

```
  DIR    *dirp;    /*  directory pointer  */
#if defined (SYS_DIR) || defined (NDIR)
  struct direct   *item;    /*  entry in directory  */
#else
  struct dirent   *item;    /*  entry in directory  */
#endif
  char    name[15];  /*  name string    */
  int    len;    /*  string length  */

  XmString   label_string;


  /*  Create MainWindow.
  */
  n = 0;
  main_window = XmCreateMainWindow (parent, "main1", args, n);
  XtManageChild (main_window);

  /*  Create MenuBar in MainWindow.
  */
  n = 0;
  menu_bar = XmCreateMenuBar (main_window, "menu_bar", args, n);
  XtManageChild (menu_bar);

  /*  Create "Exit" PulldownMenu.
  */
  n = 0;
  menu_pane = XmCreatePulldownMenu (menu_bar, "menu_pane",
                                    args, n);

  n = 0;
  button = XmCreatePushButton (menu_pane, "Quit", args, n);
  XtManageChild (button);
  XtAddCallback (button, XmNactivateCallback, QuitCB, NULL);

  n = 0;
  XtSetArg (args[n], XmNsubMenuId, menu_pane);  n++;
  cascade = XmCreateCascadeButton (menu_bar, "Exit", args, n);
  XtManageChild (cascade);
```

```
/*  Create "Help" button.
*/
n = 0;
cascade = XmCreateCascadeButton (menu_bar, "Help", args, n);
XtManageChild (cascade);
XtAddCallback (cascade, XmNactivateCallback, HelpCB, NULL);

n = 0;
XtSetArg (args[n], XmNmenuHelpWidget, cascade);  n++;
XtSetValues (menu_bar, args, n);


/*  Create Frame MainWindow and ScrolledWindow in Frame.
*/
n = 0;
XtSetArg (args[n], XmNmarginWidth, 2);  n++;
XtSetArg (args[n], XmNmarginHeight, 2);  n++;
XtSetArg (args[n], XmNshadowThickness, 1);  n++;
XtSetArg (args[n], XmNshadowType, XmSHADOW_OUT);  n++;
frame = XmCreateFrame (main_window, "frame", args, n);
XtManageChild (frame);

n = 0;
XtSetArg (args[n], XmNscrollBarDisplayPolicy, XmAS_NEEDED);
          n++;
XtSetArg (args[n], XmNscrollingPolicy, XmAUTOMATIC);  n++;
swindow = XmCreateScrolledWindow (frame, "swindow", args, n);
XtManageChild (swindow);


/*  Create RowColumn in ScrolledWindow to manage buttons.
*/
n = 0;
XtSetArg (args[n], XmNpacking, XmPACK_COLUMN);  n++;
XtSetArg (args[n], XmNnumColumns, 5);  n++;
row_column = XmCreateRowColumn (swindow, "row_column",
                                      args, n);
XtManageChild (row_column);
```

```
/*  Set MainWindow areas and add tab groups
*/
XmMainWindowSetAreas (main_window, menu_bar, NULL, NULL,
                      NULL, frame);
n = 0;
XtSetArg (args[n], XmNhorizontalScrollBar, &hsb);  n++;
XtSetArg (args[n], XmNverticalScrollBar, &vsb);  n++;
XtGetValues (main_window, args, n);
XmAddTabGroup (row_column);
if (hsb)
  XmAddTabGroup (hsb);
if (vsb)
  XmAddTabGroup (vsb);

/*  Create a PushButton widget for each font.
*/
/*  open the font directory  */
dirp = opendir (AppData.fontpath);
/*  read one entry each time through the loop  */
for (item=readdir(dirp); item!=NULL; item=readdir(dirp))
{
  len =  (strlen (item -> d_name));
/*  discard entries that don't end in ".xxx"  */
  if ((len < 5) || (item -> d_name[len-4] != '.')) continue;
/*  copy the name (except extension) from the entry  */
  strncpy (name, item -> d_name, len-4);
  name[len-4] = ' ';
/*  create PushButton in RowCol  */
  n = 0;
  label_string = XmStringCreateLtoR(name, charset);
  XtSetArg (args[n], XmNlabelString, label_string);  n++;
  button = XmCreatePushButtonGadget (row_column, name,
                                     args, n);
  XtManageChild (button);
  XtAddCallback (button, XmNarmCallback, SelectFontCB, NULL);
  XmStringFree (label_string);
}

/*  Return MainWindow.
*/
return (main_window);
}
```

```
/*----------------------------------------------------------
** CreateFontSample  - create font display window
*/
Widget CreateFontSample (parent)
Widget    parent;    /* parent widget  */
{
  Widget     message_box;    /* MessageBox Dialog  */
  Widget     button;
  Arg    args[MAX_ARGS];    /* arg list    */
  register int  n;         /* arg count    */

  char    *name = NULL;    /* font name    */
  XFontStruct  *font = NULL;   /* font pointer  */
  XmFontList  fontlist = NULL;  /* fontlist pointer  */
  static char  message[BUFSIZ];  /* text sample    */
  XmString  name_string = NULL;
  XmString  message_string = NULL;
  XmString  button_string = NULL;

  /* Get font name.
  */
  n = 0;
  XtSetArg (args[n], XmNlabelString, &name_string); n++;
  XtGetValues (parent, args, n);
  XmStringGetLtoR (name_string, charset, &name);


  /* Load font and generate message to display.
  */
  if (name)
    font = XLoadQueryFont (XtDisplay (XtParent (parent)), name);
  if (!font)
    sprintf (message, "Unable to load font: %s ", name);
  else
  {
    fontlist = XmFontListCreate (font, charset);
    sprintf (message, "\
This is font %s.0
The quick brown fox jumps over the lazy dog. ", name);
  }
  message_string = XmStringCreateLtoR (message, charset);
  button_string = XmStringCreateLtoR ("Close", charset);
```

```
/*  Create MessageBox dialog.
*/
n = 0;
if (fontlist)
{
  XtSetArg (args[n], XmNlabelFontList, fontlist);  n++;
}
XtSetArg (args[n], XmNdialogTitle, name_string);  n++;
XtSetArg (args[n], XmNokLabelString, button_string);  n++;
XtSetArg (args[n], XmNmessageString, message_string);  n++;
message_box = XmCreateMessageDialog (
    XtParent (XtParent(parent)), "fontbox", args, n);

button = XmMessageBoxGetChild (message_box,
                              XmDIALOG_CANCEL_BUTTON);
XtUnmanageChild (button);
button = XmMessageBoxGetChild (message_box,
                              XmDIALOG_HELP_BUTTON);
XtUnmanageChild (button);

/*  Free strings and return MessageBox.
*/
if (fontlist) XtFree (fontlist);
if (name_string) XtFree (name_string);
if (message_string) XtFree (message_string);
if (button_string) XtFree (button_string);
return (message_box);
}


/*--------------------------------------------------------
** CreateHelp    - create help window
*/
Widget CreateHelp (parent)
  Widget    parent;    /*  parent widget  */
{
  Widget    button;
  Widget    message_box;  /*  Message Dialog   */
  Arg    args[MAX_ARGS];  /*  arg list    */
  register int  n;    /*  arg count    */

  static char  message[BUFSIZ];  /*  help text  */
  XmString  title_string = NULL;
  XmString  message_string = NULL;
  XmString  button_string = NULL;
```

```
/*  Generate message to display.
*/
sprintf (message, "\
These are buttons for the fonts in the X11 font directory.  0
The button label is the name of the font.  When you select 0
a button, a small window will display a sample of the font.  0
Press the 'close' button to close a font window.  0
Select 'quit' from the 'exit' menu to exit this application. ");
  message_string = XmStringCreateLtoR (message, charset);
  button_string = XmStringCreateLtoR ("Close", charset);
  title_string = XmStringCreateLtoR ("xmfonts help", charset);


/*  Create MessageBox dialog.
*/
n = 0;
XtSetArg (args[n], XmNdialogTitle, title_string);  n++;
XtSetArg (args[n], XmNokLabelString, button_string);  n++;
XtSetArg (args[n], XmNmessageString, message_string);  n++;
message_box = XmCreateMessageDialog (parent, "helpbox",
                                     args, n);

button = XmMessageBoxGetChild (message_box,
                              XmDIALOG_CANCEL_BUTTON);
XtUnmanageChild (button);
button = XmMessageBoxGetChild (message_box,
                              XmDIALOG_HELP_BUTTON);
XtUnmanageChild (button);


/*  Free strings and return MessageBox.
*/
if (title_string) XtFree (title_string);
if (message_string) XtFree (message_string);
if (button_string) XtFree (button_string);
return (message_box);
}
```

```
/*--------------------------------------------------------
**   SelectFontCB    - callback for font buttons
*/
void SelectFontCB (w, client_data, call_data)
Widget     w;     /*  widget id    */
caddr_t    client_data;  /*  data from application   */
caddr_t    call_data;  /*  data from widget class  */
{
  Widget     message_box;


  /*  Create font sample window.
   */
  message_box = CreateFontSample (w);


  /*  Display font sample window.
   */
  XtManageChild (message_box);
}

/*--------------------------------------------------------
**   CloseCB        - callback for close button
*/
void CloseCB (w, client_data, call_data)
Widget     w;     /*  widget id    */
caddr_t    client_data;  /*  font pointer */
caddr_t    call_data;  /*  data from widget class   */
{
  XFontStruct  *font  = (XFontStruct *) client_data;
  Widget     message_box  = XtParent (w);
  Widget     shell  = XtParent (message_box);


  /*  Free font.
   */
  if (font) XFreeFont (XtDisplay (w), font);


  /*  Unmanage and destroy widgets.
   */
  XtUnmanageChild (message_box);
  XtDestroyWidget (shell);
}
```

```
/*----------------------------------------------------------
**   HelpCB       - callback for help button
*/
void HelpCB (w, client_data, call_data)
Widget    w;      /*  widget id     */
caddr_t   client_data;  /*  data from application   */
caddr_t   call_data;  /*  data from widget class  */
{
  Widget    message_box;     /*  MessageBox    */


  /*  Create help window.
  */
  message_box = CreateHelp (w);


  /*  Display help window.
  */
  XtManageChild (message_box);
}

/*----------------------------------------------------------
**   QuitCB        - callback for quit button
*/
void QuitCB (w, client_data, call_data)
Widget    w;      /*  widget id     */
caddr_t   client_data;  /*  data from applicaiton   */
caddr_t   call_data;  /*  data from widget class  */
{

  /*  Terminate the application.
  */
  exit (0);
}
```

3.12.3.2 The Defaults File

This file should be placed in the **/usr/lib/X11/app-defaults**
directory as a part of **XMdemos**.

```
!
!XMdemos app-defaults file
!  for Motif demo programs
!
!general appearance and behavior defaults
!
*allowShellResize:              true
*borderWidth:                   0
*highlightThickness:            2
*traversalOn:                   true
*keyboardFocusPolicy:           explicit
*menuAccelerator:               <Key>KP_F2
*fontList:                      vr-20
!
xmfonts*XmScrolledWindow.height:    432
xmfonts*XmScrolledWindow.width:     690
xmfonts*menu_bar*background:     #58f
!
```

Chapter 4

Shell Widgets

Shell widgets are used to provide communication between the widgets in an application and the window manager. An application's widgets are arranged in a hierarchy, with upper-level widgets acting as the parents of lower-level widgets. Widgets at the top of the hierarchy do not have normal parent widgets, but have a Shell as the parent. Different Shell widgets are provided for the various categories of "toplevel" widgets, including dialogs and menu panes. Figure 4-1 shows the hierarchy of the Shell widgets. Keep in mind that Shell is a subclass of Composite (see Figure 1-4).

Figure 4-1. Shell Widget Hierarchy

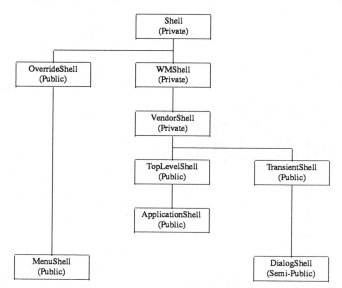

The classes Shell, WmShell, and VendorShell are private and should
not be instantiated. The other Shell classes are for public use,
although a DialogShell is normally created by a convenience
function as part of a set rather than by itself. Each of the Shell
classes has a manpage (found in the *OSF/Motif Programmer's
Reference*) that has information on the resources belonging to the
specific Shell widget.

4.1 Descriptions of Shell Widgets

The Shell widgets shown in Figure 4-1 are of two types: Private and
Public. This means that the Public widgets are those that you
should instantiate, either individually or, as in the case of
DialogShell, as part of a set. The Private widgets are those that you
should not instantiate. These widgets typically just supply
resources to Shell widgets that are lower in the hierarchy. Keep in

mind the hierarchy diagram of Figure 4-1 as you study the definitions of the Shell widgets.

- **Shell** - Shell is the base class for all Shell widgets. It provides the fields needed by all the Shell widgets. Shell is a subclass of Composite (see Figure 1-2).

- **OverrideShell** - OverrideShell is used for shell windows that bypass the window manager. Popup menus are one example of where an OverrideShell might be used.

- **WMShell** - WMShell contains fields that are needed by the common window manager protocol.

- **VendorShell** - VendorShell contains fields that are used by vendor-specific window managers.

- **TopLevelShell** - TopLevelShell is used for normal toplevel windows. It is not the root shell used by an application, rather it is normally used to create peer toplevel windows in situations where an application needs more than one set of windows. The root shell is normally the ApplicationShell.

- **ApplicationShell** - ApplicationShell is an application's toplevel or root window. This is the shell that is created by **XtAppInitialize**. An application should not have more than one ApplicationShell. Subsequent toplevel shells should be of class TopLevelShell and are created by **XtAppCreateShell**. These toplevel shells can be considered the root of a second widget tree for the application.

- **MenuShell** - MenuShell is used as the parent of pop-up and pull-down menu panes. It is a subclass of OverrideShell.

- **DialogShell** - DialogShell is the parent of Dialogs. Although it can be instantiated by itself, it is normally instantiated as part of a set by one of the convenience dialogs. For example, **XmCreateErrorDialog** creates a DialogShell and a message box as its child. See Chapter 5, ''Dialog Widgets and Functions,'' for more information.

4.2 Shell Widget Appearance

Most Shell widgets are invisible. However, the type of Shell class can have an impact on how its children are displayed. For example, children of a TransientShell (typically Dialogs) by default have no buttons on the window manager frame that surrounds the window. Also, as long as the transient window is visible, it will remain above the window from which it is transient.

Chapter 5

Dialog Widgets and Functions

Dialog widgets are container widgets that provide a means of communicating between the user of an application and the application itself. A Dialog widget will normally ask a question or present some information to the user. In some cases, the application is suspended until the user provides a response.

This chapter explains the Dialog widgets that are available and how they can be used in your application.

5.1 Dialog Widgets and Menus

There are two types of Dialog widgets: single-reply and multiple-reply. A single-reply Dialog widget consists of a single question, and a single reply is expected. A multiple-reply Dialog widget consists of a number of questions that require a number of responses. Generally speaking, a single-reply Dialog widget is modal in nature. This means that a reply is required before the application can continue. A multiple-reply Dialog widget is usually modeless. It does not require a reply and does not stop the progress of the application.

There are many similarities between Dialog widgets and menus, and knowing when to use a Dialog widget and when to use a menu may be difficult. You should understand the differences between Dialog widgets and menus in order to make this determination.

A menu is short-lived. It exists only while a selection is being made, then it disappears. A Dialog widget stays visible until it is told to disappear.

A menu is usually modal. Until the user of the application makes some selection on the menu, interaction with any other part of the application is not possible. Since multiple-reply Dialog widgets are modeless, interaction with other parts of the application is possible. Thus, if a modeless state is required, a multiple-reply or modeless single-reply Dialog widget should be used instead of a menu. A menu is faster when there is a need to identify current settings or make a single selection. When multiple selections are needed, a menu disappears after each selection and has to be displayed over and over, so in this case a Dialog widget works better.

5.2 A List of the Dialog Widgets

The following list identifies the Dialog widgets by name and provides a brief description of each widget's function. Each widget will be described in more detail in later sections of this chapter. Additional information can be found in the manpage for the respective widget. Manpages are contained in the *OSF/Motif Programmer's Reference*.

- **XmDialogShell**. This widget is used as the parent for all Dialogs. It is automatically created by Dialog convenience functions (described in a later section).

- **XmBulletinBoard**. This is a composite widget that provides simple geometry management for its child widgets. It is the base widget for most Dialog widgets, but is also used as a container widget.

- **XmCommand**. This widget is a subclass of the **XmSelectionBox** widget. It includes a command line input text field, a command line prompt, and a command history region.

- **XmFileSelectionBox**. This widget is used to traverse through file system directories. You can view the files in the directories and then select a single file on which you intend to perform some action.

- **XmForm**. This widget is a constraint-based Manager widget that establishes and maintains spatial relationships between its children. These relationships are maintained even though the Form or any of its children are resized, unmanaged, remanaged, or destroyed.

- **XmMessageBox**. This widget is used to pass information to the user of an application. It contains up to three standard push buttons (**OK**, **Cancel**, and **Help** by default), a message symbol, and the message itself.

- **XmSelectionBox**. This widget provides the capability of selecting a single item from a list of items.

5.3 Convenience Dialogs

In this guide, Dialog widget describes a particular type of widget. When used by itself, the word Dialog takes on a special meaning. A Dialog is a collection of widgets that are used for a specific purpose. A Dialog normally consists of a DialogShell, some BulletinBoard resources, and various other widgets such as Label, PushButton, and Text. The collection of widgets that forms a Dialog can be built from scratch using argument lists and creating each individual widget of the Dialog. However, there is an easier, more convenient method to create the Dialog. Functions (called, appropriately, Dialog convenience functions) exist that create the collection of widgets that make up the Dialog in one step. The Dialogs that are created by these convenience functions are referred to as convenience Dialogs. The following table identifies the convenience dialogs that are available.

Table 5-1. Convenience Dialogs

Convenience Dialog	Convenience Function Definition
BulletinBoardDialog	**XmCreateBulletinBoardDialog** Used for interactions that are not supported by the standard Dialog set.
ErrorDialog	**XmCreateErrorDialog** This Dialog instantiates a MessageBox and a DialogShell. It uses a message and a symbol (circle with backslash) to warn the user that an error has occurred.
FileSelectionDialog	**XmCreateFileSelectionDialog** This Dialog instantiates a FileSelectionBox and a DialogShell.
FormDialog	**XmCreateFormDialog** This Dialog instantiates a Form and a DialogShell.
InformationDialog	**XmCreateInformationDialog** This Dialog instantiates a MessageBox and a DialogShell. This Dialog provides information to the user and it has a symbol that consists of a large lowercase "i" that is positioned on the left side of the MessageBox.
PromptDialog	**XmCreatePromptDialog** This Dialog instantiates a SelectionBox and a DialogShell. It is used to prompt the user for input.
QuestionDialog	**XmCreateQuestionDialog** This Dialog instantiates a MessageBox and a DialogShell. It is used to get an answer from the user. It has a symbol that consists of a large question mark that is positioned on the left side of the MessageBox.

Convenience Dialog	Convenience Function Definition
SelectionDialog	**XmCreateSelectionDialog** This Dialog instantiates a SelectionBox and a DialogShell.
WarningDialog	**XmCreateWarningDialog** This Dialog instantiates a MessageBox and a DialogShell. It is used to warn the user of some potential danger. It has a symbol that consists of a large exclamation point contained within a triangle. The symbol is positioned on the left side of the MessageBox.
WorkingDialog	**XmCreateWorkingDialog** This Dialog instantiates a MessageBox and a DialogShell. It is used to inform the user that a potentially time-consuming operation is in progress. It has a symbol that is an hourglass positioned on the left side of the MessageBox.

5.4 Using Dialogs and Convenience Functions

Now that you have an idea of what Dialogs and convenience Dialogs are available, you can learn how and when to use them in an application. This section explains each Dialog and its associated convenience functions. Code segments are included to help you understand how to use them in your own applications. More detailed information about these widgets can be found in the respective manpages in the *OSF/Motif Programmer's Reference* .

5.4.1 XmDialogShell

XmDialogShell is the Shell parent widget for all Dialogs. It provides the necessary communication with the window manager to allow the Dialogs to be managed and unmanaged. **XmDialogShell** is automatically created by the Dialog convenience functions and is used as the parent widget for **XmBulletinBoard** or any subclass of **XmBulletinBoard**. It can also be directly instantiated by using either of the two create functions that are available:

```
Widget XtCreatePopupShell (name,
    xmDialogShellWidgetClass, parent,
    arglist, argcount)

Widget XmCreateDialogShell (parent, name,
    arglist, argcount)
```

Both of these create functions create an instance of a DialogShell and return the associated widget ID. The following code segment shows you how to create **XmDialogShell** using **XtCreatePopupShell**:

```
Arg        args;
int        n;
Widget     dialog_shell;
Widget     parent_shell;

n = 0;
dialog_shell = XtCreatePopupShell (
    "dialog_shell", xmDialogShellWidgetClass,
    parent_shell, args, n);
```

The next code segment shows you how to create **XmDialogShell** using **XmCreateDialogShell**:

```
Arg        args;
int        n;
Widget     dialog_shell;
Widget     parent_shell;

n = 0;
dialog_shell = XmCreateDialogShell (
    parent_shell, "dialog_shell", args, n);
```

Remember that **XmDialogShell** is automatically created for you when you create any of the convenience Dialogs. You do not need to use either of the functions previously described when you create a convenience Dialog. Also, note that **XmDialogShell** should be popped up by using **XtManageChild** on its Dialog child. If the child is created using **XtCreateManagedWidget**, it will try to pop up the shell before it has been realized. This will result in an error.

5.4.2 XmBulletinBoard

XmBulletinBoard is a composite widget that can be instantiated alone. Its main purpose with Dialog widgets, however, is as a superclass widget that supplies resources to the subclass Dialog widgets. All of the other Dialog widgets except **XmDialogShell** are built in part from **XmBulletinBoard**. Refer to the **XmBulletinBoard** manpage in the *OSF/Motif Programmer's Reference* for a description of the **XmBulletinBoard** resources.

XmBulletinBoard can be directly instantiated by using either of the two create functions that are available:

```
Widget XtCreateWidget (name,
    xmBulletinBoardWidgetClass,
    parent, arglist, argcount)

Widget XmCreateBulletinBoard (parent, name,
    arglist, argcount)
```

Both of these create functions create an instance of a BulletinBoard and return the associated widget ID. The following code segment shows you how to create an instance of **XmBulletinBoard** using **XmCreateWidget**:

```
Arg       args;
int       n;
Widget    bboard;
Widget    parent_shell;
```

```
n = 0;
bboard = XtCreateWidget ("bboard",
    xmBulletinBoardWidgetClass,
    parent_shell, args, n);
XtManageChild (bboard);
```

The next code segment shows you how to create an instance of **XmBulletinBoard** using **XmCreateBulletinBoard**:

```
Arg        args;
int        n;
Widget     bboard;
Widget     parent_shell;

n = 0;
bboard = XmCreateBulletinBoard (parent_shell,
    "bboard", args, n);
XtManageChild (bboard);
```

Remember that you do not need to use either of the create functions previously described if you are creating convenience Dialogs.

5.4.3 XmCommand

XmCommand allows you to choose one selection from a list of selections. It is very much like the **XmSelectionBox** widget except that it can record selections in a history region. The history region is accessible so that choices can be made from it as well as entering a choice from the keyboard. The following figure shows an example of a Command widget.

Figure 5-1. XmCommand Widget

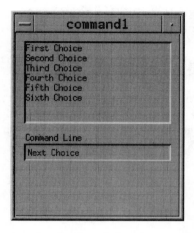

The history region is displayed in the top box and the current selection is displayed in the command line box at the bottom. The history region will scroll automatically as the need arises. In Figure 5-2 for example, more entries have been placed in the history region, causing the vertical ScrollBar to appear.

Figure 5-2. XmCommand Widget with Scrolled History Region

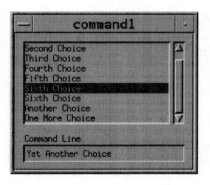

XmCommand can be directly instantiated by using either of the two create functions that are available:

```
Widget XtCreateWidget (name,
    xmCommandWidgetClass,
    parent, arglist, argcount)

Widget XmCreateCommand (parent, name, arglist,
    argcount)
```

Both of these create functions create an instance of a Command widget and return the associated widget ID. The following code segment shows you how to create an instance of **XmCommand** using **XmCreateWidget**:

```
Arg         args;
int         n;
Widget      command;
Widget      parent_shell;

n = 0;
command = XtCreateWidget ("command",
    xmCommandWidgetClass, parent_shell,
    args, n);
XtManageChild (command);
```

The next code segment shows you how to create an instance of **XmCommand** using **XmCreateCommand**:

```
Arg         args;
int         n;
Widget      command;
Widget      parent_shell;

n = 0;
command = XmCreateCommand (parent_shell,
    "command", args, n);
XtManageChild (command);
```

There are several other functions associated with **XmCommand** that perform certain operations to the command area string or the history region string. These functions are explained in the following list:

- **XmCommandAppendValue**

```
void XmCommandAppendValue (widget, command)

Widget      widget;
XmString    command;
```

This function appends the passed, null-terminated command string to the end of the string that is currently displayed in the command line. The following figure shows the resulting window from the **XmCommandAppendValue** call.

Figure 5-3. Results of XmCommandAppendValue Operation

The code segment to accomplish this is as follows.

```
XmString    str;
Widget      w;

str = XmStringCreateLtoR ("addValue",
    XmSTRING_DEFAULT_CHARSET);
XmCommandAppendValue (w, str);
```

- **XmCommandSetValue**

```
void XmCommandSetValue (widget, command)

Widget    widget;
XmString  command;
```

This function replaces the string that is currently displayed in the command line with the passed, null-terminated string.

- **XmCommandError**

```
void XmCommandError (widget, error)

Widget    widget;
XmString  error;
```

This function displays an error message in the history region.

- **XmCommandGetChild**

```
void XmCommandGetChild (widget, child)

Widget    widget;
uns char  child;
```

This function returns the widget ID of the given child. The function takes these child types:

- **XmDIALOG_PROMPT_LABEL**

- **XmDIALOG_COMMAND_TEXT**

- **XmDIALOG_HISTORY_LIST**

5.4.4 XmFileSelectionBox

XmFileSelectionBox is a widget very similar to **XmSelectionBox**. The difference is that **XmFileSelectionBox** is used to traverse through directories, viewing the names of the files and finally selecting a file on which to perform some action. One thing to remember about this widget is that you must link in the library PW (-lPW) in order for FileSelectionBox to work properly. The following figure shows an example of a FileSelectionBox.

Figure 5-4. XmFileSelectionBox

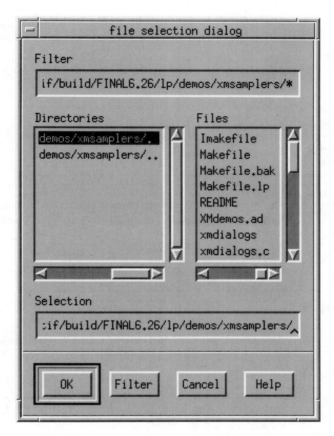

XmFileSelectionBox can be directly instantiated by using either of
the two create functions that are available:

```
Widget XtCreateWidget (name,
    xmFileSelectionBoxWidgetClass,
    parent, arglist, argcount)

Widget XmCreateFileSelectionBox (parent, name,
    arglist, argcount)
```

Both of these create functions create an instance of a FileSelectionBox widget and return the associated widget ID. The following code segment shows you how to create an instance of **XmFileSelectionBox** using **XmCreateWidget**:

```
Arg         args;
int         n;
Widget      fselbox;
Widget      parent_shell;

n = 0;
fselbox = XtCreateWidget ("fselbox",
    xmFileSelectionBoxWidgetClass,
    parent_shell, args, n);
XtManageChild (fselbox);
```

The next code segment shows you how to create an instance of **XmFileSelectionBox** using **XmCreateFileSelectionBox**:

```
Arg         args;
int         n;
Widget      fselbox;
Widget      parent_shell;

n = 0;
fselbox = XmCreateFileSelectionBox (
    parent_shell, "fselbox", args, n);
XtManageChild (fselbox);
```

In the example shown in Figure 5-4, the Filter is an asterisk following a directory name, indicating that all files in the directory should be listed. Here, all files in the directory **xmsamplers** are listed. The subdirectories appear in the Directories list, and the files appear in the Files list. The Selection window at the bottom of the **XmFileSelectionBox** specifies the directory. Once you have selected a file from the Files list, you can press the OK button and, depending on what the application has in the callback associated with this button, perform some action on the selected file. Note that you can select a file as many times as desired. The operation on that file is not performed until you select the OK push button.

You can change the Filter by moving the pointer into the Filter window and clicking **BSelect**. This activates the window and it is highlighted. You can then enter the desired filter by typing it in from the keyboard. You can also change the Filter by selecting a directory in the Directories list. This action replaces the directory portion of the Filter with the directory you select from the Directories list, leaving the search pattern in the Filter unchanged.

When you have finished entering the new filter, press **KActivate** in the Filter or move the pointer into the Filter button at the bottom of the main window and press **BSelect**. The subdirectories of the directory specified by the Filter are displayed in the Directories list, and the files that match the search pattern specified by the Filter are displayed in the Files list.

You can also generate a new file listing by double clicking on an item in the Directories list. This creates a new Filter, using the directory selected from the Directories list and the search pattern from the existing Filter. It then uses the new Filter to generate new lists of directories and files.

5.4.5 XmForm

The Form widget is a container widget that has no input characteristics of its own. Constraints are placed on the Form widget's children. These constraints define attachments for each of the four sides of each child, and the attachments determine the layout of the Form widget when any resizing occurs. The child widgets' attachments can be to the Form widget, to another child of the Form widget, to a relative position within the Form widget, or to the initial position of the child.

XmForm can be directly instantiated by using either of the two create functions that are available:

```
Widget XtCreateWidget (name,
    xmFormWidgetClass, parent,
    arglist,argcount)

Widget XmCreateForm (parent, name, arglist,
    argcount)
```

Both of these create functions create an instance of the Form widget and return the associated widget ID. The following code segment shows you how to create an instance of **XmForm** using **XmCreateWidget**:

```
Arg        args;
int        n;
Widget     form;
Widget     parent_shell;

n = 0;
form = XtCreateWidget ("form",
    xmFormWidgetClass, parent_shell,
    args, n);
XtManageChild (form);
```

The next code segment shows you how to create an instance of **XmForm** using **XmCreateForm**:

```
Arg        args;
int        n;
Widget     form;
Widget     parent_shell;

n = 0;
form = XmCreateForm (parent_shell, "form",
    args, n);
XtManageChild (form);
```

You can create a Form Dialog by using the convenience function **XmFormCreateDialog**. This function creates and returns a Form widget as a child of a DialogShell widget.

```
Arg        args;
int        n;
Widget     form;
Widget     parent_shell;

n = 0;
form = XmCreateFormDialog (parent_shell, "form",
     args, n);
XtManageChild (form);
```

The following figure shows an example of a Form widget.

Figure 5-5. Form Widget With ArrowButtons

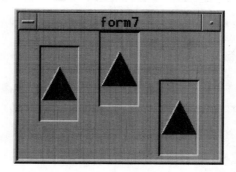

There are three ArrowButton widgets positioned within the Form widget. The ArrowButton on the left is set so that its left side position is offset an amount equal to 10 percent of the Form widget's width, its right side position is offset 30 percent of the Form widget's width, and the top is set to a fixed offset of 20 pixels from the top of the Form widget. When the Form widget is resized, the spatial relationships between the Form widget and its children remain the same. This is shown in the following figure.

Figure 5-6. Form Widget After Resizing

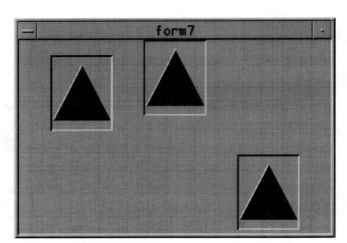

The code segment that positions the ArrowButton on the left is as follows:

```
Widget      arrow1;
int     n;
n = 0;
XtSetArg(args[n],XmNleftAttachment,XmATTACH_POSITION);
     n++;
XtSetArg(args[n],XmNleftPosition,10);  n++;
XtSetArg(args[n],XmNrightAttachment,XmATTACH_POSITION);
     n++;
XtSetArg(args[n],XmNrightPosition,30);  n++;
XtSetArg(args[n],XmNtopAttachment,XmATTACH_FORM);  n++;
XtSetArg(args[n],XmNtopOffset,20);  n++;
arrow1 = XtCreateManagedWidget("arrow1",
    xmArrowButtonWidgetClass, form, args, n);
```

Note that the position of the top side of the ArrowButton is a constant value (20 pixels in this case), regardless of any resizing operations that may occur. This is because the **XmNtopAttachment** resource is set to XmATTACH_FORM as opposed to XmATTACH_POSITION.

5.4.6 XmMessageBox

A MessageBox is used just as its name implies, to pass messages to the user of an application. **XmMessageBox** is a subclass of **XmBulletinBoard** and inherits a large number of the BulletinBoard resources. Convenience Dialogs based on **XmMessageBox** are provided for several user-interaction functions: providing information, asking questions, and notifying the user if errors occur. The figure below shows some examples of **XmMessageBox**.

Figure 5-7. MessageBox Examples

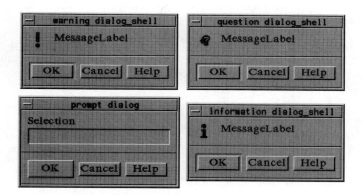

XmMessageBox can be directly instantiated by using either of the two create functions that are available:

```
Widget XtCreateWidget (name,
    xmMessageBoxWidgetClass,
    parent, arglist, argcount)

Widget XmCreateMessageBox (parent, name,
    arglist, argcount)
```

Both of these create functions create an instance of the MessageBox widget and return the associated widget ID. The following code segment shows you how to create an instance of **XmMessageBox** using **XmCreateWidget**:

```
Arg        args;
int        n;
Widget     msgbox;
Widget     parent_shell;

n = 0;
msgbox = XtCreateWidget ("msgbox",
    xmMessageBoxWidgetClass,
    parent_shell, args, n);
XtManageChild (msgbox);
```

The next code segment shows you how to create an instance of **XmMessageBox** using **XmCreateMessageBox**:

```
Arg        args;
int        n;
Widget     msgbox;
Widget     parent_shell;

n = 0;
msgbox = XmCreateMessageBox (parent_shell,
    "msgbox", args, n);
XtManageChild (msgbox);
```

You can create a MessageBox Dialog by using the convenience function **XmMessageCreateDialog**. This function creates and returns a MessageBox widget as a child of a DialogShell widget.

```
Arg        args;
int        n;
Widget     msgbox;
Widget     parent_shell;

n = 0;
msgbox = XmCreateMessageDialog (parent_shell,
    "msgbox", args, n);
XtManageChild (msgbox);
```

A MessageBox can contain a message symbol, a message, and up to three standard PushButtons (the default buttons are OK, Cancel, and Help). The symbol (if any) appears in the upper left part of the MessageBox (see Figure 5-7), the message appears in the top and center-to-right side, and the buttons appear along the bottom edge.

The defaults for the button labels and the message symbols can be changed. The button labels can be changed by setting a resource in the program or in a defaults file. For example, if you wanted to change the OK label to Close, you could use this code segment:

```
n = 0;
XtSetArg (args[n], XmNokLabelString,
    XmStringCreateLtoR ("Close",
    XmSTRING_DEFAULT_CHARSET) ); n++;
messageD = XmCreateMessageDialog (parent,
    "fontbox", args, n);
```

XmStringCreateLtoR is a compound string function. See Chapter 8, "Additional Functionality," for more information on this function and compound strings in general. You can make the same change by using the following statement in a defaults file:

```
*msgbox.okLabelString: Close
```

Note that the preceding statement applies only to the MessageBox widget whose name is msgbox as specified in the **XmCreateMessageDialog** or **XmCreateMessageBox**.

The message label can be changed in the same manner as the button. Use the resource `XmNmessageString` instead of `XmNokLabelString`.

There are several other convenience dialogs that allow you to create special versions of **XmMessageBox**. These convenience dialogs are **XmCreateErrorDialog**, **XmCreateInformationDialog**, **XmCreateQuestionDialog**, **XmCreateWarningDialog**, and **XmCreateWorkingDialog**. You use these functions to create the appropriate dialogs in exactly the same manner as described earlier for the **XmMessageBoxDialog**.

5.4.7 XmSelectionBox

A SelectionBox is a general Dialog widget that allows you to select an item from a list of items. SelectionBox can contain a label, a list of items from which to choose, a selection text edit window that allows you to enter a selection directly, and three PushButtons (OK, Cancel, and Help). An example of a SelectionBox widget is shown in the following figure.

Figure 5-8. SelectionBox Widget

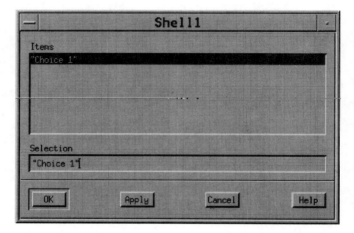

You can select an item from the SelectionBox in either of two ways:

- By scrolling through the list of items and selecting one. The item you select will be displayed in the SelectionBox text edit window.

- By entering the item name directly into the text edit window.

You can select a new item as many times as you desire since no action is taken until you move the pointer to the OK button and click mouse button 1.

XmSelectionBox can be directly instantiated by using either of the two create functions that are available:

```
Widget XtCreateWidget (name,
    xmSelectionBoxWidgetClass, parent,
    arglist,argcount)

Widget XmCreateSelectionBox (parent, name,
    arglist, argcount)
```

Both of these create functions create an instance of the SelectionBox widget and return the associated widget ID. The following code segment shows you how to create an instance of **XmSelectionBox** using **XmCreateWidget**:

```
Arg        args;
int        n;
Widget     selectbox;
Widget     parent_shell;

n = 0;
selectbox = XtCreateWidget ("selectbox",
    xmSelectionBoxWidgetClass,
    parent_shell, args, n);
XtManageChild (selectbox);
```

The next code segment shows you how to create an instance of **XmSelectionBox** using **XmCreateSelectionBox**:

```
Arg        args;
int        n;
Widget     selectbox;
Widget     parent_shell;

n = 0;
selectbox = XmCreateSelectionBox(parent_shell,
    "selectbox", args, n);
XtManageChild (selectbox);
```

You can create a SelectionBox Dialog by using the convenience function **XmSelectionBoxCreateDialog**. This function creates and returns a SelectionBox widget as a child of a DialogShell widget.

```
Arg        args;
int        n;
Widget     selectbox;
Widget     parent_shell;

n = 0;
selectbox = XmCreateSelectionBoxDialog
    (parent_shell, "selectbox", args, n);
XtManageChild (selectbox);
```

The defaults for the button labels and the list and text window labels can be changed. The button labels can be changed by setting a resource in the program or in a defaults file. For example, if you wanted to change the OK label to Close, you could use this code segment:

```
n = 0;
XtSetArg (args[n], XmNokLabelString,
    XmStringCreateLtoR ("Close",
    XmSTRING_DEFAULT_CHARSET) ); n++;
selectbox=XmCreateSelectionBoxDialog(parent,
    "selectbox", args, n);
```

The following code segment shows how to set the list items that appear in the list window.

```
XmString    item[5];
item[0] = XmStringCreateLtoR ("one",
    XmSTRING_DEFAULT_CHARSET);
item[1] = XmStringCreateLtoR ("two",
    XmSTRING_DEFAULT_CHARSET);
item[2] = XmStringCreateLtoR ("three",
    XmSTRING_DEFAULT_CHARSET);
item[3] = NULL
n = 0;
XtSetArg(args[n], XmNlistItems, item); n++;
XtSetArg(args[n], XmNlistItemCount, 3); n++;
```

An array of type **XmString** is defined to hold the list items. Since only three of the five entries in the array are used, the fourth is set to NULL to identify the end of the list. Each entry is set manually, and then the argument list is set in the normal manner.

Chapter 6

Menus

The Motif menu system provides three types of menus—Popup, Pulldown, and Option menus. This chapter describes how to implement and use these menus. The chapter includes the following:

- An overview of the Motif menu system

- Guidelines for creating and interacting with each menu type

- A description of the mouse and keyboard interfaces for each menu type

6.1 Overview of the Motif Menu System

Motif provides the ability to create three types of menu systems:

- Popup menu systems
- Pulldown menu systems
- Option menu systems

The term "menu system" refers to a combination of various widgets that create the visual and interactive behavior of a menu. For example, a Pulldown menu system characteristically consists of a MenuBar containing a number of CascadeButtons; the CascadeButtons are used to post various Pulldown MenuPanes which, in turn, contain various buttons.

The major widget components of menu systems are RowColumn widgets that are configured to behave as:

- PopupMenuPanes
- PulldownMenuPanes
- MenuBars
- Option menus

For example, a Popup MenuPane is a RowColumn widget created to behave as a Popup MenuPane; likewise, a MenuBar is a type of RowColumn widget.

The Motif menu system provides the ability to manually create the major menu widgets by creating RowColumn widgets of the appropriate types. For example, a Popup MenuPane can be created by creating a MenuShell widget and a child RowColumn widget of type XmMENU_POPUP. However, Motif provides a set of convenience functions that automatically create RowColumn widgets of the appropriate type and, when necessary, a parent MenuShell. (Popup and Pulldown MenuPanes require MenuShell parents; MenuBars and Option menus do not have MenuShell parents.) For example, the **XmCreatePopupMenu** convenience function creates a RowColumn widget configured to act as a Popup MenuPane and automatically creates its parent MenuShell.

Most of the instructions and examples in this chapter use the convenience functions. Creating menus by separately creating MenuShells and RowColumn widgets is discussed at the end of the chapter.

6.1.1 Convenience Functions and Widgets Used to Create Menus

A menu is constructed from combinations of widgets created explicitly or by using convenience functions.

The following convenience functions create RowColumn widgets that act as MenuPanes. MenuPanes are transient features in an application—they are not displayed until they are posted by a particular event, and they are unposted at the conclusion of some other event.

- **XmCreatePopupMenu** convenience function. This function automatically creates a Popup MenuPane and its required parent MenuShell.

- **XmCreateSimplePopupMenu** and **XmVaCreateSimplePopupMenu** convenience functions. These functions automatically create a Popup MenuPane and its required parent MenuShell. They also create the button children of the menu.

- **XmCreatePulldownMenu** convenience function. This function automatically creates a Pulldown MenuPane and its required parent MenuShell.

- **XmCreateSimplePulldownMenu** and **XmVaCreateSimplePulldownMenu** convenience functions. These functions automatically create a Pulldown MenuPane and its required parent MenuShell. They also create the button children of the menu.

The following convenience functions create RowColumn widgets configured to act as other components of menu systems. These are nontransient features of an application.

- **XmCreateMenuBar** convenience function. This function automatically creates a MenuBar. Menubars are typically used as the basis for building Pulldown menu systems. A MenuBar is the top-level component of a Pulldown menu system.

- **XmCreateSimpleMenuBar** and **XmVaCreateSimpleMenuBar** convenience functions. These functions automatically create a MenuBar and its button children.

- **XmCreateOptionMenu** convenience function. This function automatically creates an Option menu.

- **XmCreateSimpleOptionMenu** and **XmVaCreateSimpleOptionMenu** convenience functions. These functions automatically create an Option Menu, its Pulldown submenu, and the button children of the submenu.

- **XmCreateRadioBox** convenience function. This function automatically creates a RowColumn widget of type **XmWORK_AREA** that behaves as a RadioBox. In a RadioBox, the ToggleButton or ToggleButtonGadget children behave like buttons on an automobile radio. Only one button at a time can be set, and setting one button turns off all other buttons.

- **XmCreateSimpleRadioBox** and **XmVaCreateSimpleRadioBox** convenience functions. These functions automatically create a RowColumn widget of type **XmWORK_AREA** that behaves as a RadioBox. The functions also create the ToggleButtonGadget children of the RadioBox.

- **XmCreateSimpleCheckBox** and **XmVaCreateSimpleCheckBox** convenience functions. These functions automatically create a RowColumn widget of type **XmWORK_AREA** that behaves as a CheckBox. The functions also create the ToggleButtonGadget children of the CheckBox. A CheckBox is like a RadioBox, except that more than one button can be set at any time.

- **XmCreateWorkArea** convenience function. This function automatically creates a RowColumn widget of type **XmWORK_AREA**.

In addition to the RowColumn widgets created by convenience functions, the following widgets and gadgets are used in menu systems:

- **XmCascadeButton** and **XmCascadeButtonGadget**. CascadeButtons are used as the visual means to display Pulldown menus, Option menus, and submenus.

- **XmSeparator** and **XmSeparatorGadget**. The Separator widget is used to separate unrelated buttons or groups of buttons within a MenuPane.

- **XmLabel** and **XmLabelGadget**. The Label widget is used to provide a title for a MenuPane.

- **XmPushButton** and **XmPushButtonGadget**. PushButtons provide the means for selecting an item from a menu.

- **XmToggleButton** and **XmToggleButtonGadget**. ToggleButtons provide a way to set nontransitory states using menus.

- **XmRowColumn**. The RowColumn widget is a general-purpose RowColumn manager. Popup MenuPanes, Pulldown MenuPanes, MenuBars, and Option menus are types of RowColumn widgets. When menu RowColumn widgets are created without using convenience functions, the resource **XmNrowColumnType** specifies the type of MenuPane created.

- **XmMenuShell**. The MenuShell widget is a shell widget designed to contain a Popup or Pulldown MenuPane as its child. The convenience functions that create Popup and Pulldown menus automatically create their parent MenuShell.

Note that the Motif menu system does not implement Popup MenuPanes, Pulldown MenuPanes, Option menus, and MenuBars as separate widget classes. For example, no Popup Menu widget class exists; rather, a convenience function exists for creating the appropriately configured RowColumn widget.

6.1.2 Introducing the Three Menu Types

This section describes Popup, Pulldown, and Option menus.

6.1.2.1 Popup Menu System

A Popup menu system consists of a single Popup MenuPane containing a combination of Label, PushButton, ToggleButton, and Separator widgets or gadgets. In addition, the MenuPane can contain CascadeButtons or CascadeButtonGadgets that are used to access Pulldown MenuPanes that function as submenus of the Popup MenuPane. The following figure shows the top level of a Popup menu system.

Figure 6-1. Top Level of a Popup Menu System

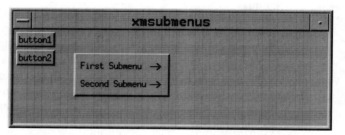

The CascadeButtons have arrows that indicate the presence of submenus. Moving the pointer to the First Submenu button displays its submenu. The following figure shows a window with a submenu for a Popup menu system.

Figure 6-2. Submenu of a Popup Menu System

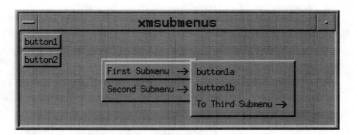

The submenu contains two PushButtons and one CascadeButton. Moving the pointer to the Third Submenu button displays its submenu. The following figure shows a window with a Popup menu system and two cascading submenus.

Figure 6-3. Popup Menu System with Two Cascading Submenus

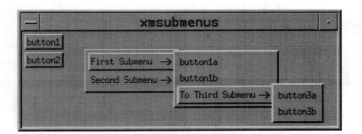

6.1.2.2 Pulldown Menu System

A Pulldown menu system typically consists of a MenuBar, a set of CascadeButtons parented from the MenuBar, and a Pulldown MenuPane attached to each CascadeButton. The CascadeButtons are displayed within the MenuBar and provide the means for displaying the MenuPanes. In addition, the menu system may include Label, PushButton, ToggleButton, and Separator widgets or gadgets.

The following figure shows a MenuBar, which is the top level of a Pulldown menu system.

Figure 6-4. MenuBar of a Pulldown Menu System

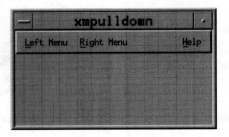

Moving the pointer to Right Menu and pressing mouse button 1 displays its Pulldown MenuPane. The following figure shows a window with a Pulldown Menupane displayed.

Figure 6-5. Displaying a Pulldown MenuPane

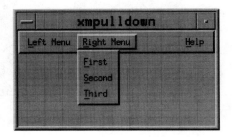

6.1.2.3 Option Menu System

Visually, an Option menu is composed of three areas:

- A descriptive LabelGadget. Typically, the label describes the types of options available.

- A Pulldown MenuPane containing PushButtons or PushButtonGadgets. The buttons represent the available options.

- A selection area consisting of a CascadeButtonGadget that contains a label string. The label string reflects the most recent option chosen from the Pulldown MenuPane.

The top level of an Option menu system shows the descriptive label and selection area. The following figure shows a window with the top level of an Option menu system.

Figure 6-6. Top Level of an Option Menu System

Pressing mouse button 1 while the pointer is in the selection area displays the Pulldown MenuPane containing the options. The following figure shows a Pulldown Menupane in an Option Menu system.

Figure 6-7. The Pulldown MenuPane in an Option Menu System

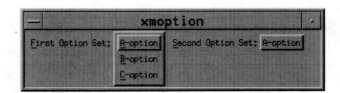

6.2 Creating Popup Menu Systems

The top level of a Popup menu system is a Popup MenuPane. Popup MenuPanes are implemented as XmRowColumn widgets configured to operate as a Popup MenuPanes. The Popup MenuPane may contain CascadeButtons or CascadeButtonGadgets, which are used to access Pulldown MenuPanes that act as submenus of the Popup MenuPane. (Submenus are discussed later in this chapter.)

A Popup MenuPane displays a 3-dimensional shadow around the edge of the MenuPane unless the feature has been disabled by the application.

The Popup MenuPane must be the child of a MenuShell widget. If the Popup MenuPane is created using the convenience function, a MenuShell is automatically created as the real parent of the MenuPane. If the Popup MenuPane is created without using the convenience function, the MenuShell widget must be created first.

6.2.1 Popup MenuPane Convenience Function

A Popup MenuPane is created using the convenience function:

Widget XmCreatePopupMenu(*parent*, *name*, *arglist*, *argcount*)

XmCreatePopupMenu creates a Popup MenuPane and a parent MenuShell, and returns the widget ID for the MenuPane. The Popup MenuPane is created as a RowColumn widget with the **XmNrowColumnType** resource set to XmMENU_POPUP. This resource cannot be changed by the application.

6.2.2 Event Handlers for Popup Menu Systems

Popup menu systems require an event-handler procedure that is called when a specified event (usually, a ButtonPress) occurs in the widget(s) to which the Popup menu system is attached. Usually, this is the *parent* specified by the **XmCreatePopupMenu** function and the parent's descendents. The event-handler procedure should test that the proper mouse button has been pressed and then display the Popup MenuPane.

The **XtAddEventHandler** function registers the event-handler procedure with the dispatch mechanism. It has the following syntax:

void XtAddEventHandler(*w*, *event_mask*, *nonmaskable*, *proc*, *client_data*)
> **Widget** *w*;
> **EventMask** *event_mask*;
> **Boolean** *nonmaskable*;
> **XtEventHandler** *proc*;
> **caddr_t** *client_data*;

w　　　　　Specifies the widget to add the callback to

event_mask　Specifies the event mask for which to call this procedure

nonmaskable Specifies whether this procedure should be called on the nonmaskable events

proc　　　　Specifies the client event-handler procedure

client_data　Specifies additional data to be passed to the client's event handler

For example, the line

```
XtAddEventHandler(rc, ButtonPressMask, False,
     PostIt, popup);
```

registers the procedure PostIt for the event ButtonPress within the widget rc and all of rc's descendents.

6.2.3 Procedure for Creating a Popup Menu

The following steps create a Popup menu. Following each step is a code segment that accomplishes the task.

1. Use the **XmCreatePopupMenu** convenience function to automatically create the Popup MenuPane and its required parent MenuShell. Register the event handler. The following lines create a Popup MenuPane as a child of widget **form1**.

```
popup = XmCreatePopupMenu(form1, "popup",
    NULL, 0);
XtAddEventHandler(form1, ButtonPressMask,
    False, PostIt, popup);
```

2. Create the contents of the MenuPane. The following segment creates a title (LabelGadget), SeparatorGadget, and three PushButtonGadgets.

```
XtSetArg(args[0], XmNlabelString,
    XmStringCreate ("Menu Title",
    XmSTRING_DEFAULT_CHARSET) );
item[0] = XmCreateLabelGadget(popup,
    "title", args, 1);
item[1] = XmCreateSeparatorGadget(popup,
    "separator", NULL, 0);
item[2] = XmCreatePushButtonGadget(popup,
    "button1", NULL, 0);
item[3] = XmCreatePushButtonGadget(popup,
    "button2", NULL, 0);
item[4] = XmCreatePushButtonGadget(popup,
    "button3", NULL, 0);
XtManageChildren(item, 5);
```

The following figure shows the parenting relationships to use when creating a Popup menu system using convenience functions.

Figure 6-8. Creating a Popup Menu System with Convenience Functions

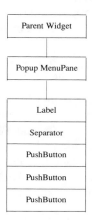

6.2.4 Interacting with Popup Menus

This section describes mouse and keyboard interactions with popup menus.

6.2.4.1 Mouse Input

Mouse button 3 is the default primary means of interacting with a Popup menu.

A Popup MenuPane is not visible until it is displayed by the user. The Popup menu system is normally associated with a particular widget and all of that widget's descendents. The Popup MenuPane is posted (displayed) by moving the pointer into the associated widget or one of its descendents and then pressing mouse button 3.

If the Popup menu system includes any Pulldown MenuPane submenus, they are not displayed until the pointer is moved into the associated CascadeButton widget or gadget.

The application is responsible for posting the Popup MenuPane by using **XtManageChild** to display the MenuPane. This is usually done in the event handler added to the Popup MenuPane's parent. All visible MenuPanes (the Popup MenuPane and any displayed submenus) are automatically unposted when the user has completed interacting with the menu.

Once a MenuPane has been posted, menu items are armed when the pointer enters them and disarmed when it leaves. If the pointer is moved into a CascadeButton or CascadeButtonGadget, the associated submenu is posted. Releasing mouse button 3 while a menu item is armed activates the menu item. If the pointer is not within a menu item when mouse button 3 is released, then all visible MenuPanes are unposted.

Ordinarily, a Popup menu is positioned to the right and beneath the pointer. However, if this placement causes a portion of the MenuPane to be inaccessible, the menu may be automatically repositioned to force the Popup MenuPane on the screen.

The mouse button used to interact with Popup menus can be changed using the RowColumn resource **XmNmenuPost**.

6.2.4.2 The Keyboard Interface

Keyboard traversal is activated and deactivated by the user. When a user is interacting with the menu using the mouse, traversal is enabled by releasing the mouse button while the pointer is within any CascadeButton or CascadeButtonGadget; releasing the mouse button posts the associated submenu and enables traversal for all the MenuPanes in the Popup menu system. When traversal is enabled

- The directional keys traverse the menu hierarchy.

- **KActivate** selects the currently armed menu item.

- **KCancel** unposts the currently posted Pulldown MenuPane. In the Popup menu, **KCancel** unposts the menu, returning focus to the tab group from which the menu was popped up.

- **KMenu** unposts all the MenuPanes in the Popup menu system, returning focus to the tab group from which the menu was popped up.

- Pressing a mnemonic for a menu item in the most recently posted MenuPane selects that item.

- Pressing an accelerator for a menu item selects that item.

- Pressing mouse button 3 disables traversal and reenables interactive operation.

An accelerator, **KMenu** by default, can be associated with a Popup menu. When **KMenu** is pressed while the pointer is located within the associated widget or one of its children, the first MenuPane in the Popup menu hierarchy is posted and traversal is enabled. The user interacts with the menu as described previously for keyboard traversal.

Use the resource **XmNmenuAccelerator** to change the accelerator.

6.2.5 Sample Program

This sample program creates a Popup menu system. The menu can be posted using the mouse or by using the accelerator **<Ctrl-P>**. Items can be selected using the mouse or by using the underlined mnemonics.

```
/* Popup Menu Example */

#include <Xm/Xm.h>
#include <Xm/LabelG.h>
#include <Xm/PushBG.h>
#include <Xm/CascadeBG.h>
#include <Xm/SeparatoG.h>
#include <Xm/RowColumn.h>
```

```
/*********** Callback for the Pushbuttons ******************/

void ButtonCB (w, client_data, call_data)
Widget      w;              /*  widget id          */
caddr_t     client_data;  /*  data from application   */
caddr_t     call_data;    /*  data from widget class  */
{
    /*  print message and terminate program  */
    printf ("Button %s selected.\n", client_data);
}

/************* Event Handler for Popup Menu *****************/

PostIt (w, popup, event)
Widget w;
Widget popup;
XButtonEvent * event;
{
    if (event->button != Button3)
        return;
    XmMenuPosition(popup, event);
    XtManageChild(popup);
}

/******************Main Logic for Program *****************/


void main (argc, argv)
int argc;
char **argv;
{
    XtAppContext app_context;
    Widget toplevel, popup, rc;
    Widget buttons[2], popupBtn[5];
    Arg args[5];

/* Initialize toolkit */

    toplevel = XtAppInitialize (&app_context, "PopupMenu", NULL,
                                0, &argc, argv, NULL, NULL, 0);
```

```
/* Create RowColumn in toplevel with two PushButtonGadgets */

    XtSetArg(args[0], XmNwidth, 150);
    XtSetArg(args[1], XmNheight, 125);
    XtSetArg(args[2], XmNresizeWidth, False);
    XtSetArg(args[3], XmNresizeHeight, False);
    XtSetArg(args[4], XmNadjustLast, False);
    rc = XmCreateRowColumn(toplevel, "rc", args, 5);
    XtManageChild(rc);

    buttons[0] = XmCreatePushButtonGadget (rc, "buttonA", NULL, 0);
    XtAddCallback(buttons[0], XmNactivateCallback, ButtonCB, "A");

    buttons[1] = XmCreatePushButtonGadget (rc, "buttonB", NULL, 0);
    XtAddCallback(buttons[1], XmNactivateCallback, ButtonCB, "B");
    XtManageChildren (buttons, 2);

/* Create popup menu with accelerator CTRL P */

    XtSetArg(args[0], XmNmenuAccelerator, "Ctrl <Key> p");
    popup = XmCreatePopupMenu(rc, "popup", args, 1);
    XtAddEventHandler(rc, ButtonPressMask, False, PostIt, popup);


/* Create title for the popup menu and a separator */

    XtSetArg(args[0], XmNlabelString,
        XmStringCreate("Menu Title", XmSTRING_DEFAULT_CHARSET) );
    popupBtn[0] = XmCreateLabelGadget(popup, "Title", args, 1);
    popupBtn[1] = XmCreateSeparatorGadget(popup, "separator",
                                          NULL, 0);
```

```
/* Create three PushButtonGadgets in the popup menu */

    XtSetArg(args[0], XmNmnemonic, '1');
    popupBtn[2] = XmCreatePushButtonGadget(popup,  "button1",
                                            args, 1);
    XtAddCallback(popupBtn[2],XmNactivateCallback,ButtonCB,"1");

    XtSetArg(args[0], XmNmnemonic, '2');
    popupBtn[3] = XmCreatePushButtonGadget(popup,  "button2",
                                            args, 1);
    XtAddCallback(popupBtn[3],XmNactivateCallback,ButtonCB,"2");

    XtSetArg(args[0], XmNmnemonic, '3');
    popupBtn[4] = XmCreatePushButtonGadget (popup, "button3",
                                            args, 1);
    XtAddCallback (popupBtn[4],XmNactivateCallback,ButtonCB,"3");
    XtManageChildren (popupBtn, 5);

/* Get and dispatch events */

    XtRealizeWidget(toplevel);

    XtAppMainLoop(app_context);
}
```

6.3 Creating a Pulldown Menu System

The basis of a Pulldown menu system is a MenuBar containing a set of CascadeButtons. (CascadeButtonGadgets are not allowed as the children of a MenuBar.) The CascadeButtons are used to display Pulldown MenuPanes. One of the CascadeButtons (typically, the one that is used to display help information) may be treated specially. This button is always positioned at the lower right corner of the MenuBar.

Two convenience functions, **XmCreateMenuBar** and **XmCreatePulldownMenu**, create the appropriate RowColumn widgets.

In addition to their use in Pulldown menu systems, Pulldown MenuPanes are used to create submenus in both Popup and Pulldown menu systems. Submenus are discussed in the next section.

6.3.1 MenuBar Create Function

A MenuBar is created using the convenience function:

Widget XmCreateMenuBar*(parent, name, arglist, argcount)*

XmCreateMenuBar creates a MenuBar as a RowColumn widget with the **XmNrowColumnType** resource set to XmMENU_BAR. This resource cannot be changed by the application. No MenuShell is created for MenuBar.

The MenuBar displays a 3-dimensional shadow around its edge unless this feature has been disabled by the application.

6.3.2 Pulldown MenuPane Create Function

A Pulldown MenuPane is created using the convenience function:

Widget XmCreatePulldownMenu*(parent, name, arglist, argcount)*

To create a Pulldown MenuPane that is displayed using a CascadeButton in a MenuBar, specify the MenuBar as the parent in the **XmCreatePulldownMenu** function.

XmCreatePulldownMenu creates a Pulldown MenuPane and a parent MenuShell, and returns the widget ID for the MenuPane. The Pulldown MenuPane is created as a RowColumn widget with the **XmNrowColumnType** resource set to XmMENU_PULLDOWN. This resource cannot be changed by the application.

6.3.3 Creating a Help Button

The MenuBar resource **XmNmenuHelpWidget** specifies a CascadeButton that will be positioned at the lower right corner of the MenuBar. Typically, this CascadeButton is used to display help information. The Pulldown menu sample program creates a Help button.

6.3.4 Procedure for Creating a Pulldown Menu

The following steps create a Pulldown menu. Following each step is a code segment that accomplishes the task.

1. Use the **XmCreateMenuBar** convenience function to create the MenuBar. The following lines create the MenuBar as the child of widget **form1**.

```
menubar        =        XmCreateMenuBar(form1,
"menubar", NULL, 0);
XtManageChild(menubar);
```

2. Create one or more Pulldown MenuPanes as submenus (children) of the MenuBar.

```
pulldown1 = XmCreatePulldownMenu(menubar,
    "pulldown1", NULL, 0);
pulldown2 = XmCreatePulldownMenu(menubar,
    "pulldown2", NULL, 0);
```

3. Create a CascadeButton widget for each Pulldown MenuPane. The CascadeButtons and MenuPanes must have the same parent (in this case, menubar). Use the resource **XmNsubMenuId** to attach each CascadeButton to its MenuPane.

```
XtSetArg(args[0],XmNsubMenuId,pulldown1);
cascade[0]=XmCreateCascadeButton(menubar,
    "cascade1",args,1);

XtSetArg(args[0],XmNsubMenuId,pulldown2);
cascade[1]=XmCreateCascadeButton(menubar,
    "cascade2",args,1);
XtManageChildren(cascade, 2);
```

4. Create one or more buttons in each Pulldown MenuPane. The following lines create two PushButtonGadgets in each MenuPane.

```
pbutton1[0] = XmCreatePushButtonGadget
    (pulldown1, "button1a", NULL, 0);
pbutton1[1] = XmCreatePushButtonGadget
    (pulldown1, "button1b", NULL, 0);
XtManageChildren(pbutton1, 2);

pbutton2[0] = XmCreatePushButtonGadget
    (pulldown2, "button2a", NULL, 0);
pbutton2[1] = XmCreatePushButtonGadget
    (pulldown2, "button2b", NULL, 0);
XtManageChildren(pbutton2, 2);
```

The following figure shows the parenting relationships and attachments (dashed lines) to use when creating a Pulldown menu system using convenience functions. The system includes a CascadeButton MenuPane designated as a Help menu.

Figure 6-9. Creating a Pulldown Menu System With Convenience Functions

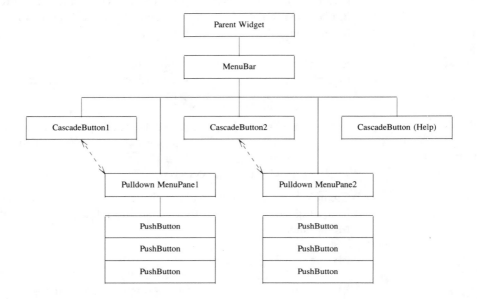

6.3.5 Interacting with Pulldown Menus

This section describes mouse and keyboard interaction with Pulldown menus.

6.3.5.1 Mouse Input

Mouse button 1 is the default primary means of interacting with a Pulldown menu. Pressing mouse button 1 while the pointer is positioned in a CascadeButton in the MenuBar arms and highlights the CascadeButton. If the CascadeButton has an associated Pulldown MenuPane, the MenuPane is posted. At this point, the pointer can be

- Moved down into the Pulldown MenuPane. Menu items are armed when the pointer enters them and disarmed when it leaves. If the pointer is moved into a CascadeButton widget or gadget, the associated submenu is posted. Releasing mouse button 1 while an item is armed activates the menu item.

- Moved to a different CascadeButton within the MenuBar. This unposts the current Pulldown MenuPane and posts the MenuPane attached to the other CascadeButton.

Releasing mouse button 1 while the pointer is outside the menu hierarchy unposts all visible submenus and disarms the MenuBar.

The mouse button used to interact with Pulldown menus can be changed using the RowColumn resource **XmNmenuPost** for the MenuBar.

6.3.5.2 The Keyboard Interface

Keyboard traversal is activated and deactivated by the user. When a user is interacting with the menu using the mouse, traversal is enabled by either of the following:

- Releasing the mouse button while the pointer is within any CascadeButton widget or gadget. Releasing the mouse button posts the associated submenu and enables traversal for all the MenuPanes in the Pulldown menu system.

- Pressing **KMenuBar**. This highlights the first CascadeButton in the MenuBar and enables traversal. **KLeft** and **KRight** traverse to other CascadeButtons in the MenuBar. **KDown** or **KActivate** posts the Pulldown MenuPane associated with the highlighted CascadeButton.

When traversal is enabled,

- The directional keys traverse the menu hierarchy.

- **KActivate** selects the currently armed menu item.

- **KCancel** unposts the currently posted Pulldown MenuPane. In the MenuBar, **KCancel** disarms the CascadeButton, returning the focus to the tab group that had focus when the MenuBar was entered.

- **KMenuBar** unposts all the submenus and disarms the CascadeButton in the MenuBar, returning the focus to the tab group that had focus when the MenuBar was entered.

- Pressing a mnemonic for a menu item in the most recently posted MenuPane selects that item.

- Pressing an accelerator for a menu item selects that item.

- Pressing mouse button 1 disables traversal and reenables interactive operation.

Mnemonics can be used to post the Pulldown MenuPanes. The mnemonics are resources of the CascadeButtons in the MenuBar. To use a mnemonic associated with a MenuBar CascadeButton, preface it with the **Meta** modifier key. Traversal is enabled when a menu is posted using a mnemonic. The user interacts with the menu as described previously for keyboard traversal.

6.3.6 Sample Program

The following sample program creates a Pulldown menu system consisting of a MenuBar containing three CascadeButtons. One CascadeButton is designated as a Help button; the other two are attached to Pulldown MenuPanes.

All the CascadeButtons and PushButtons have mnemonics.

```
/* Pulldown Menu Example */

#include <Xm/Xm.h>
#include <Xm/RowColumn.h>
#include <Xm/PushBG.h>
#include <Xm/Form.h>
#include <Xm/CascadeB.h>

/**** Callback for the pushbuttons in the pulldown menu. *****/

void ButtonCB (w, client_data, call_data)
Widget      w;                /*  widget id          */
caddr_t     client_data;  /*  data from application   */
caddr_t     call_data;    /*  data from widget class  */
{
   /*  print message and terminate program  */
   printf ("Button %s selected.\n", client_data);
}

/***************Main Logic*********************************/

void main (argc, argv)
unsigned int argc;
char **argv;

{
   XtAppContext app_context;
   Widget toplevel, form, menubar;
   Widget menubarBtn[3], pulldowns[2];
   Widget buttons1[3], buttons2[3];
   Arg args [4];
```

```
/* Initialize toolkit and create form and menubar */

   toplevel =
        XtAppInitialize (&app_context, "PulldownMenu", NULL, 0,
                         &argc, argv, NULL, NULL, 0);

   XtSetArg(args[0], XmNwidth, 250);
   XtSetArg(args[1], XmNheight, 125);
   form = XmCreateForm(toplevel, "form", (ArgList) args, 2);
   XtManageChild(form);

   XtSetArg(args[0], XmNtopAttachment, XmATTACH_FORM);
   XtSetArg(args[1], XmNrightAttachment, XmATTACH_FORM);
   XtSetArg(args[2], XmNleftAttachment, XmATTACH_FORM);
   menubar = XmCreateMenuBar(form, "menubar", args, 4);
   XtManageChild(menubar);

/* Create help button in menubar */

   XtSetArg(args[0], XmNlabelString, XmStringCreate("Help",
            XmSTRING_DEFAULT_CHARSET) );
   XtSetArg(args[1], XmNmnemonic, 'H');
   menubarBtn[0] = XmCreateCascadeButton(menubar, "help",
                                                 args, 2);
   XtAddCallback(menubarBtn[0], XmNactivateCallback, ButtonCB,
                 "Help");

   XtSetArg(args[0], XmNmenuHelpWidget, (XtArgVal)menubarBtn[0]);
   XtSetValues(menubar, args, 1);


/* Create 2 Pulldown MenuPanes and 2 CascadeButtons in menubar */

   pulldowns[0] = XmCreatePulldownMenu(menubar, "pulldown1",
                                          NULL, 0);

   XtSetArg(args[0], XmNsubMenuId, pulldowns[0]);
   XtSetArg(args[1], XmNlabelString, XmStringCreate("Left Menu",
            XmSTRING_DEFAULT_CHARSET) );
   XtSetArg(args[2], XmNmnemonic, 'L');
   menubarBtn[1] = XmCreateCascadeButton(menubar, "button1",
                                            args, 3);

   pulldowns[1] = XmCreatePulldownMenu(menubar, "pulldown2",
                                          NULL, 0);

   XtSetArg(args[0], XmNsubMenuId, pulldowns[1]);
```

```
XtSetArg(args[1], XmNlabelString, XmStringCreate("Right Menu",
        XmSTRING_DEFAULT_CHARSET) );
XtSetArg(args[2], XmNmnemonic, 'R');
menubarBtn[2] = XmCreateCascadeButton(menubar,  "button2",
                                      args, 3);
XtManageChildren(menubarBtn,  3);


XtSetArg(args[0], XmNlabelString, XmStringCreate("First",
        XmSTRING_DEFAULT_CHARSET) );
XtSetArg(args[1], XmNmnemonic, 'F');
buttons1[0] =
   XmCreatePushButtonGadget(pulldowns[0],"button1a",args,2);
XtAddCallback(buttons1[0], XmNactivateCallback,
             ButtonCB, "Left-First");

XtSetArg(args[0], XmNlabelString, XmStringCreate("Second",
        XmSTRING_DEFAULT_CHARSET) );
XtSetArg(args[1], XmNmnemonic, 'S');
buttons1[1] =
   XmCreatePushButtonGadget(pulldowns[0],"button1b",args,2);
XtAddCallback(buttons1[1], XmNactivateCallback,
             ButtonCB, "Left-Second");

XtSetArg(args[0], XmNlabelString, XmStringCreate("Third",
        XmSTRING_DEFAULT_CHARSET) );
XtSetArg(args[1], XmNmnemonic, 'T');
buttons1[2] =
   XmCreatePushButtonGadget(pulldowns[0],"button1c",args,2);
XtAddCallback(buttons1[2], XmNactivateCallback,
             ButtonCB, "Left-Third");
XtManageChildren(buttons1,  3);


XtSetArg(args[0], XmNlabelString, XmStringCreate("First",
        XmSTRING_DEFAULT_CHARSET) );
XtSetArg(args[1], XmNmnemonic, 'F');
buttons2[0] =
   XmCreatePushButtonGadget(pulldowns[1],"button2a",args,2);
XtAddCallback(buttons2[0], XmNactivateCallback,
             ButtonCB, "Right-First");

XtSetArg(args[0], XmNlabelString, XmStringCreate("Second",
        XmSTRING_DEFAULT_CHARSET) );
XtSetArg(args[1], XmNmnemonic, 'S');
buttons2[1] =
   XmCreatePushButtonGadget(pulldowns[1],"button2b",args,2);
```

```
    XtAddCallback(buttons2[1], XmNactivateCallback,
            ButtonCB, "Right-Second");

    XtSetArg(args[0], XmNlabelString, XmStringCreate("Third",
            XmSTRING_DEFAULT_CHARSET) );
    XtSetArg(args[1], XmNmnemonic, 'T');
    buttons2[2] =
        XmCreatePushButtonGadget(pulldowns[1],"button2c",args,2);
    XtAddCallback(buttons2[2], XmNactivateCallback,
            ButtonCB, "Right-Third");
    XtManageChildren(buttons2, 3);

/* Get and dispatch events */

    XtRealizeWidget(toplevel);

    XtAppMainLoop(app_context);
}
```

6.4 Creating Submenus

Submenus are implemented using Pulldown MenuPanes attached to CascadeButton widgets or gadgets. The submenu and the CascadeButton to which it is attached are children of the MenuPane (Popup or Pulldown) from which the submenu cascades.

The MenuShell of the submenu is created automatically if the submenu is created using **XmCreatePulldownMenu** convenience function:

Widget CreatePulldownMenu(*parent*, *name*, *arglist*, *argcount*);

The submenu's MenuShell is created as the child of the *parent*'s MenuShell.

6.4.1 Procedure for Creating Submenus

The following steps create a submenu of a Popup menu, and then create a submenu of that submenu. Following each step is a code segment that accomplishes the task.

1. Create the Popup MenuPane. The following line creates the Popup MenuPane as a child of widget **form1**.

```
popup = XmCreatePopupMenu(form1, "popup",
    NULL, 0);
```

2. To create a submenu, create a Pulldown MenuPane and CascadeButtonGadget as the children of the Popup MenuPane. Use the resource XmNsubMenuId to attach the CascadeButtonGadget to the MenuPane.

```
submenu1 = XmCreatePulldownMenu(popup,
    "submenu1", NULL, 0);

XtSetArg(args[0],XmNsubMenuId,submenu1);
cascade1 = XmCreateCascadeButtonGadget(
    popup, "cascade1", args, 1);
XtManageChild(cascade1);
```

3. To create a submenu of submenu1, create a Pulldown MenuPane and CascadeButtonGadget as children of submenu1.

```
submenu3 = XmCreatePulldownMenu(submenu1,
    "submenu3", NULL, 0);

XtSetArg(args[0],XmNsubMenuId,submenu3);
cascade3 = XmCreateCascadeButtonGadget
    (submenu1, "cascade3", args, 1);
XtManageChild(cascade3);
```

Figure 6-10 shows the parenting relationships and attachments (dashed lines) to use when creating submenus in a Popup menu system using convenience functions. This system contains two submenus beneath the top level Popup MenuPane. The first submenu contains two PushButtons and one CascadeButtonGadget (CascadeButton3). The CascadeButtonGadget is used to access the submenu (Pulldown MenuPane3) that cascades from the first submenu.

Figure 6-10. Creating Submenus With Convenience Functions

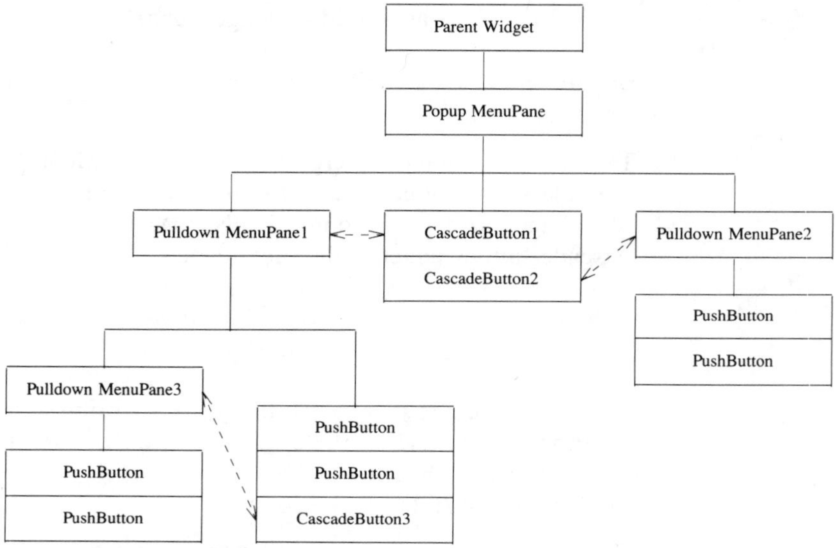

6.4.2 Interacting with Submenus

Interacting with submenus is explained earlier in of this chapter in the sections "Interacting with Popup Menus" and "Interacting with Pulldown Menus."

6.4.3 Sample Program

The following program creates the Popup menu system (with submenus) that is illustrated in Figure 6-10.

```
/* Popup Menu with Submenus Example */

#include <Xm/Xm.h>
#include <Xm/PushBG.h>
#include <Xm/CascadeBG.h>
#include <Xm/RowColumn.h>


/******** Callback for the Pushbuttons ***************/

void ButtonCB (w, client_data, call_data)
Widget      w;              /*  widget id          */
caddr_t     client_data;  /*  data from application   */
caddr_t     call_data;    /*  data from widget class  */
{
   /*  print message and terminate program  */
   printf ("Button %s selected.\n", client_data);
}

/* ******* Event Handler for Popup Menu **************/

PostIt (w, popup, event)
Widget w;
Widget popup;
XButtonEvent * event;
{
   if (event->button != Button3)
       return;
   XmMenuPosition(popup,  event);
   XtManageChild(popup);
}
```

```
/**************Main Logic for Program *************/


void main (argc, argv)
int argc;
char **argv;
{
   XtAppContext app_context;
   Widget toplevel, popup, rc;
   Widget submenu1, submenu2, submenu3, buttons[2];
   Widget popupBtn[2], sub1Btn[3], sub2Btn[2], sub3Btn[2];
   Arg args[5];

/* Initialize toolkit */
   toplevel = XtAppInitialize (&app_context, "PopupMenu", NULL,
                               0, &argc, argv, NULL, NULL, 0);

/* Create RowColumn in toplevel with two pushbuttons */

   XtSetArg(args[0], XmNwidth, 400);
   XtSetArg(args[1], XmNheight, 125);
   XtSetArg(args[2], XmNresizeWidth, False);
   XtSetArg(args[3], XmNresizeHeight, False);
   XtSetArg(args[4], XmNadjustLast, False);
   rc = XmCreateRowColumn(toplevel, "rc", args, 5);
   XtManageChild(rc);

   buttons[0]=XmCreatePushButtonGadget(rc, "button1", NULL, 0);
   XtAddCallback(buttons[0],XmNactivateCallback,ButtonCB,"1");

   buttons[1]=XmCreatePushButtonGadget(rc, "button2", NULL, 0);
   XtAddCallback(buttons[1],XmNactivateCallback,ButtonCB,"2");
   XtManageChildren(buttons, 2);

/* Create popup menu */

   popup = XmCreatePopupMenu(rc, "popup", NULL, 0);
   XtAddEventHandler(rc, ButtonPressMask, False, PostIt, popup);
```

```
/* Create two submenus and CascadeButtons in the popup menu */

    submenu1 =
        (Widget)XmCreatePulldownMenu(popup,  "submenu1", NULL, 0);

    XtSetArg(args[0], XmNsubMenuId, submenu1);
    XtSetArg(args[1], XmNlabelString, XmStringCreate(
            "First Submenu", XmSTRING_DEFAULT_CHARSET) );
    popupBtn[0] =
        XmCreateCascadeButtonGadget(popup,  "cbutton1", args, 2);


    submenu2 =
        (Widget)XmCreatePulldownMenu(popup,  "submenu2", NULL, 0);

    XtSetArg(args[0], XmNsubMenuId, submenu2);
    XtSetArg(args[1], XmNlabelString, XmStringCreate(
            "Second Submenu", XmSTRING_DEFAULT_CHARSET) );
    popupBtn[1] =
        XmCreateCascadeButtonGadget(popup,  "cbutton2", args, 2);
    XtManageChildren(popupBtn,  2);

/* Create pushbuttons in submenu1 and submenu2. */

    sub1Btn[0] =
        XmCreatePushButtonGadget(submenu1,  "button1a", NULL, 0);
    XtAddCallback(sub1Btn[0],XmNactivateCallback,ButtonCB,"1a");

    sub1Btn[1] =
        XmCreatePushButtonGadget(submenu1,  "button1b", NULL, 0);
    XtAddCallback(sub1Btn[1],XmNactivateCallback,ButtonCB,"1b");

    sub2Btn[0] =
        XmCreatePushButtonGadget(submenu2,  "button2a", NULL, 0);
    XtAddCallback(sub2Btn[0],XmNactivateCallback,ButtonCB,"2a");

    sub2Btn[1] =
        XmCreatePushButtonGadget(submenu2,  "button2b", NULL, 0);
    XtAddCallback(sub2Btn[1],XmNactivateCallback,ButtonCB,"2b");
    XtManageChildren(sub2Btn,  2);
```

```
/* Create a submenu of submenu 1 */

    submenu3 =
        (Widget) XmCreatePulldownMenu(submenu1,  "submenu3", NULL, 0);

    XtSetArg(args[0], XmNsubMenuId, submenu3);
    XtSetArg(args[1], XmNlabelString, XmStringCreate(
        "To Third Submenu", XmSTRING_DEFAULT_CHARSET) );
    sub1Btn[2] =
        XmCreateCascadeButtonGadget(submenu1, "cbutton3", args, 2);
    XtManageChildren(sub1Btn, 3);

/* Create pushbuttons in submenu 3 */

    sub3Btn[0] =
        XmCreatePushButtonGadget(submenu3, "button3a", NULL, 0);
    XtAddCallback(sub3Btn[0],XmNactivateCallback,ButtonCB,"3a");

    sub3Btn[1] =
        XmCreatePushButtonGadget(submenu3, "button3b", NULL, 0);
    XtAddCallback(sub3Btn[1],XmNactivateCallback,ButtonCB,"3b");
    XtManageChildren(sub3Btn, 2);

/* Get and dispatch events */

    XtRealizeWidget(toplevel);

    XtAppMainLoop(app_context);
}
```

6.5 Creating Option Menu Systems

The basis of an Option menu system is the following:

- An Option menu. An Option menu is created by the convenience function **XmCreateOptionMenu**. It is a specialized RowColumn manager composed of two internal gadgets:

  — A selection area. The selection area is a specialized CascadeButtonGadget. It provides the means for displaying an associated Pulldown MenuPane, and it displays the label string of the last item selected from the Pulldown MenuPane. The **XmNmenuHistory** resource defines the initial item displayed. (The default is the first item in the Pulldown MenuPane.)

  — A label. The label is a specialized LabelGadget, and is displayed to the left of the selection area.

- A Pulldown MenuPane attached to the Option menu. The Pulldown MenuPane contains a PushButton or PushButtonGadget for each available option.

The Option menu typically does not display any 3-dimensional visuals around itself or its internal label. The internal CascadeButtonGadget has a 3-dimensional shadow. This can be changed by the application using the standard visual-related resources.

6.5.1 Option MenuPane Create Function

An Option menu can be created using this convenience function:

Widget XmCreateOptionMenu(*parent*, *name*, *arglist*, *argcount*)

XmCreateOptionMenu automatically creates an Option menu and two internal gadgets—a CascadeButtonGadget (selection area) and LabelGadget (label area). The function returns the widget ID of the Option menu. The Option menu is created as a RowColumn widget with the **XmNrowColumnType** resource set to XmMENU_OPTION.

The two internal gadgets can be accessed separately using the following functions:

- **Widget XmOptionLabelGadget**(*option_menu*) returns the ID of the LabelGadget.

- **Widget XmOptionButtonGadget**(*option_menu*) returns the ID of the CascadeButtonGadget.

These functions allow the application to have more control over the visuals associated with the label and selection areas.

6.5.2 Procedure for Creating an Option Menu

The following steps create an Option menu. Following each step is a code segment that accomplishes the task.

1. Create the Pulldown MenuPane that will contain the selection items.

```
optionsubmenu = XmCreatePulldownMenu(form1,
    "optionsubmenu", NULL, 0);
```

2. Create the selection items for the Pulldown MenuPane.

```
option[0] = XmCreatePushButtonGadget
    (optionsubmenu, "option1", NULL, 0);
option[1] = XmCreatePushButtonGadget
    (optionsubmenu, "option2", NULL, 0);
XtManageChildren(option, 2);
```

3. Use the **XmCreateOptionMenu** convenience function to create the Option menu and attach it to the Pulldown MenuPane. Also specify a string for the Label area.

```
string = XmStringCreate("Options:",
    XmSTRING_DEFAULT_CHARSET);
XtSetArg(args[0], XmNlabelString, string);
XtSetArg(args[1], XmNsubMenuId,
        optionsubmenu);
option_menu = XmCreateOptionMenu(form1,
    "option_menu", args, 2);
XmStringFree(string);
XtManageChild(option_menu);
```

The components of the Option menu system must be created in the order shown. (You cannot use **XtSetValues** to specify the Option menu's submenu.)

The following figure shows the parenting relationships and attachments (dashed lines) used to create Option menu systems using convenience functions. Each Pulldown MenuPane contains three options.

Figure 6-11. Creating Option Menu Systems Convenience Functions

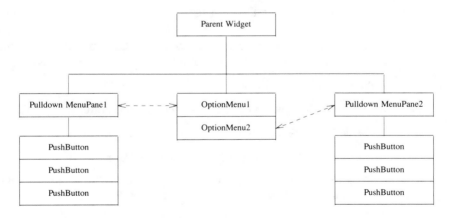

6.5.3 Interacting with Option Menus

The following sections describe mouse and keyboard interactions with option menus.

6.5.3.1 Mouse Input

The Pulldown MenuPane is posted by moving the mouse pointer over the selection area and pressing mouse button 1. The Pulldown MenuPane is positioned so that the last selected item is directly over the selection area; the MenuPane is not repositioned if a portion is inaccessible.

Menu items are armed when the pointer enters them and disarmed when it leaves. Releasing mouse button 1 while a menu item is armed selects the menu item and changes the label in the selection area.

The mouse button used to interact with Option menus can be changed using the RowColumn resource **XmNmenuPost**.

6.5.3.2 The Keyboard Interface

A mnemonic can be associated with the Option menu. Typing the mnemonic posts the Pulldown MenuPane and enables traversal.

When traversal is enabled,

- The directional keys traverse the menu hierarchy.

- **KActivate** selects the currently armed menu item.

- **KCancel** unposts the Pulldown MenuPane.

- Pressing the mouse button disables traversal and reenables interactive operation.

- Pressing a mnemonic or accelerator for a menu item selects that item.

6.5.4 Sample Program

The following sample program contains two option menus with three options each. The Pulldown MenuPanes can be posted using the mouse or by using the mnemonics **F** and **S**. When a MenuPane has been posted using a mnemonic, a mnemonic can then be used to select an option.

The source code for this program is located on your system in **./demos/xmsamplers/xmoption.c**.

```c
/* Option Menu Example */

#include <Xm/Xm.h>
#include <Xm/PushBG.h>
#include <Xm/CascadeBG.h>
#include <Xm/RowColumn.h>


/*********** Callback for the Pushbuttons *****************/

void ButtonCB (w, client_data, call_data)
Widget      w;              /*  widget id             */
caddr_t     client_data;  /*  data from application   */
caddr_t     call_data;    /*  data from widget class  */
{
   /*  print message and terminate program  */
   printf ("Option %s selected.\n", client_data);
}

/*****************Main Logic for Program *******************/


void main (argc, argv)
int argc;
char **argv;
{
   XtAppContext app_context;
   Widget toplevel, pulldown1, pulldown2, rc;
   Widget option_menus[2], options1[3], options2[3];
   Arg args[6];
```

```
/* Initialize toolkit */
   toplevel = XtAppInitialize (&app_context, "OptionMenu", NULL,
                               0, &argc, argv, NULL, NULL, 0);

/* Create RowColumn in toplevel */

   XtSetArg(args[0], XmNwidth, 375);
   XtSetArg(args[1], XmNheight, 75);
   XtSetArg(args[2], XmNresizeWidth, False);
   XtSetArg(args[3], XmNresizeHeight, False);
   XtSetArg(args[4], XmNnumColumns, 2);
   XtSetArg(args[5], XmNpacking, XmPACK_COLUMN);
   rc = XmCreateRowColumn(toplevel, "rc", args, 6);
   XtManageChild(rc);

/* Create two pulldown menus in rc */

   pulldown1 =
       (Widget)XmCreatePulldownMenu(rc, "pulldown1", NULL, 0);

   XtSetArg(args[0], XmNlabelString, XmStringCreate("A-option",
            XmSTRING_DEFAULT_CHARSET) );
   XtSetArg(args[1], XmNmnemonic, 'A');
   options1[0] =
       XmCreatePushButtonGadget(pulldown1, "option1a", args, 2);
   XtAddCallback(options1[0],XmNactivateCallback,ButtonCB,"1A");

   XtSetArg(args[0], XmNlabelString, XmStringCreate("B-option",
            XmSTRING_DEFAULT_CHARSET) );
   XtSetArg(args[1], XmNmnemonic, 'B');
   options1[1] =
       XmCreatePushButtonGadget(pulldown1, "option1b", args, 2);
   XtAddCallback(options1[1],XmNactivateCallback,ButtonCB,"1B");

   XtSetArg(args[0], XmNlabelString, XmStringCreate("C-option",
            XmSTRING_DEFAULT_CHARSET) );
   XtSetArg(args[1], XmNmnemonic, 'C');
   options1[2] =
       XmCreatePushButtonGadget(pulldown1, "option1c", args, 2);
   XtAddCallback(options1[2],XmNactivateCallback,ButtonCB,"1C");
   XtManageChildren(options1, 3);
```

```
    pulldown2 =
        (Widget)XmCreatePulldownMenu(rc,  "pulldown2", NULL, 0);

    XtSetArg(args[0], XmNlabelString, XmStringCreate("A-option",
            XmSTRING_DEFAULT_CHARSET) );
    XtSetArg(args[1], XmNmnemonic, 'A');
    options2[0] =
        XmCreatePushButtonGadget(pulldown2,  "option2a", args, 2);
    XtAddCallback(options2[0],XmNactivateCallback,ButtonCB,"2A");

    XtSetArg(args[0], XmNlabelString, XmStringCreate("B-option",
            XmSTRING_DEFAULT_CHARSET) );
    XtSetArg(args[1], XmNmnemonic, 'B');
    options2[1] =
        XmCreatePushButtonGadget(pulldown2,  "option2b", args, 2);
    XtAddCallback(options2[1],XmNactivateCallback,ButtonCB,"2B");

    XtSetArg(args[0], XmNlabelString, XmStringCreate("C-option",
            XmSTRING_DEFAULT_CHARSET) );
    XtSetArg(args[1], XmNmnemonic, 'C');
    options2[2] =
        XmCreatePushButtonGadget(pulldown2,  "option2c", args, 2);
    XtAddCallback(options2[2],XmNactivateCallback,ButtonCB,"2C");
    XtManageChildren(options2,  3);

/* Create option menus and attach the two pulldown menus */
    XtSetArg(args[0], XmNlabelString, XmStringCreate(
            "First Option Set:", XmSTRING_DEFAULT_CHARSET) );
    XtSetArg(args[1], XmNmnemonic, 'F');
    XtSetArg(args[2], XmNsubMenuId, pulldown1);
    XtSetArg(args[3], XmNmenuHistory, options1[2]);
    option_menus[0] = XmCreateOptionMenu(rc, "option_menu1",
                                        args, 4);

    XtSetArg(args[0], XmNlabelString, XmStringCreate(
            "Second Option Set:", XmSTRING_DEFAULT_CHARSET) );
    XtSetArg(args[1], XmNmnemonic, 'S');
    XtSetArg(args[2], XmNsubMenuId, pulldown2);
    XtSetArg(args[3], XmNmenuHistory, options2[0]);
    option_menus[1]=XmCreateOptionMenu(rc,"option_menu2",args,4);
    XtManageChildren(option_menus,  2);

/* Get and dispatch events */
    XtRealizeWidget(toplevel);
    XtAppMainLoop(app_context);
}
```

6.6 Selecting a Menu Cursor

OSF/Motif provides a number of menu cursors (listed at the end of this section.) An application can select a specific menu cursor that is used whenever a menu is displayed. This feature provides consistent appearance within menus that belong to the same application. The default menu cursor is **arrow**.

The menu cursor can be specified at application startup by the resource **XmNmenuCursor**. This resource is not associated with a particular widget, and can only be set at application startup. The resource can be set two ways:

- By setting a resource in a defaults file. For example:

```
*menuCursor: star
```

  sets **star** as the menu cursor.

- By using the **-xrm** command line argument. For example, the following command line specifies a clock as the menu cursor for the application named **myprog**:

  myprog -xrm "*menuCursor: clock"

The cursor can be specified programmatically using the **XmSetMenuCursor** function:

void XmSetMenuCursor(*display*, *cursorId*)
    Display **display*;
    Cursor cursorId;

display   Specifies the display for which the cursor is used

cursorId   Specifies the menu cursor

After the function is executed, any menu displayed by the application on the specified display uses the menu cursor identified in the *cursorId* variable. This allows the application to use different menu cursors on different displays.

The **XmGetMenuCursor** function returns the cursor ID of the current menu cursor for a specified display:

Cursor XmGetMenuCursor(*display*)
   Display **display*;

display   Specifies the display.

If the application has not created any menus, no cursor is defined and the function returns the value None. The following list shows the valid cursor names.

arrow	gobbler	sailboat
based_arrow_down	gumby	sb_down_arrow
based_arrow_up	hand1	sb_h_double_arrow
boat	hand2	sb_left_arrow
bogosity	heart	sb_right_arrow
bottom_left_corner	icon	sb_up_arrow
bottom_right_corner	iron_cross	sb_v_double_arrow
bottom_side	left_ptr	shuttle
bottom_tee	left_side	sizing
box_spiral	left_tee	spider
centr_ptr	leftbutton	spraycan
circle	ll_angle	star
clock	lr_angle	target
coffee_mug	man	tcross
cross	middlebutton	top_left_arrow
cross_reverse	mouse	top_left_corner
crosshair	pencil	top_right_corner
diamond_cross	pirate	top_side
dot	plus	top_tee
dotbox	question_arrow	trek
double_arrow	right_ptr	ul_angle
draft_large	right_side	umbrella
draft_small	right_tee	ur_angle
exchange	rightbutton	watch
fleur	rtl_logo	xterm

6.7 Creating Menus Without Convenience Functions

Applications that use the menu system convenience functions do not need to explicitly create MenuShell widgets; the **XmCreatePopupMenu** and **XmCreatePulldownMenu** functions create a Popup or Pulldown MenuPane and the parent MenuShell.

If an application requires access to individual MenuShells in an application, the MenuShells and MenuPanes can be created by using the standard X Toolkit create routines or by using the create functions for MenuShells and RowColumn Widgets.

6.7.1 Functions for Creating Menus

Three functions are used in creating menu systems.

- The MenuShell specific create function:

  Widget XmCreateMenuShell (*parent*, *name*, *arglist*, *argcount*)

  creates an instance of a MenuShell widget and returns the associated widget ID.

- The X Toolkit function:

  Widget XtCreatePopupShell(*name*, *widget_class*, *parent*, *args*, *num_args*)

  can be used to create a MenuShell for a Popup or Pulldown MenuPane.

- The RowColumn specific create function:

  Widget XmCreateRowColumn (*parent*, *name*, *arglist*, *argcount*)

  creates an instance of a RowColumn widget and returns the associated widget ID.

6.7.2 Parenting Relationships

The parenting relationships required to create a menu system without using convenience functions depend on the type of menu system being built:

- If the MenuShell is for a Popup MenuPane, the MenuShell must be the parent of the Popup MenuPane (see Figure 6-12).

- If the MenuShell is for a MenuPane that is pulled down from a MenuBar, the MenuShell must be created as a child of the MenuBar (see Figure 6-13).

- If the MenuShell is for a submenu MenuPane that is pulled down from a Popup or another Pulldown MenuPane, the MenuShell must be created as a child of the Popup or Pulldown MenuPane's parent MenuShell (see Figure 6-14).

- If the MenuShell is for a Pulldown MenuPane in an Option menu, the MenuShell must have the same parent as the Option menu (see Figure 6-15).

Figure 6-12. Creating a Popup Menu System Without Convenience Functions

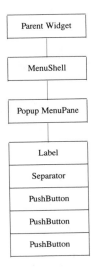

Figure 6-13. Creating a Pulldown Menu System Without Convenience
Functions

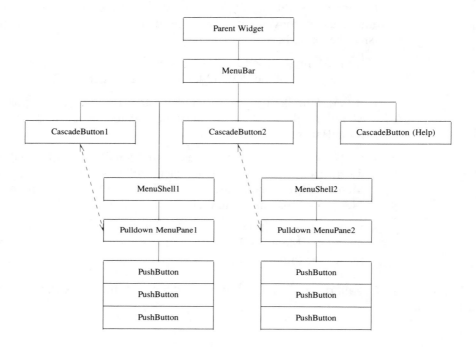

Figure 6-14. Creating Submenus Without Convenience Functions

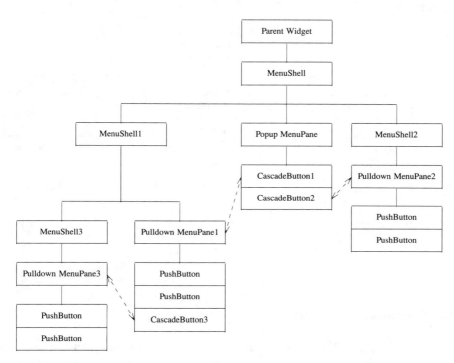

Figure 6-15. Creating an Option Menu System Without Convenience Functions

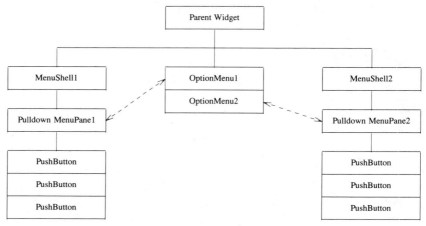

6.7.3 Sample Program

The following program creates a Popup menu system without using the convenience functions. Figure 6-14 illustrates the menu system created by this program.

The source code for this program is located on your system in **./demos/xmsamplers/xmmenushel.c**.

```
/* Popup Menu and Submenus created with MenuShells */

#include <Xm/Xm.h>
#include <Xm/MenuShell.h>
#include <Xm/PushBG.h>
#include <Xm/CascadeBG.h>
#include <Xm/RowColumn.h>
```

```
/********** Callback for the Pushbuttons *****************/

void ButtonCB (w, client_data, call_data)
Widget      w;              /*  widget id         */
caddr_t     client_data;  /*  data from application  */
caddr_t     call_data;    /*  data from widget class  */
{
   /*  print message and terminate program  */
   printf ("Button %s selected.\n", client_data);
}

/********** Event Handler for Popup Menu ******************/

PostIt (w, popup, event)
Widget w;
Widget popup;
XButtonEvent * event;
{
   if (event->button != Button3)
       return;
   XmMenuPosition(popup, event);
   XtManageChild(popup);
}



/****************Main Logic for Program *******************/


void main (argc, argv)
int argc;
char **argv;
{
   XtAppContext app_context;
   Widget toplevel, rc, buttons[2];
   Widget popupshell, mshell1, mshell2, mshell3;
   Widget popup, submenu1, submenu2, submenu3;
   Widget popupBtn[2], sub1Btn[3], sub2Btn[2], sub3Btn[2];
   Arg args[5];

/* Initialize toolkit */

   toplevel = XtAppInitialize (&app_context, "PopupMenu", NULL,
                          0, &argc, argv, NULL, NULL, 0);
```

```
/* Create RowColumn in toplevel with two pushbuttons */

    XtSetArg(args[0], XmNwidth, 150);
    XtSetArg(args[1], XmNheight, 50);
    XtSetArg(args[2], XmNresizeWidth, False);
    XtSetArg(args[3], XmNresizeHeight, False);
    XtSetArg(args[4], XmNadjustLast, False);
    rc = XmCreateRowColumn(toplevel, "rc", args, 5);
    XtManageChild(rc);

    buttons[0]=XmCreatePushButtonGadget(rc,"button1",NULL,0);
    XtAddCallback(buttons[0],XmNactivateCallback,ButtonCB,"1");

    buttons[1]=XmCreatePushButtonGadget(rc,"button2",NULL,0);
    XtAddCallback(buttons[1],XmNactivateCallback,ButtonCB,"2");
    XtManageChildren(buttons, 2);

/* Create MenuShell for a Popup MenuPane */

    XtSetArg(args[0], XmNheight, 100);
    XtSetArg(args[1], XmNwidth, 100);
    popupshell = XmCreateMenuShell(rc, "popupshell", args, 2);

/* Create RowColumn Widget configured as Popup MenuPane */

    XtSetArg(args[0], XmNrowColumnType, XmMENU_POPUP);
    popup = XmCreateRowColumn (popupshell, "popup", args, 1);
    XtAddEventHandler(rc, ButtonPressMask, False, PostIt, popup);

/* Create MenuShells and Pulldown MenuPanes for two submenus */

    XtSetArg(args[0], XmNheight, 100);
    XtSetArg(args[1], XmNwidth, 100);
    mshell1 = XmCreateMenuShell (popupshell, "mshell1", args, 2);

    XtSetArg(args[0], XmNrowColumnType, XmMENU_PULLDOWN);
    submenu1 = XmCreateRowColumn (mshell1, "submenu1", args, 1);

    XtSetArg(args[0], XmNheight, 100);
    XtSetArg(args[1], XmNwidth, 100);
    mshell2 = XmCreateMenuShell (popupshell, "mshell2", args, 2);

    XtSetArg(args[0], XmNrowColumnType, XmMENU_PULLDOWN);
    submenu2 = XmCreateRowColumn (mshell2, "submenu2", args, 1);
```

```
/* Create two Cascade Buttons in the Popup MenuPane */

    XtSetArg(args[0], XmNsubMenuId, submenu1);
    XtSetArg(args[1], XmNlabelString, XmStringCreate(
            "First Submenu", XmSTRING_DEFAULT_CHARSET) );
    popupBtn[0] =
        XmCreateCascadeButtonGadget(popup, "cbutton1", args, 2);

    XtSetArg(args[0], XmNsubMenuId, submenu2);
    XtSetArg(args[1], XmNlabelString, XmStringCreate(
            "Second Submenu", XmSTRING_DEFAULT_CHARSET) );
    popupBtn[1] =
        XmCreateCascadeButtonGadget(popup, "cbutton2", args, 2);
    XtManageChildren (popupBtn, 2);

/* Create pushbuttons in MenuPanes submenu1 and submenu2 */

    sub1Btn[0] =
        XmCreatePushButtonGadget(submenu1, "button1a", NULL, 0);
    XtAddCallback(sub1Btn[0],XmNactivateCallback,ButtonCB,"1a");

    sub1Btn[1] =
        XmCreatePushButtonGadget(submenu1, "button1b", NULL, 0);
    XtAddCallback(sub1Btn[1],XmNactivateCallback,ButtonCB,"1b");

    sub2Btn[0] =
        XmCreatePushButtonGadget(submenu2, "button2a", NULL, 0);
    XtAddCallback(sub2Btn[0],XmNactivateCallback,ButtonCB,"2a");

    sub2Btn[1] =
        XmCreatePushButtonGadget(submenu2, "button2b", NULL, 0);
    XtAddCallback(sub2Btn[1],XmNactivateCallback,ButtonCB,"2b");
    XtManageChildren (sub2Btn, 2);


/* Create a MenuShell for the submenu of submenu1 */

    XtSetArg(args[0], XmNheight, 100);
    XtSetArg(args[1], XmNwidth, 100);
    mshell3 = XmCreateMenuShell (mshell1, "mshell3", args, 2);

/* Create the MenuPane for the submenu of submenu1 */

    XtSetArg(args[0], XmNrowColumnType, XmMENU_PULLDOWN);
    submenu3 = XmCreateRowColumn (mshell3, "submenu3", args, 1);
```

```
/* Create CascadeButton in submenu1 for accessing submenu3 */

   XtSetArg(args[0], XmNsubMenuId, submenu3);
   XtSetArg(args[1], XmNlabelString, XmStringCreate(
           "To Third Submenu", XmSTRING_DEFAULT_CHARSET) );
   sub1Btn[2] =
       XmCreateCascadeButtonGadget(submenu1,"cbutton3",args,2);
   XtManageChildren(sub1Btn, 3);

/* Create pushbuttons in submenu */

   sub3Btn[0] =
       XmCreatePushButtonGadget(submenu3, "button3a", NULL, 0);
   XtAddCallback(sub3Btn[0],XmNactivateCallback,ButtonCB,"3a");

   sub3Btn[1] =
       XmCreatePushButtonGadget(submenu3, "button3b", NULL, 0);
   XtAddCallback(sub3Btn[1],XmNactivateCallback,ButtonCB,"3b");
   XtManageChildren (sub3Btn, 2);

/* Get and dispatch events */

   XtRealizeWidget(toplevel);

   XtAppMainLoop(app_context);
}
```

Chapter 7

Specialized Widgets

This chapter explains the use of the following three specialized widgets:

- List

- RowColumn

- Text

The Form widget is explained in Chapter 5, "Dialog Widgets." The others are explained in this chapter.

7.1 List Widget

The List widget allows you to make a selection from a list of items. The application defines an array of compound strings, each of which becomes an item in the list. You can set the number of items in the list that are to be visible. You can also choose to have the List appear with a ScrollBar so that you can scroll through the list of items. Items are selected by moving the pointer to the desired item and pressing the mouse button or key defined as select. The selected item is displayed in inverse color.

7.1.1 List Functions

The List widget has a number of functions that can perform a variety of tasks. These functions are listed in the following table and each has its own manpage in the *OSF/Motif Programmer's Reference*.

Table 7-1. List Widget Functions

Function	Description
XtCreateWidget	Basic widget creation function.
XmCreateList	Specific creation function for XmList.
XmCreateScrolledList	Creation function for ScrolledList.
XmListAddItem	Adds an item (possibly selected) to the list.
XmListAddItems	Adds items (possibly selected) to the list.
XmListAddItemUnselected	Adds an item (unselected) to the list.
XmListDeleteAllItems	Deletes all items from the list.
XmListDeleteItem	Deletes an item from the list.
XmListDeleteItems	Deletes items from the list.
XmListDeleteItemsPos	Deletes items from the list starting at the specified position.
XmListDeletePos	Deletes an item at the specified position.
XmListDeselectAllItems	Unhighlights all items in the list and removes them from the selected list.
XmListDeselectItem	Unhighlights the specified item and removes it from the selected list.
XmListDeselectPos	Unhighlights the item at the specified position and removes it from the selected list.
XmListGetMatchPos	Returns a list of all positions where the specified item is found in the list.
XmListGetSelectedPos	Returns a list of positions of all currently selected items in the list.
XmListItemExists	Returns True if the specified item is present in the list.
XmListItemPos	Returns the position of the specified item in the list.
XmListReplaceItems	Replaces some existing list items with new items.
XmListReplaceItemsPos	Replaces the specified number of existing items with new items, starting at the specified position.

Function	Description
XmListSelectItem	Highlights the specified item and add it to the selected list.
XmListSelectPos	Highlights the item at the specified position and adds it to the selected list.
XmListSetAddMode	Turns Add Mode on or off in the list.
XmListSetBottomItem	Makes the specified item the last visible item in the list.
XmListSetBottomPos	Makes the item at the specified position the last visible item in the list.
XmListSetHorizPos	If the horizontal ScrollBar is visible, sets the XmNvalue resource of the ScrollBar to the specified position and updates the visible portion of the list.
XmListSetItem	Makes the specified item the first visible item in the list.
XmListSetPos	Makes the item at the specified position the first visible item in the list.

The use of many of these functions will be described in the sections that follow. Actual code segments accompanied by illustrations show the results of certain programming actions.

7.1.2 Using the List Widget

The figure that follows shows an example of a List widget. You have seen other examples in earlier chapters of this guide. For example, the lists displayed in the FileSelectionBox and SelectionBox widgets are List widgets.

Figure 7-1. Example of a List Widget

The program that produces the List widget just shown can be found in the **./demos/xmsamplers/xmlist.c** file. You can compile and link this program using the procedure described in Chapter 1. Segments of this program are used in this section to describe how to accomplish certain functions associated with the List widget.

In the figure, the two lines that appear in inverse video indicate items that have been selected by the application. Any number of items can be selected. This is accomplished as shown in the following code segment.

```
Arg Args[20];

static char *CharSelectedItems[2] = {
"New Item List",
"New Policy"};

#define NUM_SELECTED_ITEMS 2
int i;
XmStringCharSet  cs = "ISOLatin1";
XmString SelectedItems[NUM_SELECTED_ITEMS];
```

```
/* Create compound strings for selected items */
for (i = 0; i < NUM_SELECTED_ITEMS; i++)
SelectedItems[i]=(XmString)XmStringCreateLtoR
                        (CharSelectedItems[i],cs);

/* Set the resource values */
i = 0;
XtSetArg(args[n], XmNselectedItems,
        (XtArgVal) SelectedItems); i++;
XtSetArg(args[n], XmNselectedCount,
        (XtArgVal) NUM_SELECTED_ITEMS); i++;
```

As you can see, you can include as many items as you want in the selected list.

In the next figure, you can see that one of the items in the list is Five Visible. To select this item, move the pointer into the window and position it anywhere on the Five Visible line. Clicking **BSelect** selects the item and it is highlighted, as shown in Figure 7-2.

Figure 7-2. List Widget Before Selection Action

When you double-click **BSelect**, the action is performed. In this case, now only five items are displayed in the list, as shown in the following figure:

Figure 7-3. List Widget After Selecting Five Visible

Note the ScrollBar in the preceding figure. There are the same number of items in the list as before, but now only five of them are visible at any given time.

7.1.2.1 Callback

The callback procedure that is executed when a double-click occurs performs the necessary steps to accomplish the task given by the selected item in the list. In the preceding situation, the task was to make only five items visible at a time. The code segments to accomplish this are as follows:

```
/* Add the callback */
XtAddCallback(outer_box, XmNdefaultActionCallback,
          DoubleClickProc, NULL);

/**********************************************************
 *
 * DoubleClickProc is the XmDEFAULT_ACTION callback.
 * It functions as a big case statement, comparing the
 * item that was double-clicked to the items in the list.
 * When it finds a match, it takes the appropriate action.
 *
 **********************************************************/
void  DoubleClickProc(w,closure,call_data)
  Widget  w;
  caddr_t  closure, call_data;
{
  int j;
```

```
XmListCallbackStruct  *cb =  (XmListCallbackStruct *)call_data;
int   i = 0;
unsigned char k;

DumpListCBStruct(call_data);

/* Set a new item list */
if (XmStringCompare(cb->item,ListItems[0]) )
{
   XtSetArg(Args[i],XmNitems,(XtArgVal)NewListItems);i+ +;
   XtSetArg(Args[i],XmNitemCount,(XtArgVal)NUM_NEW_LIST_ITEMS);
   i++;
}

/* Set the original Item List */
if (XmStringCompare(cb->item,NewListItems[0]) )
{
   XtSetArg(Args[i], XmNitems, (XtArgVal) ListItems); i++;
   XtSetArg(Args[i], XmNitemCount, (XtArgVal) NUM_LIST_ITEMS);
   i++;
}

/* Set a new Selected Item List */
if (XmStringCompare(cb->item,ListItems[1]) )
{
 XtSetArg(Args[i], XmNselectedItems, (XtArgVal)SelectedItems);
 i++;
 XtSetArg(Args[i], XmNselectedItemCount,
                         (XtArgVal) NUM_SELECTED_ITEMS); i++;
}

/* Make all items visible by getting the current item  */
/* count and making that the visible item count. */
if (XmStringCompare(cb->item,ListItems[2]) )
{
 XtSetArg(Args[0], XmNitemCount, &j);
 XtGetValues(w, Args, 1);
 XtSetArg(Args[i], XmNvisibleItemCount, (XtArgVal) j); i++;
}

/* Make five items visible */
if (XmStringCompare(cb->item,ListItems[3]) )
{
 XtSetArg(Args[i], XmNvisibleItemCount, (XtArgVal) 5); i++;
}
```

```
/* Set a new selection policy */
if (XmStringCompare(cb->item,ListItems[4]) )
{
 XtSetArg(Args[0], XmNselectionPolicy,  &k);
 XtGetValues(w, Args, 1);
 if (k == XmSINGLE_SELECT)
  k = XmMULTIPLE_SELECT;
  else
  if (k == XmMULTIPLE_SELECT)
     k = XmBROWSE_SELECT;
  else
    if (k == XmBROWSE_SELECT)
     k = XmEXTENDED_SELECT;
    else
    if (k == XmEXTENDED_SELECT)
       k = XmSINGLE_SELECT;
 XtSetArg(Args[i], XmNselectionPolicy,  (XtArgVal)k ); i++;
}

/* Increase the spacing between items */
if (XmStringCompare(cb->item,ListItems[5]) )
{
 Spacing += 2;
 XtSetArg(Args[i], XmNlistSpacing, (XtArgVal)Spacing ); i++;
}

/* Change the font the items are displayed in */
if (XmStringCompare(cb->item,ListItems[6]) )
{
 if (curfont == font1)
    curfont = font2;
 else
    if (curfont == font2)
      curfont = font3;
   else
      curfont = font1;
 XtSetArg(Args[i], XmNfontList, (XtArgVal) curfont ); i++;
}
```

```
  /* Set automatic selection ON */
  if (XmStringCompare(cb->item,ListItems[21]) )
  {
   XtSetArg(Args[i], XmNautomaticSelection, (XtArgVal) TRUE);
   i++;
  }

  if (XmStringCompare(cb->item,ListItems[22]) )
  { /* Set automatic selection OFF */
   XtSetArg(Args[i], XmNautomaticSelection, (XtArgVal) FALSE);
   i++;
  }
/***************
 *
 * If we have set any arguments, do the SetValues and return.
 *
 ***************/
  if (i > 0)
  {
    XtSetValues(w,Args,i);
    return;
  }

  /* Add an item at the first position in the list   */
  if (XmStringCompare(cb->item,ListItems[7]) )
  {
   XmListAddItem(w,FirstItem,1);
  }

  /* Add an item at the last position in the list   */
  if (XmStringCompare(cb->item,ListItems[8]) )
  {
   XmListAddItem(w,LastItem,0);
  }

  /* Add an item at the fifth position in the list   */
  if (XmStringCompare(cb->item,ListItems[9]) )
  {
   XmListAddItem(w,MiddleItem,5);
  }

  /* Delete the 'Middle Item' list element        */
  if (XmStringCompare(cb->item,ListItems[10]) )
  {
   XmListDeleteItem(w, MiddleItem);
  }
```

```
/* Delete the last item   */
if (XmStringCompare(cb->item,ListItems[11]) )
{
 XmListDeletePos(w,0);
}

/* Select the first item */
if (XmStringCompare(cb->item,ListItems[12]) )
{
  XmListSelectPos(w,1,TRUE);
}

/* Select the last item */
if (XmStringCompare(cb->item,ListItems[13]) )
{
  XmListSelectPos(w,0,TRUE);
}

/* Deselect the first item */
if (XmStringCompare(cb->item,ListItems[14]) )
{
  XmListDeselectPos(w,1);
}

/* Deselect the last item */
if (XmStringCompare(cb->item,ListItems[15]) )
{
  XmListDeselectPos(w,0);
}

/* Deselect all selected items */
if (XmStringCompare(cb->item,ListItems[16]) )
{
  XmListDeselectAllItems(w);
}

/* Make the fifth item the top */
if (XmStringCompare(cb->item,ListItems[17]) )
{
  XmListSetPos(w,5);
}
```

```
/* Make the first item the top */
if (XmStringCompare(cb->item,ListItems[18]) )
{
  XmListSetPos(w,1);
}

/* Make the fifth item bottom */
if (XmStringCompare(cb->item,ListItems[19]) )
{
  XmListSetBottomPos(w,5);
}

/* Make the last item the bottom */
if (XmStringCompare(cb->item,ListItems[20]) )
{
  XmListSetBottomPos(w,0);
}

/* End the program. */
if (XmStringCompare(cb->item,ListItems[23]) )
{
  exit(0);
}
}
```

This callback is the heart of the program. Basically, it compares the current selected item in the callback structure (see the List manpage for a description of this structure) to the the original list of items. When a match is found, the necessary action is taken.

For example, if Five Visible is the item selected from the List, the resource XmNvisibleItemCount is reset to 5 and XtSetValues is called. Note the use of the functions presented in the table at the beginning of this chapter. Continuing the example, if Add Item at Top is the item selected from the List, the function **XmListAddItem** is called with the position value set to 1. If Add Item at End is selected, **XmListAddItem** is called with the position value set to 0. You can get an idea of how other list functions are used by examining the rest of the callback code segment.

7.1.2.2 Selection Policies

The List widget has four selection policies that can be set programmatically. The policies are defined as follows:

- Single Selection. This policy allows you to move the pointer to the List item you want and when you click **BSelect**, that item is highlighted. No highlighting or selection occurs while you are moving the pointer, and only one item can be selected at a time.

  With the keyboard, you can use the navigation keys to move the location cursor to a List item and then press **KSelect** to select that item. This deselects any previous selection.

- Multiple Selection. This policy allows you to select more than one item on the List. Selection and highlighting occur only after you click mouse button 1, but you can select as many items as you want. You can deselect any selected item by clicking **BSelect** when the pointer is on that item.

  With the keyboard, you can use the navigation keys to move the location cursor to a List item. If that item is not selected, pressing **KSelect** adds that item to the current selection. If the item is already selected, pressing **KSelect** deselects it.

- Extended Selection. This policy allows you to select more than one item on the List without clicking **BSelect** for each item. When you press and hold **BSelect** on an item and then drag the pointer up or down from that point, all items between the initial item and the pointer are highlighted. Releasing **BSelect** stops the selection process and those items selected remain highlighted.

  With the keyboard, the extended selection mechanism depends on whether the List is in normal mode or add mode. Normal mode allows selection of a single range of items. In this mode, pressing a navigation key moves the location cursor and an *anchor* to a List item. It also selects that item and deselects any previous selection. Pressing a navigation key with the **MShift** modifier moves the location cursor to a List item and extends the current selection to include all items between the anchor and the location cursor.

Add mode allows selection of discontinuous ranges of items. In this mode, pressing a navigation key moves the location cursor, but not the anchor or the selection, to a new List item. Pressing **KSelect** moves the anchor to the item at the location cursor. If this item was previously selected, it is unselected; if this item was previously unselected, it is selected. Pressing **KExtend** adds all items between the anchor and the location cursor to the current selection.

- Browse selection. When you press and hold **BSelect** on an item, that item is selected and highlighted. Dragging the pointer up or down from that point causes each succeeding item to be selected and highlighted while the preceding item is unselected and unhighlighted. When you release the mouse button, the item on which the pointer rests is selected and highlighted.

  With the keyboard, pressing a navigation key moves the location cursor to a List item, selects that item, and deselects any previous selection.

The policy selections can be changed in the sample program by double-clicking on the New Policy item.

Figures 7-2 and 7-3 show single selection, Figure 7-4 shows multiple selection, and Figure 7-5 shows extended selection.

Figure 7-4. List Widget Multiple Selection

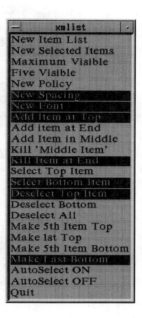

Figure 7-5. List Widget Extended Selection

The code segments shown in the Callback section provide an example of how selection policy can be changed programmatically. The appropriate segment from that section is as follows:

```
/*New Selection policy*/
if (XmStringCompare(cb->item,ListItems[4]) )
{
XtSetArg(myArgs[0], XmNselectionPolicy, &k);
XtGetValues(w, Args, 1);
if (k == XmSINGLE_SELECT)
 k = XmMULTIPLE_SELECT;
 else
  if (k == XmMULTIPLE_SELECT)
   k = XmBROWSE_SELECT;
  else
   if (k == XmBROWSE_SELECT)
    k = XmEXTENDED_SELECT;
   else
   if (k == XmEXTENDED_SELECT)
     k = XmSINGLE_SELECT;
/* Set the new values into the widget */
 XtSetArg(Args[i], XmNselectionPolicy, (XtArgVal)k);
```

The variable *k* is defined as an unsigned char to match the type of the resource **XmNselectionPolicy**. The argument array is set up with a call to **XtSetArg**, and the current selection policy is obtained by the call to **XtGetValues**. The selection policy is then changed and the new selection policy is reset into the widget with a call to **XtSetArg**.

7.2 RowColumn Widget

The RowColumn widget is a general-purpose RowColumn manager capable of containing any widget type as a child. It requires no special knowledge about how its children function, and provides nothing above and beyond support for several different layout styles.

The RowColumn widget has no 3-dimensional visuals associated with it. If an application wishes to have a 3-dimensional shadow placed around the RowColumn widget, it should create the RowColumn as a child of a Frame widget.

7.2.1 RowColumn Types

Motif provides several types of RowColumn widgets. The widget type is specified using the **XmNrowColumnType** resource. The possible settings for this resource are as follows:

- XmWORK_AREA. The XmWORK_AREA type provides the generalized RowColumn manager. It is the default type when the widget is created using the **XmCreateRowColumn** function or the **XtCreateWidget** X Toolkit function.

- Any of the following four settings, used to create Motif menus:

  — XmMENU_POPUP

  — XmMENU_BAR

  — XmMENU_PULLDOWN

  — XmMENU_OPTION

The specific create functions for Popup MenuPanes, MenuBars, Pulldown MenuPanes, and Option menus create RowColumn widgets set to these types.

The various types of menus are covered in Chapter 6. The rest of this section deals only with the XmWORK_AREA type.

7.2.2 RowColumn Functions

The following functions create RowColumn widgets of default type XmWORK_AREA:

```
Widget XtCreateWidget (name,
    xmRowColumnWidgetClass, parent,
    arglist, argcount)
```

```
Widget XmCreateRowColumn (parent,
    name, arglist, argcount)
```

Both create functions create an instance of a RowColumn widget and return the associated widget ID. **XtCreateWidget** is the standard X Toolkit Create function. **XmCreateRowColumn** is the RowColumn specific Create function.

7.2.3 Layout

RowColumn provides a variety of resources that determine the type of layout performed. For example, resources control these attributes:

- Sizing. The size of the widget can be set explicitly (by resource settings), or automatically according to requirements of the children and their specified layout.

- Orientation. RowColumn can be configured to lay out its children in columns (vertical) or rows (horizontal).

- Packing. The children can be packed together tightly (not in an organized grid of rows and columns); or all children can be placed in identically sized boxes, thus producing a symmetrical-looking arrangement of the children. Another alternative allows the application to specify the exact X and Y positions of the children.

- Spacing Between Children. The application can control the spacing between the rows and columns.

- Margin Spacing. Resources set the spacing between the edges of the RowColumn widget and the children placed along the edge.

7.2.3.1 Sizing

When **XmNresizeHeight** and/or **XmNresizeWidth** are set to True, RowColumn will request new dimensions from its parent, if necessary. The resources should be set to False if the application wants to control the dimensions.

When the **XmNpacking** resource is set to XmPACK_NONE, the RowColumn widget expands, if necessary, to enclose its children.

7.2.3.2 Orientation

The orientation is set using the **XmNorientation** resource. There are two possible settings:

- XmVERTICAL (default). This specifies a column-major orientation. In a column-major orientation, children are laid out in columns from top to bottom.

- XmHORIZONTAL. This specifies a row-major orientation. In a row-major orientation, children are laid out in rows, from left to right.

The two figures that follow show column-major and row-major orientations.

Figure 7-6. Column-Major Orientation (XmVERTICAL)

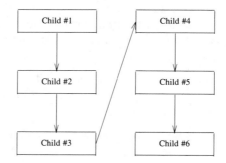

Figure 7-7. Row-Major Orientation (XmHORIZONTAL)

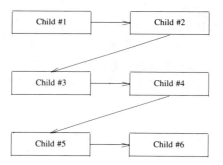

7.2.3.3 Packing

The **XmNpacking** resource determines how the items in a RowColumn widget are packed together. There are three possible settings:

- XmPACK_TIGHT (default). The layout depends on the orientation:

    — For Xm_VERTICAL orientation, items are placed one after another in a given column until there is no room left for another item. Wrapping then occurs to the next column and continues until all the children have been placed. The boxes in a given column are set to the same width, based on the widest box in that column. Thus, the items are stacked vertically but may be staggered horizontally. The following figure shows an **XmRowColumn** widget.

Figure 7-8. XmRowColumn Widget

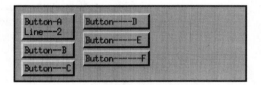

    — For Xm_HORIZONTAL orientation, items are placed one after another in a given row until there in no room left for another item. Wrapping then occurs to the next row and continues until all the children have been placed. Boxes in a given row are set to the same height, based on the highest box in that row. Thus, the items are layered horizontally but may be staggered vertically. The following figure shows a RowColumn widget with the XmPACK_TIGHT resource and XmHORIZONTAL orientation.

Figure 7-9. XmPACK_TIGHT with XmHORIZONTAL Orientation

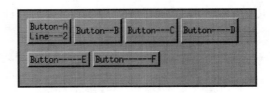

- XmPACK_COLUMN. In PACK_COLUMN packing, children are placed in identically sized boxes so that the layout becomes a grid. The height of the boxes is the height of the highest child; similarly, the width of the boxes is the width of the widest child.

  The **XmNnumColumns** resource specifies how many columns (for XmVERTICAL orientation) or rows (for XmHORIZONTAL orientation) are built. There is no automatic wrapping when a column or row is too long to fit.

  The following figures show packed, 3-column RowColumn widgets with vertical and horizontal orientations.

Figure 7-10. XmPACK_COLUMN With XmVERTICAL Orientation and XmNnumColumns = 3

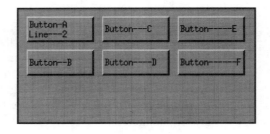

Figure 7-11. XmPACK_COLUMN With XmHORIZONTAL Orientation and XmNnumColumns = 3

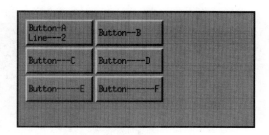

- XmPACK_NONE. When there is no packing, children are positioned according to the X and Y positions specified by their resources. If necessary, the RowColumn widget will attempt to become large enough to enclose all its children.

7.2.3.4 Spacing Between Children

The **XmNspacing** resource specifies the horizontal and vertical spacing, in pixels, between items within the RowColumn widget. The default is one pixel.

7.2.3.5 Margin Spacings

The **XmNmarginHeight** and **XmNmarginWidth** resources specify the size of the margins between the edge of the RowColumn widget and the children along the edge. The following figure shows a RowColumn widget using margins.

Figure 7-12. XmNmarginHeight and XmNmarginWidth

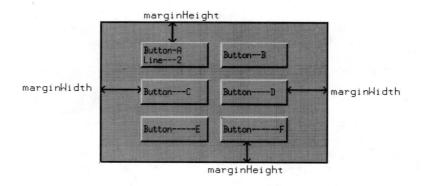

7.3 Text Widget

The Text widget can be used as a single-line or a multiline text editor. You can interact with the Text widget programmatically or by user action. You can use the Text widget for single-line entry, form entry, or full-window editing.

7.3.1 Text Functions

The following table lists the functions associated with the Text widget. Each function has its own manpage in the *OSF/Motif Programmer's Reference*.

Table 7-2. Text Widget Functions

Function	Description
XtCreateWidget	Basic widget creation function
XmCreateText	Specific creation function for XmText
XmCreateScrolledText	Creation function for ScrolledText
XmTextClearSelection	Clears the primary selection
XmTextCopy	Copies primary selection to the clipboard
XmTextCut	Copies primary selection to the clipboard and deletes selected text
XmTextGetBaseline	Finds the X position of the first baseline
XmTextGetEditable	Finds the value of the edit permission state
XmTextGetInsertionPosition	Finds the insert cursor position
XmTextGetLastPosition	Finds the position of the last character
XmTextGetMaxLength	Finds the maximum allowable length of the text string
XmTextGetSelection	Retrieves the value of the primary selection
XmTextGetSelectionPosition	Finds the position of the primary selection
XmTextGetSource	Accesses the source of the Text widget
XmTextGetString	Accesses the string value of the Text widget
XmTextGetTopCharacter	Finds the position of the first character
XmTextInsert	Inserts a character string into a text string
XmTextPaste	Inserts the clipboard selection
XmTextPosToXY	Finds the X and Y position of a character position
XmTextRemove	Deletes the primary selection
XmTextReplace	Replaces part of a string
XmTextScroll	Scrolls text in the Text widget
XmTextSetAddMode	Turns Add Mode on or off in the widget
XmTextSetEditable	Sets the value of the edit permission state
XmTextSetHighlight	Highlights text in the Text widget
XmTextSetInsertionPosition	Sets the insert cursor position

Function	Description
XmTextSetMaxLength	Sets the maximum allowable length of the text string
XmTextSetSelection	Sets the primary selection of text in the widget
XmTextSetSource	Sets the source of the Text widget
XmTextSetString	Sets the string value of the Text widget
XmTextSetTopCharacter	Sets the position of the first character
XmTextShowPosition	Forces text at a given position to be displayed
XmTextXYToPos	Finds the character position nearest an X and Y position

The use of some of these functions will be described in the sections that follow. Actual code segments accompanied by illustrations show the results of programming actions.

7.3.2 Using the Text Widget in a Program

The figure that follows shows an example of a Text widget. You have seen other examples in earlier chapters of this manual. The FileSelectionBox Selection window is a Text widget, as is the same window in the SelectionBox widget.

Figure 7-13. Text Widget

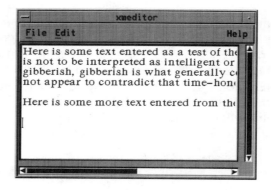

The program that generated the window shown in the preceding figure is called **xmeditor**. The source code is located on your system as **./demos/xmsamplers/xmeditor.c**. This program demonstrates how you can use the Text widget in concert with other widgets. You can create a new file, edit an old file, cut and paste text, and so on.

7.3.2.1 The File Menu

If you move the pointer so that it covers the File button in the MenuBar and then click mouse button 1, a menu appears like the following:

Figure 7-14. Text Demonstration File Menu

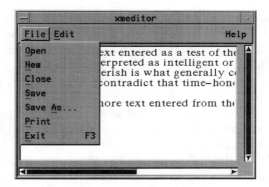

If you select Open, a FileSelectionBox will appear. You can select a file from this as described in Section 5.4.4. The other menu choices are self-explanatory.

7.3.2.2 The Edit Menu

The Edit menu allows you to use some of the cut and paste features of Motif within the Text widget. Move the pointer to Edit and click mouse button 1 to see the Edit menu. The figure that follows shows the Edit menu.

Figure 7-15. Text Demonstration Edit Menu

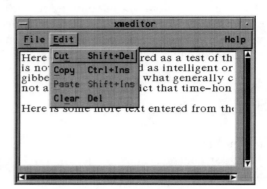

7.3.2.3 Accelerators and Mnemonics

Both the Edit and File menus contain *mnemonics*, indicated by underlined characters in the menus. You can use them instead of the mouse button to make the selection you want. For example, to choose File using its mnemonic, move the pointer into the **xmeditor** window and press **<Meta> <f>**. This will cause the Pulldown menu to appear. You can traverse the Pulldown menu by using the <↑> and <↓> keys, or use the mouse to move the pointer. You can select from the Pulldown menu by using its mnemonics as well. Just press the key that corresponds to the underlined letter in the menu. Don't worry about uppercase or lowercase as these are not case-sensitive. For example, if you want to open a file, press <o>. You need to use the **<Meta>** key only when accessing a Pulldown menu from the MenuBar.

The Edit menu also has accelerators in addition to the mnemonics. Accelerators are keys or combinations of keys that perform a specific function within an application. For example, Cut has a mnemonic of "t" and an accelerator of **<Shift><Del>**. Pressing either the <t> key or the **<Shift><Del>** keys will execute the Cut function of the menu. Note that accelerators are not part of the menu and will execute regardless of whether or not the menu is visible.

7.3.2.4 Primary Selection

The Text widget has primary selection. Primary selection is identified by highlighting the text in inverse video. You can cut out text that is the primary selection and paste it in at some other point in the Text window. Selection is described in more detail in later sections of this chapter.

7.3.2.5 Cutting Text

To remove (or cut) text, move the insert cursor to the starting point of the text you wish to remove. You can then perform any of the following actions to select the text (primary selection) to be removed:

NOTE: To position the insert cursor, move the pointer into the text window and to the desired point on a text line, then click **BSelect**.

- If you want just a single word removed, position the insert cursor before the first letter of the word and then double-click **BSelect**. The word is highlighted.

- If you want the entire line of text to be removed, triple-click mouse button 1. The entire line of text is highlighted. Note that the entire line is highlighted regardless of the initial position of the insert cursor on the line.

- If you want all of the text to be removed, quadruple-click mouse button 1. All of the text is highlighted. Note that the all of the text is highlighted regardless of the initial position of the insert cursor on the line.

- If you want more than one line (or more than one word) of text to be removed, you can drag the insert cursor to select the desired text. Begin by moving the pointer to the starting point in the text window and pressing and holding down **BSelect**. This positions the insert cursor at that point. Now drag the insert cursor along the line (or lines) of text that you want to remove. When you reach the end of the text that you want removed, release **BSelect** and that text is highlighted. (See Figure 7-16.)

- If you want to add text to the current primary selection, move the pointer to the position in the text that corresponds to the last character you want to add, and press **BExtend**. You can add text in front of or after the current primary selection.

You can also use the keyboard to select text. The selection mechanism depends on whether the text widget is in normal mode or add mode.

In normal mode, pressing a navigation key moves the location cursor to a new text element. This also sets an *anchor* at the new element and deselects any previous selection. Pressing a navigation key along with the **MShift** modifier moves the location cursor to a new text element and extends the current selection to include all items between the anchor and the location cursor. Pressing **KSelect** moves the anchor to the location cursor and deselects any previous selection. Pressing **KExtend** extends the current selection to include all items between the anchor and the location cursor.

In add mode selection works the same way as in normal mode, except that pressing a navigation key does not change the anchor or the current selection.

Figure 7-16. Selecting Text for Removal

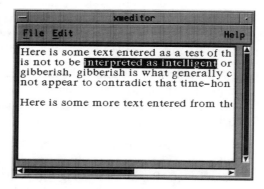

Now that you have selected the text to be removed, move the pointer to the Edit button in the MenuBar and press mouse button 1. The menu shown in Figure 7-15 appears. Move the pointer to Cut and release mouse button 1. The text you selected disappears.

The source code to accomplish this is taken from **xmeditor.c**. First, in the **MenuCB** procedure, which is the callback from PushButtons in the Pulldown menu, the case called MENU_CUT is executed.

```
case MENU_CUT:
    {
    /* needed to get the event time */
    XmAnyCallbackStruct * cb =
        (XmAnyCallbackStruct *) call_data;

    /* call routine to copy selection to clipboard */
    CopyFileToClipboard(cb->event->xbutton.time);

    /* call routine to delete primary selection */
    DeletePrimarySelection();
    }
    break;
```

The **CopyFileToClipboard** procedure copies the text you selected to the clipboard for safekeeping, then that text is deleted by the **DeletePrimarySelection** procedure. You can paste the text that was cut by using the method in the **PasteFromClipboard** procedure, which is discussed later in this chapter. Note that if you select Clear from the menu instead of Cut, the text is not copied to the clipboard before being deleted. This means that using Clear does not allow a subsequent paste of the deleted text.

The procedure **CopyFileToClipboard** uses several of the Cut and Paste functions described in Chapter 8. Keep in mind that copying to the clipboard is just a temporary measure. You can then subsequently use other Cut and Paste functions to retrieve the data.

```
/*-------------------------------------------------------------
** CopyFileToClipboard
** Copy the present file to the clipboard.
*/
void CopyFileToClipboard(time)
Time time;
{
   char *selected_string =
       XmTextGetSelection (text); /* text selection */
   unsigned long item_id = 0;        /* clipboard item id */
   int data_id = 0;           /* clipboard data id */
   int status = 0;          /* clipboard status */
   XmString clip_label;
```

```
/* using the clipboard facilities, copy
 * the selected text to the clipboard */
if (selected_string != NULL) {
clip_label = XmStringCreateLtoR ("XM_EDITOR", charset);
/* start copy to clipboard, and continue till
 * a successful start copy is made */
status = 0;
while (status != ClipboardSuccess)
   status = XmClipboardStartCopy (XtDisplay(text),
      XtWindow(text), clip_label, time, text,
      NULL, &item_id);

 /* move the data to the clipboard, and
  * continue till a successful copy is made */
status = 0;
while (status != ClipboardSuccess)
   status = XmClipboardCopy (XtDisplay(text), XtWindow(text),
    item_id, "STRING", selected_string,
    (long)strlen(selected_string)+1, 0, &data_id);

/* end the copy to the clipboard and continue till
 * a successful end copy is made */
status = 0;
while (status != ClipboardSuccess)
   status = XmClipboardEndCopy (XtDisplay(text),
      XtWindow(text), item_id);

/* allow pasting when an item is successfully copied
 * to the clipboard */
XtSetSensitive(paste_button, True);

}
}
```

The **XmTextGetSelection** function is used to set the *selected_string* variable to point to the primary selection in the Text widget. The primary selection in this case is the three words that are highlighted in inverse video shown in Figure 7-16. Note that the primary selection always appears in inverse video.

In the preceding code segment the actual copy-to-clipboard process involves three steps:

1. Prepare the clipboard for copying by executing **XmClipboardStartCopy**. This procedure must return a success before copying can occur. The *clip_label* variable is set to the string **XM_EDITOR** to identify the data item for possible use in a clipboard viewer. The variable *item_id* specifies is set to an arbitrary identification number assigned to this data item. This will be used in the calls to **XmClipboardCopy** and **XmClipboardEndCopy**.

2. Copy the data by using **XmClipboardCopy**. The copying done by this function is not actually to the clipboard but to a buffer. Copying to the clipboard occurs when the **XmClipboardEndCopy** function is executed.

3. The **XmClipboardEndCopy** function locks the clipboard to prevent access by other applications while performing the copy, copies the data to the clipboard, and then unlocks the clipboard.

7.3.2.6 Pasting Text

To paste the text you just removed, move the insert cursor to the position where you want the text to be inserted. Move the pointer to the **Edit** button in the MenuBar and press and hold down mouse button 1. Move the pointer to **Paste** and release mouse button 1. The text you deleted is restored (pasted) into the new position, as shown in the following figure:

Figure 7-17. Pasting Text

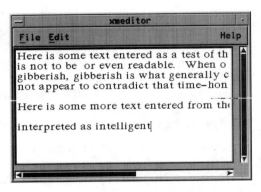

The code to accomplish this begins with that part of the **MenuCB** procedure dealing with a paste operation.

```
case MENU_PASTE:
/* call the routine that pastes the
text at the cursor position */
PasteItemFromClipboard();
break;
```

When you select Paste from the menu, **PasteItemFromClipboard** is called.

```
/*--------------------------------------------------------------
**    PasteItemFromClipboard
**       paste item from the clipboard to the current
**       cursor location
*/
void PasteItemFromClipboard()
{
   /* retrieve the current data from the clipboard
   and paste it at the current cursor position */


   int status = 0;          /* clipboard status  */
   char *buffer;            /* temporary text buffer   */
   int length;           /* length of buffer     */
   int outlength = 0;        /* length of bytes copied  */
   int private_id = 0;       /* id of item on clipboard */
   XmTextPosition cursorPos;  /* text cursor position    */
   register int ac;        /* arg count         */
   Arg al[10];            /* arg list       */
```

```
/* find the length of the paste item,
 * continue till the length is found */
while (status != ClipboardSuccess) {
status = XmClipboardInquireLength(XtDisplay(text),
        XtWindow(text), "STRING", &length);
if (status == ClipboardNoData) {
length = 0;
break;
}
}


if (length == 0) {
fprintf(stderr,
        "Warning: paste failed, no items to paste.\n");
return;
}


/* malloc to necessary space */
buffer = XtMalloc(length);

status = XmClipboardRetrieve (XtDisplay(text), XtWindow(text),
    "STRING", buffer, length, &outlength, &private_id);


/* Dialogs need to be added to indicate errors in pasting */
if (status != ClipboardSuccess) {
fprintf(stderr,
        "Warning: paste failed, status = %d\n", status);
return;
}


/* get cursor position for pasting */
XtSetArg(al[0], XmNcursorPosition, &cursorPos);
XtGetValues(text, al, 1);

/* add new text */
XmTextReplace(text, cursorPos, cursorPos, buffer);
}
```

The length of the data stored under the format name STRING is found by using the **XmClipboardInquireLength** procedure. If this procedure is successful, then space is allocated for that length by **XtMalloc**, and **XmClipboardRetrieve** is called to retrieve the text from the clipboard. Then the current cursor position in the Text widget is found through **XtGetValues** and the text is actually pasted by the function **XmTextReplace**.

7.3.2.7 Copying Text

To copy text, you move the insert cursor to the starting point of the text you want to copy and select the text in the same manner as for cutting text. When you have the text selected, move the pointer to the Edit button in the MenuBar and press and hold down mouse button 1. When the menu appears, drag the pointer to Copy and release mouse button 1. You won't see any change in the **xmeditor** window, but the text has been copied to the clipboard. In this case, the case called **MENU_COPY** is executed.

```
case MENU_COPY:
    {
    /* needed to get the event time */
    XmAnyCallbackStruct * cb = (XmAnyCallbackStruct *) call_data;

    /* call routine to copy selection to clipboard */
    CopyFileToClipboard(cb->event->xbutton.time);

    }
    break;
```

The only difference between this case and **MENU_CUT** is that the delete procedure **DeletePrimarySelection** is not called. The data is copied to the clipboard as before and can be pasted anywhere in the text.

Chapter 8
Additional Functionality

The Motif widget library provides additional functionality that you can use to perform certain tasks. The following list provides an overview of this functionality. Subsequent sections of this chapter describe each topic in detail.

- Compound strings. A compound string is designed to allow any message or text to be displayed without having to resort to hard-coding certain attributes that are language dependent. The three main attributes involved are direction, character set, and text. The Motif Intrinsics library provides a number of functions that allow you to create and manipulate compound strings.

- Cut and paste functions. The Motif Intrinsics has a clipboard that is used to hold data that is being transferred between applications. The Motif intrinsics also provide a set of cut and paste functions that allow you to modify the type and value of the data.

- Dynamic resource defaulting. This feature incorporates a processing function into a widget's resource definitions. This function is used to calculate a default resource value when the widget is created, thus overriding any static default value.

- Keyboard grabbing. Grabbing refers to an action in which an application or window isolates an input device (the keyboard in this case) from other applications or windows, thus preventing the other applications or windows from using the device.

- Localization. You can use localized defaults files in the Motif system by specifying the location of these files within certain environment variables. **XtAppInitialize** determines the proper path to the localized defaults variables.

- Pixmap naming and caching. The Motif widgets provide functions that allow you to associate any image with a unique name. With this association, the functions can generate pixmaps through references to a **.Xdefaults** file and through an argument list for all widgets with pixmap resources.

- Resolution independence. Resolution independence is a feature that allows your application to create and display images that are the same physical size regardless of the resolution of the display.

- Interacting with MWM. There are a number of functions you can use when interacting with the MWM. A sample program is available that demonstrates how to use some of these functions.

- Motif version and MWW presence. There are functions that provide information on the current version of Motif and whether or not MWM is running.

8.1 Compound Strings

A compound string is designed to allow any message or text to be displayed without having to resort to hard-coding certain attributes that are language dependent. The three main attributes involved are character set, direction, and the text of the message. For example, suppose you have a message to display in English and Arabic. This can easily be done with a compound string because you specify not only the text of the message, but character set and direction as well.

- Character set. The mapping between the string of bytes that make up the text and the font in which the text will be displayed.

- Direction. The relationship between the logical order (keystroke entry) and the display order of the characters in a string. In English, the display order is left to right; as characters are typed, they are displayed from left to right. In Arabic, the direction is right to left; as characters are typed, they are displayed from right to left.

- Text. This is simply the text of the message or string you wish to display.

In addition, you specify a font list from which to select the fonts used to display the message. The font list contains character set references that are matched with an X font. To display a compound string, the widget uses the character set specified in the compound string and searches the font list for a matching character set. Note that the font list is a widget resource.

Motif provides a set of compound string functions that enable the creation and manipulation of compound strings and font lists. This chapter discusses the compound string functions you can use to

- Create compound strings

- Compare and manipulate compound strings

- Create a font list and font list entries

8.1.1 Components of a Compound String

A compound string is a stream of data that is made up of tag-length-value (TLV) segments. Each TLV segment represents an attribute of the compound string. Within a TLV segment, the fields are

- Tag. A 1-byte field that identifies the type of Value that follows.

- Length. A 2-byte field that specifies the length of the data in the Value field.

- Value. The value of the segment. The length of this field is the number of bytes specified in the Length field.

For example, for a TLV segment that identifies the character set to be used, the Tag field identifies the segment as a character set segment, the Length field sets the length of the segment, and the Value field contains the character-set identifier.

A compound string always begins with a Tag field set to **0x7f** and a Length field set to the length of the segments that follow. Subsequent TLV segments then define the remainder of the compound string. The Value field of each of the TLV segments contains the information about the attributes of the compound string. These attributes are described below.

- A character-set identifier. This is a sequence of bytes that identifies the desired character set. This information is used by Motif to match a font with a compound string segment. All text between two character-set identifiers is interpreted to be in the first set. It is an error for a text component to precede the first character-set identifier.

    The character-set identifier has **persistence**; that is, any specified character set is used for all subsequent text segments until a new character set is encountered.

    There are times when an application must create a string without knowing what character sets will be available at the time the string is to be displayed. Motif provides a special character-set identifier that will match any available font. This universal character set is specified by the XmSTRING_DEFAULT_CHARSET identifier. If this identifier is used as the character set when a compound string is created, it will match the first font in the font list used to display the string, regardless of the character set associated with that particular font. By using the universal character set, an application can construct its strings so that they will be displayed in any font desired by the user, no matter what character set is associated with that font.

    The universal character set can also be associated with a font in a font list. When used with a font, that font will match any string, no matter what the character set of the string. An application can thus construct a multiple-font font list and specify a default font to be used when no other font is matched.

- A direction. This can have three values: left-to-right, right-to-left, and revert. Like the character-set identifier, it has persistence. The default direction is left-to-right; that is, text components preceding the first direction component will be assigned a direction of left-to-right.

- Text. This is the actual character data. There are no semantics for any bytes. Specifically this means that characters like \n do not have any meaning. As a convenience there is a function, **XmStringCreateLtoR**, which does impose this single semantic.

- A separator. This is a tag with no value. It is simply a marker that allows an array of compound string segments to be presented as a single entity.

The following is a set of useful definitions for compound strings:

```
/* an enumerated type */
typedef unsigned char XmStringDirection
```

The set of possible values for this type are:

```
XmSTRING_DIRECTION_L_TO_R
XmSTRING_DIRECTION_R_TO_L
/*octet chars, null terminated*/
typedef char * XmStringCharSet
/*opaque to users*/
typedef char * XmString
/*component tag types*/
typedef unsigned char XmStringComponentType
```

The set of currently possible values for this type are:

```
#define XmSTRING_COMPONENT_UNKNOWN  0
#define XmSTRING_COMPONENT_CHARSET  1
#define XmSTRING_COMPONENT_TEXT  2
#define XmSTRING_COMPONENT_DIRECTION  3
#define XmSTRING_COMPONENT_SEPARATOR  4
/*no more components*/
#define XmSTRING_COMPONENT_END 126
/*0-127 reserved for Motif*/
#define XmSTRING_COMPONENT_USER_BEGIN 128
#define XmSTRING_COMPONENT_USER_END 255
/*The universal character set*/
#define XmSTRING_DEFAULT_CHARSET ""
```

8.1.2 Compound String Functions

You can use a number of functions associated with compound strings. The following table lists these functions along with a brief description of what each can do. Subsequent sections describe the functions in more detail. A short sample program at the end of the list of functions shows how to use some of them.

Table 8-1. Compound String Functions

Function Name	Description
XmFontListAdd	Adds an entry to an existing font list.
XmFontListCopy	Copies a font list.
XmFontListCreate	Creates a new font list.
XmFontListFree	Recovers memory used by a font list.
XmFontListFreeFontContext	Recovers memory used by a font list context.
XmFontListGetNextFont	Accesses fonts and character sets in a font list.
XmFontListInitFontContext	Creates a context for accessing fonts and character sets in a font list.
XmStringBaseline	Returns the number of pixels between the top of the character box and the baseline of the first line of text in the specified compound string.
XmStringByteCompare	Returns True or False as the result of a byte-by-byte comparison of two specified compound strings.
XmStringCompare	Returns True if two compound strings have the same text components, directions, and separators.
XmStringConcat	Appends one compound string to another.
XmStringCopy	Returns a copy of the specified compound string.
XmStringCreate	Creates a compound string.
XmStringCreateLtoR	Creates a compound string in a left-to-right direction.

Function Name	Description
XmStringCreateSimple	Creates a compound string in the current language environment.
XmStringDirectionCreate	Creates a compound string with just one component, the specified direction.
XmStringDraw **XmStringDrawImage**	Draws a compound string in an X window. This function is identical to **XmStringDraw** except that it also paints both the foreground and background bits of each character.
XmStringDrawUnderline	Identical to **XmStringDraw** except that if the specified substring is matched in the main string, then the substring is underlined.
XmStringEmpty	Returns True if all text segments are empty.
XmStringExtent	Determines the height and width (in pixels) of the smallest rectangle that will enclose the specified compound string.
XmStringFree	Frees the memory used by a compound string.
XmStringFreeContext **XmStringGetLtoR**	Frees a previously established context. Returns True if a segment can be found in the input compound string that matches the specified character-set identifier.
XmStringGetNextComponent **XmStringGetNextSegment** **XmStringHasSubstring**	Returns the next component. Returns the bytes in the next segment. Indicates whether one compound string is contained within another.
XmStringHeight	Returns the height (in pixels) of the sum of all the line heights of the specified compound string.
XmStringInitContext	Specifies a context used to read the contents of a compound string segment-by-segment.

Function Name	Description
XmStringLength	Returns the length of the specified compound string.
XmStringLineCount	Returns the number of lines of text in the specified compound string.
XmStringNConcat	Appends a specified number of bytes from one compound string to another.
XmStringNCopy	Returns a copy of a specified portion of a compound string.
XmStringPeekNextComponent	Returns the type of the next component.
XmStringSegmentCreate	Creates a compound string segment.
XmStringSeparatorCreate	Creates a compound string with only a separator.
XmStringWidth	Returns the width (in pixels) of the longest sequence of text components in the specified compound string.

8.1.2.1 XmFontListAdd

This function adds an entry to an existing font list.

XmFontList XmFontListAdd(*oldlist, font, charset*)
   XmFontList *oldlist*;
   XFontStruct **font*;
   XmStringCharSet *charset;*

oldlist   Specifies a pointer to the font list to which an entry will be added.

font   Specifies a pointer to the font structure to be added to the list.

charset   Specifies the character-set identifier for the font being added to the list. This can be XmSTRING_DEFAULT_CHARSET.

XmFontListAdd creates a new font list consisting of the contents of *oldlist* and the new font list element being added. Note that this function de-allocates the *oldlist* after extracting the required information; *oldlist* should not be referenced thereafter. The following code segment shows you how this function is used.

```
XmFontList font list1, font list2;
XmFontStruct *font1, *font2;

font list1=XmFontListCreate(font1,"chset1");
font list2=XmFontListAdd(font list1,font2,
          "chset2");
```

The variables *chset1* and *chset2* are set in an app-default file, as shown in the sample program at the end of this section.

8.1.2.2 XmFontListCreate

This function creates a new font list. See the preceding segment for an example of how to use this function.

XmFontList XmFontListCreate(*font, charset*)
  XFontStruct **font*;
  XmStringCharSet *charset;*

font   Specifies a pointer to a font structure for which the new font list is generated.

charset   Specifies the character-set identifier for the font. This can be XmSTRING_DEFAULT_CHARSET.

The **XmFontListCreate** function creates a new font list with a single element specified by the provided font and character set. It also allocates the space for the font list.

8.1.2.3 XmFontListFree

This function frees the memory used by a font list.

void XmFontListFree *(list)*
 XmFontList *list;*

 list   Specifies the font list to be freed.

8.1.2.4 XmStringBaseline

This function returns the number of pixels between the top of the character box and the baseline of the first line of text in the specified compound string.

Dimension XmStringBaseline *(font list, string)*
 XmFontList *font list;*
 XmString *string;*

8.1.2.5 XmStringByteCompare

This function determines whether two compound strings are identical.

Boolean XmStringByteCompare *(s1, s2)*
 XmString *s1, s2;*

This function returns True if the comparison shows the two specified compound strings to be identical and False if they are not.

It is important to note that when a compound string is placed in a widget, it is converted into an internal form to allow faster processing. Part of the conversion process strips out unnecessary or redundant information. The result is that if an application subsequently executes a call to **XtGetValues** to retrieve a compound string from a widget (specifically XmLabel and all of its subclasses), no guarantee can be given that the compound string returned will be the same byte-for-byte as the original string in the widget.

8.1.2.6 XmStringCompare

This function determines whether or not two compound strings are *semantically* (but not necessarily byte-for-byte) equivalent.

Boolean XmStringCompare (*s1, s2*)
   XmString *s1, s2;*

This function returns True if the two compound strings are semantically equivalent and False otherwise. Semantically equivalent means that the strings have the same text components, directions, and separators. If character sets are specified, they must be equal as well.

8.1.2.7 XmStringConcat

This function appends a copy of one compound string to another compound string.

XmString XmStringConcat (*s1, s2*)
   XmString *s1, s2;*

XmStringConcat appends *s2* to the end of *s1* and returns the resulting compound string. The original strings are preserved. The space for the resulting compound string is allocated within the function. After using this function, you should free this space by calling **XtFree**.

8.1.2.8 XmStringCopy

This function creates a copy of a compound string.

XmString XmStringCopy (*s1*)
  XmString *s1;*

This function returns a copy of *s1*. The space for the resulting compound string is allocated within the function. The application is responsible for managing the the allocated space. The memory can be recovered by calling **XtFree**.

8.1.2.9 XmStringCreate

This function creates a compound string.

XmString XmStringCreate (*text, charset*)
  char **text;*
  XmStringCharSet *charset;*

text   Specifies a pointer to a null terminated string.

charset   Specifies the character-set identifier to be associated with the given text. This can be XmSTRING_DEFAULT_CHARSET.

This function creates a compound string with two components: a character set and text.

8.1.2.10 XmStringCreateLtoR

This function creates a compound string with a default direction of left-to-right.

XmString XmStringCreateLtoR (*text, charset*)
  char **text;*
  XmStringCharSet *charset;*

text   Specifies a pointer to a null terminated string.

charset   Specifies the character-set identifier to be associated with the given text. This can be XmSTRING_DEFAULT_CHARSET.

This function is similar to **XmStringCreate** except that it scans the text for newline characters in the text. When one is found, the text up to that point is put into a segment followed by a separator component. No final separator component is appended to the end of the compound string. The direction is defaulted to left-to-right. Finally, note that this function assumes that the encoding is single octet rather than double or quadruple octet per character of text.

8.1.2.11 XmStringDirectionCreate

This function creates a compound string with a single component, a direction with the specified value.

XmString XmStringDirectionCreate (*direction*)
  XmStringDirection *direction;*

direction   Specifies the value of the directional component.

8.1.2.12 XmStringDraw

This function is used to draw a compound string in an X window.

void XmStringDraw *(d, w, font list, string, gc, x, y,*
 width, alignment, layout_direction, clip);
 Display **d;*
 Window *w;*
 XmFontList *font list;*
 XmString *string;*
 GC *gc;*
 Position *x,y;*
 Dimension *width;*
 Byte *alignment;*
 Byte *layout_direction;*
 XRectangle **clip;*

The *x* and *y* parameters identify the top left coordinate of the rectangle that contains the displayed compound string. The *layout_direction* parameter controls the direction in which the segments of the compound string are laid out. It is also used to determine the meaning of the alignment parameter. The *clip* parameter allows the application to restrict the area into which the compound string will be drawn. If it is NULL, no clipping is done.

8.1.2.13 XmStringDrawImage

This function is identical to **XmStringDraw** except that it paints both the foreground and background bits of each character (equivalent to **XDrawImageString**).

void XmStringDrawImage *(d, w, font list, string, gc, x, y,*
    width, alignment, layout_direction, clip);
  Display **d;*
  Window *w;*
  XmFontList *font list;*
  XmString *string;*
  GC *gc;*
  Position *x,y;*
  Dimension *width;*
  Byte *alignment;*
  Byte *layout_direction;*
  XRectangle **clip;*

8.1.2.14 XmStringDrawUnderline

This function is equivalent to **XmStringDraw** with the addition that if the substring identified by *underline* can be matched in *string* then the substring will be underlined. Once a match has occurred, no further matches or underlining will be done.

void XmStringDrawUnderline *(disp, d, font list, string, gc, x, y,*
    width, alignment, layout_direction, clip, underline);
  Display **disp;*
  Drawable *d;*
  XmFontList *font list;*
  XmString *string;*
  GC *gc;*
  Position *x,y;*
  Dimension *width;*
  Byte *alignment;*
  Byte *layout_direction;*
  XRectangle **clip;*
  XmString *underline;*

8.1.2.15 XmStringEmpty

This function determines whether a compound string is empty.

Boolean XmStringEmpty *(s1)*
  XmString *s1;*

This function returns True or False depending on whether or not any nonzero text components exist in the provided compound string. It returns True if all text segments are empty or if the specified string parameter is NULL, and False otherwise.

8.1.2.16 XmStringExtent

This function determines the width and height (in pixels) of the smallest rectangle that will enclose the specified compound string.

void XmStringExtent *(font list, string, width, height)*
  XmFontList *font list;*
  XmString *string;*
  Dimension **width, *height;*

8.1.2.17 XmStringFree

This function frees the memory used by a compound string.

void XmStringFree *(string)*
  XmString *string;*

string   Specifies the compound string to be freed

8.1.2.18 XmStringFreeContext

This function instructs the Intrinsics that the context is no longer needed and will not be used without reinitialization.

void XmStringFreeContext *(context)*
  XmStringContext *context;*

8.1.2.19 XmStringGetLtoR

This function returns True if a segment can be found in the input compound string that matches the given character-set identifier.

Boolean XmStringGetLtoR *(string, charset, text)*
  XmString *string;*
  XmStringCharSet *charset;*
  char ***text;*

On return, *text* will have a null-terminated octet sequence containing the matched segment.

8.1.2.20 XmStringGetNextComponent

This function returns the type and value of the next component in the compound string identified by the specified context.

XmStringComponentType XmStringGetNextComponent *(*
    context, text, charset, direction, unknown_tag,
    unknown_length, unknown_value)
  XmStringContext **context;*
  char ***text;*
  XmStringCharSet **charset;*
  XmStringDirection **direction;*
  XmStringComponentType **unknown_tag;*
  short **unknown_length*
  char ***unknown_value;*

This is a low-level component fetch function. Components are returned one at a time. Only some output parameters will be valid on return, and this can be determined by examining the return status. In the case of *text*, *charset*, or *direction* components, only one output parameter is valid. If the return status indicates that an unknown component was encountered, the *tag*, *length* and *value* are returned. This function will allocate the space necessary to hold returned values; freeing this space is the caller's responsibility.

8.1.2.21 XmStringGetNextSegment

This function returns the bytes in the next segment of the specified compound string.

Boolean XmStringGetNextSegment *(context, text, charset,*
direction, separator)
XmStringContext **context;*
char ***text;*
XmStringCharSet **charset;*
XmStringDirection **direction;*
Boolean **separator;*

The *text*, *charset*, and *direction* of the fetched segment are returned. The separator parameter indicates whether the next component of the compound string is a *separator*. True or False is returned to indicate whether a valid segment was successfully parsed.

8.1.2.22 XmStringHeight

This function returns the height in pixels of the sum of all the line heights of the given compound string.

Dimension XmStringHeight *(font list, string)*
XmFontList *font list;*
XmString *string;*

Separator components delimit lines.

8.1.2.23 XmStringInitContext

This function establishes the context for a subsequent segment-by-segment read of the specified compound string.

Boolean XmStringInitContext *(context, string)*
  XmStringContext **context;*
  XmString *string;*

In order to allow applications to read the contents of a compound string segment-by-segment some *context* needs to be maintained. This function establishes the context for such a read. A True or False value is returned to indicate whether the input string could be parsed.

8.1.2.24 XmStringLength

This function obtains the length of a compound string.

int XmStringLength *(s1)*
  XmString *s1;*

This function returns the number of bytes in *s1*, including the string header (**0x7f**) and all tags, direction indicators, and separators. Zero is returned if the compound string has an invalid structure.

8.1.2.25 XmStringLineCount

This function returns the number of lines of text in the specified compound string.

int XmStringLineCount *(string)*
  XmString *string;*

8.1.2.26 XmStringNConcat

This function appends a specified number of bytes from one compound string to another.

XmString XmStringNConcat *(s1, s2, num_bytes)*
   XmString *s1, s2;*
   int *num_bytes;*

XmStringNConcat appends *num_bytes* bytes from *s2* to *s1*, including tags, directional indicators, and separators. It then returns the resulting compound string. If *num_bytes* is less than the length of *s2*, the resulting string will not be a valid compound string the original strings are preserved. The space for the resulting compound string is allocated within the function. The application is responsible for managing the allocated space. The memory can be recovered by calling **XtFree**.

8.1.2.27 XmStringNCopy

This function copies a specified portion of a given compound string.

XmStringNCopy *(s1, num_bytes)*
   XmString *s1;*
   int *num_bytes;*

This function creates a copy of *s1* which contains *num_bytes* bytes from *s1*, including tags, directional indicators, and separators. It then returns the resulting copy. If *num_bytes* is less than the length of *s1*, the resulting string will not be a valid compound string and the original string is preserved. For this reason, you should normally use **XmStringCopy**. The space for the resulting compound string is allocated within the function. The application is responsible for managing the allocated space. The memory can be recovered by calling **XtFree**.

8.1.2.28 XmStringPeekNextComponent

This function examines the next component that would be fetched by **XmStringGetNextComponent** and returns the component type.

XmStringComponentType XmStringPeekNextComponent *(*
context)
XmStringContext **context;*

8.1.2.29 XmStringSegmentCreate

This is a high-level function that assembles a compound string consisting of a character-set identifier, a direction component, a text component, and, optionally, a separator component. If *separator* is False, then the compound string does not have a separator component at the end. If it is True, the compound string has a separator component immediately following the text component.

XmString XmStringSegmentCreate *(text, charset, direction,*
separator)
char **text;*
XmStringCharSet *charset;*
XmStringDirection *direction;*
Boolean *separator;*

text　　　　Specifies a pointer to a null-terminated string.

charset　　Specifies the character-set identifier to be associated with the text. This can be XmSTRING_DEFAULT_CHARSET.

direction　Specifies the direction of the text.

separator　Specifies if a separator should be added to the compound string segment being constructed.

8.1.2.30 XmStringSeparatorCreate

This function creates a compound string with a single component, a *separator*.

XmString XmStringSeparatorCreate *(separator)*
  Boolean *separator;*

8.1.2.31 XmStringWidth

This function returns the width in pixels of the longest sequence of text components in the provided compound string. Separator components are used to delimit sequences of text components.

Dimension XmStringWidth *(font list, string)*
  XmFontList *font list;*
  XmString *string;*

8.1.3 A Sample Program

This section contains a listing and defaults file for a sample program that illustrates how you can use the compound string functions in applications. This program creates a PushButton, the Label for which is Hello World. Each word in the Label appears in a different font as specified in the applications-defaults file for the program.

8.1.3.1 Program Listing

The program listing follows.

```c
#include <X11/Xlib.h>
#include <Xt/Intrinsic.h>
#include <Xt/Shell.h>
#include <Xm/Xm.h>
#include <Xm/PushB.h>

Widget toplevel,pbutton;
Arg myArgs[10];

void main(argc, argv)
     unsigned int argc;
     char **argv;
{
     int i;
     XmString s1,s2,string,ButtonText;
     char *word1="Hello ",*word2="World";
     XtAppContext app_context;
     char *appclass = "LAB0";

     toplevel = XtAppInitialize(&app_context,
               appclass, NULL, 0, &argc,
               argv, NULL, NULL, 0);
     s1=XmStringSegmentCreate(word1,"chset1",
         XmSTRING_DIRECTION_L_TO_R, False);
     s2=XmStringSegmentCreate(word2,"chset2",
         XmSTRING_DIRECTION_L_TO_R, True);
     string=XmStringConcat(s1,s2);

     i=0;
     XtSetArg(myArgs[i], XmNlabelString,
               string); i++;
     pbutton = XmCreatePushButton(toplevel,
               "x01", myArgs,i);
     XtManageChild(pbutton);
     XtRealizeWidget(toplevel);
     XtAppMainLoop(app_context);
}
```

8.1.3.2 Defaults File

The applications-default file follows.

```
!
!   Apps default file LAB0 for compound string
!   function sample program
*foreground: Yellow
*background: SlateBlue
*FontList: hp8.8x16b=chset1, hp8.8x16=chset2
```

Note that font lists can be specified in a defaults file by setting the font list resource to a string of the form *fontname = character set*. The widget will build a font list consisting of the specified font and character set. If the character set is omitted, the character set will default to **XmSTRING_DEFAULT_CHARSET**.

Strings can be specified by setting the string resource to the desired text. For example, **oklabel.labelString: OK** sets a label's text to OK. Specifying a string in a defaults file is the same as creating the string using **XmStringCreateLtoR** with the default character set **XmSTRING_DEFAULT_CHARSET**.

8.2 Cut and Paste Functions

The Motif clipboard is used to hold data that is to be transferred between applications. Motif provides the functions necessary to modify the type and value of the data that is to be transferred via the clipboard. These functions are known as cut and paste functions. An application can interface to the Motif clipboard through calls to the cut and paste functions.

The table below gives a brief description of each function. Detailed information on each function is presented in the sections that follow.

Table 8-2. Cut and Paste Functions

Function Name	Description
XmClipboardStartCopy	Set up storage and data structures for clipboard copying.
XmClipboardCopy	Copies a data item to the clipboard.
XmClipboardCopyByName	Copies a data item passed by name.
XmClipboardCancelCopy	Cancels a copy to clipboard.
XmClipboardUndoCopy	Deletes the last item placed on the clipboard.
XmClipboardEndCopy	Ends copy to clipboard.
XmClipboardInquireCount	Returns the number of data item formats.
XmClipboardInquireFormat	Returns a specified format name.
XmClipboardInquireLength	Returns the length of the stored data.
XmClipboardInquirePendingItems	Returns a list of data id/private id pairs.
XmClipboardStartRetrieve	Starts copy from clipboard.
XmClipboardRetrieve	Retrieves a data item from the clipboard.
XmClipboardEndRetrieve	Ends copy from clipboard.
XmClipboardLock	Locks the clipboard.
XmClipboardRegisterFormat	Registers a new format.
XmClipboardUnlock	Unlocks the clipboard.
XmClipboardWithdrawFormat	Indicates the application no longer wants to supply a data item.

8.2.1 Clipboard Copy Functions

The following sections describe clipboard copy functions.

8.2.1.1 XmClipboardStartCopy

This function sets up storage and data structures to receive clipboard data.

int XmClipboardStartCopy (*display*, *window*, *clip_label*,
   timestamp, *widget*, *callback*, *item_id*)
Display **display*;
Window *window*;
XmString *clip_label*;
Time *timestamp*;
Widget *widget*;
VoidProc *callback*;
long **item_id*;

display	Specifies a pointer to the **Display** structure that was returned in a previous call to **XtOpenDisplay**.
window	Specifies the window ID that relates the application window to the clipboard. The same application instance should pass the same window ID to each of the clipboard functions that it calls. Note that this window must be associated with a widget.
clip_label	Specifies the label to be associated with the data item. This argument is used to identify the data item, for example, in a clipboard viewer. An example of a label is the name of the application that places the data in the clipboard.
timestamp	The time of the event that triggered the copy.
widget	Specifies the ID of the widget that will receive messages requesting data previously passed by name. This argument must be present in order to pass data by name. Any valid widget ID in your application can be used for this purpose and all the message handling is taken care of by the cut and paste functions.

callback   Specifies the address of the callback function that is called when the clipboard needs data that was originally passed by name. This is also the callback to receive the DELETE message for items that were originally passed by name. This argument must be present in order to pass data by name.

item_id   Specifies the number assigned to this data item. The application uses this number in calls to **XmClipboardCopy**, **XmClipboardEndCopy**, and **XmClipboardCancelCopy**.

The **XmClipboardStartCopy** function sets up storage and data structures to receive clipboard data. An application calls **XmClipboardStartCopy** during a cut or copy operation. The data item that these structures receive then becomes the next paste item in the clipboard.

Copying a large piece of data to the clipboard can take time. It is possible that, once copied, no application will ever request that data. Motif provides a mechanism so that an application does not need to actually pass data to the clipboard until the data has been requested by some application. Instead, the application passes format and length information in **XmClipboardCopy** to the clipboard functions, along with a widget ID and a callback function address that is passed in **XmClipboardStartCopy**. The widget ID is needed for communications between the clipboard functions in the application that owns the data and the clipboard functions in the application that requests the data. Your callback functions are responsible for copying the actual data to the clipboard (via **XmClipboardCopyByName**). The callback function is also called if the data item is removed from the clipboard, and the actual data is therefore no longer needed.

For more information on passing data by name, see **XmClipboardCopy** and **XmClipboardCopyByName**.

The *widget* and *callback* arguments must be present in order to pass data by name. The callback format is as follows:

function name(*widget*, *data_id*, *private*, *reason*)
  Widget **widget*;
  int **data_id*;
  int **private*;
  int **reason*;

widget	Specifies the ID of the widget passed to **XmClipboardStartCopy**
data_id	Specifies the identifying number returned by **XmClipboardCopy**, which identifies the pass-by-name data.
private	Specifies the private information passed to **XmClipboardCopy**.
reason	Specifies the reason, either **XmCR_CLIPBOARD_DATA_DELETE** or **XmCR_CLIPBOARD_DATA_REQUEST**.

This function can return one of the following status return constants:

ClipboardSuccess The function is successful.

ClipboardLocked The function failed because the clipboard was locked by another application. The application can continue to call the function again with the same parameters until the lock goes away. This gives the application the opportunity to ask if the user wants to keep trying or to give up on the operation.

8.2.1.2 XmClipboardCopy

This function copies a data item to temporary clipboard storage.

int XmClipboardCopy (*display*, *window*, *item_id*, *format_name*,
  buffer, *length*, *private_id*, *data_id*)
 Display **display*;
 Window *window*;
 long *item_id*;
 char **format_name*;
 char **buffer*;
 unsigned long *length*;
 int *private_id*;
 int **data_id*;

display	Specifies a pointer to the **Display** structure that was returned in a previous call to **XtOpenDisplay**.
window	Specifies the window ID that relates the application window to the clipboard. The same application instance should pass the same window ID to each of the clipboard functions that it calls. Note that this window must be associated with a widget.
item_id	Specifies the number assigned to this data item. This number was returned by a previous call to **XmClipboardStartCopy**.
format_name	Specifies the name of the format in which the data item is stored on the clipboard. Format is referred to as target in the *Inter-Client Communication Conventions Manual*.
buffer	Specifies the buffer from which the clipboard copies the data.
length	Specifies the length of the data being copied to the clipboard.
private_id	Specifies the private data that the application wants to store with the data item.

data_id   Specifies an identifying number assigned to the data item that uniquely identifies the data item and the format. This argument is required only for data that is passed by name.

The **XmClipboardCopy** function copies a data item to temporary clipboard storage. The data item is moved from temporary storage to the clipboard data structure when a call to **XmClipboardEndCopy** is made. Additional calls to **XmClipboardCopy** before a call to **XmClipboardEndCopy** add more data item formats to the same data item or append data to an existing format.

If the *buffer* argument is NULL, the data is considered passed by name. If data passed by name is later needed by another application, the application that owns the data receives a callback with a request for the data. The application that owns the data must then transfer the data to the clipboard with the **XmClipboardCopyByName** function. When a data item that was passed by name is deleted from the clipboard, the application that owns the data receives a callback that states that the data is no longer needed.

For information on the callback function, see the callback argument description for **XmClipboardStartCopy**.

This function can return one of the following status return constants:

ClipboardSuccess   The function is successful.

ClipboardLocked   The function failed because the clipboard was locked by another application. The application can continue to call the function again with the same parameters until the lock goes away. This gives the application the opportunity to ask if the user wants to keep trying or to give up on the operation.

8.2.1.3 XmClipboardCopyByName

This function copies a data item to the clipboard.

int XmClipboardCopyByName (*display*, *window*, *data_id*, *buffer*,
    length, *private_id*)
Display **display*;
Window *window*;
int *data_id*;
char **buffer*;
unsigned long *length*;
int *private_id*;

display   Specifies a pointer to the **Display** structure that was returned in a previous call to **XtOpenDisplay**.

window   Specifies the window ID that relates the application window to the clipboard. The same application instance should pass the same window ID to each of the clipboard functions that it calls. Note that this window must be associated with a widget.

data_id   Specifies an identifying number assigned to the data item that uniquely identifies the data item and the format. This number was assigned by **XmClipboardCopy** to the data item.

buffer   Specifies the buffer from which the clipboard copies the data.

length   Specifies the number of bytes in the data item.

private_id   Specifies the private data that the application wants to store with the data item.

The **XmClipboardCopyByName** function copies the actual data for a data item that was previously passed by name to the clipboard. Data is considered to be passed by name when a call to **XmClipboardCopy** is made with the *buffer* parameter is set to NULL. Additional calls to **XmClipboardCopyByName** append new data to the existing data. The clipboard should be locked before making such calls by using **XmClipboardLock** to ensure the integrity of the clipboard data.

This function can return one of the following status return constants:

ClipboardSuccess The function is successful.

ClipboardLocked The function failed because the clipboard was locked by another application. The application can continue to call the function again with the same parameters until the lock goes away. This gives the application the opportunity to ask if the user wants to keep trying or to give up on the operation.

8.2.1.4 XmClipboardCancelCopy

This function cancels any copy to the clipboard that is in progress and frees any temporary storage in use.

void XmClipboardCancelCopy (*display*, *window*, *item_id*)
  Display *display ;
  Window *window* ;
  long *item_id* ;

display   Specifies a pointer to the **Display** structure that was returned in a previous call to **XtOpenDisplay**.

window   Specifies the window ID that relates the application window to the clipboard. The same application instance should pass the same window ID to each of the clipboard functions that it calls. Note that this window must be associated with a widget.

item_id   Specifies the number assigned to this data item. This number was returned by a previous call to **XmClipboardStartCopy**.

The **XmClipboardCancelCopy** function cancels any copy-to-clipboard that is in progress and frees any temporary storage in use. When a copy is performed, **XmClipboardStartCopy** allocates temporary storage for the clipboard data. **XmClipboardCopy** places the data in the temporary storage. **XmClipboardEndCopy** copies the data to the clipboard data structure and frees the temporary data storage.

XmClipboardCancelCopy also frees up temporary storage. If **XmClipboardCancelCopy** is called, then **XmClipboardEndCopy** does not have to be called. A call to **XmClipboardCancelCopy** is valid only after a call to **XmClipboardStartCopy** and before a call to **XmClipboardEndCopy**.

8.2.1.5 XmClipboardUndoCopy

This function deletes the last item placed on the clipboard.

int XmClipboardUndoCopy (*display*, *window*)
   Display **display*;
   Window *window*;

display   Specifies a pointer to the **Display** structure that was returned in a previous call to **XtOpenDisplay**.

window   Specifies the window ID that relates the application window to the clipboard. The same application instance should pass the same window ID to each of the clipboard functions that it calls. Note that this window must be associated with a widget.

The **XmClipboardUndoCopy** function deletes the last item placed on the clipboard if the item was placed there by an application with the passed *display* and *window* arguments. Any data item deleted from the clipboard by the original call to **XmClipboardCopy** is restored. If the *display* or *window* IDs do not match the last copied item, no action is taken and this function has no effect.

This function can return one of the following status return constants:

Clipboard Success The function is successful.

ClipboardLocked The function failed because the clipboard was locked by another application. The application can continue to call the function again with the same parameters until the lock goes away. This gives the application the opportunity to ask if the user wants to keep trying or to give up on the operation.

8.2.1.6 XmClipboardEndCopy

This function has several uses: to lock the clipboard, to place data in the clipboard data structure, and to unlock the clipboard.

int XmClipboardEndCopy (*display*, *window*, *item_id*)
  Display *display;
  Window *window*;
  long *item_id*;

display   Specifies a pointer to the **Display** structure that was returned in a previous call to **XtOpenDisplay**.

window   Specifies the window ID that relates the application window to the clipboard. The same application instance should pass the same window ID to each of the clipboard functions that it calls. Note that this window must be associated with a widget.

item_id   Specifies the number assigned to this data item. This number was returned by a previous call to **XmClipboardStartCopy**.

The **XmClipboardEndCopy** function locks the clipboard from access by other applications, places data in the clipboard data structure, and unlocks the clipboard. Data items copied to the clipboard by **XmClipboardCopy** are not actually entered in the clipboard data structure until the call to **XmClipboardEndCopy**. It also frees the temporary storage that was allocated by **XmClipboardStartCopy**.

This function can return one of the following status return constants:

ClipboardSuccess The function is successful.

ClipboardLocked The function failed because the clipboard was locked by another application. The application can continue to call the function again with the same parameters until the lock goes away. This gives the application the opportunity to ask if the user wants to keep trying or to give up on the operation.

8.2.2 Clipboard Inquire Functions

This section describes the Clipboard Inquire functions, which obtain information about data in the Clipboard.

8.2.2.1 XmClipboardInquireCount

This function returns the maximum length for all data item formats.

int XmClipboardInquireCount (*display*, *window*, *count*,
   max_format_name_length)
  Display *display;
  Window *window*;
  int *count;
  int **max_format_name_length*;

display   Specifies a pointer to the **Display** structure that was returned in a previous call to **XtOpenDisplay**.

window   Specifies the window ID that relates the application window to the clipboard. The same application instance should pass the same window ID to each of the clipboard functions that it calls. Note that this window must be associated with a widget.

count   Returns the number of data item formats available for the next paste item in the clipboard. If no formats are available, this argument equals zero. The count includes the formats that were passed by name.

max_format_name_length
    Specifies the maximum length of all format names for the next paste item in the clipboard.

The **XmClipboardInquireCount** function returns the number of data item formats available for the next paste item in the clipboard. This function also returns the maximum name length for all formats in which the next paste item is stored.

This function can return one of the following status return constants:

ClipboardSuccess The function is successful.

ClipboardLocked The function failed because the clipboard was locked by another application. The application can continue to call the function again with the same parameters until the lock goes away. This gives the application the opportunity to ask if the user wants to keep trying or to give up on the operation.

ClipBoardNoData The function could not find data on the clipboard that corresponds to the format requested. This could occur because the clipboard is empty, there is no data on the clipboard in the format requested, or the data requested was passed by name and is no longer available.

8.2.2.2 XmClipboardInquireFormat

This function obtains the format name for the next paste data item in the clipboard.

int XmClipboardInquireFormat(*display*, *window*, *index*,
   format_name_buf, *buffer_len*, *copied_len*)
   Display *display;
   Window *window*;
   int *index*;
   char *format_name_buf;
   unsigned long *buffer_len*;
   unsigned long *copied_len;

display   Specifies a pointer to the **Display** structure that was returned in a previous call to **XtOpenDisplay**.

window   Specifies the window ID that relates the application window to the clipboard. The same application instance should pass the same window ID to each of the clipboard functions that it calls. Note that this window must be associated with a widget.

index Specifies which of the ordered format names is to be obtained. If this index *i* is greater than the number of formats for the data item, **XmClipboardInquireFormat** returns a zero in the *copied_len* argument.

format_name_buf
Specifies the buffer that receives the format name.

buffer_len Specifies the number of bytes in the format name buffer.

copied_len Specifies the number of bytes in the string copied to the buffer. If this argument equals zero, there is no *nth* format for the next paste item.

The **XmClipboardInquireFormat** function returns a specified format name for the next paste item in the clipboard. If the name must be truncated, the function returns a warning status. This function can return one of the following status return constants:

ClipboardSuccess The function is successful.

ClipboardLocked The function failed because the clipboard was locked by another application. The application can continue to call the function again with the same parameters until the lock goes away. This gives the application the opportunity to ask if the user wants to keep trying or to give up on the operation.

ClipboardTruncate The data returned is truncated because the user did not provide a buffer that was large enough to hold the data.

ClipBoardNoData The function could not find data on the clipboard that corresponds to the format requested. This could occur because the clipboard is empty, there is no data on the clipboard in the format requested, or the data requested was passed by name and is no longer available.

8.2.2.3 XmClipboardInquireLength

This function obtains the length of the data stored under a specified format.

> **int XmClipboardInquireLength** (*display*, *window*,
>   *format_name*, *length*)
> **Display** *display;
> **Window** *window*;
> **char** *format_name;
> **unsigned long** *length;

display   Specifies a pointer to the **Display** structure that was returned in a previous call to **XtOpenDisplay**.

window   Specifies the window ID that relates the application window to the clipboard. The same application instance should pass the same window ID to each of the clipboard functions that it calls. Note that this window must be associated with a widget.

format_name Specifies the name of the format for the next paste item.

length   Specifies the length of the next data item in the specified format. This argument equals zero if no data is found for the specified format, or if there is no item on the clipboard.

The **XmClipboardInquireLength** function returns the length of the data stored under a specified format name for the clipboard data item. This is accomplished by passing a pointer to the length in the *length* parameter in the function.

If no data is found for the specified format, or if there is no item on the clipboard, **XmClipboardInquireLength** returns a value of zero.

This function can return one of the following status return constants:

ClipboardSuccess The function is successful.

ClipboardLocked The function failed because the clipboard was locked by another application. The application can continue to call the function again with the same parameters until the lock goes away. This gives the application the opportunity to ask if the user wants to keep trying or to give up on the operation.

ClipBoardNoData The function could not find data on the clipboard that corresponds to the format requested. This could occur because the clipboard is empty, there is no data on the clipboard in the format requested, or the data requested was passed by name and is no longer available.

8.2.2.4 XmClipboardInquirePendingItems

This function obtains a format name's list of data ID or private ID pairs.

int XmClipboardInquirePendingItems(*display*, *window*,
  format_name, *item_list*, *count*)
  Display *display;
  Window *window*;
  char *format_name;
  XmClipboardPendingList *item_list;
  unsigned long *count;

display Specifies a pointer to the **Display** structure that was returned in a previous call to **XtOpenDisplay**.

window Specifies the window ID that relates the application window to the clipboard. The same application instance should pass the same window ID to each of the clipboard functions that it calls. Note that this window must be associated with a widget.

format_name Specifies a string that contains the name of the format for which the list of data ID/private ID pairs is to be obtained.

item_list Specifies the address of the array of data ID/private ID pairs for the specified format name. This argument is a type **XmClipboardPendingList**. The application is responsible for freeing the memory provided by this function for storing the list.

item_count Specifies the number of items returned in the list. If there is no data for the specified format name, or if there is no item on the clipboard, this argument equals zero.

The **XmClipboardInquirePendingItems** function returns a list of data ID/private ID pairs for a specified format name. For the purposes of this function, a data item is considered pending if the application originally passed it by name, the application has not yet copied the data, and the item has not been deleted from the clipboard.

The application is responsible for freeing the memory provided by this function to store the list.

This function is used by an application when exiting to determine if the data that it passed by name should be sent to the clipboard.

This function can return one of the following status return constants:

ClipboardSuccess The function is successful.

ClipboardLocked The function failed because the clipboard was locked by another application. The application can continue to call the function again with the same parameters until the lock goes away. This gives the application the opportunity to ask if the user wants to keep trying or to give up on the operation.

8.2.3 Clipboard Retrieve Functions

This section describes the Clipboard Retrieve functions, which you use to retrieve data from the Clipboard.

8.2.3.1 XmClipboardStartRetrieve

This function begins copying data incrementally from the clipboard.

int XmClipboardStartRetrieve *(display, window, timestamp);*
  Display **display;*
  Window *window;*
  Time *timestamp;*

display   Specifies a pointer to the **Display** structure that was returned in a previous call to **XtOpenDisplay**.

window   Specifies the window ID that relates the application window to the clipboard. The same application instance should pass the same window ID to each of the clipboard functions that it calls.

timestamp   The time of the event that triggered the copy.

This routine tells the cut and paste routines that the application is ready to start copying an item from the clipboard. The clipboard will be locked by this routine and will stay locked until **XmClipboardEndRetrieve** is called. Between an **XmClipboardStartRetrieve** and an **XmClipboardEndRetrieve**, multiple calls to **XmClipboardRetrieve** with the same format name will result in data being incrementally copied from the clipboard until the data in that format has all been copied. The return value **ClipboardTruncate** from calls to **XmClipboardRetrieve** indicates that more data remains to be copied in the given format. It is recommended that any calls to the INQUIRE functions that the application needs to make to effect the copy from the clipboard be made between the call to **XmClipboardStartRetrieve** and the first call to **XmClipboardRetrieve**. That way, the application does not need to call **XmClipboardLock** and **XmClipboardUnlock**.

8.2.3.2 XmClipboardRetrieve

This function obtains the current next paste data item from clipboard storage.

int XmClipboardRetrieve (*display*, *window*, *format_name*, *buffer*,
    length, *num_bytes*, *private_id*)
  Display *display;
  Window *window*;
  char *format_name;
  char *buffer;
  unsigned long *length*;
  unsigned long *num_bytes;
  int *private_id;

display   Specifies a pointer to the **Display** structure that was returned in a previous call to **XtOpenDisplay**.

window   Specifies the window ID that relates the application window to the clipboard. The same application instance should pass the same window ID to each of the clipboard functions that it calls. Note that this window must be associated with a widget.

format_name Specifies the name of a format in which the data is stored on the clipboard.

buffer   Specifies the buffer to which the application wants the clipboard to copy the data.

length   Specifies the length of the application buffer.

num_bytes Specifies the number of bytes of data copied into the application buffer.

private_id Specifies the private data stored with the data item by the application that placed the data item on the clipboard. If the application did not store private data with the data item, this argument returns zero.

The **XmClipboardRetrieve** function retrieves the current data item from clipboard storage. **XmClipboardRetrieve** returns a warning under the following circumstances:

- The data needs to be truncated because the buffer length is too short.

- The clipboard is locked.

- There is no data on the clipboard.

This function can return one of the following status return constants:

ClipboardSuccess The function is successful.

ClipboardLocked The function failed because the clipboard was locked by another application. The application can continue to call the function again with the same parameters until the lock goes away. This gives the application the opportunity to ask if the user wants to keep trying or to give up on the operation.

ClipboardTruncate The data returned is truncated because the user did not provide a buffer that was large enough to hold the data.

ClipboardNoData The function could not find data on the clipboard corresponding to the format requested. This could occur because (1) the clipboard is empty; (2) there is data on the clipboard but not in the requested format; and (3) the data in the requested format was passed by name and is no longer available.

8.2.3.3 XmClipboardEndRetrieve

This function suspends copying data incrementally from the clipboard.

int XmClipboardEndRetrieve *(display, window);*
  Display **display;*
  Window *window;*

display   Specifies a pointer to the **Display** structure that was returned in a previous call to **XtOpenDisplay**.

window   Specifies the window ID that relates the application window to the clipboard. The same application instance should pass the same window ID to each of the clipboard functions that it calls.

XmClipboardEndRetrieve tells the cut and paste routines the application is through copying an item to the clipboard. Until **XmClipboardEndRetrieve** is called, data items can be retrieved incrementally from the clipboard by calling **XmClipboardRetrieve**. If the application calls **XmClipboardStartRetrieve**, it has to call **XmClipboardEndRetrieve**. If data is not being copied incrementally, **XmClipboardStartRetrieve** and **XmClipboardEndRetrieve** do not need to be called.

8.2.4 Miscellaneous Clipboard Functions

This section describes several additional clipboard functions.

8.2.4.1 XmClipboardLock

This function locks the clipboard from access by other applications.

int XmClipboardLock (*display*, *window*)
   Display *display;
   Window *window*;

display   Specifies a pointer to the **Display** structure that was returned in a previous call to **XtOpenDisplay**.

window   Specifies the window ID that relates the application window to the clipboard. The same application instance should pass the same window ID to each of the clipboard functions that it calls.

The **XmClipboardLock** function locks the clipboard from access by another application until you call **XmClipboardUnlock**. All clipboard functions lock and unlock the clipboard to prevent simultaneous access. The **XmClipboardLock** and **XmClipboardUnlock** functions allow the application to keep the clipboard data from changing between calls to the inquire functions and other clipboard functions. The application does not need to lock the clipboard between calls to **XmClipboardStartCopy** and **XmClipboardEndCopy**, but it should do so before multiple calls to **XmClipboardCopyByName**.

If the clipboard is already locked by another application, **XmClipboardLock** returns an error status.

Multiple calls to **XmClipboardLock** by the same application increase the lock level.

This function can return one of the following status return constants:

ClipboardSuccess   The function is successful.

ClipboardLocked   The function failed because the clipboard was locked by another application. The application can continue to call the function again with the same parameters until the lock goes away. This gives the application the opportunity to ask if the user wants to keep trying or to give up on the operation.

8.2.4.2 XmClipboardRegisterFormat

This function registers a new format.

int ClipboardRegisterFormat *(display, format_name,*
   format_length)
   Display   **display;*
   char   **format_name;*
   unsigned long *format_length;*

display   Specifies a pointer to the **Display** structure that was returned in a previous call to **XtOpenDisplay**.

format_name Specifies the string name for the new format.

format_length
   Specifies the format length in bits (8, 16, or 32).

Each format stored on the clipboard should have a length associated with it and known to the cut and paste routines. All of the formats specified by the *Inter-Client Communication Conventions Manual* are pre-registered (formats are referred to as targets in the ICCCM). Any other format that the application wants to use must be registered via this routine. Failure to register the length of the data will result in applications not being compatible across platforms having different byte swapping orders.

8.2.4.3 XmClipboardUnlock

This function unlocks the clipboard.

int XmClipboardUnlock (*display*, *window*, *remove_all_locks*)
  Display *display;
  Window *window*;
  Boolean *remove_all_locks* ;

display   Specifies a pointer to the **Display** structure that was returned in a previous call to **XtOpenDisplay**.

window   Specifies the window ID that relates the application window to the clipboard. The same application instance should pass the same window ID to each of the clipboard functions that it calls. Note that this window must be associated with a widget.

remove_all_locks

        Specifies a Boolean value that, when True, indicates that all nested locks should be removed. If False, indicates that only one level of lock should be removed.

The **XmClipboardUnlock** function unlocks the clipboard, enabling it to be accessed by other applications.

If multiple calls to **XmClipboardLock** have occurred, then the same number of calls to **XmClipboardUnlock** is necessary to unlock the clipboard, unless the *remove_all_locks* argument is True.

This function can return one of the following status return constants:

ClipboardSuccess The function is successful.

ClipboardLocked The function failed because the clipboard was locked by another application. The application can continue to call the function again with the same parameters until the lock goes away. This gives the application the opportunity to ask if the user wants to keep trying or to give up on the operation.

8.2.4.4 XmClipboardWithdrawFormat

This function indicates that the application is no longer willing to supply a data item to the clipboard.

int XmClipboardWithdrawFormat(*display*, *window*, *data_id*)
   Display *display;
   Window *window*;
   int *data_id*;

display   Specifies a pointer to the **Display** structure that was returned in a previous call to **XtOpenDisplay**.

window   Specifies the window ID that relates the application window to the clipboard. The same application instance should pass the same window ID to each of the clipboard functions that it calls. Note that this window must be associated with a widget.

data_id   Specifies an identifying number assigned to the data item that uniquely identifies the data item and the format. This was assigned to the item when it was originally passed by **XmClipboardCopy**.

The **XmClipboardWithdrawFormat** function indicates that the application will no longer supply a data item to the clipboard that the application had previously passed by name.

This function can return one of the following status return constants:

ClipboardSuccess   The function is successful.

ClipboardLocked   The function failed because the clipboard was locked by another application. The application can continue to call the function again with the same parameters until the lock goes away. This gives the application the opportunity to ask if the user wants to keep trying or to give up on the operation.

8.3 Dynamic Resource Defaulting

Dynamic resource defaulting is a mechanism that incorporates a processing function into a widget's resource definitions. The widget can use this mechanism to calculate a default resource value when it (the widget) is created, instead of having the resource default be static. The widget set uses this capability to determine much of its visual resource defaults at run time. This allows the widget to make more sensible choices for color and pixmap defaults.

All of the color resources and pixmap resources that represent visual data are dynamically defaulted. This includes the resources **XmNforeground, XmNbackground, XmNbackgroundPixmap, XmNtopShadowColor,** **XmNtopShadowPixmap,** **XmNbottomShadowColor,** **XmNbottomShadowPixmap,** **XmNhighlightColor**, and **XmNhighlightPixmap**.

Color and pixmap data are set as follows:

- Set to black and white if a monochrome system is used

- If a color system is used:

  — A default color scheme, or

  — A color scheme based on the background resource, **XmNbackground**.

Part of the design for the widget set and window manager includes an algorithmic approach for generating color schemes. This means that by specifying the background color, the foreground and two shadowing colors are calculated.

8.4 Localization

The Motif toolkit supports the Xt Intrinsics mechanisms for localization of resource files. You can specify a language by using the **xnlLanguage** resource or the **LANG** environment variable. Elements of this variable are then used to establish a path to the proper resource files. The following substitutions are used in building the path:

- %N is replaced by class name of the application.

- %L is replaced by the display's language specification (from the **xnlLanguage** resource or, if that resource is not defined, the **LANG** environment variable).

- %l is replaced by the language part of the language specification.

- %t is replaced by the territory part of the language specification.

- %c is replaced by the codeset part of the language specification.

- %% is replaced by %.

If the **xnlLanguage** resource or the **LANG** environment variable is not defined, or if one of its parts is missing, then a % element that references it is replaced by NULL.

The paths contain a series of elements separated by colons. Each element denotes a filename, and the filenames are looked up left-to-right until one of them succeeds. Before doing the lookup, substitutions are performed.

NOTE: The Intrinsics use the X/Open convention of collapsing multiple adjoining slashes in a filename into one slash.

The **XtDisplayInitalize** function loads the resource database by merging in resources from these sources, in order:

- Application-specific class resource file on the local host

- Application-specific user resource file on the local host

- Resource property on the server or user preference resource file on the local host

- Per-host user environment resource file on the local host

- The application command line

To load the application-specific class resource file, **XtDisplayInitialize** performs the appropriate substitutions on the path specified by the **XFILESEARCHPATH** environment variable. If that fails, or if **XFILESEARCHPATH** is not defined, **XtDisplayInitialize** uses the following as the path:

/usr/lib/X11/%L/app-defaults/%N:
/usr/lib/X11/%l/app-defaults/%N:/usr/lib/X11/app-defaults/%N

If the language is not specified (or the first path lookup using the language specification fails), the lookup defaults to the current non-language-specific location (**/usr/lib/X11/app_defaults/%N**).

If no application-specific class resource file is found, **XtDisplayInitialize** looks for any fallback resources that may have been defined by a call to **XtAppInitialize** or **XtAppSetFallbackResources**.

To load the user's application resource file, **XtDisplayInitialize** performs the following steps:

1. Use **XUSERFILESEARCHPATH** to look up the file, performing appropriate substitutions.

2. If that fails, or if **XUSERFILESEARCHPATH** is not defined, and if **XAPPLRESDIR** is defined, use the following as the path:

   $XAPPLRESDIR/%L/%N:$XAPPLRESDIR/%l/%N:
   $XAPPLRESDIR/%N:$HOME/%N

   where **$XAPPLRESDIR** is the value of the **XAPPLRESDIR** environment variable and **$HOME** is the user's home directory.

3. If **XAPPLRESDIR** is not defined, use the following as the path:

   $HOME/%L/%N:$HOME/%l/%N:$HOME/%N

To load the server resource property or user preference file, **XtDisplayInitialize** first looks for a RESOURCE_MANAGER property on the root window of the display's screen 0. If that property does not exist, **XtDisplayInitialize** looks for the file **$HOME/.Xdefaults**.

To load the per-host user environment resources, **XtDisplayInitialize** uses the filename specified by the **XENVIRONMENT** environment variable. If **XENVIRONMENT** is not defined, **XtDisplayInitialize** looks for the file **$HOME/.Xdefaults-***host*, where *host* is the name of the host on which the application is running.

8.5 Pixmap Caching Functions

The pixmap caching functions provide the application and widget writer with a means of associating an image with a name. Given this association, these functions can generate pixmaps through references to a **.Xdefaults** file (by name) and through an argument list (by pixmap), for all widgets that have pixmap resources. A cache of all pixmaps is automatically maintained. This improves performance and decreases server data space when requesting identical pixmaps.

The pixmap caching provides four functions by which the application or widget writer can install images, uninstall images, create pixmaps, and destroy pixmaps.

Boolean XmInstallImage *(image, image_name)*
  XImage   * *image*;
  char   * *image_name*;

image   Points to the image structure to be installed. The installation process does not make a local copy of the image, therefore the application should not destroy the image until it is installed from the caching functions.

image_name Specifies a string that the application uses to name the image. After installation, this name can be used in a **.Xdefaults** file for referencing the image. A local copy of the name is created by the image caching functions.

XmInstallImage is used to give to the caching routines an image that can later be used to generate a pixmap. Part of the installation process is to extend the resource converter used to reference these images. The resource converter can access the image name so that the image can be referenced in a **.Xdefaults** file. Since an image can be referenced by a widget through its pixmap resources, it is up to the application to ensure that the image is installed before the widget is created. *image* is a pointer to the image structure to be installed. The installation process does not make a local copy of the image. Therefore, the application should not destroy the image until it is uninstalled from the caching functions. *image_name* is a string the application uses to name the image. After installation this name can be used in a **.Xdefaults** file for referencing the image. A local copy of the name is created by the image caching functions.

The image caching functions provide a set of eight preinstalled images. These names can be used within a **.Xdefaults** file for generating pixmaps for the resource they are provided for.

Table 8-3. Preinstalled Images

Image Name	Description
background	A tile of solid background
25_foreground	A tile of 25% foreground, 75% background
50_foreground	A tile of 50% foreground, 50% background
75_foreground	A tile of 75% foreground, 25% background
horizontal	A tile of horizontal lines of the two colors
vertical	A tile of vertical lines of the two colors
slant_right	A tile of slanting lines of the two colors
slant_left	A tile of slanting lines of the two colors

Boolean XmUninstallImage *(image)*
  XmImage **image*;

image   Points to the image structure given to the **XmInstallImage** routine

XmUninstallImage provides the mechanism by which an image can be removed from the caching routines. *image* is a pointer to the image given to the **XmInstallImage** routine.

An application or widget makes a call to extract a pixmap when the images have been installed or to access a set of the predefined images. When an application or widget is finished with a pixmap, it can call a function to destroy the pixmap. These functions are defined as follows:

Pixmap XmGetPixmap *(screen, image_name, foreground,*
    background)
  Screen * *screen*;
  char   * *image_name*;
  Pixel *foreground*;
  Pixel *background*;

screen   Specifies the display screen on which the pixmap is to
           be drawn and is used to ensure that the pixmap
           matches the visual required for the screen.

image_name Specifies the name of the image to be used to generate
           the pixmap.

foreground   Combines the image with the foreground color to
           create the pixmap if the image referenced is a bit-per-
           pixel image.

background Combines the image with the background color to
           create the pixmap if the image referenced is a bit-per-
           pixel image.

XmGetPixmap uses the parameter data to perform a lookup in the
pixmap cache to see if a pixmap has already been generated that
matches the data for the specified screen. If one is found, a
reference count is incremented and the pixmap is returned. If one is
not found, the image corresponding to *image_name* is used to
generate a pixmap which is then cached and returned. *screen*
contains the display screen on which the pixmap is to be drawn and
is used to ensure the pixmap matches the visual required for the
screen. *image_name* is the name of the image to be used to generate
the pixmap. If a bit-per-pixel image is being accessed, *foreground*
and *background* are combined with the image to create the pixmap.

Boolean XmDestroyPixmap *(screen, pixmap)*
  Screen * *screen*;
  Pixmap *pixmap*;

screen   Specifies the display screen for which the pixmap was
           requested

pixmap   Specifes the pixmap to be destroyed

XmDestroyPixmap is used to remove pixmaps that are no longer
needed. A pixmap is completely freed only when there is no further
reference to it.

8.6 Resolution Independence

The OSF/Motif widget set has a built-in mechanism called resolution independence. Resolution independence allows applications to create and display images that are the same physical size regardless of the resolution of the display. This frees the application developer from the task of ensuring that an application can be used on a wide range of systems.

The resolution independence mechanism provides resource data to the widgets in various unit types, including millimeters, inches, points, and font units. All widget resources connected with size, position, thickness, padding, and spacing can be set using the preceding unit types. The application or user of the application can provide resolution independent data through **.Xdefaults** and applications-defaults files, command line arguments, or argument lists.

8.6.1 The Resolution Independence Mechanism

The unit a widget uses is defined by the resource XmNunitType, which can be found in the base classes of XmPrimitive, XmGadget, and XmManager. Since all widgets are built from these base classes, it follows that all widgets support resolution independence. XmNunitType can have five values:

- **XmPIXELS** - All values provided to the widget are treated as normal pixel values. This is the default value for the resource.

- **Xm100TH_MILLIMETERS** - All values provided to the widget are treated as 1/100 of a millimeter.

- **Xm1000TH_INCHES** - All values provided to the widget are treated as 1/1000 of an inch.

- **Xm100TH_POINTS** - All values provided to the widget are treated as 1/100 of a point. A point is a unit typically used in text processing applications and is defined as 1/72 of an inch.

- **Xm100TH_FONT_UNITS** - All values provided to the widget are treated as 1/100 of a font unit. The value to be used for the font unit is determined in one of three ways:

— The application can use **XmSetFontUnit** to specify the font unit values. This function is described later in this section.

— If the application has not called **XmSetFontUnit**, the font units can be derived from a font. The user specifies this font by using the font resource in a defaults file or on the command line, or by using the standard command line options **-fn** and **-font**.

— If the application has not called **XmSetFontUnit** and the user has not specified a font resource, the horizontal and vertical font units default to 10.

A horizontal font unit is derived from a font as follows:

- If the font has an **AVERAGE_WIDTH** property, the horizontal font unit is the **AVERAGE_WIDTH** property divided by 10.

- If the font has no **AVERAGE_WIDTH** property but has a **QUAD_WIDTH** property, the horizontal font unit is the **QUAD_WIDTH** property.

- If the font has no **AVERAGE_WIDTH** or **QUAD_WIDTH** property, the horizontal font unit is the sum of the font struct's min_bounds.width and max_bounds.width divided by 2.3.

A vertical font unit is derived from a font as follows:

- If the font has a **PIXEL_SIZE** property, the vertical font unit is the **PIXEL_SIZE** property divided by 1.8.

- If the font has no **PIXEL_SIZE** property but has **POINT_SIZE** and **RESOLUTION_Y** properties, the vertical font unit is the product of the **POINT_SIZE** and **RESOLUTION_Y** properties divided by 1400.

- If the font has no **PIXEL_SIZE**, **POINT_SIZE**, or **RESOLUTION_Y** properties, the vertical font unit is the sum of the font struct's max_bounds.ascent and max_bounds.descent divided by 2.2.

There are two reasons for the unit types to be fractional:

- It allows all calculations to be done in integer representation. This ensures maximum performance for type conversions.

- There is no way to supply a floating-point number to a widget through an argument list. This is because the value field in the argument list is of type **char ***. When a floating-point value is forced into a **char *** variable, the fractional part is truncated.

When a widget is created and its unit type is something other than pixels, it converts the data specified by the application or the user into pixel values, taking into account the resolution of the screen. These converted pixel values are then placed into the internal data space of the widget, and the widget operates as it would normally. The same process occurs when the application issues an **XtSetValues** to a widget. The new values are converted from unit type to pixels and placed back into the widget.

When the application issues an **XtGetValues** to a widget, the pixel values are taken out of the widget, converted back to the unit type, and inserted into the argument list to be returned.

The conversion and storing of unit type values to pixel values can cause some rounding errors. Therefore, when an application issues an **XtGetValues**, it should not expect exactly the same data to be returned as was originally specified. This rounding error will only occur once and will not get progressively worse. For example, if a widget's width is set to 1000/1000 inches (1 inch), **XtGetValues** may return 993/1000 inches. If this value is then used to set the width of a second widget and the application calls **XtGetValues** on the second widget, 993/1000 inches will be returned.

8.6.2 Setting the Font Units

Applications may want to specify resolution independent data based on a global font size. The widget set provides an external function to use to initialize the font unit values. This function needs to be called before any widgets with resolution independent data are created.

XmSetFontUnit *(display, font_unit_value)*
  Display * *display;*
  int *font_unit_value;*

The parameters for this function are as follows:

display   Defines the display for which this font unit value is to be applied.

font_unit_value Specifies the value to be used for both horizontal and vertical font units in the conversion calculations.

8.6.3 Converting Between Unit Types

The widgets use a general conversion function to convert between pixels and other unit types. This function can convert values between any of the defined unit types, and is available to the application for its use.

int XmConvertUnits *(widget, orientation, from_unit_type,*
    from_value, to_unit_type)
  Widget * *widget;*
  int *orientation;*
  int *from_unit_type;*
  int *from_value;*
  int *to_unit_type;*

XmConvertUnits uses the parameter data to convert the value and return it as the return value from the function. The parameters for this function are as follows:

widget   Specifies the widget for which the data is to be converted.

orientation   Specifies whether the converter should use the horizontal screen resolution or vertical screen resolution when performing the conversions. *orientation* can have values of **XmHORIZONTAL** or **XmVERTICAL**.

from_unit_type
      Specifies the current unit type of the supplied value.

from_value   Specifies the value to be converted.

to_unit_type   Specifies the unit type into which the value should be converted.

8.7 Interacting with the Motif Window Manager

This section explains the procedures an application can use to interact with the WM_PROTOCOLS and system menu facilities provided by MWM. Be sure that you have read at least the discussion of MWM properties in the Motif Window Manager chapters before reading this section. You should also be familiar with the concepts presented in the *Inter-Client Communications Conventions Manual* (ICCCM).

8.7.1 Protocol Management

The protocol management functions are a set of general purpose routines for interacting with properties that contain atom arrays, client messages, and associated callbacks. They are used to support the existing entries for the WM_PROTOCOLS and _MOTIF_WM_MESSAGES properties. See the section about configuring the OSF/Motif window manager for more information.

NOTE: In the following discussion, the names of atoms or properties are in upper case and are obtained by interning the strings with the server. Use **XmInternAtom** to convert these strings to a 32-bit tag. The following code segment shows how to obtain the _MOTIF_WM_MESSAGES atom.

```
Atom motif_wm_messages;

    motif_wm_messages = XmInternAtom(display,
        "_MOTIF_WM_MESSAGES", true);
```

Alternatively, you could use _XA_MOTIF_WM_MESSAGES (defined in **X11/MwmUtil.h**) as the second argument to **XmInternAtom**.

A protocol is a 32-bit tag used by clients to communicate with the window manager. This tag is either an X Atom or an arbitrary long integer variable whose value is shared by the parties to the protocol communication. The client indicates interest in certain communications protocols by adding these tags to a tag array that is the value of a special property on its top-level window. For predefined ICCC protocols, this property is WM_PROTOCOLS. For MWM, this property is _MOTIF_WM_MESSAGES. The window manager sends a protocol message (when appropriate) in the form of a client message event with the *message_type* field of the **ClientMessage** structure set to the property and the *data.l[0]* field set to the protocol. The client can associate a callback list with the protocol that is invoked when the client message event is received.

Each shell can have one protocol manager per property associated with it, and the protocol manager can have multiple protocols registered. Each protocol is identified by its tag (WM_SAVE_YOURSELF, for example). The protocols can have any number of client callbacks associated with them, in addition to prehook and posthook callbacks (usually registered by the widget set) for each protocol.

The protocol manager does the following:

- Tracks the state of the protocols whether or not they are active

- Tracks the state of the Shell and creates and updates the protocol property accordingly

- Processes the client messages received and invokes the appropriate callbacks

8.7.1.1 _MOTIF_WM_MESSAGES

The client uses the _MOTIF_WM_MESSAGES property to indicate to MWM which messages (sent by MWM when an **send_msg** function is invoked from the MWM system menu) it is currently handling. A client can add **f.send_msg** entries to the menu by using the **.mwmrc** file or by using the **XmNmwmMenu** resource of VendorShell. This resource is a string that is parsed by MWM to determine what to display in the system menu and how to react to an item's selection. When the action associated with an item is **f.send_msg**, MWM sends the client a message if the specified protocol is active. The protocol is the integer argument to the **f.send_msg** action. A menu protocol is active if the protocol is in the _MOTIF_WM_MESSAGES property and the _MOTIF_WM_MESSAGES atom is in the WM_PROTOCOLS property. Otherwise, the protocol is inactive and the menu label will be grayed out.

8.7.1.2 WM_PROTOCOLS

A corresponding macro is provided for each of the general protocol manager routines to simplify their use. The only difference between them is that the general routines are passed a protocol property in all calls while the macros always force this property to WM_PROTOCOLS. These macros are useful if you want to interact with ICCC protocols such as WM_DELETE_WINDOW or WM_SAVE_YOURSELF.

Note that if you are using the protocol manager for the system menu, the property should be the atom corresponding to _MOTIF_WM_MESSAGES.

8.7.2 Protocol Manager Functions

The following sections list the protocol manager functions. A sample program, **xmprotocol**, in the **./demos** directory adds or deactivates entries to the system menu. You can use the methods presented in that program to get an idea of how to use the functions discussed in this section.

Note that the statement

```
#include <X11/Protocols.h>
```

must be present in any program using these functions.

The functions that have the letters WM are the macros referred to earlier. Each function has a corresponding macro. For example, **XmAddProtocols** has a corresponding macro **XmAddWMProtocols**. The macro simply calls **XmAddProtocols** with the *property* parameter set to XA_WM_PROTOCOL.

8.7.2.1 Add and Remove Functions

The following routine adds the protocols to the protocol manager corresponding to the specified property and allocate the internal tables. The protocols are initialized to active.

void XmAddWMProtocols *(shell, protocols, num_protocols)*
   Widget *shell*;
   Atom **protocols*;
   Cardinal *num_protocols;*

void XmAddProtocols *(shell, property, protocols, num_protocols)*
   Widget *shell;*
   Atom *property;*
   Atom **protocols;*
   Cardinal *num_protocols;*

The following routine removes the protocols from the protocol manager and deallocates the internal tables. It also updates the handlers and the property if any of the protocols are active and the shell referenced in the *shell* parameter is realized.

void XmRemoveWMProtocols *(shell, protocols, num_protocols)*
   Widget *shell;*
   Atom **protocol;*
   Cardinal *num_protocols;*

void XmRemoveProtocols *(shell, property, protocols,*
   num_protocols)
   Widget *shell;*
   Atom *property;*
   Atom **protocols;*
   Cardinal *num_protocols;*

8.7.2.2 Protocol State

It is sometimes useful to allow a protocol's state information (callback lists for example) to persist, even though the client may choose to temporarily resign from the interaction. The main use of this capability is to gray out `f.send_msg` labels in the system menu. This is supported by allowing a protocol to be in one of two states, active or inactive. If the protocol is active and the shell is realized, then the property contains the protocol atom. If the protocol is inactive, then the atom is not present in the property.

If the protocol is inactive, the following routine updates the handlers and adds the protocol to the property if the shell is realized.

> **void XmActivateWMProtocol** *(shell, protocol)*
> **Widget** *shell;*
> **Atom** *protocol;*

> **void XmActivateProtocol** *(shell, property, protocol)*
> **Widget** *shell;*
> **Atom** *property;*
> **Atom** *protocol;*

If the protocol is inactive, this routine updates the handlers and the property if the shell is realized.

> **void XmDeactivateWMProtocol** *(shell, protocol)*
> **Widget** *shell;*
> **Atom** *protocol;*

> **void XmDeactivateProtocol** *(shell, property, protocol)*
> **Atom** *property;*
> **Cardinal** *num_protocols;*

8.7.2.3 Protocol Callbacks

When a client message associated with a protocol is received by the protocol manager, it checks to see if the protocol is active. If it is, then any callbacks associated with the protocol are called. Three callback lists can be associated with a protocol. One is for client use and is accessed by **XmAddProtocolCallback** and

XmRemoveProtocolCallback. The other two (the pre-hook and post-hook callbacks) are intended for toolkit use and are accessed by the **XmSetProtocolHooks** routine. The hook routines are called before and after the client callbacks (if any) are called. The protocol callbacks have a reason field of XmCR_PROTOCOLS and a type of XmAnyCallbackStruct.

The following routine checks to see if the protocol is registered and if not, it calls **XmAddProtocols**. It then adds the callbacks to the internal list. These callbacks are called when the corresponding client message is received.

void XmAddWMProtocolCallback *(shell, protocol, callback,*
   closure)
  Widget *shell;*
  Atom *protocol;*
  XtCallbackProc *callback;*
  caddr_t *closure;*

void XmAddProtocolCallback *(shell, property, protocol,*
  callback, closure)
  Widget *shell;*
  Atom *property;*
  Atom *protocol;*
  XtCallbackProc *callback;*
  caddr_t *closure;*

The following routine removes the callback from the internal list.

void XmRemoveWMProtocolCallback *(shell, protocol, callback,*
  closure)
  Widget *shell;*
  Atom *protocol;*
  XtCallbackProc *callback;*
  caddr_t *closure;*

void XmRemoveProtocolCallback *(shell, property, protocol,*
  callback, closure)
  Widget *shell;*
  Atom *property;*
  Atom *protocol;*
  XtCallbackProc *callback;*
  caddr_t *closure;*

The following routine is used by toolkit widgets that want to have before and after actions executed when a protocol message is received from the window manager. Since there is no guaranteed ordering in execution of event handlers or callback lists, this allows the shell to control the flow while leaving the protocol manager structures private. The callback procedure's *Call_data* argument will contain the same pointer as that passed to the client callbacks.

void XmSetWMProtocolHooks *(shell, protocol, prehook,*
   pre_closure, posthook, post_closure)
  Widget   *shell;*
  XtCallbackProc *prehook, posthook;*
  caddr_t *pre_closure, post_closure;*

void XmSetProtocolHooks *(shell, protocol, property, prehook,*
   pre_closure, posthook, post_closure)
  Widget   *shell;*
  Atom   *property;*
  XtCallbackProc *prehook, posthook;*
  caddr_t   *pre_closure, post_closure;*

8.7.3 Atom Management

The atom management routines mirror the Xlib interfaces for atom management, but provide client-side caching. When (and where) caching is provided in Xlib, the routines will become pseudonyms for the Xlib routines. Note that the statement

```
#include <Xm/AtomMgr.h>
```

must be present in any program using these functions.

Atom XmInternAtom *(display, name, only_if_exists)*
  Display **display;*
  String *name;*
  Boolean *only_if_exists;*

String XmGetAtomName *(display, atom)*
  Display **display;*
  Atom   *atom;*

8.8 Motif Version Number

Motif provides a macro, **XmVersion**, that returns the current Motif version. Essentially, the macro multiplies the version number of the library by 1000 and adds the revision number. For example, in the first release of Motif Version 1.0, the macro would return 1000.

Additionally, a global variable, **XmUseVersion** is provided. The value of this variable is set to reflect the value returned by **XmVersion** as soon as the first widget is created (the setting takes place during the class initialization procedure of the widget). In the future, an application may be able to set this variable to specify the kind of behavior the widget library should provide.

8.9 Motif Window Manager Presence

Users often need to determine whether MWM is running on a given display. The Motif **XmIsMotifWMRunning** function can provide this information.

#include <Xm/Xm.h>

Boolean XmIsMotifWMRunning *(shell)*
  Widget *shell;*

shell   Specifies the shell whose screen should be tested for MWM's presence. The function returns True if MWM is running, False if it is not.

Chapter 9

Keyboard Interface

The keyboard interface allows the user to interact with an application using the keyboard in place of, or as a supplement to, the mouse. This capability is necessary in a variety of situations, such as mouseless systems or applications that do not want to force the user to switch back and forth between the keyboard and mouse.

The keyboard interface involves two major components:

- Keyboard focus and traversal from widget to widget
- Keyboard input processing to an individual widget

9.1 Keyboard Focus Models

Traversal provides the means of moving the keyboard focus within an application. The keyboard focus indicates which widget is currently active. When a particular widget has keyboard focus, all keyboard input directed at the application goes to that widget, regardless of the location of the pointer.

Motif supports two focus models:

- The pointer-driven focus model. In the pointer-driven model, a widget receives keyboard input only when the cursor is positioned within the widget's bounding rectangle; moving the cursor out of the widget causes it to lose focus.

- The click-to-type focus model. In the click-to-type model, when the window manager passes the focus to the topmost shell widget, the topmost shell widget redirects the focus to one of its descendents. The user can move the focus to another descendent of the topmost shell widget either by pressing the arrow or tab keys, or by clicking mouse button 1 in a widget. Clicking mouse button 1 in a widget may cause that widget to ask for and receive the input focus. When a descendent has focus, it continues to receive all keyboard input until either of the following occurs:

  — The user requests that the focus be moved to another descendent of the topmost shell widget.

  — The window manager takes the focus away from the topmost shell widget.

An application sets the desired model by means of the **XmNkeyboardFocusPolicy** resource, which is exported by the VendorShell widget class. The specified focus model is active for the complete widget hierarchy built from the topmost shell widget.

The functionality described in the rest of this chapter applies only to the click-to-type focus model. The Motif menu system provides its own type of keyboard traversal. This is explained in Chapter 6, ''Menus.''

Only Primitive widgets and gadgets can have the keyboard focus, since they are not merely containers; the user interacts with them. In this discussion, gadgets are considered comparable to Primitive widgets.

Each Primitive widget has a Boolean resource, XmNtraversalOn, that specifies whether or not the widget will accept the focus. The default is False, which denies focus. The resource must be set to True in order for the widget to accept the focus.

When a widget has accepted the keyboard focus, a highlight is drawn around the widget.

9.2 Grouping Widgets Into Tab Groups

Motif uses the concept of tab groups to group Primitive widgets. Any manager or Primitive widget can be defined as a tab group. If a manager widget is in a tab group, its Primitive children are part of the tab group.

Two functions manage the addition and deletion of tab groups for an application.

Tab groups are ordinarily specified by the **XmNnavigationType** resource. **XmAddTabGroup** is called to control the order of traversal of tab groups. **XmAddTabGroup** adds the specified tab group to the list of tab groups associated with a particular widget hierarchy.

XmAddTabGroup(*tab_group*)
   Widget *tab_group*;

tab_group   Specifies the manager or Primitive widget that defines a tab group.

XmRemoveTabGroup removes the tab group from the list of tab groups associated with a particular widget hierarchy.

XmRemoveTabGroup(*tab_group*)
   Widget *tab_group*;

tab_group   Specifies the manager or Primitive widget that defines a tab group.

9.3 Traversal Within and Between Tab Groups

Traversal involves two types of focus changes—changing the focus to a different widget within a particular tab group and changing the focus to another tab group.

Movement among the Primitive widgets within a tab group is controlled by the order in which the widgets were created. The following keys change the focus to another widget in the same tab group:

- The down arrow key moves the focus to the next widget for which the XmNtraversalOn resource has been set to True. When the focus reaches the end of the tab group, it wraps to the beginning. The right arrow key has the same effect unless its behavior is defined by the particular widget. For example, a Text widget configureOBd for single-line edit defines the behavior of the right arrow key; therefore, that key does not change the focus.

- The up arrow key moves the focus to the previous widget. When the focus reaches the beginning of the tab group, it wraps to the end. The left arrow key has the same effect unless its behavior is defined by the particular widget.

- The home key moves the focus to the first Primitive widget in the tab group.

Movement between tab groups is controlled by the order in which the application has registered the tab groups.

- The <Tab> moves the focus to the first widget in the next tab group. When the focus reaches the end of the tab group list, the focus wraps to the beginning of the list.

- <Shift> <Tab> moves the focus to the first widget in the previous tab group. When the focus reaches the beginning of the tab group list, it wraps to the end of the list.

Clicking mouse button 1 within certain widgets (typically, text widgets) moves the focus to the indicated widget. The focus remains there until either the widget hierarchy loses the focus, or the user moves the focus to another widget. A widget must have its XmNtraversalOn resource set to True in order to get focus this way.

Certain widgets must be placed within their own tab group; that is, the widget cannot be included in a tab group containing other widgets.

- Each List widget and the ScrollBar widget must be registered as its own tab group, since they define special behavior for the arrow keys.

- Each multiline text widget must be registered as its own tab group, since it defines special behavior for both the arrow keys and the Tab keys. Single-line text widgets do not have this requirement.

- The Option menu widget must be registered as its own tab group because it consists of two internal Primitive widgets.

9.4 Keyboard Input Processing to a Widget

Keyboard input into a widget that has focus is handled by definitions of the widget's default translations for keyboard input. Refer to the *OSF/Motif Programmer's Reference* for the default translations.

Chapter 10
Introduction to the OSF/Motif Window Manager

The next seven chapters provide information for application developers about the OSF/Motif Window Manager. The OSF/Motif Window Manager (MWM) provides window management facilities within the framework of the OSF/Motif environment. MWM provides you with an industry standard user interface, a high degree of flexibility, and a pleasing visual interface.

MWM facilitates user-computer communications in the following areas:

- MWM provides for direct manipulation of graphic objects using an object-action model. A user controls the operation of an application program by selecting a window, menu, icon, or other graphic object and then indicating an action to be done to that object.

- MWM uses several configuration files, including **.Xdefaults**, **.mwmrc**, and **.motifbind**. By editing these files, users can customize the appearance and behavior of MWM.

- MWM provides keyboard access to window management functionality in cases where a mouse is not available or the user prefers keyboard access.

- MWM provides consistent appearance and behavior using the OSF/Motif widgets as specified in the *OSF/Motif Style Guide*.

10.1 Conventions

The OSF/Motif Window Manager can be operated with either a 2-button or a 3-button mouse by observing the conventions shown in Figure 10-1. With a 2-button mouse, you can obtain a third button by pressing buttons 1 and 2 simultaneously. You can obtain five buttons from a 3-button mouse by pressing buttons 1 and 2 for a fourth button and buttons 2 and 3 for a fifth button.

Figure 10-1. Two- and Three-Button Mice

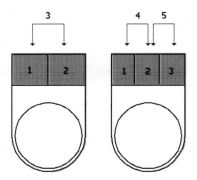

Figure 10-2. Mouse Buttons and Their Locations

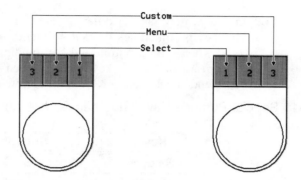

When using a keyboard instead of a mouse, follow the instructions in "Using a Keyboard" under the section "Getting User Input" in Chapter 11.

10.2 Some Window Manager Precautions

If you are new to window manager configuring, you should be aware of the following conventions:

- File and resource names used by MWM are case sensitive. Use uppercase letters where indicated and only where indicated. A file named **.xdefaults** is not the same file as **.Xdefaults**.

- Do not confuse the number "1" (one) with the lowercase "l" (el). If you are changing to the **/usr/lib/X11** directory, you need to type "X one one" and not "X el el."

- Do not confuse the number "0" (zero) with the uppercase "O" (oh) for the same reason.

- When typing a command, use the spacing indicated in the example. Although adding an extra space usually does not cause problems, omitting a space definitely brings your command to a halt.

- Some keys may have a different label on your keyboard. The **<Alt>** key is sometimes labeled **<Extend>** or **<Meta>**. "Meta" is used when setting button and key bindings. Some keys may not appear on your keyboard. When possible use the recommended substitute given in the following table:

Table 10-1. Special Purpose Keys and Their Substitutions.

Key	Substitution
<Select>	**<Space Bar>** or **<Enter>**
<Menu>	**<F4>**
<Help>	**<F1>**
<Alt>	**<Meta>** or **<Extend>**
<Page up>	**<F7>**
<Page down>	**<F8>**
<Esc>	**<F12>**
<Next Field>	**<Tab>** or **<Ctrl>+<Tab>**
<Previous Field>	**<Shift>+<Tab>** or **<Ctrl>+<Shift>+<Tab>**
<Enter>	**<Return>**

Chapter 11

Understanding the Principles of Window Management

This chapter provides you with background information. It gives you a conceptual foundation upon which to build your understanding of the more technical aspects of window management that you encounter in the following chapters.

This chapter discusses the following topics:

- Getting user input
- Focus policies: keyboard input and colormaps
- Distinguishing windows by type
- Understanding the parts of the MWM window frame
- Placing and sizing windows
- Introduction to icons

11.1 Getting User Input

The default user interface behavior of MWM is based on the *OSF/Motif Style Guide*. MWM provides all of the required elements of OSF/Motif behavior, but it is also customizable so you can modify window appearance and behavior to suit the specific needs of you and your application.

11.1.1 Using a Pointer

The pointer cursor (as distinguished from the text cursor) is controlled with a pointer device. In most cases, the pointer device is a mouse. In this guide, the term **pointer** refers to the pointer cursor and the term **mouse** refers to the pointer device.

A mouse has one or more buttons and is capable of the following actions:

Pointing   Sliding the mouse on the desktop to position the pointer on an object on the screen

Pressing   Holding down a mouse button

Clicking   Pressing and releasing a mouse button without moving the pointer

Double-Clicking   Clicking a mouse button twice in rapid succession

Dragging   Pressing and holding down a mouse button while moving the pointer

MWM has a resource, **doubleClickTime**, for controlling the maximum time (in milliseconds) that can elapse between button clicks before a double-click becomes just two clicks in a row. This resource is discussed in Section 14.5.

In conformance with OSF/Motif behavior, a mouse under MWM has the uses described in the following table:

Table 11-1. Mouse Actions and Their Effects

This action...	Does this...	For example...
Pressing Select button. (Button 1)	Initiates a drag operation.	Pressing the Select button on the window menu button of a client's window frame brings up the window menu.
Releasing Select button.	Completes an action started with a press and drag of the Select button.	Releasing the Select button after dragging the button on a title bar repositions the window and ends the move operation.
Clicking Select button.	Selects an object or action.	Clicking the Select button on a client's Window-frame Minimize button turns the client window into an icon.
Double-clicking Select button.	Provides a shortcut for doing a default action associated with an object.	Double-clicking the Select button on an icon turns the icon into the window associated with the icon.
Dragging Select button.	Performs a drag function such as resizing a window, or browsing a menu.	Pointing to the title area of a client's window frame and dragging the Select button performs a move operation.

11.1.2 Using a Keyboard

In conformity with OSF/Motif behavior, MWM allows you to perform window management functions without using a mouse.

For example, pressing <**Shift**> <**Esc**> pops up the window menu for the active window. The arrow keys are used to browse the menu items, then pressing <**Select**> selects an item. Pressing <**Esc**> cancels the current window management operation.

Window management functions performed from the keyboard generally apply to the active window, the window that is getting keyboard input. However, you can also use the keyboard for nonspecific window management functions such as changing the focus or stacking order of windows on the screen.

11.1.3 Modifying Default Behavior

While the default window management behavior is recommended for the sake of consistency, MWM allows users to modify the default behavior to suit their needs. Users can modify the default behavior of MWM by changing the entries in the resource files that it uses to configure its appearance and behavior.

Table 11-2 summarizes the resource files used by MWM. Some of the filenames in the table represent customary locations for the resource files described. In some cases the actual location can depend on environment variables and on the current language environment. For more information see the ''Creating Defaults Files'' section in Chapter 3, the ''Localization'' section in Chapter 8, and the description of the MWM **configFile** resource in Chapter 14.

Table 11-2. MWM Resource Configuration Files

File Name	Description
/usr/lib/X11/app-defaults/Mwm	Contains system-wide MWM resource configuration information. The actual file location may depend on the XFILESEARCHPATH environment variable and the current language environment.
$HOME/Mwm	Contains user-specific MWM resource configuration information. The actual file location may depend on the XUSERFILESEARCH-PATH and XAPPLRESDIR environment variables and the current language environment.
$HOME/.Xdefaults	Contains user-specific resource configuration information about MWM and other clients used by this user.
$HOME/.Xdefaults-*host*	Contains user-specific and host-specific resource configuration information about MWM and other clients used by this user. The actual file location may depend on the XEN-VIRONMENT environment variable.

File Name	Description
$HOME/.motifbind	Contains user-specific virtual key bindings.
/usr/lib/X11/$LANG/system.mwmrc or /usr/lib/X11/system.mwmrc	Contains system-wide configuration information about MWM menus and keyboard and button bindings.
$HOME/$LANG/.mwmrc or $HOME/.mwmrc	Contains user-specific configuration information about MWM menus and keyboard and button bindings used by this user.

Menus, mouse button bindings, and keyboard bindings are discussed in Chapter 14.

11.2 Using Focus Policies: Keyboard Input and Colormaps

The input focus policy determines how and when a window becomes the active window. An active window has the following characteristics:

- What you type appears in the window

- The color of the window frame changes to indicate the active focus

- Input from extended input devices goes to the window

The default methods of changing the keyboard input focus are shown in Tables 11-3 and 11-4.

Table 11-3. MWM Default Keyboard Input Focus with a Mouse

Doing this...	Does this...
Clicking the mouse Select button with the pointer on the window or window frame.	Selects that window as the focus of keyboard input.
Clicking the mouse Select button with the pointer on an icon.	Selects that icon as the focus of keyboard input.

Table 11-4. MWM Default Keyboard Input Focus with a Keyboard

Pressing these keys...	Does this...
<Alt> <Tab>	Moves the keyboard input focus to the next window in the window stack.
<Alt> <Shift> <Tab>	Moves the keyboard input focus to the previous window in the window stack.

The default input focus policy is an "explicit" selection policy; the user must perform a mouse button action or a key action to change the input focus. A "track pointer" policy, which changes the input focus to match the pointer's position (no other action is required), is also available. These policies are explained further in Chapter 13.

11.2.1 Setting the Colormap Focus Policy

The colormap focus policy dictates which client window has its colormap installed. A **colormap** is a display resource that controls the set of colors appearing on the display. Colormap focus policy is explained in Chapter 13.

11.3 Distinguishing Windows by Type

As you design your client application and write the code, you use particular types of windows to fulfill the specific needs of your design plan.

11.3.1 Choosing the Right Type of Client Window

When you design your client application, remember that MWM recognizes the following types of client windows:

Primary Window

A primary window is a top-level window, a direct descendent of the root window. MWM provides this type of client window with a window frame. By default, this frame is decorated with the full set of functional frame components (resize frame handles, title bar, and window control buttons). You can change the window decoration on primary windows either programmatically from your client or by using the **clientDecoration** resource, as explained in Section 13.11.

Secondary Window

A secondary window is a window that is transient in nature. A secondary window is associated with another window, usually a primary window, and is always over that window in the window stack. Secondary windows are iconified (minimized) together with their associated windows. A secondary window may also receive keyboard or pointer input that it does not pass on to its associated window. This is known as being "modal" with respect to the associated window. For example, you might design a secondary window as an application modal dialog box that requires an action by the user before the application continues.

The WM_TRANSIENT_FOR property indicates that a window is a secondary window and identifies the associated window. The _MOTIF_WM_HINTS property indicates the input mode of a secondary window. Window properties are discussed in more detail in the next chapter. A secondary window typically receives less window-frame decoration than a primary window, and, typically, fewer window management functions are available to control the window. For example, a secondary window may not have a minimize button in the window frame or resize frame handles.

You can configure a secondary window either programmatically, with the _MOTIF_WM_HINTS property (Chapter 12), or with the **transientDecoration** resource, (Chapter 13).

Client Icon
A client icon is supplied by a client for use as an image in an MWM icon.

Client Icon Window
A client icon window is supplied by a client for use as an alternative to a pixmap image in MWM icons (minimized windows). This window can be used while the window is in its iconic state.

Override-redirect Window
An override-redirect window is typically visible for only a short time and, while in use, the pointer should be grabbed by the client. A common example of this type of window is a pop-up menu. MWM does not place override-redirect windows in a window frame, nor does MWM support window management operations on override-redirect windows.

11.3.2 Input Modes

Certain windows constrain the user's input. There are four levels of window constraints, called "modes."

- **Modeless windows** do not constrain user input to other windows. Client primary windows are generally modeless.

- **Primary Application Modal Windows** "prevent" input from going to any of the window's ancestors. Secondary client windows are sometimes application modal with respect to their associated primary window.

- **Full Application Modal Windows** "prevent" input from going to any of the window's ancestors or to any other windows in the same application that are not in the window's hierarchy.

- **System Modal Windows** are similar to application modal windows except that they prevent input from going to any other window on the screen. For example, restart confirmation messages are displayed in system modal windows.

11.3.3 Understanding Window Manager Windows

MWM uses the following window types to provide window management services to your client application:

Client Frames

A client frame is placed around the client area.

Icon Frames

An icon is a small graphic representation of your client application window. When the window manager minimizes (iconifies) a full-sized client window, it uses an icon window frame to represent the client. Icons can be arranged on the screen by the window manager or placed in an icon box.

Icon Box

An icon box is a window used by the window manager to contain icons. An icon box window is decorated with a window frame that is typically the same as a primary window's frame.

Feedback Window

A feedback window appears at the center of the screen when a primary client window is being either resized or repositioned by the window manager. If the client is being resized, the feedback window contains the size (width and height) of the client. If the client is being relocated, the feedback window contains the new location (x-offset and y-offset).

A configuration feedback window is displayed whenever MWM is restarted or a behavior switch is requested. The confirmation window is system modal and is displayed in the center of the screen. Explicit user confirmation is required for MWM to continue the restart or behavior switch.

11.4 Understanding the Parts of the MWM Window Frame

MWM surrounds client windows with a functional frame. Positioning the pointer on a part of the frame and performing the appropriate mouse button action or key action executes the function of that frame part. The following figure shows the components of the frame.

Figure 11-1. MWM Surrounds a Client's Window with a Frame

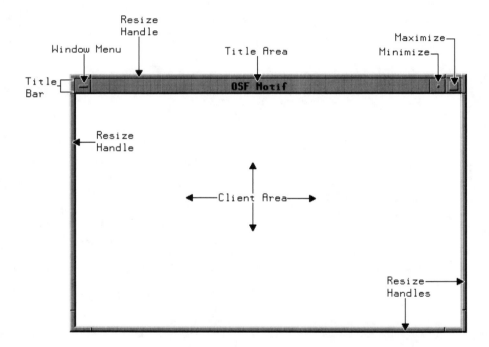

The parts of the MWM window manager frame and their functions are listed in the following table:

Table 11-5. Window Frame Parts and What They Do

This frame part...	Is used to...
Title area.	Move a window.
Window menu button.	Display the window menu.
Minimize button.	Iconify a window.
Maximize button.	Expand a window to maximum size.
Resize frame handles.	Stretch or shrink a window horizontally, vertically, or diagonally (in two directions).

11.4.1 Coloring Frame Components

MWM gives you the option of selecting varied color schemes for active and inactive client windows. Additionally, you may specify the color of a 3D matte frame. This topic is covered in Section 13.8.

11.4.2 Understanding Frame Components and Their Behavior

The components of the client window frame provide users with visual cues for direct manipulation of the window. You can configure the basic frame layout for your client application programmatically by using the _MOTIF_WM_HINTS property (Chapter 12). Users can set the **clientDecoration** (Chapter 13) and **clientFunction** (Chapter 14) resources to configure the client window frame.

11.4.2.1 Resize Handles

The function of the resize handles is to resize the window frame and your client application with it.

A user initiates a resize operation by positioning the pointer on one of the "handles," pressing the mouse Select button, and dragging the window to the desired size. A wire outline shows changing dimensions as the mouse is dragged. Also, a small configuration feedback window displays the current dimensions of the frame. The resize operation stops when the user releases the Select button. It is also canceled when the user presses **<Esc>**.

The resize handles form a frame composed of eight distinct pieces:

- Top
- Bottom
- Left side
- Right side
- Lower right corner
- Lower left corner
- Upper right corner
- Upper left corner

Each handle has a distinct cursor shape. The following figure illustrates these shapes.

Figure 11-2. Resize Handles Have Distinctive Cursor Shapes

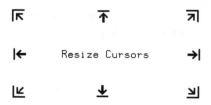

Which handle a user drags, and in which direction the user drags it, affects the outcome of the resize operation. The following table lists where to grab a handle for the desired result.

Table 11-6. Where to Grab an MWM Resize Handle

To stretch or shrink the window...	Position the pointer on the...
vertically from the...	
top	top of the frame, above the title bar
bottom	bottom of the frame
horizontally from the...	
right	right side of the frame
left	left side of the frame
diagonally from the...	
bottom left corner	frame's lower left corner
top left	frame's upper left corner
top right	frame's upper right corner
bottom right	frame's lower right corner

As an application programmer, you have several ways to control a user's ability to resize your client window:

- A window cannot be resized smaller than the minimum size specified by your client.

- A window cannot be resized smaller than the minimum size dictated by the components you select for the window frame.

- A window cannot be resized larger than the maximum window size specified by your client.

- A client can indicate that the resize function should not apply (use the _MOTIF_WM_HINTS property, Chapter 12).

Window frames can be configured to omit resize handles. The frame can then be configured to have a border or to be borderless.

11.4.2.2 The Title Area

The title area has two functions:

- It usually lists the name of the application appearing within the client area of the window.

- It provides the user with a "handle" to grab during a move operation.

A user initiates a move operation by positioning the pointer anywhere in the title area, pressing the mouse Select button, and then dragging the pointer to a new location. A wire frame outline represents the location of the window during the move. The user completes the move operation by releasing the Select button at the desired location. When the button is released, the window moves to that location. A move in progress is canceled when the user presses **<Esc>**.

11.4.2.3 The Title Bar

The title bar, which may include a title area, window menu button, and minimize and maximize buttons, is constrained so that all components in the title bar are always visible. This necessitates a minimum frame size and, by extension, a minimum size for your application's window. The size of the components in the title bar depends upon the size of the font you choose for the title area text.

As a user shrinks your client window horizontally, space is removed from the title area first. As the window is resized smaller, title text is clipped from the right. The absolute minimum size of the title bar is equal to the size of the buttons in the title bar, plus a title area equivalent to the width of one title bar button.

11.4.2.4 Window Menu Button

The function of the window menu button is to display the window menu. There are two ways to display the window menu:

1. **Using the window menu button.** Position the pointer on the window-menu button of the window frame and press the mouse Select button. (If you want the menu to remain posted, click the mouse Select button.) Once the menu appears, browse the menu by dragging the pointer down the menu. As the pointer encounters an available selection, the selection is highlighted. To choose a selection, highlight the desired selection and release the mouse Select button.

2. **Using the keyboard.** Set the keyboard input focus to a window and press **<Shift> <Esc>**, or **<Alt> <Space>**. Use arrow keys to browse the menu and **<Select>** to choose menu items. Cancel the posted menu using **<Shift> <Esc>** again, or just **<Esc>**.

There are two resources used to configure the behavior of the window menu button with respect to mouse clicks. The **wMenuButtonClick** resource indicates whether a click of the mouse when the pointer is over the window menu button posts and leaves posted the window menu. The **wMenuButtonClick2** resource indicates whether a double-click action on the window menu button closes the window and terminates the application. Both resources are discussed in Chapter 14, "Changing the Menu Associated with the Window Menu Button."

11.4.2.5 Minimize Button

The function of a window's minimize button is to iconify the window.

A user minimizes your client window by positioning the pointer on the minimize button and then clicking the mouse Select button. As a result of the minimize operation, your client window changes into an icon on the screen. If you use an icon box, the icon in the box displays its iconified client appearance.

11.4.2.6 Maximize Button

The function of a window's maximize button is to make the window its largest allowable size.

A user maximizes your client window by positioning the pointer on the maximize button and then clicking the mouse Select button. As a result of the maximize operation, the client window expands to the maximum size set by either the client or the configured resources. By default, the client fills the screen.

If a maximum size other than the default (full screen) size is important to your application, you can set the maximum size for your client by specifying values in the appropriate fields in the WM_NORMAL_HINTS property (see Chapter 12.) Users can also set a maximum size for windows by using the **maximumClientSize** resource and the **maximumMaximumSize** resource (see Chapter 13).

MWM tries to maximize your client window without moving it if your client fits on the screen at its current location. If the maximized window extends off the screen, MWM moves the maximized window onscreen, placing the window with the title bar showing so that the user still has access to the window control buttons. When a maximized window extends beyond the screen boundaries, MWM places the upper left-hand portion of the maximized window in the upper left-hand corner of the screen.

Once your client is maximized, the large square image on the maximize button appears recessed. In this state, the maximize button functions as a "restore" button. Clicking the mouse Select button on the recessed maximize button restores your client to its previous size.

11.4.2.7 Manipulating the Window Frame with a Mouse or a Keyboard

The following table summarizes the default frame manipulations available for mouse operations.

Table 11-7. Default Mouse Operations

Doing this...	With the pointer on this component...	Does this...
Clicking the Select button	Frame or window	Selects current keyboard input focus and brings window to top of the stack
Clicking the Select button	Frame or window	Brings window to top
Dragging the Select button	Resize frame handles	Resizes the window
Clicking the Select button	Window menu button	Posts window menu
Dragging the Select button	Window menu button	Pulls down window menu
Double-clicking the Select button	Window menu button	Closes the window
Dragging the Select button	Title area	Moves the window
Clicking the Select button	Minimize button	Iconifies the window
Clicking the Select button	Maximize button	Maximizes the window

The following table summarizes the default frame manipulations available for keyboard operations.

Table 11-8. Default Keyboard Operations

Pressing this key sequence...	Does this...
<Shift> <Esc> the window menu	Posts or unposts
<Alt> <Space> the window menu	Posts or unposts
When window menu is posted...	
<Esc> menu	Unposts the window
<↓> selection on a menu	Moves to the next selection
<↑> selection on a menu	Moves to the previous selection
<→> cascade button	Displays a submenu
<←> cascade button	Unposts a submenu
<Select>	Selects the highlighted menu selection

11.4.3 Selecting From the Window Menu

The window menu contains selections that provide consistent functionality from one MWM application to another. This consistency reduces the time it takes a user to learn to manage your application windows.

The window menu provides an additional way to access window manager functionality. You can select items in the window menu with either the mouse or the keyboard. The following figure shows the default menu window.

Figure 11-3. OSF/Motif Default Window Menu

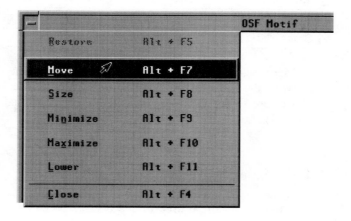

11.4.3.1 Looking at the Contents of the Window Menu

The following table describes the window menu selections.

Table 11-9. The Window Menu Selections

This selection...	Does this...
Restore	Restores a window to its normal size from an icon or after maximizing.
Move	Changes the location of a window.
Size	Changes the width and height of a window.
Minimize	Shrinks a window to its icon (graphic representation).
Maximize	Enlarges a window to its maximum size.
Lower	Places a window at the bottom of the window stack.
Close	Terminates the client.

Menu selections for functions that are not immediately applicable when the menu is displayed are grayed out. This is the case for the Restore selection when your client is in its normal state (see Figure 11-3).

11.4.3.2 Selecting with the Mouse

The mouse can be used in 2 ways to select items from the window menu: 1) press to open, drag to highlight, release to select, or, 2) click to open and post, move to desired item, and click to select.

11.4.3.3 Selecting with the Keyboard

Key actions can be used to select items from the window menu and to access functions of the window frame components. Once the menu is displayed, using the <**Shift**> <**Esc**> sequence, the user presses the <↑> and <↓> keys to highlight the appropriate selection and the <**Select**> key to make the choice.

While this completes the operation in the case of the Minimize, Maximize, and Lower operations, the Resize and Move operations require further input from the user. When the user chooses a move or resize operation, the pointer changes to a 4-headed arrow centered on the client area of the window. The user moves or resizes the window by pressing the arrow keys. Pressing <**Ctrl**> simultaneously with the arrow keys moves the pointer in multiple increments. Once the window is in the desired location or has the desired size, the user presses <**Select**> to complete the operation. Pressing <**Esc**> cancels a move or resize operation.

11.4.3.4 Accelerators and Mnemonics

Window menu items can also be selected using accelerators and mnemonics. Accelerators are key bindings that cause a menu item to be selected, and the associated function done, without posting the menu. For example, <**Alt**> <**F9**> is used to minimize (iconify) a window. Accelerators appear in the menu to the right of their associated menu items. Mnemonics are used to select a menu item once the window menu is posted. Mnemonic keys are indicated in a menu item by an underlined character in the menu item label.

11.4.3.5 Closing Your Client's Window

When a user chooses the Close selection from the window menu, the window manager executes an **f.kill** function on the client window. You can configure the **f.kill** function either to send a message to the client window or to terminate the client's X connection. Refer to WM_SAVE_YOURSELF, WM_PROTOCOLS, and WM_COMMAND in Chapter 12, and to the MWM function **f.kill** in Chapter 14.

Another way to close a window is to double-click the mouse Select button with the pointer on the window menu button. This behavior is enabled with the **wMenuButtonClick2** resource. (See Section 14.4 for more information on window menus.)

11.5 Placing and Sizing Windows

In the OSF/Motif environment you can think of client windows as existing in a stack on the screen. A new client window is initially placed on top of the window stack with a size and position specified by the client or the user.

A user can establish a different initial size and position for windows by using the procedures presented in Chapter 13, "Controlling Window Size and Position."

Users can enable interactive placement by setting the **interactivePlacement** resource. During interactive placement, the following visual clues appear on the screen:

- The pointer changes to an upper-left-corner bracket for the duration of the placement operation

- A wire frame outline shows the current size and location of the window

- A configuration feedback window appears in the center of the screen, relating location and size information

To interactively set the initial position of your client without changing its size, the user moves the pointer (and with it the wire outline) to the desired location and clicks the mouse Select button.

To interactively set the initial position *and* change the size of your client, the user performs the following steps:

1. Establishes the upper left-hand corner of your client window by moving the pointer to the desired location and pressing the mouse Select button.

2. With the mouse Select button pressed, resizes your client window to the desired size by dragging the Select button to the desired location of the lower right-hand corner of the window. The pointer changes to a lower-right-hand corner bracket for the duration of the sizing operation.

Interactive placement can also be done from the keyboard. The following table summarizes interactive placement behavior when using the keyboard.

Table 11-10. Interactive Placement Using the Keyboard.

This key press... while positioning the window...	Performs this function...
<↑>	Moves up one pixel
<↓>	Moves down one pixel
<←>	Moves left one pixel
<→>	Moves right one pixel
<Ctrl> *<arrow key>*	Move several pixels
<Space>	End positioning, start sizing operation
while sizing the window...	
<↑>	Decreases the height one pixel
<↓>	Increases the height one pixel
<←>	Decreases the width one pixel
<→>	Increases the width one pixel
<Ctrl> *<arrow key>*	Changes the height or width several pixels
<Select>	Completes the interactive placementl

The arrow keys move the pointer in the direction of the arrow. Holding down **<Ctrl>** moves the pointer in larger increments. The space bar is used to complete positioning and switch to sizing the window. Pressing **<Select>** completes the interactive placement operation.

The configuration feedback window provides position and size information as the pointer moves. The size feedback is in units that depend on the client. You can specify the units with the WM_NORMAL_HINTS property (see Chapter 12).

If window position information is specified by the user with the command-line geometry option when the client is invoked, no interactive placement takes place. The window is simply placed on the screen with the size and position specified. If the user specifies only the size of the window, MWM uses that size as the default during the interactive placement operation.

MWM does not support interactive placement on secondary windows or on the initial placement of icons.

11.5.1 Stacking Windows

With the default MWM configuration, you can change the stacking order of windows on the screen using the following methods:

- By setting the keyboard input focus so that the active window rises to the top of the stack. Set the keyboard input focus either by clicking the mouse Select button on the window or by pressing the <**Alt**> <**Tab**> accelerator sequence. For this feature to work, the **focusAutoRaise** resource should be set to "True." (See Chapter 13, "Setting Focus Policies.")

- By iconifying a window, thus effectively taking it off the stack until the icon is normalized.

- By performing a window manager stacking function such as **f.circle_up**, **f.circle_down**, **f.raise**, **f.raise_lower**, or **f.lower**. (Functions are explained and defined in Chapter 14.)

11.6 Introduction to Icons

Icons are small graphic representations of windows that are used to reduce clutter on the screen. A primary client window can be turned into an icon and restored to window form when desired. Icons can be arranged on the screen in a pattern you select, or in the default pattern (bottom left to right).

Icons can be placed into an "icon box." The icon box is an MWM window, similar to other windows, that holds icons. The icon box itself can be minimized (turned into an icon).

Information on using and configuring icons and the icon box is found in Chapter 15.

The following chapters discuss communications between your client and MWM, how a user can configure MWM resources and functions (which might affect your client application), and how to work with icons.

Chapter 12
Communicating Between MWM and Clients: MWM Properties

This chapter provides technical information you need to establish communications between MWM and your client. A typical user does not need access to this information.

Chapter 12 discusses the following topics:

- MWM programmatic interface standards

- The Inter-Client Communication Conventions

- MWM specific information

12.1 MWM Programmatic Interface Standards

The MWM programmatic interface is based on the *Inter-Client Communication Conventions Manual* (ICCCM). The ICCCM establishes the standards for "good citizenship" among clients in a multi-client environment. To avoid costly compatibility problems, you should design and code your client application to operate as a "good citizen." The OSF/Motif toolkit supports the inter-client communications conventions and facilitates appropriate communications with MWM.

MWM fully supports Version 1.0 of the ICCCM. Conventions documented in earlier editions of the ICCCM are supported by MWM only to the extent necessary to support clients that use released versions of the X11 Xlib and Xt Intrinsics libraries.

12.2 Inter-Client Communication Conventions

The ICCCM section "Client to Window Manager Communication" specifically discusses how clients communicate with a window manager. Reading the section is recommended as it gives you generally applicable information about how your client application should communicate with a window manager. The remainder of this chapter provides additional client information and MWM-specific information.

12.2.1 Programming Client Actions

As mentioned above you should design your client application to be a good citizen whether or not a window manager is present to police the environment. The following information helps you program your client application to be a good citizen in a multi-client environment.

12.2.1.1 Creating a Top-Level Window

The typical way to create a top-level window is to use an Xt Intrinsics or Xm Toolkit function (for example, **XtAppCreateShell**). These functions set up standard window properties that are used to provide the window manager with client-specific information.

At any time, your client application's top-level windows have one of three states:

Normal   A normal application window is displayed.

Iconic   An icon window is displayed instead of a normal window.

Withdrawn   No normal or iconic window is displayed.

12.2.1.2 Working with Client Properties

Each top-level window you create for your client should have several standard properties associated with it. The values of these properties are generally accessible through **WmShell** resources. These properties are what the window manager inspects to determine how it should manage the client's behavior.

This is especially important in the case where the proper operation of your client application depends on particular property values; any properties you *don't* specify are specified by the window manager *using whatever values are most convenient.*

Client applications can set up the following properties:

WM_NAME. The WM_NAME property contains a string to be displayed in the title area of the client window frame. MWM can dynamically change the window title if your client application changes the value of the string in the WM_NAME property. If you don't set the WM_NAME property, MWM looks for a title in the res_name part of the WM_CLASS property. If MWM finds no title, it uses the string "*****" as the window title. The window manager assumes that the string passed in the WM_NAME property is compatible with the font used for the window title.

WM_ICON_NAME. The WM_ICON_NAME property contains a string to be displayed in the label part of the icon that is associated with the client window. MWM can dynamically change the icon label if the WM_ICON_NAME property value is changed by the client. If you don't set the WM_ICON_NAME property, MWM uses the window title as the icon label. The window manager assumes that the string passed in the WM_ICON_NAME property is compatible with the font used for the icon label.

WM_NORMAL_HINTS. The WM_NORMAL_HINTS property contains a list of fields. MWM tracks changes to the WM_NORMAL_HINTS property. A change of the property does not affect the window configuration at the time the change is made. The change affects only subsequent configurations.

The type of the WM_NORMAL_HINTS property is WM_SIZE_HINTS. The WM_NORMAL_HINTS property contains the following fields:

flags   MWM places windows on the screen using various sources of size and position information. The order of precedence MWM uses to look for this information is as follows:

1. User specified. The client has been supplied configuration information by the user (indicated to MWM by the USSize and USPosition values).

2. Interactive placement. Interactive placement is established with the **interactivePlacement** resource (see Chapter 13).

3. Default position, current window size.

min_width, min_height

The values set for min_width and min_height (minimum width and minimum height) are used to configure a minimum size for a client window. If the values set for these fields are not greater than 0, or not set at all, then a value of 1x1 or larger is used by MWM. The actual minimum size used by MWM is based on the window size that fits in the minimum frame size for the frame type that is being used.

max_width, max_height

The values set for max_width and max_height (maximum width and maximum height) are used only if the **maximumClientSize** resource is not set. The values set with these fields are used to set a maximum size for a client window. If max_width and max_height are not configured, then MWM sizes the window and its frame to exactly fill the screen. The maximum size of a window can be limited by the

maximumMaximumSize resource. (See Chapter 13 for resource descriptions.)

width_inc, height_inc

The values set for width_inc and height_inc (width increment and height increment) determine the unit of measure used to report window size. When windows are being resized, a feedback window reports the current size in the units specified. If values are not set for these fields, then one pixel is used as the sizing increment.

min_aspect.x, min_aspect.y

The values set for min_aspect.x and min_aspect.y [minimum aspect.x (width) and minimum aspect.y (length)] determine constraints for the minimum ratio of width/length of a window. MWM applies a minimum aspect ratio sizing constraint when the x and y values are set greater than or equal to 0. The values must also be less than or equal to the max_aspect values.

max_aspect.x, max_aspect.y

The values set for max_aspect.x and max_aspect.y [maximum aspect.x (width) and maximum aspect.y (length)] determine constraints for the maximum ratio of width/length of a window. MWM applies a maximum aspect-ratio-sizing constraint when the x and y values are set greater than or equal to zero. The values must also be greater than or equal to the min_aspect values.

base_width, base_height

The values set for these fields determine the amount of "padding" (margin) between the window and the window frame. The base width value sets the amount of left and right padding. The base height value sets the amount of top and bottom padding. If these fields have a value of less than 0, or if there is no value set, then MWM uses a value of 0.

win_gravity

> The value set for win_gravity determines where the window manager tries to place windows. If the window manager decides to place a window where the client asks, the position on the parent window's border named by win_gravity will be placed where the client window would have been placed in the absence of a window manager. The default value is NorthWest.

WM_HINTS. The WM_HINTS property contains a list of fields. Except for changes to the icon_pixmap, MWM tracks changes to the WM_HINTS property only when the client window changes state from the withdrawn state to the normal or iconic state.

The type of the WM_HINTS property is WM_HINTS. The WM_HINTS property contains the following fields:

icon_pixmap   An image for icon window.

icon_window   A working window for the icon window.

icon_x   X coordinate for icon window position.

icon_y   Y coordinate for icon window position.

icon_mask   MWM does not currently use this.

input   See the following NOTE.

window_group   MWM does not currently use this.

NOTE: MWM does not set keyboard focus to the client window if any of the following conditions exist:

1. The value for input is False.

2. The value for the **enforceKeyFocus** resource is True.

3. The client has expressed an interest in the WM_TAKE_FOCUS protocol.

If the user attempts to set the keyboard focus to the window, a WM_TAKE_FOCUS client message is sent to the window. The input field also determines whether or not a window receives keyboard focus automatically. (See the following resources in Chapter 13: **autoKeyFocus**, **startupKeyFocus**, and **deiconifyKeyFocus**.)

WM_CLASS. The WM_CLASS property contains two fields. MWM tracks changes to the WM_CLASS property only when the client window changes state from the withdrawn state to the normal or iconic state.

The res_class and res_name values are used by MWM to do client-specific configuration of window decorations and icons. If the WM_CLASS property is not set, then no special client customization is done.

The type of the WM_CLASS property is STRING. The WM_CLASS property contains the following fields:

res_class
: When a client is initially managed by MWM, the res_class value is used to determine the client's class. All resources previously configured for that class are used for the new client.

res_name
: The res_name value is used by MWM to look up MWM resources for a client of a particular name. The value also determines the name used in the client's window title when the WM_NAME property is not set.

WM_TRANSIENT_FOR. MWM regards a transient window as equivalent to a secondary window. A transient window is always on top (in terms of stacking order) of its primary window. This primary window is identified by the WM_TRANSIENT_FOR property.

The window manager places transient windows on the screen without user interaction. MWM uses the window's existing size and position. The amount of decoration for a transient window is controlled by the **transientDecoration** resource. (See Section 13.11 and the _MOTIF_WM_HINTS property in this chapter for more information on window decoration.)

A transient window is normally associated with a primary window. You can design your client windows so that transient windows are arranged in a tree structure where a transient window has another transient window as its associated primary window. However, the root of the tree must be a non-transient window.

The type of the WM_TRANSIENT_FOR property is WINDOW. **WM_PROTOCOLS.** The WM_PROTOCOLS property contains a list of atoms (32-bit values that represent unique names). Each atom identifies a protocol in which the client is willing to participate. Atoms can identify standard protocols and private protocols specific to individual window managers. The **XmAddProtocols** and **XmAddWMProtocols** functions can be used to set up the WM_PROTOCOLS property for a **VendorShell**.

The type of the WM_PROTOCOLS property is ATOM. MWM tracks changes to the WM_PROTOCOLS property and supports the following standard protocols:

WM_DELETE_WINDOW   Clients are notified when the MWM **f.kill** function is invoked by the user. MWM does not terminate the client or destroy the window when a WM_DELETE_WINDOW notification is done.

WM_SAVE_YOURSELF   Clients with this atom are notified when a session manager or a window manager wishes the window's state to be changed. The typical change is when the window is about to be deleted or the session terminated.

The **quitTimeout** resource specifies the amount of time (in milliseconds) that MWM waits for a client to update the WM_COMMAND property after it has sent the WM_SAVE_YOURSELF message. This protocol is used only for clients that have a WM_SAVE_YOURSELF atom in the WM_PROTOCOLS client window property. The default time is 1000 (ms). (Since **quitTimeout** is a resource, not a property, a user can change its value.)

WM_TAKE_FOCUS   Clients with this atom are notified when a window manager believes that the client should explicitly set the input focus to one of its windows.

_MOTIF_WM_MESSAGES   Clients with this atom indicate to the window manager which messages (sent by the window manager when the **f.send_msg** function is invoked) are currently being handled by the client.

WM_COLORMAP_WINDOWS.   The WM_COLORMAP_WINDOWS property contains a list of IDs of windows that may need colormaps installed that differ from the colormap of the top-level window. The type of the WM_COLORMAP_WINDOWS property is WINDOW.

12.2.1.3 Working with Window Manager Properties

MWM uses properties to supply configuration and state information to clients (usually session managers).

WM_STATE. The type of the WM_STATE property is WM_STATE. The WM_STATE property contains the following fields:

state   NormalState, IconicState, and WithdrawnState are the values defined for MWM.

icon   The icon window value is set to the window ID of the top-level icon window; this window is not the icon window supplied by the client. (The icon window, if it is set in WM_HINTS, is a child of the top-level, MWM-created icon window.)

The information in the WM_STATE property is generally used only by session management clients.

WM_ICON_SIZE. MWM sets the WM_ICON_SIZE property of the root window. The type of the WM_ICON_SIZE property is WM_ICON_SIZE. WM_ICON_SIZE contains the following fields:

min_width, min_height

> The values set for min_width and min_height (minimum width and minimum height) of an icon window are based on the value of (or default value for) the **iconImageMinimum** resource.

max_width, max_height

> The values set for max_width and max_height (maximum width and maximum height) of an icon window are based on the value of (or default value for) the **iconImageMaximum** resource.

width_inc, height_inc

> The values set for width_inc and height_inc (width increment and height increment) determine the unit of measurement for changing the size of an icon window. MWM sets this value to one pixel.

12.2.1.4 Changing Window States

Windows are normal (full sized), iconic (small symbol), or withdrawn (not visible). You can control many attributes of normal and icon windows. See Chapter 13 for information on the appearance and behavior of windows in the NormalState. See Chapter 15 for information on the appearance and behavior of windows in the IconicState.

12.2.1.5 Configuring the Window

Clients can request to be notified, with **ConfigureNotify** events, when windows change size or position. The X,Y coordinates in these events may be relative to either the root window or the frame provided by MWM. Use **XTranslateCoordinates** to determine absolute coordinates.

12.2.1.6 Changing Window Attributes

If the client requests save unders with the **saveUnder** resource, MWM sets this attribute for the MWM frame instead of the client window.

12.2.1.7 Controlling Input Focus

Use the **keyboardFocusPolicy** resource to control the input focus. Clients can request to be notified when given the input focus. See "WM_PROTOCOLS."

Windows that supply a WM_PROTOCOLS property containing the WM_TAKE_FOCUS atom receive a ClientMessage from the window manager.

12.2.1.8 Establishing Colormaps

If more than one colormap is needed for client subwindows, then set the WM_COLORMAP_WINDOWS property to the list of windows with colormaps.

12.2.2 Client Responses to MWM Actions

MWM redirects the following top-level window requests: **MapWindow, ConfigureWindow, CirculateWindow**. MWM may not immediately execute (or execute at all) redirected requests.

12.2.2.1 Window Size and Position

Clients can request sizes and positions by doing a window configuration operation, but MWM may not satisfy these requests.

12.2.2.2 Window and Icon Mapping

Client windows in the normalized state are mapped. Client windows in the iconified state are not mapped.

12.2.2.3 Colormap Changes

Clients can request to be notified when their colormap is in use (or no longer in use), by using **ColormapNotify**.

12.2.2.4 Input Focus

Distribution of input within a client window can be handled using Xt Intrinsics and the Xm Widgets. Clients should generally avoid using **XSetInputFocus**.

12.2.2.5 ClientMessage Events

Clients cannot prevent being sent **ClientMessage** events, but clients can ignore these if they are not useful.

12.3 MWM Specific Information

The following information details window manager conventions not covered by the ICCCM, but which are required for supporting OSF/Motif behavior. Properties on the client window are used to communicate client preferences to MWM. These properties are settable using **VendorShell** and **XmBulletinBoard** resources. Value definitions for MWM-specific properties are set in the **Xm/MwmUtil.h** file.

12.3.1 The _MOTIF_WM_HINTS Property

A client may communicate certain preferences directly to MWM via the _MOTIF_WM_HINTS property. The type of the _MOTIF_WM_HINTS property is _MOTIF_WM_HINTS. The following table shows the contents of this property.

Table 12-1. Contents of _MOTIF_WM_HINTS Property

Field	Type
flags	CARD32
decorations	CARD32
functions	CARD32
input_mode	INT32

12.3.1.1 The flags Field

The flags field indicates which fields in the _MOTIF_WM_HINTS property contain data. The following table shows the supported values.

Table 12-2. Values of the flags Field

Name	Value	Field
MWM_HINTS_FUNCTIONS	1	MWM functions applicable to client
MWM_HINTS_DECORATIONS	2	Client window frame decorations
MWM_HINTS_INPUT_MODE	4	Client input mode

12.3.1.2 The decorations Field

The decorations field indicates how the client window frame should be decorated (for example, whether the window should have a title bar or window menu button). The information in this field is combined with the value of the **clientDecoration** resource (see Section 13.11). Only decorations that are indicated by both **clientDecoration** and _MOTIF_WM_HINTS are displayed. Decorations for inapplicable functions are not displayed (for example, if a window cannot be minimized, the minimize window button is not displayed).

The following table shows the supported values.

Table 12-3. Values of the decorations Field

Name	Value	Comments
MWM_DECOR_ALL	1	If set, remove decorations from full set
MWM_DECOR_BORDER	2	Client window border
MWM_DECOR_RESIZEH	4	Resize frame handles
MWM_DECOR_TITLE	8	Title bar
MWM_DECOR_MENU	16	Window menu button
MWM_DECOR_MINIMIZE	32	Minimize window button
MWM_DECOR_MAXIMIZE	64	Maximize window button

12.3.1.3 The functions Field

The functions field indicates which MWM functions should apply to the client window (for example, whether the window should be resized). The information in this field is combined with the value of the **clientFunctions** resource (see Section 14.3.4). Only functions that are indicated by both **clientFunctions** and _MOTIF_WM_HINTS are applied. Also, decorations that support a particular function (for example, the minimize button) are not be shown if the associated function is not applicable. The following table shows the supported values for the functions field.

Table 12-4. Values of the functions Field

Name	Value	Comments
MWM_FUNC_ALL	1	If set, remove functions from full set
MWM_FUNC_RESIZE	2	f.resize
MWM_FUNC_MOVE	4	f.move
MWM_FUNC_MINIMIZE	8	f.minimize
MWM_FUNC_MAXIMIZE	16	f.maximize
MWM_FUNC_CLOSE	32	f.kill

12.3.1.4 The input_mode Field

The input_mode field indicates the keyboard input focus constraints that are imposed by the client window. The following table shows the values of the input_mode field.

Table 12-5. Values of the input_mode Field

Name	Value	Comments
MWM_INPUT_MODELESS	0	Input goes to any window
MWM_INPUT_PRIMARY_APPLICATION_MODAL	1	Input does not go to ancestors of this window
MWM_INPUT_SYSTEM_MODAL	2	Input goes only to this window
MWM_INPUT_FULL_APPLICATION_MODAL	3	Input does not go to other windows in this application

12.3.1.5 The _MOTIF_WM_MENU Property

The client uses the _MOTIF_WM_MENU property to add menu items to the end of the window menu for the client window. The contents of the property are a list of lines separated by new line characters (\n) , with the following format:

label [mnemonic] [accelerator] function \n
label [mnemonic] [accelerator] function

Interpretation of the strings is the same as for menu items (see Section 14.3.2 for more information on menu items).

12.3.1.6 The _MOTIF_WM_MESSAGES Property

The client uses the _MOTIF_WM_MESSAGES property to indicate to the window manager which messages (sent by the window manager when the **f.send_msg** function is invoked) are currently being handled by the client. Menu items that have **f.send_msg** specified as the function have grayed-out labels when the associated message is not being handled by the client.

This client property is tracked by the window manager if the _MOTIF_WM_MESSAGES atom is included in the client's WM_PROTOCOLS property. The _MOTIF_WM_MESSAGES property contains a list of integers (for XChangeProperty: type atom is INTEGER, format is 32). A client places the property on a client window and it is processed by MWM when the client window goes from withdrawn state to normalized or iconified state. Changes to the property are processed while the client window is not in the withdrawn state.

12.3.1.7 The _MOTIF_WM_INFO Property

The client receives MWM-specific information via the _MOTIF_WM_INFO property. This property is placed by MWM on the root window and is used by clients. The _MOTIF_WM_INFO property is set up as part of MWM initialization.

The type of the _MOTIF_WM_INFO property is _MOTIF_WM_INFO. The following table shows the contents of the _MOTIF_WM_INFO property.

Table 12-6. Contents of the _MOTIF_WM_INFO Property

Field	Type
flags	CARD32
wmWindow	CARD32

The following table shows the values that may be set:

Table 12-7. Values for the flags Field

Name	Value	Field
MWM_INFO_STARTUP_STANDARD	1	Set for startup with standard behavior.
MWM_INFO_STARTUP_CUSTOM	2	Set for startup with customized behavior.

The wmWindow field is always set to the window ID of a window that is used by MWM. When MWM is running, the _MOTIF_WM_INFO property is present on the root window and wmWindow is an ID for a window that exists.

12.3.2 Window Management Calls

Clients communicate with the window manager through properties associated with top-level windows, synthetic events (generated using **XSendEvent** and standard X events. Programmatically this communication involves Xlib routines (directly or through libraries such as the Xt Intrinsics or the Xm OSF/Motif toolkit). Clients may programmatically interact with MWM (or any X11 window manager) in one of the following ways:

- **No explicit programmatic access.** In this case, clients do not set up any window properties or do any call that directly communicates to the window manager. Communication occurs (indirectly) when the state of the client window is changed (that is, the window is mapped, unmapped, configured, has a colormap change, and so on.). To work with MWM, clients are not required to do anything more than what is required when a window manager is not being used.

- **Low-level programmatic access.** Clients with special window management requirements can use such low-level Xlib calls as **XStoreName** or **XSetWMHints** to communicate with the window manager.

- **High-level programmatic access.** Clients can make calls to certain libraries built on Xlib (Xt Intrinsics, Xm OSF/Motif toolkit) to establish and maintain standard communications with MWM. Client developers are encouraged to use these interfaces unless the client has some specialized window management requirements.

12.3.2.1 Xlib Routines

The following Xlib routines are supported in revision 4 of the X Window System, Version 11 (refer to *Xlib — C Language X Interface* for more information).

XGetIconSizes	**XSetCommand**	**XSetWMIconName**
XGetRGBColormap	**XSetTransientForHint**	**XSetWMNormalHints**
XSetClassHint	**XSetWMHints**	**XStoreName**

Chapter 13
Managing Windows with MWM

This chapter presents information users need if they want to customize the appearance and behavior of MWM windows. Although you, as a programmer, will not usually be setting values for MWM resources, knowing about the resources can help you avoid user-caused problems in your application.

MWM is an X11 client that manages the appearance and behavior of objects on the workspace (screen). MWM and its management operations are controlled by using a mouse, a keyboard, and a functional window frame as they are used by Presentation Manager.

Chapter 13 discusses the following topics:

- Starting up MWM

- Using resources to configure MWM

- Setting focus policies for active windows

- Managing clients

- Managing the general appearance of window frames and mattes

- Specifying a different font for the window manager

- Coloring window frames

- Making window frame pixmaps

- Specifying a matte for client windows

- Using frameless or reduced-element windows

- Controlling window size and position

13.1 Starting Up MWM

MWM clients receive configuration information from the configuration resource files described in preceding chapters. Users can copy to their home directory as **.mwmrc** the file **/usr/lib/X11/system.mwmrc**. By editing **.mwmrc** and their **.Xdefaults** file, they can customize the window manager to fit their needs.

MWM is often started by a display or session manager. The following syntax is used to specify display information and start-up resources:

mwm **-display** *host:display.screen* **-xrm** *resourcestring* **-multiscreen** **-name** *name* **-screens** *name* [*name* [...]]

-display   Specifies the display to use

-xrm   Enables the named resources when starting MWM

-multiscreen Causes MWM to manage all screens on the display; the default is to manage one screen

-name   Causes MWM to retrieve its resources using the specified name, as in *name*resource*

-screens Specifies the resource names to use for the screens managed by MWM

The **-display** option has the following syntax:

host   Specifies the hostname of a valid system on the network. Depending on the situation, this could be the hostname of the user's, or the hostname of a remote system.

display   Specifies the number (usually 0) of the display on the system on which the output is to appear.

screen   Specifies the number of the screen where the output is to appear. This number is 0 for single-screen systems.

13.2 Using Resources to Configure MWM

The appearance and behavior of windows, window frames, menus, and icons are controlled with **resources**. Resources are always named for the elements they affect, such as **fontList** for setting the font. Users do not need to specify values for any resources; MWM can run with its default appearance and behavior. However, to customize the appearance and/or behavior of MWM, users need to specify values for some resources.

13.2.1 The Hierarchy of Resource Configuration Files

The following diagram illustrates the path MWM travels when looking for resource values:

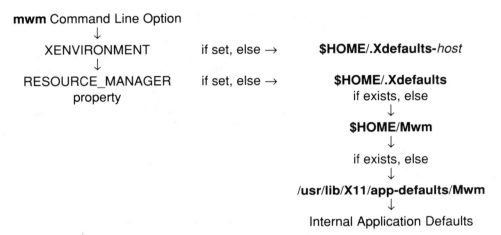

mwm Command Line Option
↓
XENVIRONMENT   if set, else →   **$HOME/.Xdefaults-**_host_
↓
RESOURCE_MANAGER   if set, else →   **$HOME/.Xdefaults**
property   if exists, else
↓
$HOME/Mwm
↓
if exists, else
↓
/usr/lib/X11/app-defaults/Mwm
↓
Internal Application Defaults

The filenames **$HOME/Mwm** and **/usr/lib/X11/app-defaults/Mwm** represent the customary locations for these files. The actual locations may depend on several environment variables and the current language environment. For more information see the "Localization" section in Chapter 8.

Entries in the resource database may refer to other resource files, such as **.mwmrc**, that contain specific types of resources. This includes files that contain bitmaps, fonts, and MWM-specific resources such as menus and behavior specifications (for example, button and key bindings).

13.2.2 Classification of Resources

MWM uses the three types of resources described in the following sections.

13.2.2.1 Component Appearance Resources

These resources are used to specify appearance attributes of window manager user interface components. They can be applied to the appearance of window manager menus, feedback windows, client window frames, and icons. Among the resources of this type are those that set frame colors (for example, background, foreground, shadows).

13.2.2.2 Specific Appearance and Behavior Resources

These resources are used to specify MWM appearance and behavior (for example, colormap and keyboard input focus policies). They are not set separately for different MWM user-interface components.

13.2.2.3 Client Specific Resources

These MWM resources can be set for a particular client window or class of client windows. They specify client-specific icon and client window frame appearance and behavior (for example, client decoration and client functions).

Resource identifiers can be either a resource name beginning with a lowercase letter, **foreground**, or a resource class beginning with an uppercase letter, **Foreground**. The resource class for MWM is **Mwm** and the resource name is **mwm**.

If the value of a resource is a filename and if the filename is prefixed by ~/ , then it is relative to the path contained in the HOME environment variable (generally the user's home directory).

13.2.3 Order of Precedence

In general, a more detailed specification takes precedence over a less detailed specification. For example, suppose the **.Xdefaults** file includes the following lines:

```
*Foreground:          red
XClock*Foreground:    DarkSlateGray
XClock*foreground:    coral
XClock*hands:         green
```

The first line makes all resources of the class **Foreground** red. The second line overrules the first line, but only in the case of clients of class **Xclock** (of which there is only one — the xclock itself). Line two specifies that when the client is **XClock**, all resources of the class **Foreground** are DarkSlateGray. Lines three and four give **Xclock** clients a coral foreground and green hands, while the other **XClock** resources (if there were any) of class **Foreground** (pointerColor, cursorColor, foreground and bottomShadowColor of the softkeys, and foreground and bottomShadowColor of the scroll bars) would remain DarkSlateGray.

13.2.4 The Syntax for Declaring Resources

The syntax used to declare a resource depends on the type of the resource. Following is an example for each type of resource:

Component appearance resource:

Mwm*menu*foreground: white

Specific appearance and behavior resource:

Mwm*useIconBox: True

Client specific resource:

Mwm*XClock*clientDecoration: None

More examples for each type of resource are presented at the end of the section in which the resources are discussed. See Chapter 16 for quick reference tables of resources.

13.3 Managing Screens

The following resources control management of single or multiple screens on the display:

multiScreen. This resource, if True, causes MWM to manage all the screens on the display. If False, MWM manages only a single screen. The default value is False.

screens. This resource specifies the resource names to use for the screens mananged by MWM. If MWM is managing a single screen, only the first name in the list is used. If MWM is managing multiple screens, the names are assigned to the screens in order, starting with screen 0. Screen 0 gets the first name, screen 1 the second name, and so on. The default screen names are 0, 1, and so on.

13.4 Setting Focus Policies for Active Windows

Two focus policy resources allow the user to choose the colormap and keyboard input focus policies **colormapFocusPolicy** and **keyboardFocusPolicy**.

13.4.1 Colormap Focus Policy

colormapFocusPolicy. The colormap focus policy can be set using the **colormapFocusPolicy** resource and one of the following three values:

keyboard   (Default value) The window manager tracks keyboard input and installs a client's colormap when the client window gets the keyboard input focus.

explicit   The window manager tracks a specific focus-selection action and installs a client's colormap when the focus-selection action is done in the client window. The focus-selection action can be a key press, a mouse button action, or a menu selection. Key and mouse button actions must be created with bindings. (See "Mouse Button Bindings" and "Keyboard Bindings" in Chapter 14.)

pointer   The window manager tracks the pointer and installs a client's colormap when the pointer moves into the client window or the window frame around the client.

13.4.1.1 Using Multiple Colormaps

MWM does all colormap installation based on the colormap focus policy and any hints from the client about which colormap the client wants installed. Clients that require only one colormap at a time can indicate the colormap they want installed by setting the colormap attribute of the clients top-level window to that colormap.

Clients that have subwindows with colormaps that differ from that of the top-level window or that would like to have more than one colormap installed must use the WM_COLORMAP_WINDOWS property on the top-level window. Subwindow colormaps for the window with the colormap focus can be installed interactively by binding the **f.next_cmap** function to a button, key, or menu selection. The user can then cycle through (shuffle) the subwindow colormaps.

13.4.2 Keyboard Focus Policy

keyboardFocusPolicy. Use the **keyboardFocusPolicy** resource to specify the conditions under which you want a window to become active and the focus of keyboard input:

explicit   (Default value) The window manager tracks a specific focus-selection action and sets the keyboard focus to a client window when the focus-selection action is done in that client window. Keyboard input goes to the selected window regardless of the location of the pointer until the user explicitly selects another window for keyboard-input focus. The default focus-selection action is a mouse Button 1 press. The focus-selection action can be a key press or a different mouse button action, but these must be configured using bindings. (See "Mouse Button Bindings" and "Keyboard Bindings" in Chapter 14.) Explicit selection is also known by the terms "click-to-type" and "explicit-listener."

pointer   The window manager tracks the pointer and sets the keyboard focus to a client window when the pointer moves into that window or the window frame around the client. The **pointer** policy is also known by the terms "track pointer," "real-estate driven," and "tracked-listener."

autoKeyFocus. This resource is available only when the keyboard input focus policy is explicit. If the **autoKeyFocus** resource is given a value of True, then when a window with the keyboard input focus is withdrawn from window management or is iconified, the focus is set to the window that previously had the focus. If there was no previous window, or if the value given is False, then the user must select a window or icon to receive the focus. The default value is True.

autoRaiseDelay. This resource is available only when the value for the **focusAutoRaise** resource is True and the keyboard focus policy is pointer. The **autoRaiseDelay** resource specifies the amount of time (in milliseconds) that MWM waits before raising a window after it gets the keyboard focus. The default value is 500 msec.

deiconifyKeyFocus. This resource is available only when the keyboard input focus policy is explicit. If the **deiconifyKeyFocus** resource is given a value of True, a window receives the keyboard input focus when it is normalized (changed from an icon to a normal window). The default value is True.

enforceKeyFocus. If the **enforceKeyFocus** resource value is True, then the keyboard input focus is always explicitly set to selected windows even if there is an indication that they are "globally active" input windows. If the resource value is False, the keyboard input focus is not explicitly set to globally active windows. The default value is True. (An example of a globally active client window would be a window with scroll bars that allows users to scroll the window without disturbing the input focus.)

focusAutoRaise. When the value of the **focusAutoRaise** resource is True, clients are raised when they get the keyboard-input focus. If the value is False, the stacking of windows on the display is not changed when a window gets the keyboard input focus. If **keyboardFocusPolicy** is explicit, the default value is True. If **keyboardFocusPolicy** is pointer, the default value is False.

passButtons. The **passButtons** resource indicates whether button press events are passed to clients after they are used to do a window manager function in the "client" context. If the resource value is False, the button press is not passed to the client. If the value is True, the button press is passed to the client window. The window manager function is done in either case. The default value is False.

passSelectButton. This resource indicates whether or not to pass the select button press events to clients after they are used to do a window manager function in the client context. If the resource value is False, then the button press will not be passed to the client. If the value is True, the button press is passed to the client window. The window manager function is done in either case. The default value for this resource is True.

startupKeyFocus. This resource is available only when the keyboard input focus policy is "explicit." If the **startupKeyFocus** resource is given the value of True, a window gets the keyboard input focus when the window is mapped (that is, initially managed by the window manager). The default value is True.

13.4.3 The Syntax of Focus Policy Resource

Focus policy resources have the following syntax:

Mwm**focusPolicyResource*:   *policy*

For example, by adding the following line to your **.Xdefaults** file, you could change the **keyboardFocusPolicy** so that moving the pointer into a window moves the keyboard input focus there (no other action is needed):

```
Mwm*keyboardFocusPolicy:    pointer
```

13.5 Managing Clients

Two unique resources allow the user to refine management of clients: **quitTimeout** sets the amount of time MWM waits for a client to save information and close; **saveUnder** controls the repainting of windows that are uncovered after being obscured.

quitTimeout. The **quitTimeout** resource specifies the amount of time (in milliseconds) that MWM waits for a client to update the WM_COMMAND property after it has sent the WM_SAVE_YOURSELF message. This protocol is used only for those clients that have a WM_SAVE_YOURSELF atom in the WM_PROTOCOLS client window property. (Refer to the sections on each property in Chapter 12.) The default time is 1000 msec.

saveUnder. The **saveUnder** resource is used to indicate whether "save unders" are used for MWM components. For this to have any effect, save unders must be implemented by the X server. If save unders are implemented, the X server saves the contents of windows obscured by windows that have the save under attribute set. If the **saveUnder** resource has a value of True, MWM sets the save under attribute on the window manager frame for any client that has it set. If the value is False, save unders are not used on any window manager frames. The default value is False.

13.6 Managing the Appearance and Behavior of Window Frames and Mattes

The appearance and behavior of window frames and mattes in the user's environment are controlled by editing the user's **.Xdefaults** file.

The following aspects of the appearance and behavior of window frames and mattes are under the user's control:

Font
: The style (including size) of the text characters in the title area, menus, and icon labels.

Color
: The color of foreground, background, top shadow, bottom shadow, and side shadows.

Pixmap
: The mixture of foreground and background color that composes the pattern of the window frame or matte surface. (This is particularly useful for monochrome displays.)

Elements
: The number of frame pieces used to decorate a client window.

Size
: The maximum size a window can be in certain situations.

Position
: The initial position of a window on the screen and whether it can be moved interactively.

The rest of this chapter describes the resources, their values, and any special syntax that applies.

13.7 Specifying a Different Font for the Window Manager

fontList. The default font for the text of MWM is the fixed font. However, you can use the **fontList** resource to specify a different font if you desire. The **fontList** resource can use any valid X11 R4 font description as its value. Keep in mind that the font size affects the size of window frames, icons and menus.

13.8 Coloring Window Frames

Any of the standard X11 colors listed in **/usr/lib/X11/rgb.txt** can be used to color frame elements. Additionally, custom colors can be created using hexadecimal values. Frame elements and resources exist for inactive windows (any window not having the current keyboard focus) and for the active window (the window having the current keyboard focus). This enables the user to distinguish the active window by giving it special "active window" colors.

Figure 13-1. MWM Frame Showing Frame Elements and Matte

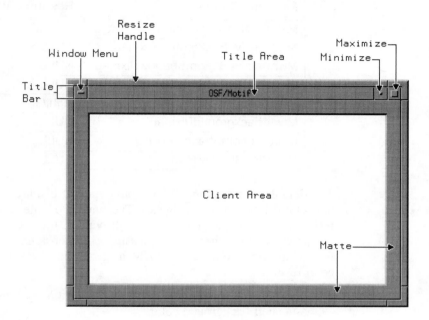

The default values for color resources are based on the visual type of the screen (for example, monochrome, 8-bit pseudocolor, and so on) and the values given to related resources. The following table indicates default values for a color display. On a monochrome display the default value for these resources is White.

Table 13-1. Default Values for Appearance on a Color Display

Resource Name	Resource Value
Mwm*activeBackground	CadetBlue
Mwm*activeBackgroundPixmap	NULL
Mwm*activeBottomShadowPixmap	NULL
Mwm*activeTopShadowPixmap	NULL
Mwm*background	LightGrey
Mwm*backgroundPixmap	NULL
Mwm*bottomShadowPixmap	NULL
Mwm*topShadowPixmap	NULL

The default menu colors (for various types of displays) are set by the OSF/Motif menu widgets. The value of the **background** resource is used to generate default values for the other color resources so that there is a pleasing 3-dimensional effect. The following rules are used by MWM in generating default values for color resources:

- A top shadow color is generated by proportionally lightening the associated background color.

- A bottom shadow color is generated by proportionally darkening the associated background color.

- The foreground color is black or white depending on the background color.

The following table indicates default values for appearance resources on a monochrome display.

Table 13-2. Default Values for Appearance on a Monochrome Display

Resource Name	Resource Value
Mwm*activeBackground	White
Mwm*activeBackgroundPixamp	NULL
Mwm*activeBottomShadowPixmap	NULL
Mwm*activeTopShadowPixmap	50_foreground
Mwm*background	White
Mwm*backgroundPixmap	75_foreground
Mwm*bottomShadowColor	Black
Mwm*bottomShadowPixmap	NULL
Mwm*topShadowColor	White
Mwm*topShadowPixmap	50_foreground

The standard pixmap names in the OSF/Motif widget library (Xm) can be used in specifying pixmap resources such as **topShadowPixmap** (refer to **XmInstallImage**).

13.8.1 Coloring Individual Frame Elements

The following table lists the individual elements of inactive and active window frames, and the resources that control their color:

Table 13-3. MWM Color Resources and What They Color

Inactive Window and Icon Resources	Active Window and Icon Resources	Area Colored
foreground	activeForeground	Foreground areas (text)
background	activeBackground	Background areas
topShadowColor	activeTopShadowColor	Top and left 3-D bevels
bottomShadowColor	activeBottomShadowColor	Bottom and right 3-D bevels

Although the active and inactive color schemes can be made the same, it is usually more effective to pick contrasting color schemes that make the active window readily distinguishable from its inactive counterparts.

13.8.2 Syntax for Resources Controlling Frame Appearance Element

The following syntax in **.Xdefaults** is used to specify the general appearance of frame elements:

Mwm**resource:* *value*

For example, suppose the user wants the foreground and background of inactive window frames to be the reverse of the foreground and background of the active window frame, and chooses the colors

SteelBlue for background and VioletRed for foreground. Also, the user wants to specify a different font. To produce this appearance, the user puts the following lines in the **.Xdefaults** file.

```
Mwm*background:          SteelBlue
Mwm*foreground:          VioletRed
Mwm*activeBackground:    VioletRed
Mwm*activeForeground:    SteelBlue
Mwm*fontList:            6x10
```

The user can specify the appearance of window-frame elements for four particular objects.

- Menus

- Icons (includes the frame elements of all icons)

- Clients (includes the frame elements of all clients)

- Feedback windows

This allows the user to select a different color or font for a particular object, perhaps menus, while the other objects (icons and clients) remain the same. To do this, the following syntax is used:

Mwm*{menu |icon |client |feedback}**resource:*   *value*

In addition, the user can specify resource values for the title area of a client window and for menus with specific names:

Mwm*client*title**resource:*   *value*

Mwm*menu**menuname*resource:*   *value*

For example, users who want the general appearance of the clients in the environment to be as above, SteelBlue and VioletRed, but want the menus to be different, can add the following lines to the **.Xdefaults** file:

```
Mwm*background:          SteelBlue
Mwm*foreground:          VioletRed
Mwm*activeBackground:    VioletRed
Mwm*activeForeground:    SteelBlue
Mwm*fontList:            6x10
Mwm*menu*background:     SkyBlue
Mwm*menu*foreground:     White
```

Information on menus and icons appears in later chapters.

13.9 Making Window Frame Pixmaps

Making a pixmap is a way of creating shades of colors. The pixmap is composed of tiles that provide a surface pattern or a visual texture. The concept is analogous to using ceramic tiles to make a pattern or texture on a floor or countertop.

Generally, the fewer colors a display produces, the more important the pixmap resource becomes. This is because a pixmap provides a way to mix foreground and background colors into a third color pattern.

For example, with a monochrome display (two colors—black and white), one could use the pixmap resource to color window frame elements with shades of gray to achieve a 3-dimensional look.

The following table shows the MWM pixmap resources that let the user create a pattern for the frame background and bevels of both inactive and active windows.

Table 13-4. Creating a Pixmap for Window Frames

Use this resource...	To pattern these elements...
backgroundPixmap	Background and bevel for inactive frames.
bottomShadowPixmap	Right and bottom bevels of inactive frames.
topShadowPixmap	Left and upper bevels of inactive frames.
activeBackgroundPixmap	Background of the active frame.
activeBottomShadowPixmap	Right and lower bevels of the active frame.
activeTopShadowPixmap	Left and upper bevels of the active frame.

The following figure illustrates various pixmap values:

Figure 13-2. Illustrations of Valid Pixmap Values

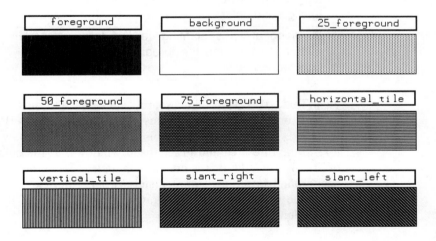

The following table lists the acceptable values for obtaining the pixmap styles illustrated above:

Table 13-5. Valid Pixmap Values

To pattern an element in this manner...	Use this value...
The foreground color	foreground
The background color	background
A mix of 25% foreground to 75% background	25_foreground
A mix of 50% foreground to 50% background	50_foreground
A mix of 75% foreground to 25% background	75_foreground
In horizontal lines alternating between the foreground and background color	horizontal_tile
In vertical lines alternating between the foreground and background color	vertical_tile
In diagonal lines slanting to the right, alternating between the foreground and background color	slant_right
In diagonal lines slanting to the left, alternating between the foreground and background color	slant_left

cleanText. The **cleanText** resource can be used to make text easier to read on monochrome systems where a **backgroundPixmap** is specified. This resource controls the display of window manager text in the title area and in feedback windows. If the default value of True is used, the text is drawn with a clear background. Only the background in the area immediately around the text is cleared. If the value is False, the text is drawn directly on top of the existing background.

13.10 Specifying a Matte for Client Windows

OSF/Motif has "matte" resources that allow further decoration of windows. A **matte** is a 3-dimensional border between the client's window area and the window frame. A matte can give an individual client, or class of clients, a distinct appearance. To configure a matte, the **WmatteWidth** resource must first be given a positive value.

matteWidth. The **matteWidth** resource defines the width of the matte between the client and the window frame. The width is given in pixels. For example, to specify a matte of 10 pixels around all xload windows, the following line must be in the **.Xdefaults** file:

```
Mwm*XLoad.matteWidth:    10
```

The default value of 0 disables the matte.

13.10.1 Coloring Individual Matte Elements

Matte resources use the same wording as window frame resources, but begin with the term "matte." The following table lists the matte resources that control color.

Table 13-6. MWM Matte Resources and What They Color

Matte Resource	Area Colored
matteBackground	Background areas
matteTopShadowColor	Top and left 3-dimensional bevels
matteBottomShadowColor	Bottom and right 3-dimensional bevels
matteForeground	Foreground areas

13.10.2 Changing the Pixmap of Mattes

As with frame colors, the fewer colors a display can produce, the more value there is in creating a pixmap for mattes. Again, a pixmap provides a way to "mix" foreground and background colors into a third color. For a 2-color (monochrome) display, one can create a pixmap for a window matte in shades of gray to achieve a pleasing 3-dimensional look.

The following table lists the resources that are used to create a pixmap for mattes.

Table 13-7. MWM Resources for Creating a Pixmap

Use this resource...	To pattern these elements...
matteBottomShadowPixmap	Right and lower bevels of matte
matteTopShadowPixmap	Left and upper bevels of matte

See Section 13.9 for a chart and an illustration of the values for pixmap resources.

13.10.3 The Syntax for Matte Resources

Matte resources can have any of three syntaxes, depending on the situation.

1. To matte all clients regardless of class, the syntax is

   Mwm*matteResource: *value*

   For example, to create a 10-pixel-wide yellow matte for every client window, the user adds the following lines to the **.Xdefaults** file:

```
Mwm*matteWidth:        10
Mwm*matteBackground:   Yellow
```

2. To matte specific classes of clients, the syntax is

    Mwm**clientclass.matteResource*:   *value*

3. To matte any client of an unknown class, the syntax is

    Mwm*defaults*matteResource: *value*

4. To matte a specific client, the syntax is

    Mwm**clientname*matteResource*:   *value*

13.11 Using Frameless or Reduced-Element Windows

For some applications the full complement of window decorations may not be desirable. For example, a clock may not need resize frame handles. MWM has two resources for such situations: **clientDecoration** and **transientDecoration**.

The **clientDecoration** resource allows the user to choose how much decoration to put around each client. The default value is "all."

The **transientDecoration** resource allows the user to choose how much or how little decoration to put around each transient window. (A **transient window** is a relatively short-lived window, for example, a dialog box.) The default value for this resource is "menu title resizeh" (that is, transient windows have a title bar with a window menu button and resize borders). Even if a decoration is specified by the **transientDecoration** resource, MWM does not put it around a transient window unless that decoration is also specified by the **clientDecoration** resource.

The user can still use any function associated with the window decoration removed either by binding the function to a button or to a key press, or by adding it to the window menu (as explained in Chapter 14).

There are two sets of constraints when configuring window decoration:

1. You, the applications programmer, can use the functions field of the _MOTIF_WM_HINTS property to limit which MWM functions are to be used by the client window. If a function is not to be applied to a window, the decoration that does that function is not shown, even if it is specified by the **clientDecoration** resource.

   The user can further limit the functions to be used by configuring the **clientFunctions** resource (or **transientFunctions** resource if the window is a transient window).

   If the functions field of the _MOTIF_WM_HINTS client window property is set, it is combined with the **clientFunctions** resource value. Functions can be removed but not added in doing this combination.

   The default value for allowed functions (to be used if no specification is done by the client or user) is that all functions are allowable.

2. The decoration specification for a window is adjusted based on the limits set by the _MOTIF_WM_HINTS property and the **clientDecoration** resource (as previously explained). Decorations that are associated with functions that are not allowed are not shown. The **clientDecoration** resource (or **transientDecoration** resource if the window is a transient window) is used to indicate the decoration specification for a window.

   If the decorations field of the _MOTIF_WM_HINTS client window property is set, it is combined with the **clientDecorations** resource value. Decorations can be removed but not added in doing this combination.

The default decoration for the client window frame is all title bar decorations and the resize frame handles.

For more discussion of how the **clientFunctions** resource is used, see Section 14.3.4. The _MOTIF_WM_HINTS property is discussed in Section 12.3.

13.11.1 Adding or Removing Elements

The **clientDecoration** and **transientDecoration** resources are configured as a list of frame elements:

- If the first element in the list is preceded by nothing or by a + (plus sign), the window manager starts with no frame and assumes that the list contains those elements to be added.

- If the list begins with a – (minus sign), the window manager starts with a complete frame and assumes that the list contains elements to be removed from the frame.

The following table lists the valid window frame elements.

Table 13-8. Valid MWM Frame Elements

Frame Element	Description
all	Includes all decoration elements (default value).
maximize	Maximize button (includes title bar).
minimize	Minimize button (includes title bar).
none	No decorations.
resizeh	Resize frame handles (includes border).
border	Window border.
menu	Window menu (includes title bar).
title	Title bar (includes border).

13.11.2 The Syntax for clientDecoration and transientDecoration Resources

The **clientDecoration** resource has three syntaxes:

- To add or remove elements from all classes of clients, the syntax is

  Mwm*clientDecoration: *value*

  For example, remove the maximize button from all windows by adding the following line to the **.Xdefaults** file:

  ```
  Mwm*clientDecoration: —maximize
  ```

- To add or remove elements from specific classes of clients, the syntax is

  Mwm*clientclass**.clientDecoration:** *value*

  For example, to remove just the resize handles and the maximize button from all clocks displayed on the screen, add the following:

  ```
  Mwm*XClock.clientDecoration: \
      —resizeh —maximize
  ```

- To add or remove elements from any client with an unknown class, the syntax is

  Mwm*defaults*clientDecoration: *value*

The **transientDecoration** resource has the following syntax:

Mwm*transientDecoration: *value*

For example, remove the menu button from all transient windows by adding the following line to the **.Xdefaults** file:

```
Mwm*transientDecoration: title resizeh
```

13.12 Controlling Window Size and Position

MWM has a number of resources that allow the user to refine control of the size and position of windows.

13.12.1 Window Size Resources

The following resources configure the size of windows:

frameBorderWidth. The **frameBorderWidth** resource specifies the width (in pixels) of a client window frame border with shadow elements, but without resize handles. The default value is 5 pixels.

limitResize. The **limitResize** resource controls the ability to enlarge a window beyond the client's maximized size. The default value of True limits a window's size to no greater than the maximum size specified by the **maximumClientSize** resource, or the WM_NORMAL_HINTS window property, or the default maximum size assigned by MWM. The value of "False" allows a window to be resized to any size.

maximumClientSize. The **maximumClientSize** resource controls the maximum size of a maximized client. Its value is a width × height, interpreted in terms of the units that the client uses. If this resource is not specified, the maximum size is taken from the WM_NORMAL_HINTS window property, or the default size (the size of the screen) is used.

maximumMaximumSize. The **maximumMaximumSize** resource controls the maximum size of a client window as set by the client. The dimensions are given in pixels. The default value of this resource is twice the screen width and height.

resizeBorderWidth. The **resizeBorderWidth** resource specifies the width of a client window frame border with resize handles and shadow elements. The default value is 10 pixels.

resizeCursors. The **resizeCursors** resource indicates whether the resize cursors are displayed when the pointer is in the window resize border. The default value True causes the appropriate resize cursor to appear when the pointer enters a resize handle in the window frame. The value of False prevents resize cursors from being displayed.

13.12.2 Window Position Resources

The following resources configure the position of windows:

clientAutoPlace. The **clientAutoPlace** resource determines the position of a window when the window has not been given a user specified position. The default value of True positions a window with the top left corner of the frame offset horizontally and vertically. The value of False causes the currently configured position of the window to be used. In either case, MWM attempts to place the window totally on the screen.

interactivePlacement. The **interactivePlacement** resource controls the initial placement of new windows on the screen. The value of True changes the shape of the pointer (to an upper-left-corner bracket) before a new window displays, so a position can be chosen for the window. When the default value of False is used, the window is placed according to its initial configuration attributes and/or the values of other MWM resources (for example, **clientAutoPlace**).

moveThreshold. The **moveThreshold** resource controls the sensitivity of dragging operations. The value of the **moveThreshold** resource is the number of pixels that the pointer must be moved with a button pressed before a drag operation is initiated. This resource is used to prevent window or icon movement when the user unintentionally moves the pointer during a click or double-click action. The default value is 4 pixels.

positionIsFrame. The **positionIsFrame** resource determines how client window-position information is reported. When the default value True is used, the position information (from WM_NORMAL_HINTS and configuration files) refers to the position of the window frame. When the value is False, the position information refers to the position of the client window itself.

positionOnScreen. The **positionOnScreen** resource controls clipping of new windows by screen edges. The default value True causes a window to be placed, if possible, so that it is not clipped. If clipping cannot be avoided, a window is placed so that at least the upper left corner of the window is on the screen. The value of False causes a window to be placed at the requested position even if it is totally off the screen.

showFeedback. The **showFeedback** resource controls when feedback information is displayed. It controls both window position and size feedback during move or resize operations and initial client placement. It also controls window manager message and dialog boxes.

The value for this resource is a list of names of the feedback options to be enabled or disabled; the names must be separated by a space. If an option is preceded by a minus sign, that option is excluded from the list. The *sign* of the first item in the list determines the initial set of options. If the sign of the first option is minus, **mwm** assumes all options are present and starts subtracting from that set. If the sign of the first decoration is plus (or not specified), **mwm** starts with no options and builds up a list from the resource.

The following table lists the names of the feedback options.

Table 13-9. Feedback Options

Name	Description
all	Show all feedback (Default value)
behavior	Confirm behavior switch
kill	Confirm on receipt of KILL signal
move	Show position during move
none	Show no feedback
placement	Show position and size during initial placement
quit	Confirm quitting MWM
resize	Show size during resize
restart	Confirm MWM restart

The following resource specification illustrates the syntax for **showFeedback**:

```
Mwm*showFeedback: placement resize behavior restart
```

This command line provides feedback for initial client placement and resize, and enables the dialog boxes to confirm the restart and set behavior functions. It disables feedback for the move function.

13.12.3 Other Resources

The following resource applies to sizing and positioning of windows:

enableWarp. The default value of this resource, True, causes MWM to "warp" the pointer to the center of the selected window during keyboard-controlled resize and move operations. Setting the value to False causes MWM to leave the pointer at its original place on the screen, unless the user explicitly moves it with the cursor keys or pointing device.

13.12.4 The Syntax for Size and Position Refinement Resources

The resources that refine control over the size and position of windows have the following syntax:

Mwm*resource: *value*

For example, to place each new window on the screen interactively, add the following line to the **.Xdefaults** file:

```
Mwm*interactivePlacement:   True
```

In addition to this syntax, the **maximumClientSize** resource has two more syntaxes:

1. To specify the maximum client size for specific classes of clients the syntax is

    Mwm*clientclass.**maximumClientSize:**   *width×height*

    For example, to specify that **xload** clients should be maximized to no more than one sixty-fourth of the size of a 1024×768 display, add the line:

    ```
    Mwm*XLoad.maximumClientSize:   128×96
    ```

2. To specify the maximum client size for any client with an unknown class, the syntax is:

    Mwm*defaults*maximumClientSize: *width×height*

Chapter 14

Managing Menus, Mouse Buttons, and Keyboard Bindings

This chapter presents information users need if they want to customize or create window menus, button bindings, and key bindings. As an applications programmer, you can also customize and create menus and bindings. However, be aware that users can modify your configurations.

This chapter discusses the following topics:

- The MWM resource description file

- Modifying menus and default menus

- Making new menus: item strings, mnemonics, accelerators, and MWM functions

- Changing the menu associated with the window menu button

- Mouse button bindings

- Keyboard bindings

14.1 MWM Resource Description File

The MWM resource description file is a supplementary resource file that contains resource descriptions that are referred to by entries in the defaults files (such as **.Xdefaults** and **/usr/lib/X11/app-defaults/Mwm**).

The following types of resources can be described in the MWM Resource Description File:

Buttons   Window manager functions can be bound (associated) with button press events.

Keys   Window manager functions can be bound (associated) with key press events.

Menus   Menus can be posted using key and button bindings.

configFile. A specific MWM resource description file can be selected using the **configFile** resource. The value for this resource is the pathname for an MWM resource description file.

If the pathname begins with ~/ (tilde followed by slash), MWM considers it to be relative to the user's home directory (as specified by the HOME environment variable). If the LANG environment variable is set, MWM looks for **$HOME/$LANG**/*configFile*. If that file does not exist or if LANG is not set, MWM looks for **$HOME**/*configFile*.

If the *configFile* pathname does not begin with ~/ (tilde followed by slash) MWM considers it to be relative to the current working directory.

If no value for the resource is specified or if the specified file does not exist, MWM uses several default paths to find a configuration file. If the LANG environment variable is set, MWM looks for the configuration file first in **$HOME/$LANG/.mwmrc**. If that file does not exist or if LANG is not set, MWM looks for **$HOME/.mwmrc**. If that file does not exist and if LANG is set, MWM next looks for **/usr/lib/X11/$LANG/system.mwmrc**. If that file does not exist or if LANG is not set, MWM looks for **/usr/lib/X11/system.mwmrc**.

An MWM resource description file is a standard text file containing items of information separated by blanks, tabs, and newline characters. Blank lines are ignored. Items or characters can be quoted to avoid special interpretation (for example, the comment character can be quoted to prevent it from being interpreted as the comment character). A quoted item can be contained in " (double quotation marks). Single characters can be quoted by preceding them with \ (the backslash character). All text from an unquoted # (comment) character to the end of the line is regarded as a comment and is not interpreted as part of a resource description. If an ! (exclamation poin) is the first character of a line, the line is regarded as a comment.

bitmapDirectory. You can also, using the **bitmapDirectory** resource, direct the window manager to search a specified directory for bitmaps. The **bitmapDirectory** resource causes the window manager to search the specified directory whenever a bitmap is named with no complete path. The default value for **bitmapDirectory** is **/usr/include/X11/bitmaps**.

14.2 Modifying Menus and Default Menus

All window manager menus, regardless of the mechanism that calls them to the screen, have the same syntax:

Menu   *menu_name*
{
item1   *[mnemonic]*   *[accelerator]*   *function*   *[argument]*
item2   *[mnemonic]*   *[accelerator]*   *function*   *[argument]*
   .
   .
item#   *[mnemonic]*   *[accelerator]*   *function*   *[argument]*
}

The menu is given a name, and then each **item** to be listed in the menu is given a name or graphic representation (bitmap). The item is followed by an optional mnemonic and/or accelerator, and then by a **function** from Table 14-1. The function is the action the window manager takes when that menu item is selected. Some functions require an argument. To illustrate menu syntax, the following default window menu is presented as it appears in **/usr/lib/X11/system.mwmrc** and in the home directory in **.mwmrc**. The default window menu illustrates the default OSF/Motif behavior.

```
Menu DefaultWindowMenu
{
Restore              _R     Meta<Key>F5     f.normalize
Move                 _M     Meta<Key>F7     f.move
Size                 _S     Meta<Key>F8     f.resize
Minimize             _n     Meta<Key>F9     f.minimize
Maximize             _x     Meta<Key>F10    f.maximize
Lower                _L     Meta<Key>F3     f.lower
no-label                                    f.separator
Close                _C     Meta<Key>F4     f.kill
}
```

You might want to create a workspace menu that gives some control over the entire workspace (screen area). A sample workspace menu is illustrated below:

```
Menu RootMenu
{
"Root Menu"         f.title
"New Window"        f.exec "mterm"
"Shuffle Up"        f.circle_up
"Shuffle Down"      f.circle_down
Refresh             f.refresh
no-label            f.separator
Restart             f.restart
}
```

You can modify either menu to suit the specific needs of your application. However, for the sake of consistency in window operation, it's usually better to modify the workspace menu and keep the window menu the same. (See _MOTIF_WM_MENU in Section 12.3.1.5 for instructions on modifying the window menu.)

14.3 Making New Menus

You may modify the window and workspace menus, but you also have another option. You can make a completely new menu, calling it to the screen by a mouse button press, by a key press, or by selecting it from an existing menu.

To create a completely new menu, use the general menu syntax as a model to do the following:

1. Fill in a menu name

2. Make up item names

3. Choose a mnemonic and accelerator (optional)

4. Give each item a function to perform from Table 14-1

14.3.1 Menu Titles

A menu title is created with the **f.title** function. The **f.title** function automatically places separators above and below the title.

14.3.2 Menu Items

An item may be either a character string or a graphic representation (bitmap).

A character string for items must be compatible with the menu font that is used. Character strings must be typed precisely, using one of the following styles:

- Any character string containing a space must be enclosed in " (double quotation marks), for example, "Menu name."

- Single-word strings do not have to be enclosed, but it is probably a good idea for the sake of consistency, for example, Menuname.

- An alternate method of dealing with 2-word selection names is to use an underbar in place of the space, for example, Menu_name.

A bitmap for an item can be created using the **bitmap** client. Using the @/ (at sign and slash) in the menu syntax tells the window manager that what follows is the full path to a bitmap file:

@/bitmapfile   function [argument]

Here is an example of a user-made menu. The menu is named "Graphics Projects." The menu items are all bitmaps symbolizing different graphics projects. The bitmaps are kept in the directory **/users/pat/bits**. When the user, Pat, selects a symbol, the graphics program starts and opens the appropriate graphics file.

```
Menu "Graphics Projects"
{
"Graphics Projects"          f.title
@/users/pat/bits/fusel.bits f.exec "cad /spacestar/fusel.e12
@/users/pat/bits/lwing.bits f.exec "cad /spacestar/lwing.s05
@/users/pat/bits/rwing.bits f.exec "cad /spacestar/rwing.s04
@/users/pat/bits/nose.bits  f.exec "cad /spacestar/nose.e17
}
```

Another method for specifying the path is to replace **/users/pat/** with the ˜/ (tilde and slash) characters. The ˜/ specifies the user's home directory. Yet another method is to use the **bitmapDirectory** resource, described in Section 14.1, "MWM Resource Description File." If the **bitmapDirectory** is set to **/users/pat/bits**, then the bitmap file could be specified as:

```
@fusel.bits   f.exec "cad /spacestar/fusel.e12
```

14.3.3 Mnemonics and Accelerators

You can use mnemonics and keyboard accelerators. Mnemonics are functional only when the menu is posted. Accelerators are functional whether or not the menu is posted. A mnemonic specification has the following syntax:

mnemonic = _*character*

The _ (underbar) is placed under the first matching *character* in the label. If there is no matching *character* in the label, no mnemonic is registered with the window manager for that label. The accelerator specification is a key action with the same syntax as is used for binding keys to window manager functions:

key context function [argument]

When choosing accelerators, be careful not to use key actions that are already used in key bindings. (Keyboard bindings are discussed in greater detail in Section 14.6.)

The following line from the Default Window Menu illustrates mnemonic and accelerator syntax:

```
Restore   _R   Meta<Key>F5   f.normalize
```

14.3.4 MWM Functions

Each MWM function operates in one or more of the following contexts:

root   Operates the function when the workspace or "root window" is selected.

window   Operates the function when a client window is selected. All sub-parts of a window are considered as "windows" for function contexts. Note that some functions operate only when the window is in its normalized state (f.maximize), or its maximized or iconified state (f.normalize).

icon   Operates the function when an icon is selected.

Additionally, each function is operated by one or more of the following devices:

- Mouse button

- Keyboard key

- Menu item

Any selection that uses an invalid context, an invalid function, or a function that does not apply to the current context is grayed out. This is the case with the Restore selection of a terminal window's window menu or the Minimize selection of an icon's menu. Also, menu items are grayed out if they do the **f.nop** (no operation performed) function.

All window manager functions are available for use in a menu, except **f.post_wmenu**. MWM can be configured to disallow the use of five of the functions: **f.resize**, **f.move**, **f.minimize**, **f.maximize**, and **f.kill.** You (the programmer) indicate disallowed functions with the _MOTIF_WM_HINTS client window property (see Chapter 12). The user indicates disallowed functions with the **clientFunctions** resource, or the **transientFunctions** resource if the window is transient (see "Functions and Clients," which appears later).

The following table lists the valid functions for MWM. Items followed by an asterisk are described in more detail following the table. Under the heading Contexts, R stands for Root, I stands for Icon, and W stands for Window. Under the heading Devices, MO stands for Mouse, K stands for Key, and ME stands for Menu.

Table 14-1. Valid Window Manager Functions

Functions		Contexts			Devices		
Name	Description	R	I	W	MO	K	ME
f.beep	Causes a beep to sound.	x	x	x	x	x	x
f.circle_down [icon | window]	Puts window on bottom of stack.*	x	x	x	x	x	x
f.circle_up [icon | window]	Puts window on top of stack.*	x	x	x	x	x	x
f.exec (or) ! command	Uses **/bin/sh** to execute a command.	x	x	x	x	x	x
f.focus_color	Sets colormap focus when colormap focus policy is explicit.*	x	x	x	x	x	x

Functions		Contexts			Devices		
Name	Description	R	I	W	MO	K	ME
f.focus_key	Sets keyboard input focus when keyboard focus policy is explicit.*	x	x	x	x	x	x
f.kill	Terminates a client.*		x	x	x	x	x
f.lower [-*client*]	Lowers a window to bottom of stack.	x	x	x	x	x	x
f.maximize	Enlarges a window to its maximum size.		x	x	x	x	x
f.menu *menu_name*	Associates a menu with a selection or binding.	x	x	x	x	x	x
f.minimize	Changes a window into an icon.			x	x	x	x
f.move	Enables the interactive moving of a window.		x	x	x	x	x
f.next_cmap	Installs the next colormap in the window with the colormap focus.	x	x	x	x	x	x
f.next_key [icon | window | transient]	Sets keyboard focus to the next window/icon in the stack.	x	x	x	x	x	x
f.nop	No operation performed.	x	x	x	x	x	x

Functions		Contexts			Devices		
Name	**Description**	**R**	**I**	**W**	**MO**	**K**	**ME**
f.normalize	Displays a window in normal size.		x	x	x	x	x
f.normalize_and_raise	Displays a window in normal size and raises it to the top of the stack.		x	x	x	x	x
f.pack_icons	Tidies up icon rows on the root window or in the icon box.	x	x	x	x	x	x
f.pass_keys	Toggles between enabling and disabling the processing of key bindings.	x	x	x	x	x	x
f.post_wmenu	Posts the window menu.	x	x	x	x	x	
f.prev_cmap	Installs the previous colormap in the window with the colormap focus.	x	x	x	x	x	x
f.prev_key [icon | window | transient]	Sets keyboard focus to the previous window/icon in the stack.	x	x	x	x	x	x
f.quit_mwm	Terminates OSF/Motif Window Manager.	x			x	x	x

Functions		Contexts			Devices		
Name	**Description**	**R**	**I**	**W**	**MO**	**K**	**ME**
f.raise [-*client*]	Lifts a window to top of stack.	x	x	x	x	x	x
f.raise_lower	Raises a partially concealed window; lowers an unconcealed window.		x	x	x	x	x
f.refresh	Redraws all windows.	x	x	x	x	x	x
f.refresh_win	Redraws a client window.			x	x	x	x
f.resize	Enables interactive resizing of windows.			x	x	x	x
f.restart	Restarts the OSF/Motif Window Manager.	x			x	x	x
f.send_msg *message_name*	Sends a client message.*		x	x	x	x	x
f.separator	Draws a line between menu selections.	x	x	x			x
f.set_behavior	Restarts MWM with default or custom behavior.*	x	x	x	x	x	x
f.title	Inserts a title into a menu at the position specified.	x	x	x			x

f.circle-down [icon | window] This function causes the window or icon that is on the top of the window stack to be put on the bottom of the window stack, so that it is no longer obscuring any other window or icon. This function affects only those windows and icons that are obscuring other windows and icons or that are themselves obscured. Secondary windows (transients) are restacked with their associated primary window. Secondary windows always stay on top of the associated primary window and there can be no other primary windows between the secondary windows and their primary window.

If an icon function argument is specified, the function applies only to icons. If a window function argument is specified, the function applies only to windows.

f.circle_up [icon | window] This function raises the window or icon on the bottom of the window stack so that it is not obscured by any other windows. It affects only those windows and icons that are obscuring other windows and icons or that are themselves obscured. Secondary windows (transients) are restacked with their associated primary window.

If an icon function argument is specified, the function applies only to icons. If a window function argument is specified, the function applies only to windows.

f.focus_color This function sets the colormap focus to a client window or icon (for icons, the default colormap for the screen is installed). If this function is done in a root context, the default colormap (set by the X Window System for the screen where MWM is running) is installed and there is no specific client window colormap focus. This function is ignored if **colormapFocusPolicy** is not "explicit."

f.focus_key This function sets the keyboard input focus to a client window or icon and is ignored if **keyboardFocusPolicy** is not "explicit." See also the description of the **focusAutoRaise** resource in Section 13.4, "Setting Focus Policies for Active Windows." A button binding for this function can be set up with a window context without the side-effect of having the button made unavailable to the client window.

f.kill This function sends a client message event to a client indicating that the client window should be deleted. This occurs only if the WM_DELETE_WINDOW protocol is set up. If the WM_SAVE_YOURSELF protocol is set up and the WM_DELETE_WINDOW protocol is not set up, the client is sent a client message event, indicating that the client needs to prepare to be terminated. If the client has neither the WM_DELETE_WINDOW nor WM_SAVE_YOURSELF protocol set up, **f.kill** causes a client's X connection to be terminated (usually resulting in termination of the client and possibly resulting in a loss of data). Refer to the description of the **quitTimeout** resource in Section 13.5, "Managing Clients," and the WM_PROTOCOLS property in Section 12.2, "Inter-Client Communications Conventions."

f.send_msg *message_name* This function sends a client message of the type WM_PROTOCOLS with the protocols type indicated by the *message_name* function argument. The client message is sent only if *message_name* is included in the client's WM_PROTOCOLS property. A menu item label is grayed-out if the menu item wants to send a message that is not included in the client's WM_PROTOCOLS property.

f.set_behavior This function causes MWM to restart with the default OSF/Motif behavior (if a custom behavior is configured) or a custom behavior (if an OSF/Motif default behavior is configured).

A key binding for doing the **f.set_behavior** function is included in the built-in default set of key bindings for MWM. If the user specifies a custom set of key bindings to replace the default set, then the **f.set_behavior** key binding is added automatically to the custom set (and is always processed first). The following table shows the key binding for **f.set_behavior**.

Table 14-2. Key Binding for f.set_behavior

Key Action	Function Description
<Meta><Shift><Ctrl><!>	Switch (toggle) between the default and custom behaviors

When the user switches to the default OSF/Motif behavior, a number of MWM resources assume their default values and MWM restarts. When the user switches back to the custom behavior, the resource values that were changed to default values are reset with the custom values and MWM restarts.

When an **f.set_behavior** function is done, the following user interaction occurs:

1. A system modal dialog box appears asking the user for confirmation of the **f.set_behavior** action. The user may cancel the action at this point.

2. The window manager restarts.

3. The window manager applies the new (custom or default) configuration values.

4. Window manager components are mapped.

When the default OSF/Motif behavior is being set, default resource values are applied, and client properties that control window manager behavior are applied if specified. This includes the _MOTIF_WM_HINTS and _MOTIF_WM_MENU properties. These properties may alter default OSF/Motif behavior, but in a way that is consistent for all users.

14.3.4.1 Functions and Clients

clientFunctions. This resource is used to indicate which window management functions are allowed or not allowed. The resource value is a list of items, with each item preceded by a + (plus) or - (minus) sign. The sign of the first item in the list determines the initial functionality. If the sign of the first item is minus, then MWM starts with all functions and subtracts from that set. If the sign of the first item is plus (or not specified), then MWM starts with no functions and builds up a list from the resource. The following table lists the name and description for each client function.

Table 14-3. Client Functions

Name	Description
all	Include all functions (Default value)
none	Include no functions
resize	**f.resize**
move	**f.move**
minimize	**f.minimize**
maximize	**f.maximize**
close	**f.kill**

Note that the five functions listed in the previous table are the only functions that can be individually specified.

transientFunctions. This resource is used to indicate which window management functions are allowed or not allowed with respect to transient windows. The function specification is exactly the same as for the **clientFunctions** resource. The default value for this resource is "-minimize -maximize."

14.3.5 Size of Menu Window

The size of the menu window is affected not only by the number of items in the menu, but also by the font you use. The size and resolution of the display determine the default value MWM uses.

14.3.6 Binding a Menu to a Mouse Button or Key

If you want your new menu to appear whenever a certain mouse button or keyboard key is pressed, follow these steps:

1. Choose the mouse button or keyboard key that you want to use.

2. Choose the action on the button or key that causes the menu to appear.

3. Use the **f.menu** function with the new menu's name as an argument to bind the menu to the button or key.

For more information on mouse button and keyboard bindings, including examples, see the Section 14.5, "Mouse Button Bindings," and Section 14.6, "Keyboard Bindings."

14.4 Changing the Menu Associated with the Window Menu Button

windowMenu. The **windowMenu** resource enables you (and the user) to change the menu that appears when the user presses the mouse Select button on the window frame's window menu button. This allows you to display a menu of your choice from the window menu button without having to extensively remodel the window menu to do it. All you need do is make a new menu, then use the **windowMenu** resource to associate this new menu with the window menu button.

The **windowMenu** resource has three syntaxes. Which one you use depends on the situation.

1. To specify the menu for all classes of clients, the syntax is

   Mwm*windowMenu: *MenuName*

   For example, if you want to associate a special **CADCAMMenu** menu with the window menu button, you add the following line to your **.Xdefaults** file:

   ```
   Mwm*windowMenu:    CADCAMMenu
   ```

2. To specify the menu for a specific class of clients, the syntax is

   Mwm*clientclass***.windowMenu**:   *MenuName*

   For example, you may want to associate a particular **EditorMenu** of your own creation with a terminal emulator window called **mterm**:

   ```
   Mwm*Mterm.windowMenu:    EditorMenu
   ```

3. To specify a menu for any client whose class is unknown, the syntax is

   Mwm*defaults***windowMenu**:   *MenuName*

The default is DefaultWindowMenu.

There are two resources involving the window menu button: **wMenuButtonClick** and **wMenuButtonClick2**.

The **wMenuButtonClick** resource indicates whether a click of the mouse when the pointer is over the window menu button posts and leaves posted the window menu. The default value of True posts and leaves posted the menu. A value of False disables this action.

The **wMenuButtonClick2** resource indicates whether the window menu button double-click action is to do an **f.kill** function. The default value of True causes an **f.kill** action. A value of False disables this action.

14.5 Mouse Button Bindings

The mouse offers a quick way to make things happen in the user's window environment without the time-consuming process of typing commands on the keyboard (and retyping misspelled commands). The window manager recognizes the following button actions:

Press   Holding down a mouse button

Release   Releasing a pressed mouse button

Click   Pressing and releasing a mouse button

Double-click   Pressing and releasing a mouse button twice in rapid succession

Drag   Pressing a mouse button and moving the pointer/mouse device

You can associate a mouse button action with a window management function by using a **button binding**. A button binding is a command line you put in the **system.mwmrc** or **.mwmrc** file that associates a button action with a window manager function.

User defined button bindings are added to built-in button bindings and are always done first.

14.5.1 Default Button Bindings

MWM has built-in default button bindings. These button bindings define the functions of the window frame components. The user-specified button bindings that are defined with the **buttonBindings** resource are added to the built-in button bindings. The default value for this resource is DefaultButtonBindings. The built-in button bindings are described by the button bindings specifications shown in the following table.

Table 14-4. Default Button Bindings

Button Action	Context*	Function
<Btn1Down>	menu	f.post_wmenu
<Btn1Click2>	menu	f.kill
<Btn1Click>	minimize	f.minimize
<Btn1Click>	maximize	f.maximize
<Btn1Down>	title	f.move
<Btn1Down>	window|icon	f.focus_key
<Btn1Down>	border	f.resize
<Btn1Click>	icon	f.post_wmenu
<Btn1Click2>	icon	f.normalize
<Btn1Down>	icon	f.move

*Context is explained in the next section.

The following special handling applies to the built-in button bindings.

- The menu, minimize, maximize, and border contexts are internal-only MWM contexts.

- The window menu is posted just below the window menu button and not at the pointer position. When the window menu is posted with a Button 1 press and the Button 1 release is done with the pointer on the window menu button, then the window menu remains posted and can be traversed from the keyboard.

- The **f.resize** function for the resize frame handles has a behavior that is specific to the resize handle contexts.

The default button binding shown in the following table is built into MWM, but can be replaced by user specified button bindings:

Table 14-5. Replaceable Default Button Binding

Button Action	Context	Function
<Btn1Down>	icon|frame	f.raise

14.5.2 Button Binding Syntax and Modifying Button Bindings

The syntax for button bindings is as follows:

Buttons   *ButtonBindingSetName*
{
button   context [| context]   function   [argument]
button   context [| context]   function   [argument]

   .
   .

button   context [| context]   function   [argument]
}

Each line identifies a certain mouse button action, followed by the context in which the button action is valid, followed by the function to be done. Some functions require an argument.

To modify the default button bindings, you need to edit either **system.mwmrc** (to make system-wide changes) or **.mwmrc** (to make changes to the local environment). The easiest way to modify button bindings is to change the default bindings or to insert extra lines in the DefaultButtonBindings section.

When modifying or creating a button binding, you need to first decide which mouse button to use and which action is performed on the button. Make sure you do not use button-action combinations already used by OSF/Motif. You might want to require a simultaneous key press with the mouse button action. This is called modifying the button action. **Modifiers** increase the number of possible button bindings you can make. The following table shows the available modifier keys and their abbreviations (for use in the button binding command line).

Table 14-6. Button Binding Modifier Keys

Modifier	Description
Ctrl	Control Key
Shift	Shift Key
Meta	Meta/Alt Key
Lock	Lock Key
Mod1	Modifier1
Mod2	Modifier2
Mod3	Modifier3
Mod4	Modifier4
Mod5	Modifier5

You can bind up to five buttons if you have a 3-button mouse. Button 4 is the simultaneous press of Buttons 1 and 2. Button 5 is the simultaneous press of Buttons 2 and 3. Each button can be bound with one of four actions. The following table describes the button actions and their abbreviations.

Table 14-7. Button Actions for Button Bindings

Button	Description
Btn1Down	Button 1 Press
Btn1Up	Button 1 Release
Btn1Click	Button 1 Press and Release
Btn1Click2	Button 1 Double-Click
Btn2Down	Button 2 Press
Btn2Up	Button 2 Release
Btn2Click	Button 2 Press and Release
Btn2Click2	Button 2 Double-Click
Btn3Down	Button 3 Press
Btn3Up	Button 3 Release
Btn3Click	Button 3 Press and Release
Btn3Click2	Button 3 Double-Click

After choosing the optional modifier and the mouse button action, you must decide under which context(s) the binding works. The following table lists the button-binding contexts that are recognized by the window manager.

Table 14-8. Contexts for Mouse Button Bindings

This context...	For mouse action at this pointer position...
root	Workspace (root window)
window	Client window
frame	Window frame
icon	Icon
title	Title bar
border	Frame minus title bar
app	Application window (inside the frame)

The context indicates where the pointer must be for the button binding to be effective. For example, a context of *window* indicates that the pointer must be over a client window or window frame for the button binding to be effective. The *frame* context is for the window frame around a client window (including the border and title bar), the *border* context is for the border part of the window frame (not including the title bar), the *title* context is for the title bar of the window frame, and the *app* context is for the application window or client area (not including the window frame).

Here is an example of a button binding. Pat, the user who created his own Graphics Projects menu, can display the menu with a button action. Pat chooses **Meta<Key>** as a modifier, and mouse custom-button press, **Btn3Down**, as the button action. He decides the pointer must be on the workspace. The function name for posting a special menu is **f.menu**, and the argument is the menu name Graphics Projects. He needs only to insert one line into his **.mwmrc** file to make this happen. The DefaultButtonBindings section of his **.mwmrc** file then looks like the following:

```
Buttons DefaultButtonBindings
{
<Btn3Down>       root   f.menu "DefaultRootMenu"
<Btn3Down>       frame  f.post_wmenu
Meta<Btn3Down>   root   f.menu "Graphics Projects"
}
```

14.5.3 Making a New Button Binding Set

Perhaps inserting a new button binding into the DefaultButtonBindings set is not enough. You might need to make a complete new set of button bindings. To do this, use the DefaultButtonBindings section of the **.mwmrc** file as a model. After you have created the new button binding set, use the **buttonBindings** resource to tell the window manager about it.

buttonBindings. The **buttonBindings** resource is used to specify a button binding set. The default is DefaultButtonBindings. The syntax of the added **.Xdefaults** line is as follows:

Mwm*buttonBindings: NewButtonBindingSetName

This line directs the window manager to use NewButtonBindingSetName as the source of its button binding information. The button bindings are assumed to exist in the file named by the **Mwm*configFile:** resource, the default being **.mwmrc**.

For example, suppose Pat, our graphics user, wants to specify a completely new button binding set instead of inserting a line in the existing DefaultButtonBindings set. He needs to create a new button binding set, such as the following, modeled after the default set:

```
Buttons         GraphicsButtonBindings
{
<Btn3Down>      root   f.menu  "Graphics Projects"
}
```

In his **.Xdefaults** file, Pat then inserts the following line:

```
Mwm*buttonBindings:   GraphicsButtonBindings
```

To display his graphics menu, Pat needs only to press button 3 on the mouse when the pointer is on the workspace.

14.5.4 Modifying Button Click Timing

doubleClickTime. This is another MWM resource for controlling mouse button behavior. The **doubleClickTime** resource sets the maximum time (in milliseconds) that can elapse between button clicks before a double-click becomes just two clicks in a row. The default value is the display's multiclick time.

14.6 Keyboard Bindings

In a manner similar to mouse button bindings, you (or the user) can bind (associate) window manager functions to keys on the keyboard using keyboard bindings.

14.6.1 Default Keyboard Bindings

OSF/Motif has default key bindings. These key bindings are replaced with user-specified key bindings specified with the **keyBindings** resource. The following table lists the default key binding specifications.

Table 14-9. Default Keyboard Bindings

Keys	Context	Function
Shift\<Key>Escape	window|icon	**f.post_wmenu**
Meta\<Key>Space	window|icon	**f.post_wmenu**
Meta\<Key>Tab	root|icon|window	**f.next_key**
Meta Shift\<Key>Tab	root|icon|window	**f.prev_key**
Meta\<Key>Escape	root|icon|window	**f.circle_down**
Meta Shift\<Key>Escape	root|icon|window	**f.circle_up**
Meta\<Key>F6	window	**f.next_key transient**
Meta Ctrl Shift\<Key>Exclam	root|icon|window	**f.set_behavior**

14.6.2 Keyboard Binding Syntax and Modifying Keyboard Bindings

The syntax for keyboard bindings is as follows:

Keys *KeyBindingSetName*
{
key   context [| *context*]   *function   [argument]*
key   context [| *context*]   *function   [argument]*

  .

  .

key   context [| *context*]   *function   [argument]*
}

Each line identifies a unique key press sequence, followed by the context in which that sequence is valid, followed by the function to be done. Some functions require an argument. Context refers to the location of the keyboard input focus when the keys are pressed: window, icon, or root (workspace).

To modify the default keyboard bindings, you need to edit either **system.mwmrc** (to make system-wide changes) or **.mwmrc** (to make changes to the local environment). The easiest way is to change the default bindings or to insert extra lines in the DefaultKeyBindings section.

Next, decide which key you want to bind. Then choose the context in which the key binding is to work. The following table shows the contexts for key bindings.

Table 14-10. Contexts for Key Bindings

Use this context...	When the keyboard focus is here...
root	Workspace (root window)
window, frame, border, title, or application	Client window (includes frame, title, border, and application window)
icon	Icon

Note that if **f.post_wmenu** or **f.menu** is bound to a key, MWM automatically uses the same key for removing the menu from the screen after it has been popped up.

To illustrate key bindings, suppose Pat, the user who created his own "Graphics Projects" menu, kept pressing the **<Shift> <Esc>** sequence and accidentally displaying the window menu. He might decide that he is better off without that particular keyboard binding. To disable it, he must delete (or comment out) the proper line in his **.mwmrc** file. The "DefaultKeyBindings" section of his **.mwmrc** file might then look like the following:

```
Keys      DefaultKeyBindings
{
#Shift<Key>Escape  icon|window   f.post_wmenu
Meta<Key>Tab       window        f.next_key
}
```

Pat has chosen simply to comment out the line by placing a # (comment) character in the left margin of the line.

14.6.3 Making a New Keyboard Binding Set

With keyboard bindings, as with button bindings, you have the option of creating a whole new binding set. To do so, you can use the DefaultKeyBindings section of your **.mwmrc** as a model. After you have created the new keyboard binding set, use the **keyBindings** resource to explain your modification to the window manager.

keyBindings. This resource is used to specify a key binding set. The default is DefaultKeyBindings. The syntax of the **.Xdefaults** line is as follows:

Mwm*keyBindings: *NewKeyboardBindingSetName*

This line directs the window manager to get its keyboard binding information from the *NewKeyboardBindingSetName* section of the **.mwmrc** file. You can have the window manager look in any file if you specify the path and filename with the **Mwm*configFile:** resource in the **.Xdefaults** file.

Chapter 15

Working with Icons

This chapter presents information users need to customize the appearance and behavior of icons. Icons provide the user with a handy way to straighten up a cluttered workspace, and are a great tool for efficient multiprocessing. Information is also presented on configuring the MWM icon box. As a programmer, being aware of this information can help you avoid user-caused problems in your application.

This chapter discusses the following topics:

- Studying icon anatomy
- Manipulating icons
- Controlling icon appearance and behavior
- Coloring icons
- Using the icon box to hold icons

15.1 Studying Icon Anatomy

As shown in the following figure, icons consist of two parts: a text label and a graphic image. Like the other objects appearing on the workspace, the user can configure the appearance of all icons in **.Xdefaults**.

Figure 15-1. Icons Have Two Parts

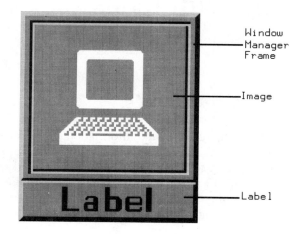

15.1.1 The Image

An icon image (a bitmap) is the actual graphic illustration in the icon. An image can come from any one of the following three sources:

Client A client can use the WM_HINTS window property to specify either an icon window or a bitmap for the window manager to use as the icon image.

User The user can specify an icon image using the **Mwm*iconImage** or **Mwm*default*iconImage** resources.

Default The window manager uses its own built-in default icon image if an image is not specified elsewhere.

bitmapDirectory. You can also, using the **bitmapDirectory** resource, direct the window manager to search a specified directory for bitmaps. The **bitmapDirectory** resource causes the window manager to search the specified directory whenever a bitmap is named with no complete path. The default value for **bitmapDirectory** is **/usr/include/X11/bitmaps**.

iconImage. The **iconImage** resource tells the window manager to use a particular bitmap for an icon image. The value that follows this resource is the path to the bitmap file. Note that, if specified, this resource overrides any client-specified image.

useClientIcon. The **useClientIcon** resource determines whether a client-supplied icon image takes precedence over a user-supplied image. If the value is True, then a client-supplied icon image takes precedence over a user-supplied icon image. The default value is False, making the user-supplied icon image have higher precedence than the client-supplied icon image.

15.1.2 The Label

The icon **label** is a rectangle, located beneath the icon image, containing the name of the icon. A label is usually supplied by the client (via the WM_ICON_NAME window property), but some clients, for example **xclock**, provide a command-line option enabling you to write in your own label.

Icon labels are truncated on the right to the width of the icon image when the icon is not active. When the icon becomes active, the full text of the label appears.

15.2 Manipulating Icons

Icons can be manipulated like windows: by positioning the pointer on the icon and clicking, double-clicking, or dragging a mouse button. The keyboard can also be used to manipulate icons. The following table describes the operations that can be performed on icons with a mouse.

Table 15-1. Manipulating Icons with a Mouse

To do this...	Position the pointer on the icon and...	Result
Turn an icon into a window.	Double-click the mouse Select button.	Restores the window to its former size and location.
Move an icon around on the root window.	Press the mouse Select button and drag.	Moves a wire frame with the pointer, showing where the icon is be moved.
Move keyboard input focus.	Press the mouse Select button.	Makes the icon the focus of input.
Move an icon to the top of the window stack.	Press the mouse Select button on an icon that has keyboard input focus.	Moves a partially concealed icon to the top of the window stack.
Display the icon's window menu.	Click the mouse Select button; or, press **<Shift><ESC>** or **<Alt><Space>**.	The window menu for an icon is like the window menu of its associated window. No window is active while an icon has the keyboard focus.

The following table describes the operations that can be performed on icons with the keyboard. Keyboard actions apply only to active icons.

Table 15-2. Manipulating Icons with the Keyboard

To do this...	Use this key action...
Display or remove icon menu.	<Shift> <ESC> or <Alt> <Space>
When the menu is posted...	**Use this key action...**
Move the cursor to different items	Arrow keys
Accept the highlighted menu item	<Select>
Remove the icon menu	<ESC>

The icon's window menu contains the same items as the window menu of the associated client window. Menu items that do not apply to icons are grayed out (for example, Minimize and Size).

The following figure shows the appearance of an icon with the input focus.

Figure 15-2. Appearance of an Icon with the Input Focus

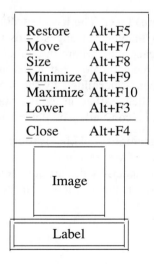

iconClick. The **iconClick** resource controls the posting of the window menu when the mouse Select button is clicked with the pointer on the icon. The value of True causes the icon window menu to be posted and remain posted. The value of False results in the icon window menu not remaining posted.

lowerOnIconify. The **lowerOnIconify** resource can be used to control the stacking order of icons. The default value of True places a window's icon on the bottom of the window stack when the window is minimized (iconified). A value of False places the icon in the stacking order at the same place as its associated window.

15.2.1 Controlling Icon Placement

By default, the window manager places icons in the lower left corner of the workspace. Successive icons are placed in a row proceeding toward the right. Icons are prevented from overlapping. An icon is placed in the position it last occupied if no icon is already there. If that place is taken, the icon is placed at the next free location.

The following three resources enable the user to control the placement of icons:

iconAutoPlace. The **iconAutoPlace** resource indicates whether the window manager arranges icons in a particular area of the screen or places each icon where the window was when it was iconified. The value True indicates that icons are arranged in a particular area of the screen, determined by the **iconPlacement** resource. The value False indicates that an icon is placed at the location of the window when it is iconified. The default is True.

iconPlacement. This resource is available only when the **iconAutoPlace** resource has the value True. The **iconPlacement** resource specifies the arrangement scheme the window manager is to use when placing icons on the workspace. The default value is "left bottom."

The following table lists options for **iconPlacement** values.

Table 15-3. Options for iconPlacement Values

If you want this icon placement...	Choose this scheme...
From left to right across the top of the screen, new rows below.	left top
From right to left across the top of the screen, new rows below.	right top
From left to right across the bottom of the screen, new rows above.	left bottom
From right to left across the bottom of the screen, new rows above.	right bottom
From bottom to top along the left of the screen, new columns to right.	bottom left
From bottom to top along the right of the screen, new columns to left.	bottom right
From top to bottom along the left of the screen, new columns to right.	top left
From top to bottom along the right of the screen, new columns to left.	top right

iconPlacementMargin. The **iconPlacementMargin** resource specifies the distance between the screen edge and icons. The unit of measurement is pixels. The default value is equal to the default space between icons.

15.2.2 The Syntax for Icon Placement Resources

The resources that place icons share a common syntax:

Mwm*resource: *value*

For example, if the user wants automatic placement of icons starting at the top of the screen and proceeding down the right side, the following lines must be added in the user's **.Xdefaults** file:

```
Mwm*iconPlacement:    top right

Mwm*iconAutoPlace:    True
```

15.3 Controlling Icon Appearance and Behavior

MWM offers a number of resources to control the appearance and behavior of icons. Among these are resources that enable the user to select icon decoration, control icon size, and create new icon pixmaps.

15.3.1 Selecting Icon Decoration

iconDecoration. The **iconDecoration** resource indicates which parts of an icon are to be displayed. The following table shows the possible values for **iconDecoration** and the results.

Table 15-4. The Values for Controlling Icon Appearance

For an icon that looks like this...	Use this value...
Just the label	label
Just the image	image
Both label and image	label image (default value when icon box is used.)
The label of an active icon is not truncated	activelabel label image (default value when icon box is not used.)

15.3.2 Sizing Icons

Each icon image has a maximum and minimum size. MWM has maximum and minimum default sizes as well as maximum and minimum allowable sizes. The following two resources control icon image size:

iconImageMaximum. The **iconImageMaximum** resource limits the maximum size of an icon image. The largest value allowed is 128x128 pixels. The default value is 50x50 pixels.

iconImageMinimum. The **iconImageMinimum** resource limits the minimum size of an icon image. The smallest value allowed is 16x16 pixels. The default value is 16x16 pixels.

When calculating limits for image size, remember that the width of an icon is the image width plus the icon frame plus the space between icons. The height of an icon is the image height plus the icon frame plus the space between icons. The amount of icon decoration and the size of font used in the icon label also affects the height of the icon.

How the window manager treats an icon depends on the size of the image in relation to the maximum and minimum sizes, as shown in the following table.

Table 15-5. Icon Size Affects Treatment of Icon

If an icon image is...	The window manager...
Smaller than the minimum size	Acts as if no image were specified
Within maximum and minimum limits	Centers the image within the maximum area
Larger than the maximum size	Clips the right side and bottom of the image to fit the maximum size

15.3.3 The Syntax for Resources that Control Icon Appearance

The resources that control icon appearance have the following syntax:

Mwm*resource*:   *value*

For example, the label part of the icon can be eliminated using the **iconDecoration** resource:

Mwm*iconDecoration: image

The **iconImage** resource has three syntaxes available:

1. To use the image for all classes of clients, the syntax is

    Mwm*iconImage: *path/bitmap*

2. To use the image for a specific class of clients, or a specific client, the syntax is

    Mwm*clientclass***iconImage:** *path/bitmap*

    Mwm*clientname***iconImage:** *path/bitmap*

3. To use the image as the default image whenever the client class is unknown, the syntax is

    Mwm*defaults*iconImage: *path/bitmap*

For example, users who want to use a personal **kaleidoscope** bitmap for a terminal emulator window (say, **mterm**) and see a complete label whenever any icon is active, must add the following lines in their **.Xdefaults** file:

```
Mwm*mterm*iconImage:    /users/username/Bitmaps/kaleid.bits

Mwm*iconDecoration:     label activelabel image
```

15.4 Coloring Icons

Icon window frame elements are colored with the same resources as normalized window frame elements. (These resources are discussed in Chapter 13.) The following table lists the color resources.

Table 15-6. MWM Color Resources and What They Color

Inactive Window and Icon Resources	Active Window and Icon Resources	Area Colored
foreground	activeForeground	Foreground areas
background	activeBackground	Background areas
topShadowColor	activeTopShadowColor	Top and left 3D bevels
bottomShadowColor	activeBottomShadowColor	Bottom and right 3D bevels

The image part of an icon can be displayed with client specific colors. The following table lists icon image elements and the resources that control their color.

Table 15-7. Coloring Icon Images with MWM Resources

To color this...	Use this resource...
Icon image background	iconImageBackground
Left and upper 3D bevels	iconImageTopShadowColor
Right and lower three-dimensional bevels	iconImageBottomShadowColor
Icon image foreground	iconImageForeground

Two pixmap resources are available for use in shading icon images:

iconImageTopShadowPixmap. The default value for **iconImageTopShadowPixmap** is the icon top shadow pixmap (specified by **Mwm*icon*topShadowPixmap**).

iconImageBottomShadowPixmap.. The default value for **iconImageBottomShadowPixmap** is the icon bottom shadow pixmap (specified by **Mwm*icon*bottomShadowPixmap**).

Procedures for making pixmaps for frame elements are described in Section 13.9.

15.4.1 The Syntax for Icon Coloring Resources

The resources that color icons can have any of three different syntaxes.

1. To color all clients regardless of class, the syntax is

   Mwm*icon*resource*:   *color*

   For example, a proper use of this syntax is to ensure that all icon backgrounds were the same color, a good thing for consistency:

   Mwm*icon*background: Cadet Blue

2. To color specific classes of clients, the syntax is

   Mwm*icon*clientclass or clientname*resource*:   *color*

   The colors specified with this resource take precedence over any other specification for this resource for this class of clients.

3. To color any client with an unknown class, the syntax is

   Mwm*icon*default*resource: *color*

15.5 Using the Icon Box to Hold Icons

The user may want to use an icon box to contain icons instead of having standalone icons on the workspace. An icon box is an MWM window and frame that can reduce the amount of "real estate" taken up by client icons. The icon box is a scrollable window that displays icons in a grid (rows and columns).

useIconBox. The **useIconBox** resource enables the icon box window manager facility. The value of True places icons in an icon box. The default value of False places icons on the root window.

iconBoxName. The **iconBoxName** resource specifies the name that is used to look up icon box resources. The default name is iconbox.

iconBoxTitle. The **iconBoxTitle** resource specifies the name that is used in the title area of the icon box frame. The default name is Icons.

15.5.1 Controlling Icon Box Appearance and Behavior

The icon box is displayed in a standard window management client frame. Client-specific resources for the icon box can be specified using "iconbox" as the client name.

Mwm*iconbox*resource: value*

Resources that may be used with the icon box are: **clientDecoration**; all window resources dealing with color, shadow, and matte; and **windowMenu**.

iconBoxGeometry. The **iconBoxGeometry** resource is used to set the initial size and placement of the icon box. If the **iconBoxGeometry** resource is set, the largest dimension of the size determines if the icons are placed in a row or a column. The default policy is to place icons in rows going from left to right, top to bottom.

The value of the resource is a standard window geometry string with the following syntax:

[=][*<width>*x*<height>*][{+-}*<xoffset>*{+-}*<yoffset>*]

If the width and height are not provided, the **iconPlacement** policy is used to determine the initial size and orientation (horizontal and vertical).

The actual size of the icon box window depends on the **iconImageMaximum** (size) and **iconDecoration** resources. The default value for size is (6 * iconWidth + padding) wide by (1 * iconHeight + padding) high. The default location (value) is +0-0.

15.5.1.1 The Icon Box Window Menu

The window menu for the icon box differs from the standard window menu in that it does not contain the "Close" selection. In its place is the "PackIcons" selection, as shown in the following figure.

Figure 15-3. The System Menu for the Icon Box

Restore	Alt+F5
Move	Alt+F7
Size	Alt+F8
Minimize	Alt+F9
Maximize	Alt+F10
Lower	Alt+F3
PackIcons	Alt+Shift+F7

f.pack_icons The function **f.pack_icons** shifts icons to fill empty spaces in the icon placement grid so that the icons appear in neat, complete rows. Icons in the icon box do not overlap.

If there are icons that cannot be displayed in the visible part of the icon box, the user can scroll to see the icons. The sliders within the scroll bars show the extent of the icon grid that is visible.

The icon box can be minimized (iconified) just like any other window. If the icon box is minimized, it is placed into the icon grid on the workspace.

15.5.2 Controlling Icons in the Icon Box

Every client window that can be iconified has an icon in the icon box, even when the window is in the normal state. The icon for a client is put into the icon box when the client becomes managed by the window manager and is removed from the icon box when the client withdraws from being managed.

fadeNormalIcon. Icons for windows in the normal state are visually distinct from icons for windows that are iconified. Icons for windows that are iconified look like standalone icons. Icons for windows that are in the normal state appear flat and are optionally grayedout. The value of True for the **fadeNormalIcon** resource grays out normalized windows. The default value is False.

The text and image attributes of icons in icon boxes are determined in the same way as for standalone icons, using the **iconDecoration** resource.

A standard "control" location cursor is used to indicate the particular icon in the icon box to which keyboard actions apply. The location cursor is a rectangle outline that surrounds the icon.

Icons contained in the icon box can be manipulated with the mouse and from the keyboard. Mouse button actions apply whenever the pointer is on any part of the icon. The following table describes the mouse button actions for controlling icons.

Table 15-8. Controlling Icons in the Icon Box with a Mouse

Button Action	Function Description
Click the mouse Select button	Selects the icon
Double-click mouse Select button with pointer on an icon of an iconified window	Normalizes the iconified window
Double-click mouse Select button with pointer on an icon of a normalized window	Raises the normalized window to the top of the stack

An icon is manipulated from the keyboard by making the icon box the active window and then using the arrow keys to traverse the icons in the icon box. Pressing <**Enter**> does the default action for the selected icon: for an icon of a normalized window, the window is raised; for an icon of an iconified window, the window is normalized.

Pressing <**Tab**> moves the keyboard input focus around the box in this order: icons, scroll bars, icons. Pressing the <**Shift**> <**Tab**> sequence moves the focus in the opposite direction.

Chapter 16

Quick Reference Tables

The reference tables in this chapter provide a quick way to look up information on resources and functions. All of this information is covered in more detail in Chapters 13, 14, and 15. The chapter begins with a review of the syntax patterns used with MWM resources.

16.1 Syntax for Resources

There are four syntax patterns used with OSF/Motif resources:

1. Resources controlling the general appearance of elements use this syntax:

   Mwm*resource: value*

2. Resources controlling elements of particular objects use this syntax:

   Mwm*[menu | icon | client | feedback]* *resource: value*

   To specifically configure the title area of a client window frame, use this syntax:

   Mwm*client*title*resource: value*

   To specifically configure the appearance of a menu, use this syntax:

   Mwm*menu*menuname*resource: value*

3. Resources to be used for specific clients use this syntax:

   Mwm*[clientclass / clientname]*resource: value*

4. Resources controlling appearance and behavior in default situations use this syntax:

   Mwm*defaults*resource: value*

16.2 Resource Tables

In the resource tables that follow, the number(s) in the syntax column refer to the preceding syntax patterns.

The following tables are presented:

- Coloring (Table 16-1)
- Shading (Table 16-2)
- Configuring Window Decorations (Table 16-3)
- Configuring Focus Policies (Table 16-4)
- Controlling Windows (Table 16-5)
- Controlling Window Size and Position (Table 16-6)
- Configuring Icons (Table 16-7)
- Configuring the Icon Box (Table 16-8)
- Valid Window Manager Functions (Table 16-9)

16.2.1 Coloring Windows, Icons, Menus, and Mattes

Resources used to color elements of active and inactive frames, mattes, and icon images are listed in the following table. Coloring is discussed in Chapter 13 (windows, icons, menus, and mattes) and Chapter 15 (icon images).

Table 16-1. Coloring

Name	Class	Value Type	Default	Syntax
Windows, Icons, and Menus				
activeBackground	Background	color	varies*	1,2
activeBottomShadowColor	Foreground	color	varies*	1,2
activeForeground	Foreground	color	varies*	1,2
activeTopShadowColor	Background	color	varies*	1,2
background	Background	color	varies*	1,2
bottomShadowColor	Foreground	color	varies*	1,2
foreground	Foreground	color	varies*	1,2
topShadowColor	Background	color	varies*	1,2
Mattes				
matteBackground	Background	color	background	1,3,4
matteBottomShadowColor	Foreground	color	bottom shadow color	1,3,4
matteForeground	Foreground	color	foreground	1,3,4
matteTopShadowColor	Background	color	top shadow color	1,3,4
matteWidth	MatteWidth	pixels	0	1,3,4
Icon Images				
iconImageBackground	Background	color	icon background	1,3,4
iconImageBottom\ ShadowColor	Foreground	color	icon bottom shadow	1,3,4
iconImageForeground	Foreground	color	varies	1,3,4
iconImageTopShadowColor	Background	color	icon top shadow color	1,3,4

*The default is chosen based on the visual type of the screen.

16.2.2 Shading

Resources used to shade elements of windows, icons, menus, mattes, and icon images are presented in the following table. Shading resources are most valuable when used with a monochrome display. In addition, the **cleanText** resource is available to reduce interference between shading used in the title bar and the title. Shading is discussed in Chapter 13 (windows, icons, menus, and mattes) and Chapter 15 (icon images).

Table 16-2. Shading

Name	Class	Value Type	Default	Syntax
Windows, Icons, and Menus				
activeBackground\ Pixmap	BackgroundPixmap	string	varies*	1,2
activeBottom\ ShadowPixmap	BottomShadowPixmap	string	varies*	1,2
activeTop\ ShadowPixmap	TopShadowPixmap	string	varies*	1,2
backgroundPixmap	BackgroundPixmap	string	varies*	1,2
bottomShadow\ Pixmap	BottomShadowPixmap	string	varies*	1,2
topShadowPixmap	TopShadowPixmap	string	varies*	1,2
cleanText	CleanText	T/F	T	1
Mattes				
matteBottom\ ShadowPixmap	BottomShadowPixmap	color	bottom shadow pixmap	1,3,4
matteTop\ ShadowPixmap	TopShadowPixmap	color	top shadow pixmap	1,3,4
Icon Images				
iconImageBottom\ ShadowPixmap	BottomShadowPixmap	color	icon bottom shadow pixmap	1,3,4
iconImageTop\ ShadowPixmap	TopShadowPixmap	color	icon top shadow pixmap	1,3,4

*The default is chosen based on the visual type of the screen.

16.2.3 Window Decorations

Resources used to declare applicable functions and decoration elements for a client are presented in the following table. (Window Decoration is discussed in Chapter 13.)

Table 16-3. Configuring Window Decorations

Name	Class	Value Type	Default	Syntax
clientDecoration	ClientDecoration	string	all	1,3,4
clientFunctions	ClientFunctions	string	all	1,3,4
transientDecoration	TransientDecoration	string	menu title resizeh	1
transientFunctions	TransientFunctions	string	-minimize -maximize	1

16.2.4 Focus Policies

Resources used to control colormap and keyboard input focus policies are presented in the following table. (Focus policies are discussed in Chapter 13.)

Table 16-4. Configuring Focus Policies

Name	Class	Value Type	Default	Syntax
autoKeyFocus	AutoKeyFocus	T/F	T	1
colormapFocusPolicy	ColormapFocusPolicy	string	keyboard	1
deiconifyKeyFocus	DeiconifyKeyFocus	T/F	T	1
enforceKeyFocus	EnforceKeyFocus	T/F	T	1
focusAutoRaise	FocusAutoRaise	T/F	varies*	1,3,4
keyboardFocusPolicy	KeyboardFocusPolicy	string	explicit	1
passButtons	PassButtons	T/F	F	1
passSelectButton	PassSelectButton	T/F	T	1
startupKeyFocus	StartupKeyFocus	T/F	T	1

*The default depends on the value of keyboardFocusPolicy.

16.2.5 Controlling Windows

Resources used to control miscellaneous aspects of window management and behavior are presented in the following table. (These resources are discussed in the chapters indicated after the subheadings in the table.)

Table 16-5. Controlling Windows

Name	Class	Value Type	Default	Syntax
Bindings (Chapter 14)				
buttonBindings	ButtonBindings	string	"DefaultButton\ Bindings"	1
keyBindings	KeyBindings	string	"DefaultKey\ Bindings"	1
Screen Management (Chapter 13)				
multiScreen screens	MultiScreen Screens	T/F string	F varies*	
Client Management (Chapter 13)				
quitTimeout	QuitTimeout	millisec.	1000	1
saveUnder	SaveUnder	T/F	F	1,2
Font (Chapter 13)				
fontList	FontList	string	display based	1,2
Mouse Timing (Chapter 14)				
doubleClickTime	DoubleClickTime	millisec.	500	1

Name	Class	Value Type	Default	Syntax
Resource Directories (Chapters 14 and 15)				
bitmapDirectory	BitmapDirectory	directory	/usr/include\ X11/bitmaps	1
configFile	ConfigFile	<file>	.mwmrc	1
Window Menus (Chapter 14)				
wMenuButton\ Click	WMenuButton\ Click	T/F	T	1
wMenuButton\ Click2	WMenuButton\ Click2	T/F	T	1
windowMenu	WindowMenu	string	"Default\ WindowMenu"	1,3,4

*The default depends on the number of screens available.

16.2.6 Controlling Window Size and Position

Resources used to control the size and position of windows are presented in the following table. (Window size and position are discussed in Chapter 13.)

Table 16-6. Controlling Window Size and Position

Name	Class	Value Type	Default	Syntax
Size Resources				
frameBorderWidth	FrameBorderWidth	pixels	5	1
limitResize	LimitResize	T/F	T	1
maximumClientSize	MaximumClientSize	wxh	fill the screen	1,3,4
maximumMaximum\ Size	MaximumMaximumSize	wxh	2X screen w&h	1
resizeBorderWidth	ResizeBorderWidth	pixels	10	1
resizeCursors	ResizeCursors	T/F	T	1
Position Resources				
clientAutoPlace	ClientAutoPlace	T/F	T	1
interactivePlacement	InteractivePlacement	T/F	F	1
moveThreshold	MoveThreshold	pixels	4	1
positionIsFrame	PositionIsFrame	T/F	T	1
positionOnScreen	PositionOnScreen	T/F	T	1
showFeedback	ShowFeedback	string	all	1
Other resources				
enableWarp	EnableWarp	T/F	T	1

16.2.7 Configuring Icons

Resources used to configure icons are presented in the following table. (Icons are discussed in Chapter 15.)

Table 16-7. Configuring Icons

Name	Class	Value Type	Default	Syntax
iconAutoPlace	IconAutoPlace	T/F	T	1
iconClick	IconClick	T/F	T	1
iconDecoration	IconDecoration	string	all*	1
iconImage	IconImage	pathname	varies†	1,3,4
iconImage\ Maximum	IconImageMaximum	wxh	50x50	1
iconImage\ Minimum	IconImageMinimum	wxh	16x16	1
iconPlacement	IconPlacement	string	left bottom	1
iconPlacement\ Margin	IconPlacementMargin	number	varies‡	1
lowerOnIconify	LowerOnIconify	T/F	T	1
useClientIcon	UseClientIcon	T/F	F	1,3,4

*MWM defaults are "label image" when an icon box is used and "activelabel label image" when an icon box is not used.

†The default value is determined by the client's WM_HINTS values and MWM defaults.

‡The default value is equal to the space between icons as they are placed on the screen.

16.2.8 Configuring the Icon Box

Resources used to configure the icon box are presented in the following table. (The icon box is discussed in Chapter 15.)

Table 16-8. Configuring the Icon Box

Name	Class	Value Type	Default	Syntax
fadeNormalIcon	FadeNormalIcon	T/F	F	1
iconBoxGeometry	IconBoxGeometry	string	6x1+0-0	1
iconBoxName	IconBoxName	string	iconbox	1
iconBoxTitle	IconBoxTitle	string	Icons	1
useIconBox	UseIconBox	T/F	F	1

16.3 MWM Functions

Window manager functions can be accessed with a mouse button binding, a keyboard binding, and/or a menu item. (Functions, menus, and bindings, including the contexts in which they can be used, are discussed in Chapter 14.)

The following table lists the valid functions for the OSF/Motif Window Manager. In the Contexts column, R stands for Root, I stands for Icon, and W stands for Window. In the Devices column, M stands for Mouse, K stands for Key, and ME stands for Menu.

Table 16-9. Valid Window Manager Functions

Functions		Contexts			Devices		
Name	**Description**	**R**	**I**	**W**	**MO**	**K**	**ME**
f.beep	Causes a beep to sound.	x	x	x	x	x	x
f.circle_down [icon | window]	Puts window on bottom of stack.	x	x	x	x	x	x
f.circle_up [icon | window]	Puts window on top of stack.	x	x	x	x	x	x
f.exec (or) ! command	Uses **/bin/sh** to execute a command.	x	x	x	x	x	x
f.focus_color	Sets colormap focus when colormap focus policy is explicit.	x	x	x	x	x	x
f.focus_key	Sets keyboard input focus when keyboard focus policy is explicit.	x	x	x	x	x	x

Functions		Contexts			Devices		
Name	**Description**	**R**	**I**	**W**	**MO**	**K**	**ME**
f.kill	Terminates a client.		x	x	x	x	x
f.lower [-*client*]	Lowers a window to bottom of stack.	x	x	x	x	x	x
f.maximize	Enlarges a window to its maximum size.		x	x	x	x	x
f.menu *menu_name*	Associates a menu with a selection or binding.	x	x	x	x	x	x
f.minimize	Changes a window into an icon.			x	x	x	x
f.move	Enables the interactive moving of a window.		x	x	x	x	x
f.next_cmap	Installs the next colormap in the window with the colormap focus.	x	x	x	x	x	x
f.next_key [icon | window | transient]	Sets keyboard focus to the next window/icon in the stack.	x	x	x	x	x	x
f.nop	No operation performed.	x	x	x	x	x	x
f.normalize	Displays a window in normal size.		x	x	x	x	x

Functions		Contexts			Devices		
Name	**Description**	**R**	**I**	**W**	**MO**	**K**	**ME**
f.normalize_and_raise	Displays a window in normal size and raises it to the top of the stack.		x	x	x	x	x
f.pack_icons	Tidies up icon rows on the root window or in the icon box.	x	x	x	x	x	x
f.pass_keys	Toggles between enabling and disabling the processing of key bindings.	x	x	x	x	x	x
f.post_wmenu	Posts the window menu.	x	x	x	x	x	
f.prev_cmap	Installs the previous colormap in the window with the colormap focus.	x	x	x	x	x	x
f.prev_key [icon | window | transient]	Sets keyboard focus to the previous window/icon in the stack.	x	x	x	x	x	x
f.quit_mwm	Terminates OSF/Motif Window Manager.	x			x	x	x
f.raise [-*client*]	Lifts a window to top of stack.	x	x	x	x	x	x

Functions		Contexts			Devices		
Name	**Description**	**R**	**I**	**W**	**MO**	**K**	**ME**
f.raise_lower	Raises a partially concealed window; lowers an unconcealed window.		x	x	x	x	x
f.refresh	Redraws all windows.	x	x	x	x	x	x
f.refresh_win	Redraws a client window.			x	x	x	x
f.resize	Enables interactive resizing of windows.			x	x	x	x
f.restart	Restarts the OSF/Motif Window Manager.	x			x	x	x
f.send_msg *message_name*	Sends a client message.		x	x	x	x	x
f.separator	Draws a line between menu selections.	x	x	x			x
f.set_behavior	Restarts MWM with default or custom behavior.	x	x	x	x	x	x
f.title	Inserts a title into a menu at the position specified.	x	x	x			x

Chapter 17

Introduction to the User Interface Language

This chapter describes the features and benefits of the User Interface Language (UIL) and provides an overview of UIL and the Motif Resource Manager (MRM).

17.1 Overview of UIL and MRM

UIL is a specification language for describing the initial state of a user interface for a Motif application. The specification describes the objects (for example, menus, form boxes, labels, and push buttons) used in the interface and specifies the functions to be called when the interface changes state as a result of user interaction.

To create a user interface with UIL and MRM, you perform the following:

1. Specify the user interface in a UIL module, which you store in a UIL specification file.

2. Compile the UIL specification file to generate a User Interface Definition (UID) file.

3. In your application program, use MRM run-time functions to open the UID file and access the interface definitions. MRM builds the necessary argument lists and calls widget creation functions in the Motif Toolkit.

Using UIL, you can specify the following:

- Objects (widgets and gadgets) that comprise your interface

- Arguments (attributes) of the widgets and gadgets you specify

- Callback functions for each object

- The widget tree for your application

- Literal values that can be fetched by the application at run time

The UIL compiler has built-in tables containing information about widgets. For every widget in the Motif Toolkit, the UIL compiler knows the widgets that are valid children of the widget, the widget arguments, and the valid callback reasons for the widget. The UIL compiler uses this information to check the validity of your interface specification at compilation time, to help you reduce run-time errors.

17.2 Benefits of Using UIL and MRM

Creating a user interface for a Motif application using UIL and MRM offers the following advantages:

- Easier coding

- Earlier error detection

- Separation of form and function

- Faster prototype development

- Interface customization

17.2.1 Easier Coding

You can specify an interface faster using UIL because you do not have to know the specific widget creation functions or the format of their arguments lists. You need to include only those object arguments you want to change. In general, you can specify these arguments in any order.

Because UIL is a specification language that describes the characteristics of an interface, it has no need for control flow. Therefore, you can define objects in your UIL specification in roughly the same order that the objects are arranged in the widget tree for your application interface. This makes it easier for a programmer reading the UIL specification to interpret the design of the interface.

At run time, when the interface objects are created, MRM performs some Motif Toolkit function calls for you as a convenience, simplifying your programming tasks.

17.2.2 Earlier Error Detection

The UIL compiler does type checking for you that is not available with the Motif or the X Toolkits, so that the interface you specify has fewer errors.

The UIL compiler issues diagnostics if you specify any of the following:

- The wrong type of value for an argument

- An argument to an object that is not supported by that object

- A reason for an object that the object does not support

- A child of an object that the object does not support

17.2.3 Separation of Form and Function

When you use UIL, you define your application interface in a separate UIL module rather than by directly calling Motif Toolkit creation functions in your application program. This lets you separate the form your interface takes from the functions provided by the application. By separating form and function, you can design multiple interfaces that share a common set of functions. This is useful, for example, in building an international application for people who speak different languages.

In general, you can freely change the appearance of the interface (for example, by repositioning widgets or changing their borders or colors) without recompiling the application program.

17.2.4 Faster Prototype Development

UIL helps you develop prototypes of user interfaces for an application. You can create a variety of interfaces in a fairly short time, and get an idea of the look of each interface before the functional routines are written.

The ability to specify the user interface separately lets designers work with end users at the same time programmers are coding the functions of the application. Because both groups can work more or less independently, the complete application can be delivered in less time than if the interface design were part of the application code.

17.2.5 Interface Customization

You can customize an interface by putting in place a hierarchy of UID files, called a UID hierarchy. At run time, MRM searches this file hierarchy in the sequence you specify to build the appropriate argument lists for the widget creation functions.

One use of this feature would be to provide an interface in several languages. The text on title bars, menus, and so on, can be displayed in the language of the end user without altering anything in the application. In this case, the files in the UID hierarchy represent alternative interfaces.

Another use of the UID hierarchy feature would be to isolate individual, department, and division customizations to an interface. In this case, you can think of the files in the UID hierarchy as superimposed, with the definitions in the first file listed in the array supplied to the MRM function **MrmOpenHierarchy** taking precedence.

17.3 Features of UIL

UIL offers the following features to increase productivity and the flexibility of your programs:

- Named values
- Compile-time expressions
- Identifiers
- Lists
- Support for compound strings
- Include files for useful constants

17.3.1 Named Values

Instead of directly specifying the values for widget and gadget attributes, you can use named values, which are similar to variables in a programming language. You give a literal value (such as an integer or string) a name and then use the name in place of the value specification. Using named values makes your UIL specification easier to understand and isolates changes.

In addition, you can use MRM functions to fetch named values from the UID file for use at run time.

17.3.2 Compile-Time Expressions

You can use expressions to specify values in UIL. A valid UIL expression can contain integers, strings, floating-point numbers, Boolean values, named values, and operators. Using expressions can make values more descriptive (for example, *bulletin_board_width*/2) and can help you avoid recomputing values (for example, if you needed to change the size or position of the bulletin board).

17.3.3 Identifiers

Identifiers provide a mechanism for referencing values in UIL that are provided by the application at run time. In the application program, you use an MRM function to associate a value with the identifier name. Unlike a named value, an identifier does not have an associated data type. You can use an identifier as an attribute value or callback procedure tag, regardless of the data type specified in the object or procedure declaration. Identifiers are useful for specifying position based on the type of terminal on which the interface will be displayed or for passing a data structure (as opposed to a constant) to a private callback function.

17.3.4 Lists

UIL allows you to create named lists of attributes, sibling widgets, and callback procedures that you can later refer to by name. This feature allows you to easily reuse common definitions by simply referencing these definitions by name.

17.3.5 Support for Compound Strings

Most Motif Toolkit widgets require strings used in the user interface (labels, menu items, and so on) to be compound strings. UIL fully supports the use of compound strings, including left-to-right and right-to-left writing direction and choice of fonts.

Chapter 18

UIL Language Syntax

This chapter and the next chapter provide reference information on UIL. This chapter describes syntax rules for low-level elements of the language. Chapter 19 describes syntax rules for building a UIL module using these low-level elements.

This chapter describes the syntax rules for the following:

- Character set
- Names
- Keywords
- Literals
- Value-generating functions
- The **any** data type
- Compile-time value expressions

UIL is a free-form language. This means that high-level constructs such as object and value declarations do not need to begin in any particular column and can span any number of lines. Low-level constructs such as keywords and punctuation characters can also begin in any column; however, except for string literals and comments, they cannot span lines.

The UIL compiler accepts input lines up to 132 characters in length.

18.1 Character Set

Use the character set described in the following table to construct elements of UIL.

Table 18-1. UIL Legal Character Set

Element	Characters
Letters	ABCDEFGHIJKLMNOPQRSTUVWXYZ abcdefghijklmnopqrstuvwxyz
Digits	0123456789
Formatting and punctuation characters	Space, tab, form-feed, _ ' ( ) * , + - . / ; : = ! $ { }
Other characters	Remaining 8-bit character codes in the range 160 to 255 decimal, & [ ] | < > % " # ? @ ˜ ' ˆ

Alphabetic, numeric, and punctuation and formatting characters are used to build the elements of UIL. Other characters are valid only in comments and string literals.

Control characters, except for the form-feed character, are not permitted in a UIL module. You must use escape sequences (described in Section 18.4.1) to construct a string literal containing a control character.

18.1.1 Punctuation Characters

You use the character sequences shown in the following table to punctuate a UIL module. These characters cannot be used in UIL names.

Table 18-2. Punctuation Characters

(	Left parenthesis	)	Right parenthesis
{	Left brace	}	Right brace
\	Backslash	!	Exclamation mark
/*	Slash asterisk	*/	Asterisk slash
;	Semicolon	:	Colon
'	Apostrophe	,	Comma
=	Equal sign		

Punctuation in a UIL module resembles that used in C programs. For example, statements end in a semicolon, braces are used to delimit definitions, and comments can be delimited by the /* (slash and asterisk) and */ (asterisk and slash) character sequences.

Spaces, tabs, and comments are special elements in the language. They are a means of delimiting other elements, such as two names. One or more of these elements can appear before or after any other element in the language. However, spaces, tabs, and comments that appear in string literals are treated as character sequences rather than delimiters.

Comments can take one of two forms, as follows:

- The comment is introduced with the sequence /* followed by the text of the comment and terminated with the sequence */. This form of comment can span multiple source lines.

- The comment is introduced with an ! (exclamation point), followed by the text of the comment and terminated by the end of the source line.

Neither form of comment can be nested.

The form-feed character is a control character and therefore cannot appear directly in a UIL specification file. You must use the escape sequence \12\ instead (see Section 18.4.1 for information on specifying other escape sequences in string literals). There is one exception to this rule: a form-feed can appear in column 1 of a source line due to the common practice of some editors separating parts of a program with a form-feed. The form-feed causes a page break in the module listing.

18.2 Names

Each entity in the UIL language, such as a value, procedure, or object, can be identified by a name. This name can also be used to reference the entity elsewhere in the UIL module.

Names can consist of any of the characters A to Z, a to z, 0 to 9, $ (dollar sign), and _ (underscore). Names cannot begin with a digit (0 to 9). The maximum length of a name is 31 characters.

UIL gives you a choice of either case-sensitive or case-insensitive names through a clause in the MODULE header (described in Section 19.1.2). For example, if names are case sensitive, the names "sample" and "Sample" are distinct from each other. If names are case insensitive, these names are treated as the same name and can be used interchangeably. By default, UIL assumes names are case sensitive.

In case-insensitive mode, the compiler outputs all names in the UID file in uppercase form. In case-sensitive mode, names appear in the UIL file exactly as they appear in the source.

You must define any referenced name exactly once in a UIL module; if you define the same name more than once or omit a definition, the UIL compiler issues an error at compile time.

18.3 Keywords

Keywords are names that have special meaning in UIL. They are of two types, reserved and nonreserved. You cannot use a reserved keyword to name an entity. Nonreserved keywords can be used as names.

If you specify case-insensitive mode, you can type UIL keywords in uppercase, lowercase, or mixed case. If you specify case-sensitive mode, you must type UIL keywords in lowercase.

You cannot abbreviate keywords by truncating characters from the end.

The following table lists the UIL reserved keywords.

Table 18-3. Reserved Keywords

Keyword	Description
ARGUMENTS	Identifies an arguments list
CALLBACKS	Identifies a callbacks list
CONTROLS	Identifies a controls list
END	Signifies the end of the module
EXPORTED	Specifies that this object or value can be referenced by other UIL modules
FALSE	Represents the Boolean value zero; synonym for Off
GADGET	For objects having a widget and a gadget variant, specifies this object as the gadget variant
IDENTIFIER	Indicates an identifier declaration
INCLUDE	Used with the nonreserved keyword FILE to specify an include file
LIST	Identifies a list declaration
MODULE	Signifies the start of a UIL module

Keyword	Description
OFF	Represents the Boolean value zero; synonym for FALSE
ON	Represents the Boolean value 1; synonym for TRUE
OBJECT	Identifies an object declaration
PRIVATE	Specifies that this object or value cannot be referenced by other UIL modules
PROCEDURE	Identifies a procedure declaration
PROCEDURES	Identifies a procedures list
TRUE	Represents the Boolean value 1; synonym for On
VALUE	Identifies a value (literal) declaration
WIDGET	For objects having a widget and a gadget variant, specifies this object as the widget variant

Keywords listed in Table 18-4 are nonreserved keywords, which you can use as names without generating an error. However, if you use any keyword as a name, you cannot use the UIL-supplied usage of that keyword. For example, if you use the name of an argument (such as **XmNx**) as the name of a value, you cannot specify the **XmNx** argument in any object definitions.

Table 18-4. Nonreserved Keywords

Keyword	Description
Built-in argument names (for example: XmNx, XmNheight)	Identifies an object argument (widget-specific attribute)
Built-in reason names (for example: XmNactivateCallback, XmNhelpCallback)	Identifies a callback reason
Character set names (for example: ISO_LATIN1, ISO_HEBREW_LR)	Identifies a character set and its (implicit) writing direction
Constant value names (for example: XmMENU_OPTION, XmBROWSE_SELECT)	Identifies a constant value defined in the Motif toolkit
Object types (for example: XmPushButton, XmBulletinBoard)	Identifies a Motif Toolkit interface object
ANY	Suppresses data type checking
ARGUMENT	Identifies the built-in ARGUMENT function
ASCIZ_STRING_TABLE	Specifies a value as the UIL data type **asciz_table**
ASCIZ_TABLE	Specifies a value as the UIL data type **asciz_table**
BACKGROUND	In a color table, specifies monochrome mapping to the background color
BOOLEAN	Specifies a literal as the UIL data type **boolean**
CASE_INSENSITIVE	Used with the nonreserved keyword NAMES to specify that names and keywords in the module are case insensitive
CASE_SENSITIVE	Used with the nonreserved keyword NAMES to specify that names and keywords in the module are case sensitive

Keyword	Description
CHARACTER_SET	Identifies the default character-set clause; identifies the built-in CHARACTER_SET function
COLOR	Specifies a value as the UIL data type **color**
COLOR_TABLE	Specifies a value as the UIL data type **color_table**
COMPOUND_STRING	Specifies a value as the UIL data type **compound_string**; identifies the built-in COMPOUND_STRING data conversion function
COMPOUND_STRING_TABLE	Specifies a value as the UIL data type **string_table**
FILE	Used with the reserved keyword INCLUDE to specify an include file
FLOAT	Specifies a literal as the UIL data type **float**; identifies the FLOAT data conversion function
FONT	Specifies a value as the UIL data type **font**
FONT_TABLE	Specifies a value as the UIL data type **font_table**
FOREGROUND	In a color table, specifies monochrome mapping to the foreground color
ICON	Specifies a value as the UIL data type **pixmap**; identifies the built-in ICON function
IMPORTED	Specifies that this literal takes its value from a corresponding literal in another UIL module
INTEGER	Specifies a literal as the UIL data type **integer**; identifies the INTEGER data conversion function
INTEGER_TABLE	Specifies a value as the UIL data type **integer_table**
KEYSYM	Specifies a literal as the UIL data type **keysym**
MANAGED	Specifies that a child is managed by its parent at run time

Keyword	Description
NAMES	Identifies the case sensitivity clause
OBJECTS	Identifies the default object-variant clause
REASON	Identifies the built-in REASON function
RGB	Specifies a color using RGB values
RIGHT_TO_LEFT	Specifies the writing direction in the COMPOUND_STRING function
SINGLE_FLOAT	Specifies a literal as the UIL data type **single_float**
STRING	Specifies a literal as the UIL data type **string**
STRING_TABLE	Specifies a value as the UIL data type **string_table**
TRANSLATION_TABLE	Specifies a value as the UIL data type **translation_table**
UNMANAGED	Specifies that a child is unmanaged by its parent at run time
USER_DEFINED	Specifies that the object is a user-defined type
VERSION	Identifies the version clause
XBITMAPFILE	Specifies a value as the UIL data type **pixmap**; identifies the XBITMAPFILE function

In this chapter, all examples assume case-insensitive mode. Keywords are shown in uppercase to distinguish them from user-specified names, which are shown in lowercase; however, this use of uppercase is not required in case-insensitive mode. In the following example, ARGUMENTS is a keyword and *circle-radius* is a user-specified value. In your UIL module, you could type the keyword ARGUMENTS in lowercase, uppercase, or mixed-case as long as you specified that names are case insensitive. If you specify that names are case sensitive, you must enter the keyword in lowercase.

```
        .
        .
        .
{ ARGUMENTS
    { circle_radius = 1000 };
        .
        .
        .
        .
};
```

18.4 Literals

Literals are one means of specifying a value. UIL provides literals for several of the value types it supports. Some of the value types are not supported as literals (for example, pixmaps and string tables). You can specify values for these types by using functions provided by UIL (discussed in Section 18.5). Literal types directly supported by UIL are as follows:

- String

- Integer

- Boolean

- Floating-point

You can designate UIL values as exported, imported, or private. An exported object or value can be referenced in another UIL module that uses the same name for the object or value and indicates that the object or value is to be imported. By default, top-level objects are exported, and all other objects and values are private and are not accessible by other UIL modules. Section 19.2 explains the scope of UIL objects and values in more detail.

18.4.1 String Literals

A string literal is a sequence of zero or more 8-bit or 16-bit characters or a combination delimited by ' (single quotation marks) or " (double quotation marks). String literals can be no more than 2000 characters long.

A single-quoted string literal can span multiple source lines. To continue a single-quoted string literal, terminate the continued line with a \ (backslash). The literal continues with the first character on the next line.

Double-quoted string literals cannot span multiple source lines. (Because double-quoted strings can contain escape sequences and other special characters, you cannot use the backslash character to designate continuation of the string.) To build a string value that must span multiple source lines, use the concatenation operator. See Section 18.4.2 for a description of how to concatenate strings.

The syntax of a string literal is one of the following:

'[*char...*]'

[#*char-set*]"[*char...*]"

Both string forms associate a character set with a string value. UIL uses the following rules to determine the character set and storage format for string literals:

- A string declared as *'string'* is equivalent to #*cur_charset*"*string*", where *cur_charset* will be the codeset portion of the value of the LANG environment if it is set or the value of **XmFALLBACK_CHARSET** if **LANG** is not set or has no codeset component. By default **XmFALLBACK_CHARSET** is ISO8859-1 (equivalent to ISO_LATIN1), but vendors may define a different default. See Section 20.2 for more information.

- A string declared as "*string*" is equivalent to #*char-set*"*string*" if you specified *char-set* as the default character set for the module. Otherwise, "*string*" is equivalent to #*cur_charset*"*string*", where *cur_charset* is interpreted as described above.

18–11

- A string of the form *"string"* or #*char-set"string"* is stored as a null-terminated string.

Table 18-5 gives examples of valid and invalid string literal syntax. Note that the COMPOUND_STRING function (described in Section 18.5.9) forces the UIL compiler to generate a compound string.

Table 18-5. Examples of String Literal Syntax

Form	Storage Format
'*string*'	Null-terminated string. Character set is *cur_charset* (see Section 20.2).
#*char-set*'*string*'	Invalid syntax. Does not compile.
COMPOUND_STRING('*string*')	Compound string. Character set is *cur_charset* (see Section 20.2).
"*string*"	Null-terminated string. If specified, the string has the default character set for the module. Otherwise, the character set is *cur_charset* (see Section 20.2).
#ISO_GREEK"*string*"	Null-terminated string. Character set is ISO_GREEK.
COMPOUND_STRING("*string*")	Compound string. If specified, the string has the default character set for the module. Otherwise, the character set is *cur_charset* (see Section 20.2).
COMPOUND_STRING (#ISO_ARABIC"*string*")	Compound string. Character set is ISO_ARABIC.

Form	Storage Format
'string'&*"string"*	If the character sets and writing directions of the operands match, the resulting string is null-terminated; otherwise, the result is a multiple-segment compound string. The string has the character set or sets specified for the individual segments.
"string"&#ISO_HEBREW*"string"*	If the implicit character set and writing direction for the left operand matches the explicit character set (ISO_HEBREW) and writing direction (right to left) for the right operand, the resulting string is a null-terminated string; otherwise, the result is a multiple-segment compound string.

String literals can contain characters with the eighth (high-order) bit set. You cannot type control characters (00..1F, 7F, and 80..9F) directly in a single-quoted string literal. However, you can represent these characters with escape sequences. The characters listed in Table 18-6 cannot be directly entered in a UIL module. You must use the indicated escape sequence to enter these characters in a string literal.

Table 18-6. Escape Sequences

Escape Sequence	Meaning
\b	Backspace
\f	Form-feed
\n	Newline†
\r	Carriage return
\t	Horizontal tab
\v	Vertical tab
\'	Single quotation mark
\"	Double quotation mark
\\	Backslash
integer\\	Character whose internal representation is given by *integer* (in the range 0 to 255 decimal)

† The UIL compiler does not process newline characters in compound strings. The effect of a newline character in a compound string depends only on the character set of the string, and the result is not guaranteed to be a multiline string.

18.4.2 Concatenated String Literals

The & (ampersand) concatenation operator takes two strings as operands and creates a new string made up of the left operand followed immediately by the right operand.

For example:

```
'abcd' & 'xyz'
```

becomes the following:

```
'abcdxyz'
```

The operands of the concatenation operator can be null-terminated strings, compound strings, or a combination of both. The operands can hold string values of the same or different character sets.

The string resulting from the concatenation is a null-terminated string unless one or more of the following conditions exists:

- One of the operands is a compound string

- The operands have different character set properties

- The operands have different writing directions

Then the resulting string is a compound string. You cannot use imported or exported values as operands of the concatenation operator. (See Section 19.2 for information on declaring values as private, exported, or imported.)

18.4.2.1 Compound String Literals

A compound string consists of a string of 8-bit or 16-bit characters, a named character set, and a writing direction. Its UIL data type is **compound_string**.

The writing direction of a compound string is implied by the character set specified for the string. You can explicitly set the writing direction for a compound string by using the COMPOUND_STRING function (discussed in Section 18.5.9). Section 18.4.2.2 describes the character sets supported in UIL for compound strings.

A compound string can consist of a sequence of concatenated compound strings, null-terminated strings, or a combination of both, each of which can have a different character set property and writing direction. Use the concatenation operator & (ampersand) to create a sequence of compound strings. The following is an example of concatenated compound strings:

```
#ISO_HEBREW"txet werbeh"&#ISO_LATIN8"latin text"
```

Each string in the sequence is stored, including the character set and writing direction information. You can manipulate a compound string with the Motif Toolkit routines for compound strings.

Generally, a string literal is stored in the UID file as a compound string when the literal consists of concatenated strings having different character sets or writing directions, or when you use the string to specify a value for an argument that requires a compound string value. If you want to guarantee that a string literal is stored as a compound string, you must use the COMPOUND_STRING function (discussed in Section 18.5.9).

Because the results of the newline character depend on the character set of a compound string, there is no guarantee that an embedded '\n' will generate a multiline string. To ensure that you create a multiline string, use the SEPARATE clause as follows:

```
VALUE
   sample_string: COMPOUND_STRING( "Hello", SEPARATE = TRUE )
                                 & "world!";
```

18.4.2.2 Character Sets for String Literals

Table 18-7 lists the character sets supported by the UIL compiler for string literals.

The first column shows the UIL name for the character set. The second column gives a brief description of the character set. Note that several UIL names map to the same character set. In some cases, the UIL name influences how string literals are read. For example, strings identified by a UIL character set name ending in _LR are read left-to-right. Names that end in a different number reflect different fonts (for example, ISO_LATIN1 or ISO_LATIN6). All character sets in this table are represented by 8 bits.

Table 18-7. Supported Character Sets

UIL Name	Description
ISO_LATIN1	GL: ASCII, GR: Latin-1 Supplement
ISO_LATIN2	GL: ASCII, GR: Latin-2 Supplement
ISO_ARABIC	GL: ASCII, GR: Latin-Arabic Supplement
ISO_LATIN6	GL: ASCII, GR: Latin-Arabic Supplement
ISO_GREEK	GL: ASCII, GR: Latin-Greek Supplement
ISO_LATIN7	GL: ASCII, GR: Latin-Greek Supplement
ISO_HEBREW	GL: ASCII, GR: Latin-Hebrew Supplement
ISO_LATIN8	GL: ASCII, GR: Latin-Hebrew Supplement
ISO_HEBREW_LR	GL: ASCII, GR: Latin-Hebrew Supplement
ISO_LATIN8_LR	GL: ASCII, GR: Latin-Hebrew Supplement
JIS_KATAKANA	GL: JIS Roman, GR: JIS Katakana

The parsing rules for each of the character sets are described in Table 18-8.

```
#ISO_HEBREW "tfel ot thgir morf og sretcarahc"
```

In this example, the characters in the string value are presented right to left. Since the character set for the literal is ISO_HEBREW, the characters in quotation marks can be any legal character as defined by the ISO_HEBREW character set.

Table 18-8. Parsing Rules for Character Sets

Character Set	Parsing Rules
All character sets	Character codes in the range 00...1F, 7F, and 80...9F are control characters including both bytes of 16-bit characters. The compiler flags these as illegal characters.
ISO_LATIN1 ISO_LATIN2 ISO_ARABIC ISO_LATIN3 ISO_GREEK ISO_LATIN4	These sets are parsed from left to right. The escape sequences for null-terminated strings are also supported by these character sets. See Table 18-6 for more information on escape sequences.
ISO_HEBREW ISO_LATIN8	These sets are parsed from right to left; for example, the string #ISO_HEBREW "012345" generates a primitive string "543210" with character set ISO_HEBREW. A DDIS descriptor for such a string has this segment marked as being right_to_left. The escape sequences for null-terminated strings in Table 18-6 are also supported by these character sets, and the characters that compose the escape sequences are in left-to-right order. For example, you type \n, not n\.
ISO_HEBREW_LR ISO_LATIN8_LR	These sets are parsed from left to right; for example, the string #ISO_HEBREW_LR "012345" generates a primitive string "012345" with character set ISO_HEBREW. A DDIS descriptor for such a string marks this segment as being left_to_right. The escape sequences for null-terminated strings, given in Table 18-6, are also supported by these character sets.

Character Set	Parsing Rules
JIS_KATAKANA	This set is parsed from left to right. The escape sequences for null-terminated strings in Table 18-6 are also supported by this character set. Note that the \ (backslash) may be displayed as a yen symbol.

In addition to designating parsing rules for strings, character set information remains an attribute of a compound string. If the string is included in a string consisting of several concatenated segments, the character set information is included with that string segment. This gives the Motif Toolkit the information it needs to decipher the compound string and choose a font to display the string.

For an application interface displayed only in English, UIL lets you ignore the distinctions between the two uses of strings. The compiler recognizes by context when a string must be passed as a null-terminated string or as a compound string.

The UIL compiler recognizes enough about the various character sets to correctly parse string literals. The compiler also issues errors if you use a compound string in a context that supports only null-terminated strings.

Since the character set names are keywords, you must put them in lowercase if case-sensitive names are in force. If names are case insensitive, character set names can be uppercase, lowercase, or mixed case.

In addition to the built-in character sets recognized by UIL, you can define your own character sets with the CHARACTER_SET function. You can use the CHARACTER_SET function anywhere a character set can be specified. See Section 18.5.1. for more information on the CHARACTER_SET function.

18.4.2.3 Data Storage Consumption for String Literals

The way a string literal is stored in the UID file depends on how you declare and use the string. The UIL compiler automatically converts a null-terminated string to a compound string if you use the string to specify the value of an argument that requires a compound string. However, this conversion is costly in terms of storage consumption.

Private, exported, and imported string literals require storage for a single allocation when the literal is declared; thereafter, storage is required for each reference to the literal. Literals declared inline require storage for both an allocation and a reference.

The following table summarizes data storage consumption for string literals. The storage requirement for an allocation consists of a fixed portion and a variable portion. The fixed portion of an allocation is roughly the same as the storage requirement for a reference (a few bytes). The storage consumed by the variable portion depends on the size of the literal value (that is, the length of the string). To conserve storage space, avoid making string literal declarations that result in an allocation per use.

Table 18-9. Data Storage for String Literals

Declaration	Data Type	Used As	Storage Requirements Per Use
Inline	Null-terminated	Null-terminated	An allocation and a reference (within the module)
Private	Null-terminated	Null-terminated	A reference (within the module)
Exported	Null-terminated	Null-terminated	A reference (within the UID hierarchy)
Imported	Null-terminated	Null-terminated	A reference (within the UID hierarchy)

Declaration	Data Type	Used As	Storage Requirements Per Use
Inline	Null-terminated	Compound	An allocation and a reference (within the module)
Private	Null-terminated	Compound	An allocation and a reference (within the module)
Exported	Null-terminated	Compound	A reference (within the UID hierarchy)
Imported	Null-terminated	Compound	A reference (within the UID hierarchy)
Inline	Compound	Compound	An allocation and a reference (within the module)
Private	Compound	Compound	A reference (within the module)
Exported	Compound	Compound	A reference (within the UID hierarchy)
Imported	Compound	Compound	A reference (within the UID hierarchy)

18.4.3 Integer Literals

An integer literal represents the value of a whole number. Integer literals have the form of an optional sign followed by one or more decimal digits. An integer literal must not contain embedded spaces or commas.

Integer literals are stored in the UID file as long integers. Exported and imported integer literals require a single allocation when the literal is declared; thereafter, a few bytes of storage are required for each reference to the literal. Private integer literals and those declared inline require allocation and reference storage per use. To conserve storage space, avoid making integer literal declarations that result in an allocation per use.

The following table shows data storage consumption for integer literals.

Table 18-10. Data Storage for Integer Literals

Declaration	Storage Requirements Per Use
Inline	An allocation and a reference (within the module)
Private	An allocation and a reference (within the module)
Exported	A reference (within the UID hierarchy)
Imported	A reference (within the UID hierarchy)

18.4.4 Boolean Literals

A Boolean literal represents the value True (reserved keyword TRUE or On) or False reserved keyword FALSE or Off). These keywords are subject to case-sensitivity rules.

In a UID file, TRUE is represented by the integer value 1 and FALSE is represented by the integer value 0.

Data storage consumption for Boolean literals is the same as that for integer literals.

18.4.5 Floating-Point Literals

A floating-point literal represents the value of a real (or float) number. Floating-point literals have one of the following forms:

[+ | -] *digit*... . [*digit*...] [{ **E** | **e** } [+ | -] *digit*...
[+ | -] . *digit*... [{ **E** | **e** } [+ | -] *digit*...]

For maximum portability a floating-point literal can represent values in the range 1.0E-37 to 1.0E+37 with at least 6 significant digits. On many machines this range will be wider, with more significant digits. A floating-point literal must not contain embedded spaces or commas.

Floating-point literals are stored in the UID file as double-precision, floating-point numbers. The following table gives examples of valid and invalid floating-point notation for the UIL compiler.

Table 18-11. Floating-Point Notation

Valid Floating-Point Literals	Invalid Floating-Point Literals
1.0	1e1 (no decimal point)
.1	E-1 (no decimal point or digits)
3.1415E-2 (equals .031415)	2.87 e6 (embedded blanks)
-6.29e7 (equals -62900000)	2.0e100 (out of range)

Data storage consumption for floating-point literals is the same as that for integer literals.

18.5 Value-Generating Functions

UIL provides functions to generate the following types of values:

- Character sets
- Keysyms
- Colors
- Pixmaps
- Single-precision, floating-point numbers
- Double-precision, floating-point numbers
- Fonts
- Font tables
- Compound strings
- Compound string tables
- ASCIZ (null-terminated) string tables
- Integer tables

- Arguments

- Reasons

- Translation tables

Remember that all examples in the following sections assume case-insensitive mode. Keywords are shown in uppercase letters to distinguish them from user-specified names, which are shown in lowercase letters. This use of uppercase letters is not required in case-insensitive mode. In case-sensitive mode, keywords must be in lowercase letters.

18.5.1 The CHARACTER_SET Function

You can define your own character sets with the **CHARACTER_SET** function. You can use the **CHARACTER_SET** function anywhere a character set can be specified. The **CHARACTER_SET** function has the following syntax:

CHARACTER_SET (*string-expression* [*,property*]...);

The result of the **CHARACTER_SET** function is a character set with the name *string-expression* and the properties you specify. *String-expression* must be a null-terminated string. You can optionally include one or both of the following clauses to specify properties for the resulting character set:

RIGHT_TO_LEFT = *boolean-expression*
SIXTEEN_BIT = *boolean-expression*

The **RIGHT_TO_LEFT** clause sets the default writing direction of the string from right to left if *boolean-expression* is True, and right to left otherwise.

The **SIXTEEN_BIT** clause allows the strings associated with this character set to be interpreted as 16-bit characters if *boolean-expression* is True, and 8-bit characters otherwise.

18.5.2 The KEYSYM Function

The **KEYSYM** function is used to specify a keysym for a mnemonic resource. It has the following syntax:

KEYSYM (*string-literal*)

The *string-literal* must contain exactly one character.

The following example shows how to use the **KEYSYM** function:

```
OBJECT push_button_1:
    XmPushButton
      { ARGUMENTS
            { XmNmnemonic = KEYSYM( "Q" );
              XmNlabelString = COMPOUND_STRING( "Quit" ); };
      };
```

18.5.3 Functions for Specifying Colors

Color values are designed to let you designate a value to specify a color and then use that value for arguments requiring a color value.

18.5.3.1 The COLOR Function

The **COLOR** function supports the definition of colors. Using the **COLOR** function, you can designate a value to specify a color and then use that value for arguments requiring a color value.

The **COLOR** function has the following syntax:

COLOR (*string-expression* [,**FOREGROUND**|,**BACKGROUND**])

The string expression names the color you want to define; the optional keywords **FOREGROUND** and **BACKGROUND** identify how the color is to be displayed on a monochrome device when the color is used in the definition of a color table.

The following example shows how to use the **COLOR** function:

```
VALUE red: COLOR( 'Red' );
VALUE green: COLOR( 'Green' );
VALUE blue: COLOR( 'Blue' );
OBJECT primary_window:
  XmMainWindow
    { ARGUMENTS
        { XmNforeground = green;
          XmNbackground = COLOR( 'Black' ); };
      };
```

In this example, the **COLOR** function is used with the **VALUE** declaration (described in Section 19.3) to define three colors and give them each a name. One of these colors, green is then used to specify the foreground color of the main window.

A second use of the **COLOR** function defines the background color for the main window as the color associated with the string 'Black'.

The UIL compiler does not have built-in color names. Colors are a server-dependent attribute of an object. Colors are defined on each server and may have different red-green-blue (RGB) values on each server. The string you specify as the color argument must be recognized by the server on which your application runs.

In a UID file, UIL represents a color as a character string. MRM calls X translation routines that convert a color string to the device-specific pixel value. If you are running on a monochrome server, all colors translate to black or white. If you are on a color server, the color names translate to their proper colors if the following conditions are met:

- The color is defined.

- The color map is not yet full.

If the color map is full, even valid colors translate to black or white (foreground or background).

Interfaces do not, in general, specify colors for widgets, so that the selection of colors can be controlled by the user through the **.Xdefaults** file.

To write an application that runs on both monochrome and color devices, you need to specify which colors in a color table (defined with the **COLOR_TABLE** function) map to the background and which colors map to the foreground. UIL lets you use the **COLOR** function to designate this mapping in the definition of the color. The following example shows how to use the **COLOR** function to map the color red to the background color on a monochrome device:

```
VALUE c: COLOR ( 'red',BACKGROUND );
```

The mapping comes into play only when the MRM is given a color and the application is to be displayed on a monochrome device. In this case, each color is considered to be in one of the following three categories:

- The color is mapped to the background color on the monochrome device.

- The color is mapped to the foreground color on the monochrome device.

- Monochrome mapping is undefined for this color.

If the color is mapped to the foreground or background color, MRM substitutes the foreground or background color, respectively. If you do not specify the monochrome mapping for a color, MRM passes the color string to the Motif Toolkit for mapping to the foreground or background color.

18.5.3.2 The RGB Function

The **RGB** function has the following syntax:

RGB (*integer, integer, integer*);

The three integers define the values for the red, green, and blue components of the color, in that order. The values of these components can range from 0 to 65,535, inclusive.

The following example shows how to use the **RGB** function:

```
VALUE green : RGB( 0, 65535, 0 );
OBJECT primary_window:
 XmMainWindow
  { ARGUMENTS
    { XmNforeground = green;
      XmNbackground = RGB(65025, 12996, 7396); };
    };
```

In a UID file, UIL represents an **RGB** value as three integers. MRM calls X translation routines that convert the integers to the device-specific pixel value. If you are running on a monochrome server, all colors translate to black or white. If you are on a color server, **RGB** values translate to their proper colors if the colormap is not yet full. If the colormap is full, values translate to black or white (foreground or background).

18.5.4 Functions for Specifying Pixmaps

Pixmap values are designed to let you specify labels that are graphic images rather than text. Pixmap values are not directly supported by UIL. Instead, UIL supports icons, which are a simplified form of pixmap. You use a character to describe each pixel in the icon.

Pixmap support in the UIL compiler is provided by the following functions: **COLOR_TABLE**, **ICON**, and **XBITMAPFILE**.

In a UIL module, any argument of type **pixmap** should have an icon or an **xbitmap** file specified as its value.

18.5.4.1 The COLOR_TABLE Function

The **COLOR_TABLE** function has the following syntax:

COLOR_TABLE ({ *color-expression = character* },...)

The color expression is a previously defined color, a color defined in line with the **COLOR** function, or the phrase **BACKGROUND COLOR** or **FOREGROUND COLOR**. The character can be any valid UIL character (see Table 18-1).

The following example shows how to specify a color table:

```
VALUE
  rgb : COLOR_TABLE ( red = 'r', green = 'g', blue = 'b' );
  bitmap_colors : COLOR_TABLE ( BACKGROUND COLOR = '0',
                                FOREGROUND COLOR = '1' );
```

The **COLOR_TABLE** function provides a device-independent way to specify a set of colors. The **COLOR_TABLE** function accepts either previously defined UIL color names or in line color definitions (using the **COLOR** function). A color table must be private because its contents must be known by the UIL compiler to construct an icon. The colors within a color table, however, can be imported, exported, or private. See Section 19.2 for more information on scope of reference to values.

The single letter associated with each color is the character you use to represent that color when creating an icon. Each letter used to represent a color must be unique within the color table.

18.5.4.2 The ICON Function

The **ICON** function has the following syntax:

ICON ([COLOR_TABLE=*color-table-name* ,] *row*,...)

The color table name must refer to a previously defined color table and the row is a character expression giving one row of the icon.

The following example shows how to define a pixmap using the **COLOR_TABLE** and **ICON** functions:

```
VALUE
   rgb      : COLOR_TABLE ( red = '=', green = '.', blue = ' ' );
   x_icon   : ICON( COLOR_TABLE=rgb, '=========',
                                     '==.   .==',
                                     '== . . ==',
                                     '==  .  ==',
                                     '== . . ==',
                                     '==.   .==',
                                     '=========' );
```

The **ICON** function describes a rectangular icon that is x pixels wide and y pixels high. The strings surrounded by single quotation marks describe the icon. Each string represents a row in the icon; each character in the string represents a pixel.

The first row in an icon definition determines the width of the icon. All rows must have the same number of characters as the first row. The height of the icon is dictated by the number of rows. For example, the x_icon defined in the previous example is 9 pixels wide and 7 pixels high.

The first argument of the **ICON** function (the color table specification) is optional and identifies the colors that are available in this icon. By using the single letter associated with each color, you can specify the color of each pixel in the icon. In the example, an = (equal sign) represents the color red, a . (dot) is green, and a space is blue. The icon must be constructed of characters defined in the specified color table. In the example, the color table named rgb specifies colors for the = (equal sign), . (dot), and space. The x_icon is constructed with these three characters.

A default color table is used if you omit the argument specifying the color table. To make use of the default color table, the rows of your icon must contain only spaces and asterisks. The default color table is defined as follows:

```
COLOR_TABLE( BACKGROUND COLOR = ' ', FOREGROUND COLOR = '*' )
```

You can define other characters to represent the background color and foreground color by replacing the space and asterisk in the **BACKGROUND COLOR** and **FOREGROUND COLOR** clauses shown in the previous statement. You can specify icons as private, imported, or exported. Use the MRM function **MrmFetchIconLiteral** to retrieve an exported icon at run time.

18.5.4.3 The XBITMAPFILE Function

The **XBITMAPFILE** function is similar to the **ICON** function in that both describe a rectangular icon that is x pixels wide and y pixels high. However, **XBITMAPFILE** allows you to specify an external file containing the definition of an X bitmap, whereas all **ICON** function definitions must be coded directly within UIL. X bitmap files can be generated by many different X applications. UIL reads these files through the **XBITMAPFILE** function, but does not support creation of these files. The X bitmap file specified as the argument to the **XBITMAPFILE** function is read at application run time by MRM.

The **XBITMAPFILE** function returns a value of type **pixmap** and can be used anywhere a pixmap data type is expected. The **XBITMAPFILE** function has the following syntax:

XBITMAPFILE(*string-expression*);

The following example shows how to use the **XBITMAPFILE** function:

```
VALUE
    background_pixmap=XBITMAPFILE('myfile_button.xbm');
```

In this example, the X bitmap specified in **myfile_button.xbm** is used to create a pixmap, which can be referenced by the value *background_pixmap*.

18.5.5 The SINGLE_FLOAT Function

The **SINGLE_FLOAT** function lets you store floating-point literals in UIL files as single-precision, floating-point numbers. Single-precision floating-point numbers can often be stored using less memory than double-precision, floating-point numbers.

The function has the following syntax:

SINGLE_FLOAT (*real_number_literal*)

The *real_number_literal* can be either an integer literal or a floating-point literal. A value defined using this function cannot be used in an arithmetic expression.

18.5.6 The FLOAT Function

The **FLOAT** function lets you store floating-point literals in UIL files as double-precision, floating-point numbers.

The function has the following syntax:

FLOAT (*real_number_literal*)

The *real_number_literal* can be either an integer literal or a floating-point literal.

18.5.7 The FONT Function

You define fonts with the **FONT** function. Using the **FONT** function, you designate a value to specify a font and then use that value for arguments that require a font value. The UIL compiler has no built-in fonts. You must define all fonts using the **FONT** function.

Each font makes sense only in the context of a character set. The **FONT** function has an additional parameter to let you specify the character set for the font. This parameter is optional; if you omit it, the default character set depends on the value of the **LANG** environment variable if it is set of the value of **XmFALLBACK_CHARSET** if **LANG** is not set. The font function has the following syntax:

FONT(*string-expression* [, **CHARACTER_SET** = *char-set*])

The string expression specifies the name of the font and the clause **CHARACTER_SET** = *char-set* specifies the character set for the font. The string expression used in the **FONT** function cannot be a compound string.

The following example shows how to use the **FONT** function:

```
VALUE big:
      FONT('-ADOBE-Times-Medium-R-Normal--*-140-*-*-P-*-ISO8859-1');
VALUE bold:
      FONT('-ADOBE-Helvetica-Bold-R-Normal--*-100-*-*-P-*-ISO8859-1');
OBJECT danger_window:
    XmWarningDialog
    { ARGUMENTS
        { XmNdialogTitle = 'You are about to lose all changes';
          XmNlabelFontList = bold;
        };
    };
```

In this example, the FONT function is used with the **VALUE** declaration (described in Section 19.3) to define two fonts and give them names. One of these fonts, *bold*, is automatically converted to a font table by the compiler (because the argument **XmNlabelFontList** requires a font table) and is used to specify the text font of the warning dialog.

Use the wildcard character * (an asterisk) to specify fonts in a device-independent manner.

If possible, you should not specify fonts for objects in your application interface. This allows end users to control font selection through the **.Xdefaults file**.

18.5.8 The FONT_TABLE Function

A font table is a sequence of pairs of fonts and character sets. At run time when an object needs to display a string, the object scans the font table for the character set that matches the character set of the string to be displayed.

UIL provides the **FONT_TABLE** function to let you supply such an argument. The syntax of the **FONT_TABLE** function is as follows:

FONT_TABLE(*font expression,...*)

The font expression is created with the **FONT** function.

If you specify a single font value to specify an argument that requires a font table, the UIL compiler automatically converts a font value to a font table.

18.5.9 The COMPOUND_STRING Function

Use the **COMPOUND_STRING** function to set properties of a null-terminated string and to convert it into a compound string. The properties you can set are the character set, writing direction, and separator.

The **COMPOUND_STRING** function has the following syntax:

COMPOUND_STRING(*string-expression* [, *property*]...);

The result of the **COMPOUND_STRING** function is a compound string with the string expression as its value. You can optionally include one or more of the following clauses to specify properties for the resulting compound string:

RIGHT_TO_LEFT = *boolean-expression*
SEPARATE = *boolean-expression*

The **RIGHT_TO_LEFT** clause sets the writing direction of the string from right to left if *boolean-expression* is True, and left to right otherwise. Specifying this argument does not cause the value of the string expression to change. If you omit the **RIGHT_TO_LEFT** argument, the resulting string has the same writing direction as *string-expression*.

The **SEPARATE** clause appends a separator to the end of the compound string if *boolean-expression* is True. If you omit the **SEPARATE** clause, the resulting string does not have a separator.

You cannot use imported or exported values as the operands of the **COMPOUND_STRING** function.

18.5.10 The COMPOUND_STRING_TABLE Function

A compound string table is an array of compound strings. Objects requiring a list of string values, such as the **XmNitems** and **XmNselectedItems** arguments for the list widget, use string table values. The **COMPOUND_STRING_TABLE** function builds the values for these two arguments of the list widget. The **COMPOUND_STRING_TABLE** function generates a value of type **string_table**. The name **STRING_TABLE** is a synonym for **COMPOUND_STRING_TABLE**.

The **COMPOUND_STRING_TABLE** function has the following syntax:

COMPOUND_STRING_TABLE(*string-expression,...*)

The following example shows how to specify a string table:

```
OBJECT file_privileges: XmList
    { ARGUMENTS
        { XmNitems = COMPOUND_STRING_TABLE("owner  read",
                                    "owner write",
                                    "owner delete",
                                    "system read",
                                    "system write",
                                    "system delete",
                                    "group read",
                                    "group write",
                                    "group delete" );
        XmNselectedItems = COMPOUND_STRING_TABLE
                                    ("owner read",
                                    "owner write",
                                    "system read",
                                    "system write" );
        };
    };
```

This example creates a list box with nine menu choices. Four of the choices are initially displayed as having been selected.

The strings inside the string table can be simple strings, which the UIL compiler automatically converts to compound strings.

18.5.11 The ASCIZ_STRING_TABLE Function

An ASCIZ string table is an array of ASCIZ (null-terminated) string values separated by commas. This function allows you to pass more than one ASCIZ string as a callback tag value. The **ASCIZ_STRING_TABLE** function generates a value of type **asciz_table**. The name **ASCIZ_TABLE** is a synonym for **ASCIZ_STRING_TABLE**.

The **ASCIZ_STRING_TABLE** function has the following syntax:

ASCIZ_STRING_TABLE(*string-expression*,...);

The following example shows how to specify an ASCIZ string table passed as a callback tag:

```
VALUE
  v1 = "my_value_1";
  v2 = "my_value_2";
  v3 = "my_value_3";
OBJECT press_my: XmPushButton {
 CALLBACKS {
  XmNactivateCallback =
        PROCEDURE my_callback(asciz_table(v1, v2, v3));
  };
 };
```

18.5.12 The INTEGER_TABLE Function

An integer table is an array of integer values separated by commas. This function allows you to pass more than one integer per callback tag value. The **INTEGER_TABLE** function generates a value of type **integer_table**.

The **INTEGER_TABLE** function has the following syntax:

INTEGER_TABLE(*integer-expression,...*);

The following example shows the **INTEGER_TABLE** function used to define an array of integers to be passed as a callback tag to the procedure *my_callback*:

```
VALUE
  v1 =  1;
  v2 =  2;
  v3 =  3;
OBJECT press_my: XmPushButton {
 ARGUMENTS {
  XmNheight = 30;
  XmNwidth =  10;
 };
 CALLBACKS {
  XmNactivateCallback =
       PROCEDURE my_callback(integer_table(v1,  v2,  v3));
 };
};
```

18.5.13 The ARGUMENT Function

The **ARGUMENT** function defines the arguments to a user-defined widget. Each of the objects that can be described by UIL permits a set of arguments, listed in Appendix B. For example, **XmNheight** is an argument to most objects and has integer data type. To specify height for a user-defined widget, you can use the built-in argument name **XmNheight**, and specify an integer value when you declare the user-defined widget. You do not use the **ARGUMENT** function to specify arguments that are built into the UIL compiler.

The **ARGUMENT** function has the following syntax:

ARGUMENT(*string-expression* [, *argument_type*])

The *string-expression* name is the name the UIL compiler uses for the argument in the UID file. the *argument_type* is the type of value that can be associated with the argument. If you omit the second argument, the default type is **any** and no value type checking occurs. Use one of the following keywords to specify the argument type:

- ANY
- ASCIZ_TABLE
- BOOLEAN
- COLOR
- COLOR_TABLE
- COMPOUND_STRING
- FLOAT
- FONT
- FONT_TABLE
- ICON
- INTEGER
- INTEGER_TABLE
- REASON
- SINGLE_FLOAT
- STRING
- STRING_TABLE
- TRANSLATION_TABLE

For example, suppose you built a user-defined widget that draws a circle and takes four arguments: *my_radius*, *my_color*, **XmNx**, and **XmNy**. The following example shows how to use the **ARGUMENT** function to define the arguments to this user-defined widget. Note that the **ARGUMENT** function is not used to specify arguments **XmNy** and **XmNy** because these are built-in argument names. The data type of **XmNx** and **XmNy** is Position.

When you declare the *circle* widget, you must use the **ARGUMENT** function to define the name and data type of the arguments that are not built-ins (*my_radius* and *my_color*). Arguments are specified in an arguments list, identified by the keyword **ARGUMENTS** in the following example:

```
VALUE circle_radius: ARGUMENT( 'my_radius', INTEGER );
VALUE circle_color:  ARGUMENT( 'my_color', COLOR );
OBJECT circle:
    USER_DEFINED  PROCEDURE CircleCreate
      { ARGUMENTS
          { circle_radius = 1000;
            circle_color = color_blue
            XmNx = 1050;
            XmNy = 1050;
          };
      };
```

In this example, the **ARGUMENT** function is used in a value declaration (described in Section 19.3) to define the two arguments that are not UIL built-ins: *circle-radius*, which takes an integer value, and *circle-color*, which takes a color value. When referenced in the arguments list of the circle widget, the UIL compiler verifies that the value you specify for each of these arguments is of the type specified in the **ARGUMENT** function. The following table shows the argument list placed in the UID file (and supplied to the creation function for the circle widget at run time).

Argument	Argument Value
my_radius	1000
my_color	Value associated with the UIL name *color_blue*

You can use the **ARGUMENT** function to allow the UIL compiler to recognize extensions to the Motif Toolkit. For example, an existing widget may accept a new argument. Using the **ARGUMENT** function, you can make this new argument available to the UIL compiler before the updated version of the compiler is released.

18.5.14 The REASON Function

The **REASON** function is useful for defining new reasons for user-defined widgets.

Each of the objects in the Motif Toolkit defines a set of conditions under which it calls a user-defined function. These conditions are known as callback reasons. The user-defined functions are termed callback procedures. In a UIL module, you use a callbacks list to specify which user-defined functions are to be called for which reasons.

Appendix B lists the callback reasons supported by the Motif Toolkit objects.

When you declare a user-defined widget, you can define callback reasons for that widget using the **REASON** function. The **REASON** function has the following syntax:

REASON(*string-expression*)

The string expression specifies the argument name stored in the UID file for the reason. This reason name is supplied to the widget creation routine at run time.

Suppose you built a new widget that implements a password system to prevent a set of windows from being displayed unless a user enters the correct password. The widget might define the following callbacks:

```
VALUE passed: REASON('AccessGrantedCallback');
VALUE failed: REASON('AccessDeniedCallback');
OBJECT guard_post:
   USER_DEFINED  PROCEDURE guard_post_create
{ CALLBACKS
   { passed = PROCEDURE display_next_level();
     failed = PROCEDURE logout(); };
   };
```

In this example, the **REASON** function is used in a value declaration to define two new reasons, *passed* and *failed*. The callback list of the widget named *guard_post* specifies the procedures to be called when these reasons occur.

A widget specifies its callbacks by defining an argument for each reason that it supports. The argument to the **REASON** function gives the name of the argument that supports this reason. Therefore, the argument list placed in the UID file for the *guard_post* widget includes the arguments listed in the following table.

Argument	Argument Value
AccessGrantedCallback	Callback structure for procedure *display_next_level*
AccessDeniedCallback	Callback structure for procedure *logout*

18.5.15 The TRANSLATION_TABLE Function

Each of the Motif Toolkit widgets has a translation table that maps X events (for example, mouse button 1 being pressed) to a sequence of actions. Through widget arguments, such as the common translations argument, you can specify an alternate set of events or actions for a particular widget. The **TRANSLATION_TABLE** function creates a translation table that can be used as the value of a argument that is of the data type **translation_table**. The **TRANSLATION_TABLE** function has the following syntax:

TRANSLATION_TABLE(*string-expression,...*)

Each of the string expressions specifies the run-time binding of an X event to a sequence of actions, as shown in the following example (arguments lists are discussed in Section 19.5.1):

```
LIST new_translations:
 ARGUMENTS
 { XmNtranslations =
   TRANSLATION_TABLE
   (
    '#override',
    '<Btn1Down>: XMPBFILLHIGHLIGHT() XMPBARM() XMPBUNGRAB()',
    '<Btn1Up>:   XMPBFILLUNHIGHLIGHT() XMPBACTIVATE() \
                XmSelectionDialog(self_destruct) XMPBDISARM()',
    '<Btn3Up>:   XMPBHELP()',
    'Any<LeaveWindow>: XMPBFILLUNHIGHLIGHT() XMPBUNGRAB() \
                XMPBDISARM()'
   );
 };
OBJECT self_destruct:
       XmPushButton
        { ARGUMENTS new_translations; };
```

This example defines an argument list, called *new_translations*. The first translation specifies that pressing the left button **<Btn1Down>** should result in the sequence of procedures **XMPBFILLHIGHLIGHT**(), **XMPBARM**(), and **XMPBUNGRAB**() executing. The *self_destruct* push button widget defines *new_translations* as its translation table.

In this example, the first line of the definition is a translation table directive that indicates that the current translations are to be overridden with those specified in the translation table. The translations defined by *new_translations* will override the current translations for the *self_destruct* PushButton.

You can use one of the following translation table directives with the **TRANSLATION_TABLE** function: #override, #augment, or #replace. The default is #replace. If you specify one of these directives, it must be the first entry in the translation table.

The #override directive causes any duplicate translations to be ignored. For example, if a translation for <**Btn1Down**> is already defined in the current translations for a PushButton, the translation defined by *new_translations* overrides the current definition. If the #augment directive is specified, the current definition takes precedence. The #replace directive replaces all current translations with those specified in the **XmNtranslations** resource.

18.6 The any Data Type

The purpose of the **any** data type is to shut off the data-type checking feature of the UIL compiler. You can use the **any** data type for the following:

- Specifying the type of a callback procedure tag
- Specifying the type of a user-defined argument

You can use the **any** data type when you need to use a type not supported by the UIL compiler or when you want the data-type restrictions imposed by the compiler to be relaxed. For example, you might want to define a widget having an argument that can accept different types of values, depending on run-time circumstances.

If you specify that an argument takes an **any** value, the compiler does not check the type of the value specified for that argument; therefore, you need to take care when specifying a value for an argument of type **any**. You could get unexpected results at run time if you pass a value having a data type that the widget does not support for that argument.

18.7 Compile-Time Value Expressions

UIL provides literal values for a diverse set of types (integer, string, real, Boolean) and a set of Motif Toolkit-specific types (for example, colors and fonts). These values are used to provide the value of Motif Toolkit arguments.

UIL includes compile-time value expressions. These expressions can contain references to other UIL values, but cannot be forward referenced.

Compile-time value expressions are useful for implementing relative positioning of children without using the Form widget. For example, suppose you wanted to create a message box inside a bulletin board, and you want the message box to be half as wide and half as tall as the bulletin board, and centered within it. Using compile-time expressions, you can specify the coordinates of the message box by referring to the values you already defined for the bulletin board. If you do not use compile-time value expressions in this case, you must compute the x and y location and the height and width of the message box, and recompute these values if the bulletin board changes size or location. Furthermore, the computed values are absolute numbers rather than descriptive expressions like "bulletin_board_width / 2".

Note that the Motif Toolkit provides direct support for resolution independence with the millimeter, inch, and point unit types; the preceding example could be implemented using this feature.

The concatenation of strings is also a form of compile-time expression. Use the concatenation operator to join strings and convert the result to a compound string.

The following table lists the set of operators in UIL that allow you to create integer, real, and Boolean values based on other values defined with the UIL module. In the table, a precedence of 1 is the highest.

Table 18-12. Operators

Operator	Operator Type	Operand Types	Meaning	Precedence
~	Unary	Boolean	NOT	1
		integer	One's complement	
-	Unary	float	Negate	
		integer	Negate	1
+	Unary	float	NOP	1
		integer	NOP	1
*	Binary	float,float	Multiply	2
		integer,integer	Multiply	2
/	Binary	float,float	Divide	2
		integer,integer	Divide	2
+	Binary	float,float	Add	3
		integer,integer	Add	3
-	Binary	float,float	Subtract	3
		integer,integer	Subtract	3
>>	Binary	integer,integer	Shift right	4
<<	Binary	integer,integer	Shift left	4

Operator	Operator Type	Operand Types	Meaning	Precedence
&	Binary	Boolean,Boolean	AND	5
		integer,integer	Bitwise AND	5
		string,string	Concatentate	5
|	Binary	Boolean,Boolean	OR	6
		integer,integer	Bitwise OR	6
^	Binary	Boolean,Boolean	XOR	6
		integer,integer	Bitwise XOR	6

A string can be either a single compound string or a sequence of compound strings. If the two concatenated strings have different properties (such as writing direction or character set), the result of the concatenation is a multisegment compound string.

The result of each operator has the same type as its operands. You cannot mix types in an expression without using conversion routines.

You can use parentheses to override the normal precedence of operators. In a sequence of unary operators, the operations are performed in right-to-left order. For example, - + -A is equivalent to -(+(-A)). In a sequence of binary operators of the same precedence, the operations are performed in left-to-right order. For example, A*B/C*D is equivalent to ((A*B)/C)*D.

A value declaration gives a value a name. You cannot redefine the value of that name in a subsequent value declaration. You can use a value containing operators and functions anywhere you can use a value in a UIL module. You cannot use imported values as operands in expressions.

Several of the binary operators are defined for multiple data types. For example, the operator for multiplication (*) is defined for both floating-point and integer operands.

For the UIL compiler to perform these binary operations, both operands must be of the same type. If you supply operands of different data types, the UIL compiler automatically converts one of the operands to the type of the other according to the conversions rules listed in the following table.

Table 18-13. Automatic Data Type Conversions

Data Type of Operand 1	Data Type of Operand 2	Conversion Rule
Boolean	Integer	Operand 1 converted to integer
Integer	Boolean	Operand 2 converted to integer
Integer	Floating-point	Operand 1 converted to floating-point
Floating-point	Integer	Operand 2 converted to floating-point

You can also explicitly convert the data type of a value by using one of the functions listed in the following table.

Table 18-14. Conversion Functions

Result	Function	Comments
Integer	INTEGER(Boolean)	TRUE->1, FALSE->0
Integer	INTEGER(integer)	
Integer	INTEGER(float)	Integer part of the floating-point number (truncate toward zero); this can result in overflow.
Double-precision floating-point	FLOAT(Boolean)	
Double-precision floating-point	FLOAT(integer)	Double-precision floating-point representation of an integer; there should not be any loss of precision.

Result	Function	Comments
Double-precision floating-point	FLOAT(float)	
Single-precision floating-point	SINGLE_FLOAT(Boolean)	
Single-precision floating-point	SINGLE_FLOAT(integer)	Single-precision floating-point representation of an integer; there should not be any loss of precision.
Single-precision floating-point	SINGLE_FLOAT(float)	

The following example shows a value section from a UIL module containing compile-time expressions and data conversion functions.

```
VALUE
  value outer_box_width:   200;
  value outer_box_height:  250;
  value box_size_ratio:    0.5;
  value inner_box_width:
                 integer(outer_box_width * box_size_ratio);
  value inner_box_height:
                 integer(outer_box_height * box_size_ratio);
  value inner_box_x:
                 (outer_box_width - inner_box_width) >> 1;
  value inner_box_y:
                 (outer_box_height - inner_box_height) / 2;
  value type_field:        0;
  value class_field:       16;
  value type1:             1;
  value type2:             2;
  value type3:             3;
  value class1:            1;
  value class2:            2;
  value class3:            3;
  value combo1:   (type1 << type_field) | (class3 << class_field);
```

Chapter 19

UIL Module Structure

This chapter describes how to build a UIL module using the language elements described in the previous chapter. This chapter also explains the scope of references to values and objects defined in UIL, and describes the syntax and use of the following UIL module components:

- Value section
- Procedure section
- List section
- Object section
- Identifier section
- Include directive

In addition, this chapter describes the following features of UIL:

- Argument definitions for constraint widgets
- Symbolic references to widget IDs

In this chapter, all examples assume case-insensitive mode. Keywords are shown in uppercase to distinguish them from user-specified names, which are shown in lowercase. This use of uppercase is not required in case-insensitive mode. In case-sensitive mode, keywords must be in lowercase.

19.1 Structure of a UIL Module

A UIL module contains definitions of objects that are to be stored in a User Interface Definition (UID) file, the compiled output of the UIL compiler. A UIL module consists of a module block, which contains a series of value, procedure, list, identifier, and object sections. There can be any number of these sections in a UIL module. A UIL module can also contain include directives, which can be placed anywhere in the module, except within a value, procedure, list, identifier, or object section.

The structure of a UIL module is as follows:

```
uil_module  ::=
     MODULE module_name
          [ version-clause ]
          [ case-sensitivity-clause ]
          [ default-character-set-clause ]
          [ default-object-variant-clause ]
          { value-section
          | procedure-section
          | list-section
          | object-section
          | identifier-section
          | include-directive }...
     END MODULE ";"
version-clause  ::=
     VERSION "=" character-expression
case-sensitivity-clause  ::=
     NAMES "=" { CASE_SENSITIVE
                 CASE_INSENSITIVE }
default-character-set-clause  ::=
     CHARACTER_SET "=" char-set
default-object-variant-clause  ::=
     OBJECTS "=" "{" object-type "=" WIDGET | GADGET";" ... "}"
```

The module name is the name by which this UIL module is known in the UID file. This name is stored in the UID file for later use in the retrieval of resources by the MRM. This name is always stored in uppercase in the UID file.

The following is an example of the UIL module structure.

```
!+
!         Sample UIL module
!-
MODULE example                    ! module name
  VERSION = 'V1.0'                ! version
  NAMES = CASE_INSENSITIVE        ! keywords and names are
                                  ! not case sensitive
  CHARACTER_SET = ISO_LATIN6      ! character set for compilation
                                  ! is ISO_LATIN6
  OBJECTS = { XmPushButton = GADGET; }   ! push buttons are
                                         ! gadgets by default
!+
!       Declare the VALUES, PROCEDURES, LISTS,
!       IDENTIFIERS, and OBJECTS here...
!-
END MODULE;
```

19.1.1 Version Clause

The version clause specifies the version number of the UIL module. It is provided so that the programmer can verify the correct version of a UIL module is being accessed by MRM. The character expression you use to specify the version can be up to 31 characters in length.

19.1.2 Case-Sensitivity Clause

The case-sensitivity clause indicates whether names are to be treated as case sensitive or case insensitive. The default is case sensitive.

The case-sensitivity clause should be the first clause in the module header, and in any case must precede any statement that contains a name.

If names are case sensitive in a UIL module, UIL keywords in that module must be in lowercase. Each name is stored in the UIL file in the same case as it appears in the UIL module. If names are case insensitive, then keywords can be in uppercase, lowercase, or mixed case, and the uppercase equivalent of each name is stored in the UID file. The following table summarizes these rules.

Table 19-1. Rules for Case Sensitivity in a UIL Module

Case Sensitivity	Keyword Treatment in UIL Module	Name Treatment in UID File
Case sensitive	Must be entered in lowercase	Stored in the same case as they appear in the UIL module
Case insensitive	Can be entered in lowercase, uppercase, or mixed case	Stored in uppercase

19.1.3 Default Character Set Clause

The default character set clause specifies the default character set for string literals in the module. The use of the default character set clause is optional.

If specified, the character set clause designates the character set used to interpret an extended string literal if you did not specify a character set for that literal. If you do not include the character set clause in the module header, the default character set for the compilation is the codeset portion of the value of the **LANG** environment variable if it is set or the value of **XmFALLBACK_CHARSET** if LANG is not set or has no codeset component. By default, **XmFALLBACK_CHARSET** is ISO8859-1 (equivalent to ISO_LATIN1), but vendors may define a different default. See Section 20.2 for more information.

19.1.4 Default Object Variant Clause

A gadget is a simplified version of a widget that consumes less resources (and therefore enhances application performance) but offers limited customization. The following types of user interface object types have both a widget and a gadget variant:

- Cascade button

- Label

- Push button

- Separator

- Toggle button

For the most part, the widget and gadget variants are interchangeable. To use gadgets in your application, you need to specify to the UIL compiler that you want that particular variant. Otherwise, by default, the UIL compiler assumes you want to use widgets. There are three ways to specify that you want to use a gadget instead of a widget:

- Add the default object-variant clause to the module header.

- Add the keyword GADGET to particular object declarations.

- Use the Motif toolkit object name of the gadget variant (usually **Xm**<*object*>**Gadget**).

By using the default object-variant clause in the UIL module header, you can declare all cascade buttons, labels, push buttons, separators, and toggle buttons, or any combination of these types, to be gadgets. In the sample module declaration shown previously in this section, only push buttons are declared as gadgets.

To change these objects from one variant to the other, you need only change the default object-variant clause. For example, suppose you used the default object-variant clause to declare all push buttons as gadgets. To change all push button objects from gadgets to widgets, remove the type **XmPushButton** from the clause.

Because you do not specify the variant for imported objects (discussed in the next section), the variant (whether a widget or gadget) of imported objects is unknown until run time.

See Section 19.6 for more information on specifying the variant of objects in a UIL module.

19.2 Scope of References to Values and Objects

UIL values can have one of the following levels of scope of reference:

- EXPORTED: A value that you define as exported is stored in the UID file as a named resource, and therefore can be referenced by name in other UID files. When you define a value as exported, MRM looks outside the module in which the exported value is declared to get its value at run time.

- IMPORTED: A value that you define as imported is one that is defined as a named resource in a UID file. MRM resolves this declaration with the corresponding exported declaration at application run time.

- PRIVATE: A private value is a value that is not imported or exported. A value that you define as private is not stored as a distinct resource in the UID file. You can reference a private value only in the UIL module containing the value declaration. The value or object is directly incorporated into anything in the UIL module that references the declaration.

EXPORTED, IMPORTED, and PRIVATE are reserved UIL keywords. By default, values and objects are private.

19.3 Structure of a Value Section

A value section consists of the keyword VALUE followed by a sequence of value declarations. It has the following syntax:

value-section ::=
    VALUE *value-declaration...*
value-declaration ::=
    value-name ":"
        { **EXPORTED** *value-expression*
        | **PRIVATE** *value-expression*
        | *value-expression*
        | **IMPORTED** *value-type* } ";"

A value declaration provides a way to name a value expression or literal. The value name can be referred to by declarations that occur later in the UIL module in any context where a value can be used. Values can be forward referenced.

Value sections can include a keyword defining the scope of references to the value (see Section 19.2). The following table describes the supported value types in UIL.

Table 19-2. Value Types

Value Type	Description
ANY	Prevents the UIL compiler from checking the type of an argument value
ARGUMENT	Defines a value as a user-defined argument
BOOLEAN	Defines a value as True (On) or False (Off)
COLOR	Defines a value as a color
COLOR_TABLE	Provides a device-independent way to define a set of colors (usually for a pixmap)

Value Type	Description
COMPOUND_STRING	Defines a value as a compound string
FLOAT	Defines a value as a double-precision, floating-point number
FONT	Defines a value as a font
FONT_TABLE	Defines a value as a sequence of font and character set pairs
ICON	Describes a rectangular pixmap using a character to represent each pixel
INTEGER	Defines a value as an integer
INTEGER_TABLE	Defines a value as an array of integers
KEYSYM	Defines a value as a keysym
REASON	Defines a condition under which a widget is to call an application function
SINGLE_FLOAT	Defines a value as a single-precision, floating-point number
STRING	Defines a value as a null-terminated (ASCIZ) string
STRING_TABLE	Defines a value as an array of compound strings
TRANSLATION_TABLE	Defines an alternative set of events or actions for a widget

The following example shows how to declare values:

```
VALUE
    k_main              : EXPORTED 1;
    k_main_menu         : EXPORTED 2;
    k_main_command      : EXPORTED 3;
VALUE
    white           : IMPORTED COLOR;
    blue            : IMPORTED COLOR;
    arg_name        : PRIVATE 'new_argument_name';
VALUE
    main_prompt     : 'next command'; ! PRIVATE by default
    main_font       : IMPORTED FONT;
```

Because the values *k_main k_main_menu* and *k_main_command* are defined as exported, you can use these values in another UIL module as follows:

```
VALUE
     k_main               : IMPORTED  integer;
```

19.4 Structure of a Procedure Section

A procedure section consists of the keyword **PROCEDURE** followed by a sequence of procedure declarations. It has the following syntax:

procedure-section ::=
    PROCEDURE *procedure-declaration*...
procedure-declaration ::=
    procedure-name
        [*formal-parameter-spec*]";"
formal-parameter-spec ::=
        "(" [*value-type*] ")" ";"

Use a procedure declaration to declare the following:

- A routine that can be used as a callback routine for a widget

- The creation function for a user-defined widget

You can reference a procedure name in declarations that occur later in the UIL module in any context where a procedure can be used. Procedures can be forward referenced. You cannot use a name you used in another context as a procedure name.

In a procedure declaration, you have the option of specifying that a parameter will be passed to the corresponding callback routine at run time. This parameter is called the callback tag. You can specify the data type of the callback tag by putting the data type in parentheses following the procedure name. When you compile the module, the UIL compiler checks that the argument you specify in references to the procedure is of this type. Note that the data type of the callback tag must be one of the valid UIL data types (see Table 19-2). Note also that you cannot use a widget as a callback tag.

The following table summarizes how the UIL compiler checks argument type and argument count, depending on the procedure declaration.

Table 19-3. Rules for Checking Argument Type and Count

Declaration	Rules
No parameters	No argument type or argument count checking occurs. You can supply any number of arguments in the procedure reference.
( )	Checks that the argument count is 0.
(**any**)	Checks that the argument count is 1. Does not check the argument type. Use the **any** type to prevent type checking on procedure tags.
(*type*)	Checks for one argument of the specified type.

For example, in the following procedure declaration, the callback procedure named *toggle_proc* will be passed an integer tag at run time. The UIL compiler checks that the parameter specified in any reference to procedure *toggle_proc* is an integer.

```
PROCEDURE
    toggle_proc (INTEGER);
```

While it is possible to use any UIL data type to specify the type of a tag in a procedure declaration, you must be able to represent that data type in the programming language you are using. Some data types (such as integer, Boolean, and string) are common data types recognized by most programming languages. Other UIL data types (such as string tables) are more complicated and may require you to set up an appropriate corresponding data structure in the application in order to pass a tag of that type to a callback routine.

You can also use a procedure declaration to specify the creation function for a user-defined widget. In this case, you specify no formal parameters. The procedure is invoked with the standard three arguments passed to all widget creation functions. (See the Motif Toolkit documentation for more information about widget creation functions.)

The following example shows how to declare a procedure:

```
PROCEDURE
     app_help (INTEGER);
     app_destroy (INTEGER);
```

19.5 Structure of a List Section

A list section consists of the keyword LIST followed by a sequence of list declarations. It has the following syntax:

list-section ::=
    LIST *list-declaration...*
list-declaration ::=
    list-name ":" *list-definition* ";"
list-definition ::=
    list-type list-spec
list-type ::=
    { **ARGUMENTS**
    | **CONTROLS**
    | **CALLBACKS**
    | **PROCEDURES** }
list-spec ::=
    { *list-name*
    | "{" *list-entry...* "}" }
list-entry ::=
    { *list-definition*
    | *argument-list-entry*
    | *control-list-entry*
    | *callback-list-entry*
    | *procedure-list-entry* } ";"

You use list sections to group together a set of arguments, controls (children), callbacks, or procedures for later use in the UIL module. Lists can contain other lists, so that you can set up a hierarchy to clearly show which arguments, controls, callbacks, and procedures are common to which widgets. You cannot mix the different types of lists; a list of a particular type cannot contain entries of a different list type or reference the name of a different list type.

A list name is always private to the UIL module in which you declare the list and cannot be stored as a named resource in a UID file.

There are four types of lists in UIL:

- Arguments list, having the list type **ARGUMENTS**
- Callbacks list, having the list type **CALLBACKS**
- Controls list, having the list type **CONTROLS**
- Procedures list, having the list type **PROCEDURES**

These list types are described in the following sections.

19.5.1 Arguments List Structure

An arguments list defines which arguments are to be specified in the arguments-list parameter when the creation routine for a particular object is called at run time. An arguments list also specifies the values for those arguments. Each entry in the arguments list has the following syntax:

argument-list-entry ::=
    argument-name "=" *value-expression*

The argument name must be either a built-in argument name or a user-defined argument name that is specified with the **ARGUMENT** function (see Section 18.5.13). If you use a built-in argument name, the type of the value expression must match the allowable type for the argument.

If you use a built-in argument name as an arguments list entry in an object definition, the UIL compiler checks the argument name to be sure that it is supported by the type of object that you are defining. If the same argument name appears more than once in a given arguments list, the last entry that uses that argument name supersedes all previous entries with that name, and the compiler issues a message.

Some arguments are coupled by the UIL compiler. When you specify one of the arguments, the compiler also sets the other. The coupled argument is not available to you. The coupled arguments are listed in the following table.

Table 19-4. Coupled Arguments

Supported Argument	Coupled Argument
XmNitems	XmNitemCount
XmNselectedItems	XmNselectedItemCount

See Appendix B for information about which arguments are supported by which widgets. See Appendix C for information about what the valid value type is for each built-in argument.

The following example shows how to declare and reference an arguments list:

```
LIST
    default_size: ARGUMENTS {
        XmNheight = 500;
        XmNwidth = 700;
    };
    default_args: ARGUMENTS {
        ARGUMENTS default_size;
        XmNforeground = white;
        XmNbackground = blue;
    };
```

19.5.2 Callbacks List Structure

Use a callbacks list to define which callback reasons are to be processed by a particular widget at run time. Each callbacks list entry has the following syntax:

callback-list-entry ::=
    reason-name "=" *procedure-reference*
procedure-reference ::=
    PROCEDURE *procedure-name*
      ["(" [*value-expression*] ")" ";"
       | *procedure-list-specification*]

For Motif Toolkit widgets, the reason name must be a built-in reason name. For a user-defined widget, you can use a reason name that you previously specified using the **REASON** function (see Section 18.5.14). If you use a built-in reason in an object definition, the UIL compiler ensures that reason is supported by the type of object you are defining. Appendix B shows which reasons each object supports.

If the same reason appears more than once in a callbacks list, the last entry referring to that name supersedes all previous entries using the same reason, and the UIL compiler issues a diagnostic message.

If you specify a named value for the procedure argument (callback tag), the data type of the value must match the type specified for the callback tag in the corresponding procedure declaration. See Section 19.4 for a detailed explanation of argument type checking for procedures.

The following example shows how to declare a callbacks list:

```
LIST
    default_callbacks : CALLBACKS {
        XmNdestroyCallback = PROCEDURE app_destroy (k_main);
        XmNhelpCallback = PROCEDURE app_help (k_main);
    };
```

The following lines of pseudocode show the interface to the callback procedure:

```
PROCEDURE procedure-name (widget by reference,
                         tag by reference,
                         reason by reference
           RETURNS: no-value);
```

Because the UIL compiler produces a UID file rather than an object module (.o), the binding of the UIL name to the address of the entry point to the procedure is not done by the loader, but is established at run time with the MRM function **MrmRegisterNames**. You call this function before fetching any objects, giving it both the UIL names and the procedure addresses of each callback. The name you register with MRM in the application program must match the name you specified for the procedure in the UIL module.

Each callback procedure receives three arguments. The first two arguments have the same form for each callback. The form of the third argument varies from object to object.

The first argument is the address of the data structure maintained by the Motif Toolkit for this object instance. This address is called the widget ID for this object.

The second argument is the address of the value you specified in the callbacks list for this procedure. The XmNdestroyCallback callback in this example has *app_destroy* as its callback procedure. The second argument is address of the integer *k_main*. If you do not specify an argument, the address is NULL.

Consult Chapter 3 of this guide to find the structure of the third argument. The reason name you specified in the UIL module is the first field in this structure.

19.5.3 Controls List Structure

A controls list defines which objects are children of, or controlled by, a particular object. Each entry in a controls list has the following syntax:

control-list-entry ::=
    [**MANAGED** I **UNMANAGED**] *object-definition*

If you specify the keyword **MANAGED** at run time, the object is created and managed; if you specify **UNMANAGED** at run time, the object is only created. Objects are managed by default.

Unlike the arguments list and the callbacks list, a controls list entry that is identical to a previous entry does not supersede the previous entry. At run time, each controls list entry causes a child to be created when the parent is created. If the same object definition is used for multiple children, multiple instances of the child are created at run time. See Appendix B for a list of which widget types can be controlled by which other widget types.

The following example shows how to declare a controls list:

```
LIST
        default_main_controls : CONTROLS {
            XmCommand main_command;
            XmMenuBar main_menu;
            UNMANAGED XmList file_menu;
            UNMANAGED XmOptionMenu edit_menu;
        };
```

19.5.4 Procedures List Structure

You can specify multiple procedures for a callback reason in UIL by defining a procedures list. Just as with other list types, lists can be defined inline or in a list section and referenced by name.

If you define a reason more than once (for example, when the reason is defined both in a referenced procedures list and in the callbacks list for the object), previous definitions are overridden by the latest definition. The syntax for a procedures list is as follows:

procedure-list-specification ::=
   PROCEDURES *procedure-list-spec*
procedure-list-spec ::=
   { *procedure-list-name*
   | "{" [*procedure-list-clause*...] "}" }
procedure-list-clause ::=
   { *procedure-list-specification* | *procedure-list-ref* }
procedure-list-ref ::=
   procedure-list-name ["(" [*tag-value-expression*] ")"]
callback-list-entry ::=
   reason-name "=" *procedure-list-spec*

You can specify multiple procedures for each callback reason in UIL by defining the procedures as a type of list. Just as with other list types, you can define procedures lists either inline, or in a list section and referenced by name. If you define a reason more than once (for example, when the reason is defined both in a referenced procedures list and in the callbacks list for the object), previous definitions are overridden by the latest definition.

The following example shows how to specify multiple procedures per callback reason in an object declaration for the push button gadget. In the example, both functions *quit_proc* and *shutdown* are called in response to the XmNactivateCallback callback reason.

```
OBJECT m_quit_button: XmPushButton {
    ARGUMENTS {
                    .
                    .
                };
    CALLBACKS {
        XmNactivateCallback = PROCEDURES
            {
                quit_proc ('normal exit');
                shutdown ();
            };
    };
};
```

19.6 Structure of an Object Section

An object section consists of the keyword OBJECT followed by a sequence of object declarations. It has the following syntax:

object-section ::=
    OBJECT *object-declaration...*
object-declaration ::=
    object-name ":"
        { **EXPORTED** *object-definition*
        I **PRIVATE** *object-definition*
        I *object-definition*
        I **IMPORTED** *object-type* } ";"
object-definition ::=
    object-type [*procedure-reference*] *object-spec*
object-spec ::=
    { *object-name* [**WIDGET** I **GADGET**]
    I "{" *list-definition...* "}" }
procedure-reference ::=
    PROCEDURE *creation_function*

Use an object declaration to define the objects that are to be stored in the UID file. You can reference the object name in declarations that occur elsewhere in the UIL module in any context where an object name can be used (for example, in a controls list, as a symbolic reference to a widget ID, or as the tag_value argument for a callback procedure). Objects can be forward referenced; that is, you can declare an object name after you reference it. All references to an object name must be consistent with the type of the object, as specified in the object declaration. You can specify an object as exported, imported, or private.

The object definition contains a sequence of lists that define the arguments, hierarchy, and callbacks for the widget. You can specify only one list of each type for an object. If you want to specify more than one list of arguments, controls, or callbacks, you can do so within one list, as follows:

object some_widget:
  arguments {
    arguments_list1;
    arguments_list2;
  };

When you declare a user-defined widget, you must include a reference to the widget creation function for the user-defined widget. See Section 22.5 for more information.

In this example, *arguments_list1* and *arguments_list2* are lists of arguments that were previously defined in a list section. The following example shows how to declare an object:

```
OBJECT
    app_main : EXPORTED XmMainWindow {
        ARGUMENTS {
            ARGUMENTS default_args;
            XmNheight = 1000;
            XmNwidth = 800;
        };
        CALLBACKS default_callbacks;
        CONTROLS {
            XmMenuBar main_menu;
            user_defined my_object;
        };
    };
```

The following sections detail UIL syntax for specifying object variants, show an example of a UIL module in which gadgets are specified (using both the default object-variant clause and explicit declaration methods), and describe UIL compiler diagnostics related to gadgets.

19.6.1 Specifying the Object Variant in the Module Header

You can include a default object-variant clause in the module header to specify the default variant of objects defined in the module on a type-by-type basis. The object type can be any user interface object type that has a gadget variant (cascade button, label, push button, separator, or toggle button). If you specify any other object type as a gadget, the UIL compiler issues a diagnostic.

When you include an object type in the default object-variant clause, all objects of that type default to the variant you specified in the clause. For example, the following default object-variant clause specifies that all push buttons in the module are gadgets:

```
OBJECTS = { XmPushButton = GADGET; }
```

The UIL compiler issues an informational diagnostic if you attempt to specify an object type more than once in the default object-variant clause.

You can override the specification you made in the default object-variant clause when you declare a particular object. If you omit the default object-variant clause, or omit an object type from the clause, the UIL compiler assumes you want the omitted type to be a widget. You can also explicitly override this default in an object declaration. The example in Section 19.6.2 shows how to use the default object-variant clause and how to override the variant specification in an object declaration.

19.6.2 Specifying the Object Variant in the Object Declaration

You can use one of the keywords WIDGET or GADGET as an attribute of an object declaration. You include the keyword between the object type and the left brace of the object specification. Use the GADGET or WIDGET keyword to specify the object type or to override the default variant for this object type.

The syntax of the object declaration is as follows:

OBJECT
   object-name : *object-type* GADGET | WIDGET {
     .
     .
     .
   };

The object type can be any user interface object type that has a gadget variant (cascade button, label, push button, separator, or toggle button). If you specify any other object type as a gadget, the UIL compiler issues a diagnostic.

You can use the Motif Toolkit name of an object type that has a gadget variant (for example, **XmLabelGadget**) as an attribute of an object declaration. The syntax of the object declaration is as follows:

OBJECT
   object-name : *object-type* {
     .
     .
     .
   };

The *object_type* can be any object type, including gadgets.

The following example shows how to specify gadgets:

```
MODULE sample
    NAMES = case_insensitive
    OBJECTS =
        { XmSeparator = GADGET; XmPushButton = WIDGET; }
    OBJECT
        a_button : XmPushButton GADGET {
            ARGUMENTS { XmNlabelString = 'choice a'; };
        };
        a_menu : XmPulldownMenu {
            ARGUMENTS { XmNborderWidth = 2; };
            CONTROLS {
                XmPushButton a_button;
                XmSeparator GADGET {};
                XmPushButton {
                    ARGUMENTS { XmNlabelString = 'choice b'; };
                };
                XmSeparator WIDGET {};
                XmPushButton c_button;
                XmSeparator {};
            };
        };
        c_button : XmPushButtonGadget {
            ARGUMENTS { XmNlabelString = 'choice c'; };
        };
END MODULE;
```

In this example, the default object-variant clause specifies that all separator objects are gadgets and all push button objects are widgets, unless overridden. Object *a_button* is explicitly specified as a gadget. Object *a_menu* defaults to a widget. Object *c_button* is explicitly specified as a gadget using the toolkit name.

Notice that the reference to *a_button* in the controls list of *a_menu* refers to the *a_button* gadget; you need to include the gadget attribute only on the declaration of *a_button*, not on each reference to *a_button*. The same holds true for *c_button*, even though the reference to *c_button* in the controls list for *a_menu* is a forward reference. The unnamed push button definition in the controls list for *a_menu* is a widget because of the default object-variant clause; the last separator is a gadget for the same reason.

You need to specify the GADGET or WIDGET keyword only in the declaration of an object, not when you reference the object. You cannot specify the GADGET or WIDGET keyword for a user-defined object; user-defined objects are always widgets.

19.7 Structure of an Identifier Section

The identifier section allows you to define an identifier, a mechanism that achieves run-time binding of data to names that appear in a UIL module. The identifier section consists of the reserved keyword IDENTIFIER, followed by a list of names, each name followed by a semicolon. You can later use these names in the UIL module as either the value of an argument to a widget or the tag value to a callback procedure. At run time, you use the MRM functions **MrmRegisterNames** and **MrmRegisterNamesInHierarchy** to bind the identifier name with the address of the data associated with the identifier. (See Chapter 21 for information about MRM functions.)

Each UIL module has a single name space; therefore, you cannot use a name you used for a value, object, or procedure as an identifier name in the same module.

The following example shows how to use an identifier section in a UIL module:

```
IDENTIFIER
    my_x_id;
    my_y_id;
    my_destroy_id;
```

The UIL compiler does not do any type checking on the use of identifiers in a UIL module. Unlike a UIL value, an identifier does not have a UIL type associated with it. Regardless of what particular type a widget argument or callback procedure tag is defined to be, you can use an identifier in that context instead of a value of the corresponding type.

To reference these identifier names in a UIL module, you use the name of the identifier wherever you want its value to be used.

Identifiers can be referenced in any context where a value can be referenced in UIL, although the primary uses for identifiers are as callback procedure tags and widget argument values.

The UIL module in the following example, the identifiers *my_x_id* and *my_y_id* are used as argument values for the main window widget, *my_main*. The position of the main window widget may depend on the screen size of the terminal on which the interface is displayed. Using identifiers, you can provide the values of the XmNx and XmNy arguments at run time. The identifier named *my_destroy_id* is specified as the tag to the callback procedure *my_destroy_callback*. In the application program, you could allocate a data structure and use *my_destroy_id* to store the address of the data structure. When the XmNdestroyCallback reason occurs, the data structure is passed as the tag to procedure *my_destroy_callback*.

```
MODULE id_example
  NAMES = CASE_INSENSITIVE
    IDENTIFIER
        my_x_id;
        my_y_id;
        my_destroy_id;
    PROCEDURE
        my_destroy_callback ( STRING );
    OBJECT my_main : XmMainWindow {
        ARGUMENTS {
          XmNx = my_x_id;
          XmNy = my_y_id;
        };
        CALLBACKS {
          XmNdestroyCallback = PROCEDURE my_destroy_callback
                ( my_destroy_id );
        };
    };
END MODULE;
```

19.8 Include Directive

The include directive incorporates the contents of a specified file into a UIL module. This mechanism allows several UIL modules to share common definitions. The syntax for the include directive is as follows:

include-directive ::=
    INCLUDE FILE *character-expression* ";"

The file specified in the include directive is called an include file. The UIL compiler replaces the include directive with the contents of the include file and processes it as if these contents had appeared in the current UIL source file.

You can nest include files; that is, an include file can contain include directives. The UIL compiler can process up to 100 references (including the file containing the UIL module). Therefore, you can include up to 99 files in a single UIL module, including nested files. Each time a file is opened counts as a reference, so including the same file twice counts as two references.

The character expression is a file specification that identifies the file to be included. The rules for finding the specified file are similar to the rules for finding header, or **.h** files using the include directive, **#include**, with a quoted string in C.

If you do not supply a directory, the UIL compiler searches for the include file in the directory of the main source file; if the compiler does not find the include file there, the compiler looks in the same directory as the source file. If you supply a directory, the UIL compiler searches only that directory for the file.

The following example shows how to use the include directive:

```
INCLUDE FILE 'constants';
```

19.9 Definitions for Constraint Arguments

The Motif Toolkit and the X Toolkit (intrinsics) support constraint arguments. A constraint argument is one that is passed to children of an object, beyond those arguments normally available. For example, the Form widget grants a set of constraint arguments to its children. These arguments control the position of the children within the Form.

Unlike the arguments used to define the attributes of a particular widget, constraint arguments are used exclusively to define additional attributes of the children of a particular widget. These attributes affect the behavior of the children within their parent. To supply constraint arguments to the children, you include the arguments in the arguments list for the child, as shown in the following example:

```
OBJECT
   my_form : XmForm {
      arguments {
           XmNx = 70;
           XmNy = 20;
           XmNrows = 35;
      };
      CONTROLS {
          XmPushButton {
               ARGUMENTS {
                   ! Constraint argument
                   XmNleftAttachment = XmATTACH_WIDGET;
                   ! Constraint argument
                   XmNleftOffset = 10;
               };
          };
      };
   };
```

19.10 Symbolic Referencing of Widget IDs

The UIL compiler allows you to reference a widget ID symbolically by using its name. This mechanism addresses the problem that the UIL compiler views widgets by name and the Motif Toolkit views widgets by widget ID. Widget IDs are defined at run time and are therefore unavailable for use in a UIL module.

When you need to supply an argument that requires a widget ID, you can use the UIL name of that widget (and its object type) as the argument. For example, the children of a Form widget can have an argument that references a widget as the anchor point for a top attachment. You give the type and name of the object you want to use for the top attachment as the value for this argument.

The widget name you reference must be a descendant of the widget being fetched for MRM to find the referenced widget; you cannot reference an arbitrary widget. MRM checks this at run time. For example, a practical use of symbolic references is to specify the default push button (in a bulletin board or radio box).

The following example shows how to use a symbolic reference:

```
MODULE
    NAMES = CASE_INSENSITIVE
        OBJECT my_dialog_box : XmBulletinBoard {
            ARGUMENTS {
                XmNdefaultButton = XmPushButton yes_button;
            };
            CONTROLS {
                XmPushButton yes_button;
                XmPushButton no_button;
            };
        };
        OBJECT yes_button : XmPushButton {
            ARGUMENTS {
                XmNlabelString = 'yes';
            };
        };
        OBJECT no_button : XmPushButton {
            ARGUMENTS {
                XmNlabelString = 'no';
            };
        };
END MODULE;
```

In this example, two PushButton widgets are defined, named *yes_button* and *no_button*. In the definition of the BulletinBoard widget, the name *yes_button* is given as the value for the **XmNdefaultButton** argument. Usually, this argument accepts a widget ID. When you use a symbolic reference (the object type and name of the *yes_button* widget) as the value for the **XmNdefaultButton** argument, MRM substitutes the widget ID of the *yes_button* PushButton for its name at run time.

Symbolic referencing of widget IDs is acceptable for any argument whose resource class is **XmCWidget**. See the *OSF/Motif Programmer's Reference* for resource names and classes.

Chapter 20

Using the UIL Compiler

This chapter discusses the following:

- Invoking the compiler
- Default character sets for string literals
- Interpreting diagnostics issued by the compiler
- Reading the listing produced by the compiler

20.1 Invoking the Compiler

This section describes how to invoke the UIL compiler from the command line using the **uil** command, or from within an application using the **Uil** function.

20.1.1 Invoking the Compiler by Command

You invoke the UIL compiler with the **uil** command. The **uil** command has the following syntax:

uil [*option...*] *input-file*

The input file contains the UIL specification to be compiled. You can use the options to control the output of the UIL compiler.

The supported options are listed in the following table.

Table 20-1. UIL Command Line Options

Option	Default	Description
-ofilename	a.uid	Directs the compiler to produce a User Interface Definition (UID) file. By default, UIL creates a UID file with the name a.uid.
		No UID file is produced if the compiler issues any diagnostics categorized as error or severe.
-vfilename	No listing is generated	Directs the compiler to produce a listing file. If the -v option is not present, no listing is generated by the compiler.
-m	No machine code is listed	Directs the compiler to place in the listing file a description of the records that it added to the UID file. This helps you isolate errors.
-w	Warning messages are generated	Directs the compiler to suppress all warning and informational messages. Error messages and severe messages are generated.

Option	Default	Description
-Ipathname	/usr/include	If you specify the -I option followed by a pathname, with no intervening spaces, the compiler uses the specified pathname to locate include files when the include directive is used. A trailing / (slash) on the specified pathname is optional; if it is omitted, the compiler inserts it for you. For example: -I/usr/include/myuilpath Causes the compiler to look for include files in the directory /usr/include/myuilpath if the include file has not been found in the paths that have already been searched.

20.1.2 Invoking the Compiler by Function

This section describes the **Uil** callable interface routine. This routine allows you to invoke the UIL compiler from within an application, and returns a data structure, describing the UIL module that was compiled. This section also describes the **UilDumpSymbolTable** routine, used to perform a symbol table dump.

The **Uil** function invokes the UIL compiler from within an application. It has the following syntax:

#include <uil/UilDef.h>
Uil_status_type Uil(*command_desc, compile_desc,*
  message_cb, message_data, status_cb, status_data)
  Uil_command_type *command_desc;
  Uil_compile_desc_type *compile_desc;
  Uil_continue_type (*message_cb) ();
  char *message_data;
  Uil_continue_type (*status_cb) ();
  char *status_data;

The **Uil** function provides a callable entry point for the UIL compiler. The callable interface can be used to process a UIL source file and to generate UID files, as well as return a detailed description of the UIL source module in the form of a symbol table (parse tree).

command_desc	Specifies the UIL command line.
compile_desc	Returns the results of the compilation.
message_cb	Specifies a callback function that is called when the compiler encounters errors in the UIL source.
message_data	Specifies user data that is passed to the message callback function (*message_cb*). Note that this argument is not interpreted by UIL, and is used exclusively by the calling application.
status_cb	Specifies a callback function that is called to allow X applications to service X events such as updating the screen. This function is called at various check points, which have been hardcoded into the UIL compiler. The status_update_delay argument in *command_desc* specifies the number of check points to be passed before the *status_cb* function is invoked.

status_data   Specifies user data that is passed to the status callback function (*status_cb*). Note that this argument is not interpreted by the UIL compiler, and is used exclusively by the calling application.

The data structures **Uil_command_type** and **Uil_compile_desc_type** are detailed in the text that follows this example.

```
typedef struct Uil_command_type {
    char *source_file; /* single source to compile */
    char *resource_file; /* name of output file */
    char *listing_file; /* name of listing file */
    unsigned int *include_dir_count; /* number of directories in
                    /* include_dir array */
    char *((*include_dir) []); /* directory to search for
                    /* include files */
    unsigned listing_file_flag: 1; /* produce a listing */
    unsigned resource_file_flag: 1; /* generate UID output */
    unsigned machine_code_flag: 1; /* generate machine code */
    unsigned report_info_msg_flag: 1; /* report info messages */
    unsigned report_warn_msg_flag: 1; /* report warnings */
    unsigned parse_tree_flag: 1; /* generate parse tree */
    unsigned int status_update_delay; /* number of times a */
                    /* status point is passed before */
                    /* calling status_cb function */
                    /* 0 means called every time */

    }


typedef struct Uil_compile_desc_type {
    unsigned int compiler_version; /* version number */
                    /* of compiler */
    unsigned int data_version; /* version number of structures */
    char *parse_tree_root; /* parse tree output */
    unsigned int message_count [Uil_k_max_status+1];
                    /* array of severity counts /*

    }
```

Following is a description of the message callback function specified by *message_cb*:

Uil_continue_type   (**message_cb*)   (*message_data, message_number, severity, msg_buffer, src_buffer, ptr_buffer, loc_buffer, message_count*)

char	**message_data*;
int	*message_number*;
int	*severity*;
char	**msg_buffer*, **src_buffer*;
char	**ptr_buffer*, **loc_buffer*;
int	*message_count*[];

Specifies a callback function that UIL invokes instead of printing an error message when the compiler encounters an error in the UIL source. The callback should return one of these values:

Uil_k_terminate   Tells UIL to terminate processing of the source file

Uil_k_continue   Tells UIL to continue processing the source file

Following are the arguments:

message_data   Data supplied by the application as the *message_data* argument to the **Uil** function. UIL does not interpret this data in any way; it just passes it to the callback.

message_number   An index into a table of error messages and severities, for internal use by UIL.

severity   An integer that indicates the severity of the error. The possible values are the status constants returned by the **Uil** function.

msg_buffer   A string that describes the error.

src_buffer   A string consisting of the source line where the error occurred. This is not always available; the argument is then NULL.

ptr_buffer   A string consisting of white space and a printing character in the character position corresponding to the column of the source line where the error occurred. This string may be printed beneath the source line to provide a visual indication of the column where the error occurred. This is not always available; the argument is then NULL.

loc_buffer   A string identifying the line number and file of the source line where the error occurred. This is not always available; the argument is then NULL.

message_count   An array of integers containing the number of diagnostic messages issued thus far for each severity level. To find the number of messages issued for the current severity level, use the *severity* argument as the index into this array.

Following is a description of the status callback function specified by *status_cb*:

Uil_continue_type (**status_cb*) (*status_data, percent_complete, lines_processed, current_file, message_count*)

char	**status_data*;
int	*percent_complete*;
int	*lines_processed*;
char	**current_file*;
int	*message_count*[];

Specifies a callback function that is invoked to allow X applications to service X events such as updating the screen. The callback should return one of these values:

Uil_k_terminate   Tells UIL to terminate processing of the source file

Uil_k_continue   Tells UIL to continue processing the source file

Following are the arguments:

status_data   Data supplied by the application as the *status_data* argument to the **Uil** function. UIL does not interpret this data in any way; it just passes it to the callback.

percent_complete   An integer indicating what percentage of the current source file has been processed so far.

lines_processed   An integer indicating how many lines of the current source file have been read so far.

current_file	A string containing the pathname of the current source file.
message_count	An array of integers containing the number of diagnostic messages issued thus far for each severity level. To find the number of messages issued for a given severity level, use the severity level as the index into this array. The possible severity levels are the status constants returned by the **Uil** function.

This function returns one of the following status return values:

Uil_k_success_status	The operation succeeded.
Uil_k_info_status	The operation succeeded, and an informational message is returned.
Uil_k_warning_status	The operation succeeded, and a warning message is returned.
Uil_k_error_status	The operation failed due to an error.
Uil_k_severe_status	The operation failed due to an error.

The **UilDumpSymbolTable** function dumps the contents of a named UIL symbol table. It has the following syntax:

#include <uil/UilDef.h>
void UilDumpSymbolTable UIL(*root_ptr***)**
    sym_root_entry_type **root_ptr*;

The **UilDumpSymbolTable** function dumps the contents of a UIL symbol table pointer that was returned from the UIL callable interface.

root_ptr	Returns a pointer to the the symbol table root entry.

By following the link from the root entry, you can traverse the entire parse tree. Symbol table entries are in the following format:

hex.address symbol.type symbol.data
  prev.source.position
  source.position
  modification.record

where:

hex.address	Specifies the hexadecimal address of this entry in the symbol table.
symbol.type	Specifies the type of this symbol table entry. Some possible types are **root**, **module**, **value**, **procedure**, and **widget**.
symbol.data	Specifies data for the symbol table entry. The data varies with the type of the entry. Often it contains pointers to other symbol table entries, or the actual data for the data type.
prev.source.position	Specifies the endpoint in the source code for the previous source item.
source.position	Specifies the range of positions in the source code for this symbol.

The exact data structures for each symbol type are defined in the include file **<uil/UilSymDef.h>**. Note that this file is automatically included when an application includes the file **<uil/UilDef.h>**.

20.2 Default Character Set for String Literals

Every string literal has a character set associated with it. The character set is determined when the UIL file is compiled.

For a string declared as '*string*,' the character set is the codeset component of the value of the **LANG** environment variable at compile time if **LANG** is set. If **LANG** is not set or if it has no codeset component, the character set is the value of **XmFALLBACK_CHARSET** at compile time. The default value of **XmFALLBACK_CHARSET** is ISO8859-1 (equivalent to ISO-LATIN1), but a vendor may set a different default.

For a string declared as "*string*," the character set is the default character set of the module if specified (see Section 19.1.3). If no character set is specified for the module, the character set is determined as for a string declared as '*string*.'

20.3 Interpreting Diagnostics Issued by the Compiler

The compiler issues diagnostics to the standard error file. The following example shows the form of these messages:

```
value d: font( 1 );
                 *
Error: found integer value when expecting string value
             line: 10  file: value_error.uil
```

The first line is the source line that produced the diagnostic. If the compiler cannot retrieve the source line from the input file, this line is omitted. Any control characters in the text of the line are printed as ? (question marks).

The second line of the diagnostic marks the start of the construct that resulted in the diagnostic. In this case the literal 1 is marked. If the error is not associated with a particular construct, the second line is omitted. If the source line cannot be retrieved, this line is also omitted, and the column information is included with the line and file information following the diagnostic message.

The third line is the diagnostic being issued.

The fourth line specifies the file containing the source line being diagnosed and the line number of the source line within that file.

The following table lists the four levels of diagnostics that are issued by the compiler, in ascending order of severity.

Table 20-2. Levels of Diagnostic Messages

Severity	Compilation Status
Informational	Accompanies other diagnostics that should be investigated.
Warning	Compilation continues: check that the compiler did what you expected.
Error	Compilation continues: no UID file will be generated.
Severe	Compilation terminates immediately.

20.4 Reading the Compiler Listing

The listing produced by the compiler contains:

- A title giving miscellaneous information about the compilation
- Source lines of the input file
- Source lines of any include files
- Diagnostics issued by the compiler
- A summary of the diagnostics issued
- A summary of the files read

The following example shows the contents of a sample listing file:

```
MOTIF UIL Compiler V1.0-000     Wed Dec 16 11:13:31 1989  Page 1
Module: EXAMPLE           Version: X-1
  1 (0)         MODULE example VERSION = 'X-1'
  2 (0)
  3 (0)          INCLUDE FILE 'colors.uil';
  1 (1)
  2 (1)          VALUE red: COLOR( 1 );  VALUE green: COLOR( 2 );
                            1                              2
Error:  (1) found integer value when expecting string value
Error:  (2) found integer value when expecting string value
  3 (1)          VALUE blue: COLOR( 'XcolorBlue' ;
  4 (1)
  4 (0)
  5 (0)         OBJECT primary_window:
  6 (0)            XmMainWindow
  7 (0)             { ARGUMENTS
  8 (0)                    { XmNforeground = pink;
                                        1
Error:  (1) value PINK must be defined before this reference
Error:  (1) found error value when expecting color value
  9 (0)                      XmNbackground = blue; }};
                                                   1
Error:  (1) unexpected RIGHT_BRACE token seen - parsing resumes
        after ";"
 10 (0)                 };
 11 (0)        END MODULE;
Info:  (0) errors: 5  warnings: 0  informationals: 0
   File (0)   a.uil
   File (1)   colors.uil
```

20.4.1 Title

Each new page of the listing starts with a title:

```
MOTIF UIL Compiler V1.0-000     Wed Dec 16 11:13:31 1989  Page 1
Module: EXAMPLE           Version: X-1
```

The first line of the title identifies the compiler by name, the version of the compiler used for the compilation, and the time the compilation started. In this case, the version of the compiler used was **V1.0-000**.

The second line of the title lists the module name for the UIL specification and the version of that module if provided in the source.

20.4.2 Source Line

The printing of each source line is preceded by two numbers:

```
1 (0)    MODULE example VERSION = 'X-1'
```

The number in parentheses designates which file the source line was read from. By looking at the file summary at the end of the listing, you will see that file (0) is a.uil. The first number on the source line is the line number within the source file.

If a source line contains any control characters other than tabs, they are replaced in the listing by ? (question marks).

20.4.3 Diagnostics

Diagnostics for a particular source line follow that line in the listing.

```
2 (1)    VALUE red: COLOR( 1 );   VALUE green: COLOR( 2 );
                   1                            2
Error:   (1) found integer value when expecting string value
Error:   (2) found integer value when expecting string value
    8 (0)                        { XmNforeground = pink;
                                                   1
Error:   (1) value PINK must be defined before this reference
Error:   (1) found error value when expecting color value
```

The line following the source line points to the position in the source line where each of the diagnostics occurred. You can determine the position of each diagnostic by looking at the number in parentheses that follows the diagnostic severity. For example, diagnostic 1 for source line 2 is at position (1), and diagnostic 2 for the same source line is at position (2). Both the diagnostics for source line 8 occur at position (1).

If a diagnostic has no associated position on the line, the position is given as (0). If a diagnostic is not associated with a source line, it appears following the last source line. The summary diagnostic, which tallies the number of diagnostics of each severity level, is an example of a diagnostic with no source line association.

20.4.4 Summaries

The following listing contains two summaries:

```
Info: (0) errors: 5 warnings: 0 informationals: 0
      file (0)    a.uil
      file (1)    colors.uil
```

The first summary is in the form of a diagnostic that tallies the number of error, warning, and informational diagnostics.

The second summary lists the files that contributed to the UIL specification. This list is useful in determining from which file a source line in the listing was read. A source line preceded by the sequence 532 (3) in the listing was read from line 532 of file (3) in the summary list.

Chapter 21
Motif Resource Manager Functions

The functions discussed in this chapter define the application interface to Motif Resource Manager (MRM). MRM is responsible for creating widgets based on definitions contained in the UID files created by the UIL compiler. MRM interprets the output of the UIL compiler and generates the appropriate argument lists for widget creation functions. Specifically, the functions discussed in this chapter allow your application to

- Initialize MRM.

- Provide information required by MRM to successfully interpret information contained in UID files.

- Create widgets using UID file definitions.

- Read literal definitions from UID files. These definitions are created by using the exported value definitions in the UIL, and the resulting literals may be used for any purpose the application requires.

The representation of widgets in a UID file is not exposed in these functions. All management and translation of these representations is done internally.

All definitions required to use MRM facilities are contained in the include file **<Mrm/MrmPublic.h>**.

21.1 Setting Up Storage and Data Structures

To initialize the internal data structures needed by MRM, use **MrmInitialize**.

void MrmInitialize ()

The **MrmInitialize** function must be called to prepare an application to use MRM widget-fetching facilities. You must call this function prior to fetching a widget. However, it is good programming practice to call **MrmInitialize** prior to performing any MRM operations. **MrmInitialize** initializes the internal data structures that MRM needs to successfully perform type conversion on arguments and to successfully access widget creation facilities. An application must call **MrmInitialize** before it uses other MRM functions.

21.2 Obtaining UID Database File IDs

A Motif application can access different UID files based on the language preferences of the user. This capability is provided by MRM in a way that is consistent with the existing NLS standards as specified in the *XOpen Portability Guide* (issue 3, draft 2). In particular, the capability is compatible with the searching and naming conventions used to access message catalogs. To specify the UID files to be opened in Motif applications, use **MrmOpenHierarchy**:

#include <Mrm/MrmPublic.h>
Cardinal MrmOpenHierarchy (*num_files*, *file_names_list*,
        ancillary_structures_list, *hierarchy_id*)
  MrmCount *num_files*;
  String *file_names_list* [];
  MrmOsOpenParamPtr **ancillary_structures_list* ;
  MrmHierarchy **hierarchy_id*;

num_files   Specifies the number of files in the name list.

file_names_list
        Specifies an array of pointers to character strings that identify the .uid files.

ancillary_structures_list
        A list of operating system dependent ancillary structures corresponding to such things as file names, clobber flag, and so forth. This argument should be NULL for most operations. If you need to reference this structure, see the definition of MrmOsOpenParamPtr in MrmPublic.h for more information.

hierarchy_id   Returns the search hierarchy ID. The search hierarchy ID identifies the list of **.uid** files that MRM searches (in order) when performing subsequent fetch calls.

The **MrmOpenHierarchy** function allows the user to specify the list of UID files that MRM searches in subsequent fetch operations. All subsequent fetch operations return the first occurrence of the named item encountered while traversing the UID hierarchy from the first list element (UID file specification) to the last list element. This function also allocates a hierarchy ID and opens all the UID files in the hierarchy. It initializes the optimized search lists in the hierarchy. If **MrmOpenHierarchy** encounters any errors during its execution, it closes any files that were opened.

Each UID file string in *file_names_list* can specify either a full pathname or a filename. If a UID file string has a leading / (slash), it specifies a full pathname, and MRM opens the file as specified. Otherwise, the UID file string specifies a filename. In this case MRM looks for the file along a search path specified by the **UIDPATH** environment variable or by a default search path, which varies depending on whether or not the **XAPPLRESDIR** environment variable is set. The filename is substituted for each occurrence of **%U** in the search path.

The **UIDPATH** environment variable specifies a search path and naming conventions associated with UID files. It can contain the substitution field **%U**, where the UID file string from the *file_names_list* argument to **MrmOpenHierarchy** is substituted for **%U**. It can also contain the substitution fields accepted by **XtResolvePathname**. For example, the following **UIDPATH** value and **MrmOpenHierarchy** call cause MRM to open two separate UID files:

```
UIDPATH=/uidlib/%L/%U.uid:/uidlib/%U/%L
  static char *uid_files[] =
      {"/usr/users/me/test.uid", "test2"};
    MrmHierarchy  *Hierarchy_id;
    MrmOpenHierarchy( (MrmCount)2,uid_files,
      NULL, Hierarchy_id)
```

MRM opens the first file, **/usr/users/me/test.uid**, as specified in the *file_names_list* argument to **MrmOpenHierarchy** because the UID file string in the *file_names_list* argument specifies a full pathname. MRM looks for the second file, **test2**, first as **/uidlib/%L/test2.uid** and second as **/uidlib/test2/%L**, where the current setting of the **xnlLanguage** resource or the **LANG** environment variable is substituted for **%L**.

If **UIDPATH** is not set but the environment variable **XAPPLRESDIR** is set, MRM searches the following pathnames:

```
%U
$XAPPLRESDIR/%L/uid/%N/%U
$XAPPLRESDIR/%l/uid/%N/%U
$XAPPLRESDIR/uid/%N/%U
$XAPPLRESDIR/%L/uid/%U
$XAPPLRESDIR/%l/uid/%U
$XAPPLRESDIR/uid/%U
$HOME/uid/%U
$HOME/%U
/usr/lib/X11/%L/uid/%N/%U
/usr/lib/X11/%l/uid/%N/%U
/usr/lib/X11/uid/%N/%U
/usr/lib/X11/%L/uid/%U
/usr/lib/X11/%l/uid/%U
/usr/lib/X11/uid/%U
/usr/include/X11/uid/%U
```

If neither **UIDPATH** nor **XAPPLRESDIR** is set, MRM searches the following pathnames:

```
%U
$HOME/%L/uid/%N/%U
$HOME/%l/uid/%N/%U
$HOME/uid/%N/%U
$HOME/%L/uid/%U
$HOME/%l/uid/%U
$HOME/uid/%U
$HOME/%U
/usr/lib/X11/%L/uid/%N/%U
/usr/lib/X11/%l/uid/%N/%U
/usr/lib/X11/uid/%N/%U
/usr/lib/X11/%L/uid/%U
/usr/lib/X11/%l/uid/%U
/usr/lib/X11/uid/%U
/usr/include/X11/uid/%U
```

The following substitutions are used in these paths:

%U   The UID file string, from the *file_names_list* argument

%N   The class name of the application

%L   The value of the **xnlLanguage** resource or the **LANG** environment variable

%l   The language component of the **xnlLanguage** resource or the **LANG** environment variable

After **MrmOpenHierarchy** opens the UID hierarchy, you should not delete or modify the UID files until you close the UID hierarchy by calling **MrmCloseHierarchy**.

The **MrmOpenHierarchy** function returns one of these status return constants:

MrmSUCCESS   The function executed successfully.
MrmNOT_FOUND File not found.
MrmFAILURE   The function failed.

21.3   Closing a MRM Search Hierarchy

To close an MRM search hierarchy, use **MrmCloseHierarchy**:

#include <Mrm/MrmPublic.h>
Cardinal MrmCloseHierarchy (*hierarchy_id*)
   MrmHierarchy *hierarchy_id*;

hierarchy_id   Specifies the ID of a previously opened UID hierarchy. The *hierarchy_id* was returned in a previous call to **MrmOpenHierarchy**.

The **MrmCloseHierarchy** function closes a UID hierarchy previously opened by **MrmOpenHierarchy**. All files associated with the hierarchy are closed by MRM and all associated memory is returned. The **MrmCloseHierarchy** function returns one of these status return constants:

MrmSUCCESS   The function executed successfully.
MrmFAILURE   The function failed.

21.4 Registering MRM Information and Callbacks

This section discusses the MRM functions you can use to

- Save the information needed to access the widget creation function

- Register a vector of callback functions

21.4.1 Registering MRM Information

To save the information needed to access the widget creation function, use **MrmRegisterClass**:

#include <Mrm/MrmPublic.h>
Cardinal MrmRegisterClass (*class_code, class_name, create_name,*
            create_proc, class_record)
    MrmType *class_code*;
    String *class_name*;
    String *create_name*;
    Widget (* *create_proc*) ();
    WidgetClass *class_record*;

class_code   Specifies the code name of the class. For all application-defined widgets, this code name is **MRMwcUnknown**. For all Motif Toolkit widgets, each code name begins with the letters **MRMwc**. The code names for all application widgets are defined in **Mrm.h**.

class_name   Specifies the case-sensitive name of the class. The class names for all Motif Toolkit widgets are defined in **Mrm.h**. Each class name begins with the letters **MRMwcn**.

create_name   Specifies the case-sensitive name of the low-level widget creation function for the class. An example from the Motif Toolkit is **XmCreateLabel**. Arguments are *parent_widget*, *name*, *override_arglist*, and *override_argcount*.

For user-defined widgets, *create_name* is the creation procedure in the UIL that defines this widget.

create_proc   Specifies the address of the creation function that you named in *create_name*.

class_record   Specifies a pointer to the class record.

The **MrmRegisterClass** function allows MRM to access user-defined widget classes. This function registers the necessary information for MRM to create widgets of this class. You must call **MrmRegisterClass** prior to fetching any user-defined class widget.

MrmRegisterClass saves the information needed to access the widget creation function and to do type conversion of argument lists by using the information in MRM databases.

This function returns one of these status return constants:

MrmSUCCESS The function executed successfully.
MrmFAILURE The allocation of the class descriptor failed.

21.4.2 Registering a Vector of Callback Functions

To register a vector of names of identifiers or callback functions for access in MRM, use **MrmRegisterNames** or **MrmRegisterNamesInHierarchy**:

#include <Mrm/MrmPublic.h>
Cardinal MrmRegisterNames (*register_list*, *register_count*)
  MrmRegisterArglist *register_list*;
  MrmCount *register_count*;

register_list   Specifies a list of name/value pairs for the names to be registered. Each name is a case-sensitive, NULL-terminated ASCII string. Each value is a 32-bit quantity, interpreted as a procedure address if the name is a callback function, and uninterpreted otherwise.

register_count Specifies the number of entries in *register_list*.

The **MrmRegisterNames** function registers a vector of names and associated values for access in MRM. The values can be callback functions, pointers to user-defined data, or any other values. The information provided is used to resolve symbolic references occurring in UID files to their run-time values. For callbacks, this information provides the procedure address required by the Motif Toolkit. For names used as identifiers in UIL, this information provides any run-time mapping the application needs.

The names in the list are case-sensitive. The list can be either ordered or unordered.

Callback functions registered through **MrmRegisterNames** can be either regular or creation callbacks. Regular callbacks have declarations determined by Motif Toolkit and user requirements. Creation callbacks have the same format as any other callback:

void CallBackProc(*widget_id*, *tag*, *callback_data*)
    Widget **widget_id*;
    Opaque *tag*;
    XmAnyCallbackStruct **callback_data*;

widget_id   Specifies the widget ID associated with the widget performing the callback (as in any callback function).

tag   Specifies the tag value (as in any callback function).

callback_data Specifies a widget-specific data structure. This data structure has a minimum of two members, event and reason. The reason member is always set to **MrmCR_CREATE**.

Note that the widget name and parent are available from the widget record accessible through *widget_id*.

This function returns one of these status return constants:

MrmSUCCESS The function executed successfully.
MrmFAILURE Memory allocation failed.

#include <Mrm/MrmPublic.h>
Cardinal MrmRegisterNamesInHierarchy (*hierarchy_id*,
    register_list, *register_count*)
  MrmHierarchy *hierarchy_id* ;
  MrmRegisterArglist *register_list* ;
  MrmCount *register_count* ;

hierarchy_id Specifies the hierarchy with which the names are to be associated.

register_list Specifies a list of name/value pairs for the names to be registered. Each name is a case-sensitive, NULL-terminated ASCII string. Each value is a 32-bit quantity, interpreted as a procedure address if the name is a callback function, and uninterpreted otherwise.

register_count Specifies the number of entries in *register_list*.

The **MrmRegisterNamesInHierarchy** function registers a vector of names and associated values for access in MRM. The values can be callback functions, pointers to user-defined data, or any other values. The information provided is used to resolve symbolic references occurring in UID files to their run-time values. For callbacks, this information provides the procedure address required by the Motif Toolkit. For names used as identifiers in UIL, this information provides any run-time mapping the application needs.

This function is similar to **MrmRegisterNames,** except that the scope of the names registered by **MrmRegisterNamesInHierarchy** is limited to the hierarchy specified by *hierarchy_id*, whereas the names registered by **MrmRegisterNames** have global scope. When MRM looks up a name, it first tries to find the name among those registered for the given hierarchy. If that lookup fails, it tries to find the name among those registered globally.

This function returns one of these status return constants:

MrmSUCCESS The function executed successfully.
MrmFAILURE Memory allocation failed.

21.5 Fetching Widgets

This section discusses the MRM functions you can use to

- Fetch all the widgets defined in some interface
- Fetch values stored in UID files
- Fetch any indexed application widget

21.5.1 Fetching Values Stored in UID Files

To fetch the values to be set from literals stored in UID files, use
MrmFetchSetValues:

#include <Mrm/MrmPublic.h>
Cardinal MrmFetchSetValues(*hierarchy_id*, *widget*, *args*,
    num_args)
  MrmHierarchy *hierarchy_id*;
  Widget *widget*;
  ArgList *args*;
  Cardinal *num_args*;

hierarchy_id Specifies the ID of the UID hierarchy that contains
                the specified literal. The *hierarchy_id* was returned
                in a previous call to **MrmOpenHierarchy**.

widget   Specifies the widget that is modified.

args   Specifies an argument list that identifies the widget
                arguments to be modified as well as the index (UIL
                name) of the literal that defines the value for that
                argument. The name part of each argument
                (*args*[*n*].*name*) must begin with the string **XmN**
                followed by the name that uniquely identifies this

attribute tag. For example, **XmNwidth** is the attribute name associated with the core argument *width*. The value part (*args*[*n*].*value*) must be a string that gives the index (UIL name) of the literal. You must define all literals in UIL as exported values.

num_args   Specifies the number of entries in *args*.

The **MrmFetchSetValues** function is similar to **XtSetValues**, except that the values to be set are defined by the UIL named values that are stored in the UID hierarchy. **MrmFetchSetValues** fetches the values to be set from literals stored in UID files.

This function sets the values on a widget, evaluating the values as literal references that can be resolved from a UID hierarchy. Each literal is fetched from the hierarchy, and its value is modified and converted as required. This value is then placed in the argument list and used as the actual value for an **XtSetValues** call. **MrmFetchSetValues** allows a widget to be modified after creation using UID file values exactly as is done for creation values in **MrmFetchWidget**.

As in **MrmFetchWidget**, each argument whose value can be evaluated from the UID hierarchy is set in the widget. Values that are not found or values in which conversion errors occur are not modified.

Each entry in the argument list identifies an argument to be modified in the widget. The name part identifies the tag, which begins with **XmN**. The value part must be a string whose value is the index of the literal. Thus, the following code modifies the XmLabel resource of the widget to have the value of the literal accessed by the index OK_button_label in the hierarchy:

```
args[n].name  = XmNlabel;
args[n].value = "OK_button_label";
```

This function returns one of these status return constants:

MrmSUCCESS The function executed successfully.
MrmFAILURE The function failed.

21.5.2 Fetching Indexed Application Widgets

To fetch an indexed application widget, use **MrmFetchWidget**.

#include <Mrm/MrmPublic.h>
Cardinal MrmFetchWidget (*hierarchy_id*, *index*, *parent_widget*,
        widget, *class*)
  MrmHierarchy *hierarchy_id*;
  String *index*;
  Widget *parent_widget*;
  Widget *widget;
  MrmType *class;

hierarchy_id   Specifies the ID of the UID hierarchy that contains the interface definition. The *hierarchy_id* was returned in a previous call to **MrmOpenHierarchy**.

index   Specifies the UIL name of the widget to fetch.

parent_widget Specifies the parent widget ID.

widget   Returns the widget ID of the created widget. If this is not NULL when you call **MrmFetchWidgetOverride,** MRM assumes that the widget has already been created and **MrmFetchWidgetOverride** returns **MrmFAILURE**.

class   Returns the class code identifying MRM's widget class. The widget class code for the main window widget, for example, is **MRMwcMainWindow**. Literals identifying MRM widget class codes are defined in **Mrm.h**.

The **MrmFetchWidget** function fetches and then creates an indexed application widget and its children. The indexed application widget is any widget that is named in UIL and that is not the child of any other widget in the UID hierarchy. In fetch operations, the fetched widget's subtree is also fetched and created. This widget must not appear as the child of a widget within its own subtree. **MrmFetchWidget** does not execute **XtManageChild** for the newly created widget.

An application can fetch any named widget in the UID hierarchy using **MrmFetchWidget**. **MrmFetchWidget** can be called at any time to fetch a widget that was not fetched at application startup. **MrmFetchWidget** determines if a widget has already been fetched by checking *widget* for a NULL value. Non-NULL values signify that the widget has already been fetched, and **MrmFetchWidget** fails. **MrmFetchWidget** can be used to defer fetching pop-up widgets until they are first referenced (presumably in a callback), and then used to fetch them once.

MrmFetchWidget can also create multiple instances of a widget (and its subtree). In this case, the UID definition functions as a template; a widget definition can be fetched any number of times. An application can use this to make multiple instances of a widget, for example, in a dialog box box or menu.

The index (UIL name) that identifies the widget must be known to the application.

This function returns one of these status return constants:

MrmSUCCESS The function executed successfully.
MrmNOT_FOUND Widget not found in UID hierarchy.
MrmFAILURE The function failed.

21.5.3 Overriding MrmFetchWidget Arguments

To fetch any indexed application widget and override the **MrmFetchWidget** arguments, use **MrmFetchWidgetOverride**:

#include <Mrm/MrmPublic.h>
Cardinal MrmFetchWidgetOverride (*hierarchy_id*, *index*,
  parent_widget, *override_name*, *override_args*,
  override_num_args, *widget*, *class*)
 MrmHierarchy *hierarchy_id*;
 String *index*;
 Widget *parent_widget*;
 String *override_name*;
 ArgList *override_args*;
 Cardinal *override_num_args*;
 Widget **widget*;
 MrmType **class*;

hierarchy_id Specifies the ID of the UID hierarchy that contains the interface definition. The *hierarchy_id* was returned in a previous call to **MrmOpenHierarchy**.

index Specifies the UIL name of the widget to fetch.

parent_widget Specifies the parent widget ID.

override_name Specifies the name to override the widget name. Use a NULL value if you do not want to override the widget name.

override_args Specifies the override argument list, exactly as given to **XtCreateWidget** (conversion complete and so forth). Use a NULL value if you do not want to override the argument list.

override_num_args
 Specifies the number of arguments in *override_args*.

widget Returns the widget ID of the created widget. If this is not NULL when you call **MrmFetchWidgetOverride**, MRM assumes that the widget has already been created and **MrmFetchWidgetOverride** returns MrmFAILURE.

class   Returns the class code identifying MRM's widget class. For example, the widget class code for the main window widget is **MRMwcMainWindow**. Literals identifying MRM widget class codes are defined in **Mrm.h**.

The **MrmFetchWidgetOverride** function is the extended version of **MrmFetchWidget**. It is identical to **MrmFetchWidget**, except that it allows the caller to override the widget's name and any arguments that **MrmFetchWidget** otherwise retrieves from the UID file or one of the defaulting mechanisms. That is, the override argument list is not limited to those arguments in the UID file.

The override arguments apply only to the widget fetched and returned by this function. Its children (subtree) do not receive any override parameters.

This function returns one of these status return constants:

MrmSUCCESS The function executed successfully.
MrmNOT_FOUND Widget not found in UID hierarchy.
MrmFAILURE   The function failed.

21.6 Fetching Literals

The Motif Toolkit provides functions with which you can fetch literals from UID files. Specifically, the section discusses how to fetch:

- A named color literal

- An icon literal

- A literal value

21.6.1 Fetching a Named Color Literal

To fetch a named color literal, use **MrmFetchColorLiteral**:

#include <Mrm/MrmPublic.h>
int MrmFetchColorLiteral (*hierarchy_id*, *index*, *display*,
              colormap_id, *pixel*)
  MrmHierarchy *hierarchy_id*;
  String *index*;
  Display **display*;
  Colormap *colormap_id*;
  Pixel **pixel*;

hierarchy_id	Specifies the ID of the UID hierarchy that contains the specified literal. The *hierarchy_id* was returned in a previous call to **MrmOpenHierarchy**.
index	Specifies the UIL name of the color literal to fetch. You must define this name in UIL as an exported value.
display	Specifies the display used for the pixmap. The *display* argument specifies the connection to the X server. For more information on the Display structure, see the Xlib function **XOpenDisplay**.
colormap_id	Specifies the ID of the colormap. If NULL, the default colormap is used.
pixel	Returns the ID of the color literal.

The **MrmFetchColorLiteral** function fetches a named color literal from a UID file, and converts the color literal to a pixel color value.

This function returns one of these status return constants:

MrmSUCCESS The function executed successfully.
MrmNOT_FOUND The color literal was not found in the UIL file.
MrmFAILURE The function failed.

21.6.2 Fetching an Icon Literal

To fetch an icon literal, use **MrmFetchIconLiteral**:

#include <Mrm/MrmPublic.h>
int MrmFetchIconLiteral (*hierarchy_id*, *index*, *screen*,
        display, *fgpix*, *bgpix*, *pixmap*)
  MrmHierarchy *hierarchy_id*;
  String *index*;
  Screen **screen*;
  Display **display*;
  Pixel *fgpix*;
  Pixel *bgpix*;
  Pixmap **pixmap*;

hierarchy_id   Specifies the ID of the UID hierarchy that contains the specified icon literal. The *hierarchy_id* was returned in a previous call to **MrmOpenHierarchy**.

index   Specifies the UIL name of the icon literal to fetch.

screen   Specifies the screen used for the pixmap. The *screen* argument specifies a pointer to the Xlib structure Screen that contains the information about that screen and is linked to the Display structure. For more information on the Display and Screen structures, see the Xlib function **XOpenDisplay** and the associated screen information macros.

display   Specifies the display used for the pixmap. The *display* argument specifies the connection to the X server. For more information on the Display structure, see the Xlib function **XOpenDisplay**.

fgpix   Specifies the foreground color for the pixmap.

bgpix   Specifies the background color for the pixmap.

pixmap   Returns the resulting X pixmap value.

The **MrmFetchIconLiteral** function fetches an icon literal from an Mrm.hierarchy, and converts the icon literal to an X pixmap.

This function returns one of these status return constants:

MrmSUCCESS The function executed successfully.
MrmNOT_FOUND The icon literal was not found in the hierarchy.
MrmFAILURE The function failed.

21.6.3 Fetching a Literal Value

To fetch a literal value, use **MrmFetchLiteral**:

#include <Mrm/MrmPublic.h>
int MrmFetchLiteral (*hierarchy_id*, *index*, *display*, *value*, *type*)
    MrmHierarchy *hierarchy_id*;
    String *index*;
    Display *display*;
    caddr_t *value*;
    MrmCode *type*;

hierarchy_id	Specifies the ID of the UID hierarchy that contains the specified literal. The *hierarchy_id* was returned in a previous call to **MrmOpenHierarchy**.
index	Specifies the UIL name of the literal (pixmap) to fetch. You must define this name in UIL as an exported value.
display	Specifies the display used for the pixmap. The *display* argument specifies the connection to the X server. For more information on the Display structure, see the Xlib function **XOpenDisplay**.
value	Returns the ID of the named literal's value.
type	Returns the named literal's data type.

The **MrmFetchLiteral** function reads and returns the value and type of a literal (named value) that is stored as a public resource in a single UID file. This function returns a pointer to the value of the literal. For example, an integer is always returned as a pointer to an integer, and a string is always returned as a pointer to a string.

Applications should not use **MrmFetchLiteral** for fetching icon or color literals. If this is attempted, **MrmFetchLiteral** returns an error.

This function returns one of these status return constants:

MrmSUCCESS The function executed successfully.

MrmWRONG_TYPE The operation encountered an unsupported literal type.

MrmNOT_FOUND The literal was not found in the UID file.

MrmFAILURE The function failed.

Chapter 22

Creating User Interfaces with UIL and MRM

This chapter shows how to build a UIL specification file for the Motifburger demo, compile the file, and access it with MRM functions. It also provides programming tips for developing international applications, working on large projects, and using user-defined widgets.

22.1 Specifying a User Interface Using UIL

The examples in this section are based on the demo application called Motifburger, shown in Figure 22-1. In this section, only relevant portions of the UIL module for the Motifburger application are shown. The complete UIL and C source code for the Motifburger application is shipped with the Motif software kit. You can copy these source files from **./demos/motifburger**.

Note that although the Motifburger application is designed to show as many different widgets and UIL coding techniques as possible, this application does not use every feature of UIL. Figure 22-5 shows the steps involved at run time to set up an interface that was specified with UIL.

To specify an interface using UIL, you create one or more UIL specification files with names that end with the characters .uil. Each file contains one UIL module block, or a legal portion of a module block (such as an object definition). The number of files you use to completely specify the interface depends on the complexity of the application; the need for variations (for example, English and French versions); and the size of the development project team (on large projects, the UIL module can be distributed over several files to avoid access competition).

For each UIL module, do the following:

1. Declare the UIL module (begin a module block).

2. Include the supplied UIL constants file.

3. Declare the callback procedures referenced in the object declarations.

4. Declare the values (integers, strings, colors, and so on) to be used in the object declarations.

5. Declare the interface objects (widgets and gadgets).

6. End the module block.

The following sections describe how to write each component of a UIL module.

22.1.1 Creating a UIL Specification File

A UIL specification file contains a module block that consists of a series of value, identifier, procedure, list, and object sections. There can be any number of these sections in a UIL module. The UIL include directive allows you to include the contents of another file in your UIL module. To specify one or more complete sections, place the include directive wherever a section is valid. You cannot use an include directive to specify a part of a section.

You can also use the include directive to have access to the supplied UIL constants that are useful for specifying values for some arguments such as **XmNdialogStyle** and **XmNalignment**. Section 22.1.3 describes this constants file.

The following example shows the overall structure of a UIL module.

```
!+
!    Sample UIL module
!-

module example    ! Module name
!+
!   Place module header clauses here.
!-

!+
!   Declare the VALUES, IDENTIFIERS,
!   PROCEDURES, LISTS, and OBJECTS here.
!-
end module;
```

22.1.2 Declaring the UIL Module

In the module declaration, you name the module and make module-wide specifications using module header clauses. The following table explains optional UIL module header clauses used in the module declaration.

Table 22-1. Optional UIL Module Header Clauses

Clause	Purpose	Default	Example
Version	Allows you to ensure the correct version of the UIL module is being used.	None	version = 'v1.1'
Case sensitivity	Specifies whether names in the UIL module are case sensitive or not.	Case insensitive	names = case_sensitive

Clause	Purpose	Default	Example
Default character set	Specifies the default character set for string literals in the compiled UIL module.	*cur_charset* (see Section 20.2)	character_set = iso_latin6
Object variant	Specifies the default variant of objects defined in the module on a type-by-type basis.	Widget	objects = (XmSeparator = gadget; XmPushButton = widget;)

The following example shows the module declaration for the Motifburger UIL module. The name you specify in the UIL module declaration is stored in the UID file when you compile the module. The module declaration for Motifburger specifies the following:

- MRM identifies the Motifburger interface by the name *motifburger_demo*.

- This is the first version of this module.

- Names are case sensitive.

- All separator, label, push-button, and toggle-button objects are gadgets unless overridden in specific object declarations. All other types of objects are widgets.

```
module motifburger_demo

version = 'v1.0'
names = case_sensitive
objects = {
     XmSeparator = gadget ;
     XmLabel = gadget ;
     XmPushButton = gadget ;
     XmToggleButton = gadget ;
       }
```

If you specify that names are case sensitive in your UIL module, you must put UIL keywords in lowercase letters. For more information on keywords, see Chapter 18. Do not use reserved keywords as names in a UIL module.

22.1.3 Using Constants Defined in the Motif Toolkit

The UIL module for the Motifburger application makes use of some of the constants defined in the Motif Toolkit. For example, the constants XmDIALOG_MODELESS and XmVERTICAL shown in the following example come from the toolkit.

```
object
! The control panel.  All order entry
! is done through this bulletin board dialog.
 control_box : XmBulletinBoardDialog {
    arguments {
        XmNdialogTitle = k_motifburger_title;
        XmNdialogStyle = XmDIALOG_MODELESS;
        XmNx = 600;
        XmNy = 200;
        XmNmarginWidth = 20;
        XmNbackground = lightblue;
    };
    controls {
            ! Some labels and decoration.
        XmLabel          burger_label;
        XmLabel          fries_label;
        XmLabel          drink_label;
        XmSeparator      {arguments {
            XmNx = 220;
            XmNy = 20;
            XmNunitType = XmPIXELS;
            XmNorientation = XmVERTICAL;
            XmNheight = 180; };};
```

22.1.4 Declaring Procedures

Use a procedure declaration to declare a function that can be used as a callback procedure for an object. You can reference the procedure name in object declarations that occur anywhere in the UIL module.

Callback procedures must be defined to accept three parameters: the widget identifier of the widget triggering the callback, a tag for user-defined information, and the callback data structure (which is unique to each widget). The widget identifier and callback structure parameters are under the control of the Motif Toolkit; the tag is under the control of the application program.

In a UIL module, you can specify the data type of the tag to be passed to the corresponding callback procedure at run time by putting the data type in parentheses following the procedure name. When you compile the module, the UIL compiler checks that the argument you specify in references to the procedure is of this type. The data type of the tag must be one of the valid UIL types (see Section 22.1.5).

For example, in the following procedure declaration, the callback procedure named *toggle_proc* is passed an integer tag at run time. The UIL compiler checks that the parameter specified in any reference to procedure *toggle_proc* is an integer.

```
PROCEDURE
    toggle_proc (INTEGER);
```

While you can use any UIL data type to specify the type of a tag in a procedure declaration, you must be able to represent that data type in the high-level language you are using to write your application program. Some data types (such as integer, Boolean, and string) are common data types recognized by most programming languages. Other UIL data types (such as string tables) are more complex and may require you to set up an appropriate corresponding data structure in the application to pass a tag of that type to a callback procedure.

The following table summarizes the rules the UIL compiler follows for checking the argument type and count. The way you declare the procedure determines which rule the UIL compiler uses to perform this checking.

Table 22-2. UIL Compiler Rules for Checking Argument Type and Count

Declaration Type	Description of Rule
No parameters	No argument type or argument-count checking. You can supply no arguments or one argument in the procedure reference.
( )	Checks that the argument count is 0.
(any)	Checks that the argument count is 1. Does not check the argument type. Use **any** to prevent type checking on procedure tags.
(*value_type*)	Checks for one argument of the specified value type.

The following example shows that all procedures in the Motifburger UIL module specify that argument type and argument count are to be checked when the module is compiled.

```
procedure
    toggle_proc      (integer);
    activate_proc    (integer);
    create_proc      (integer);
    scale_proc       (integer);
    list_proc        (integer);
    quit_proc         (string);
    show_hide_proc   (integer);
    pull_proc        (integer);
```

You can also use a procedure declaration to specify the creation function for a user-defined widget. In this case, you must not specify any parameters. The procedure is invoked with the standard three arguments passed to all widget creation functions (widget identifier, tag, and callback structure unique to the calling object).

22.1.5 Declaring Values

A value declaration is a way of giving a name to a value expression. The value name can be referenced by declarations that occur anywhere in the UIL module in any context where a value can be used.

You should use meaningful names for values to help you recall their purpose easily. See Section 22.1.8 for recommended coding techniques.

The supported data types for UIL values are

- any
- argument
- asciz_table
- Boolean
- color
- color_table
- compound_string
- float
- font
- font_table
- integer
- integer_table
- keysym
- pixmap
- reason
- single_float
- string
- string_table
- translation_table

You can control whether values are local to the UIL module or globally accessible by MRM by specifying one of the keywords

EXPORTED, IMPORTED, or PRIVATE in the value declaration. (Section 19.2 provides details on how these keywords determine the scope of references to named values and objects.)

The Motifburger application makes use of several kinds of values, as shown in the following examples. There is a separate value section for each type of value to make it easier to find the value declaration during debugging.

22.1.5.1 Defining Integer Values

Integer values are defined together in a single value section of the Motifburger UIL module. These integers are used as tags in the callback procedures. A tag provides information to the callback procedure concerning the circumstances under which the procedure is being called. The following example shows a segment of this value section:

```
value
      k_create_order          : 1;
      k_order_pdme            : 2;
      k_file_pdme             : 3;
      k_edit_pdme             : 4;
      k_nyi                   : 5;
      k_apply                 : 6;
      k_dismiss               : 7;
      k_noapply               : 8;
      k_cancel_order          : 9;
      k_submit_order          : 10;
      k_order_box             : 11;
      k_burger_rare           : 12;
      k_burger_medium         : 13;
```

22.1.5.2 Defining String Values

The following example shows the Motifburger value section containing string value declarations. These strings are the labels for the various widgets used in the interface. Using values for widget labels rather than hardcoding the labels in the specification makes it easier to modify the interface (for example, from English to German). Putting all label definitions together at the beginning of the module makes it easier to find a label if you want to change it later. Also, a string resource declared as a value can be shared by many objects, thereby reducing the size of the UID file.

```
value
  k_motifburger_title
          : "Motifburger Order-Entry Box";
  k_nyi_label_text
          : "Feature is not yet implemented";
  k_file_label_text              : "File";
  k_quit_label_text              : "Quit";
  k_edit_label_text              : "Edit";
  k_cut_dot_label_text           : "Cut";
  k_copy_dot_label_text          : "Copy";
```

All the string values in this value section, except one, are used as labels. Because the XmNlabelString argument requires a compound string value, the UIL compiler automatically converts these strings to compound strings (although the strings are declared as null-terminated strings).

The exception, k_0_label_text, is used to define an argument for the text widget; since this widget does not accept compound strings, the value for k_0_label_text must be a null-terminated string.

Because there is no default character set specified in the module header and the individual string values do not specify a character set, the default character set associated with all these compound strings is the codeset portion of the value of the **LANG** environment variable if it is set, or the value of **XmFALLBACK_CHARSET** if **LANG** is not set or has no codeset component (see Section 20.2).

The indentation shown in the example is not required but improves the readability of the UIL module by giving an indication of the widget tree. For example, the widgets labeled Cut, Copy, Paste,

Clear, and Select All are children of the widget labeled Edit. Section 22.1.6.2 explains how to define the widget tree. Section 22.1.8.2 describes recommended coding techniques to improve the readability of your UIL modules.

By convention, a label followed by ellipses (...) indicates that a DialogBox appears when the object bearing this label is selected.

22.1.5.3 Defining String Table Values

A string table is a convenient way to express a table of strings. Some widgets require a *string_table* argument (such as the list widget, which is used for drink selection in the Motifburger application).

The following example shows the definition of *string_table* values in Motifburger. The labels for the types of drinks are elements of the string table named k_drink_list_text. Notice that Apple Juice is a single element in the string table named k_drink_list_select. This value is passed to the drink_list_box widget to show apple juice as the default drink selection.

The UIL compiler automatically converts the strings in a string table to compound strings, regardless of whether the strings are delimited by double or single quotation marks.

```
value
    .
    .
    .

  k_drinks_label_text          : "Drinks";
  k_0_label_text               : '0';
  k_drink_list_text            :
       string_table ('Apple·Juice',
       'Orange Juice', 'Grape Juice',
       'Cola', 'Punch','Root beer',
       'Water', 'Ginger Ale', 'Milk',
       'Coffee', 'Tea');
  k_drink_list_select          :
       string_table('Apple Juice');
```

22.1.5.4 Defining Font Values

Use the **FONT** function to declare a UIL value as a font. (See
Chapter 18 for more information on defining font values.)

The following example shows the declaration of a font value in the
Motifburger UIL module. This value is used later as the value for
the **XmNfontList** attribute of the apply_button, can_button, and
dismiss_button push button widgets.

```
value
 k_button_font   :
    font('-ADOBE-Courier-Bold-R-Normal-\
        -14-140-75-75-M-90-ISO8859-1');
```

The UIL compiler converts a font to a font table when the font value
is used to specify an argument that requires a font-table value.

Font names are server dependent. If you specify a font name that is
not defined on your server, the system issues a warning and uses the
default font. (See Chapter 18 for more information on defining font
values.)

22.1.5.5 Defining Color Values

The following example shows the value section in the Motifburger
module containing color declarations. By using the **COLOR**
function, you can designate a string as specifying a color and then
use that string for arguments requiring a color value. The optional
keywords **FOREGROUND** and **BACKGROUND** identify how the
color is to be displayed on a monochrome device. (See Chapter 18
for more information on defining color values.)

```
value
   yellow     : color('yellow', foreground);
   red        : color('red', background);
   green      : color('green', foreground);
   magenta    : color('magenta', background);
   gold       : color('gold', foreground);
   lightblue  : color('lightblue', background);
```

22.1.5.6 Defining Pixmap Values

Pixmap values let you specify labels that are graphic images rather than text strings. Pixmap values are not directly supported by UIL. Instead, UIL supports icons, a simplified form of pixmap (which you define directly in UIL), or **xbitmap** files (which you create outside UIL).

You can generate pixmaps in UIL in two ways:

- Define an icon inline using the **ICON** function (and optionally use the **COLOR_TABLE** function to specify colors for the icon). You use a character to describe each pixel in the icon.

- Use the **XBITMAPFILE** function, specifying the name of an X bitmap file that you created outside UIL to be used as the pixmap value.

The following example shows the value section in the Motifburger module containing a color table declaration.

The colors you specify when defining a color table must have been previously defined with the **COLOR** function. For example, the colors yellow and red were previously defined in the example in Section 22.1.5.5. Color tables must be private because the UIL compiler must be able to interpret their contents at compilation time to construct an icon. The colors within a color table, however, can be imported, exported, or private.

```
value
    button_ct    : color_table(
                     yellow='o'
                     ,red='.'
                     ,background color=' ');
```

The following example shows how the button_ct color table is used to specify an icon pixmap. Referring to the color table shown in the previous example, each lowercase "o" in the icon definition is replaced with the color yellow, and each . (dot) is replaced with the color red. Whatever color is defined as the background color when the application is run replaces the spaces.

In UIL, if you define an argument of type pixmap, you should specify an icon or an **xbitmap** file as its value. For example, the icon defined in the following example is given as the value of the label on the drink quantity push button. (Refer to the definition of the drink_quantity form widget in Section 22.1.7.)

```
value

    drink_up_icon:  icon(color_table=button_ct,
                    '                                 ',
                    '..........OO..........',
                    '.........OOOO.........',
                    '........OOOOOO........',
                    '.......OO....OO.......',
                    '......OO......OO......',
                    '.....OO........OO.....',
                    '....OO..........OO....',
                    '...OO............OO...',
                    '..OO..............OO..',
                    '.OO................OO.',
                    'OOOOOOOOOOOOOOOOOOOOOOOO',
                    'OOOOOOOOOOOOOOOOOOOOOOOO',
                    '.........OOOO.........',
                    '.........OOOO.........',
                    '.........OOOO.........',
                    '.........OOOO.........',
                    '.........OOOO.........',
                    '.........OOOO.........',
                    '                                 ');
```

Each row in the icon must contain the same number of pixels and therefore must contain the same number of characters. The height of the icon is dictated by the number of rows. For example, the preceding arrow icon is 24 pixels wide and 20 pixels tall. (The rows of spaces at the top and bottom of the pixmap and the spaces at the start and end of each row are included in this count and are defined as the background color in the button_ct color table.

A default color table is used if you omit the color table argument from the **ICON** function. The definition of the default color table is as follows:

```
color_table( background color = ' ',
             foreground color = '*' );
```

You can specify icons as private, imported, or exported.

22.1.6 Declaring Interface Objects in a UIL Module

Use an object declaration to define an instance of a widget or gadget that is to be stored in the UID file. You can reference the object name in declarations that occur elsewhere in the UIL module, usually to specify one object as a child of another object. Some widgets accept a widget name as an argument. This use of a widget name is called a symbolic reference to a widget identifier and is explained in Section 19.10.

The object declaration contains a sequence of lists that define the arguments (attributes), children, and callback functions for the object. You can specify only one list of each type for an object.

Objects can be forward referenced; that is, you can declare an object name after you refer to it. This is useful for declaring a parent first, followed by the declarations for all its children. (The declaration of the parent includes a list of the names of its children.) In this way, the structure of your UIL module resembles the widget tree of your interface.

All references to an object name must be consistent with the type you specified when you declared the object. As with values, you can specify an object as exported, imported, or private.

The following example shows how the file_menu widget is declared in the Motifburger UIL module.

```
object
    file_menu : XmPulldownMenu {

        arguments {
           XmNlabelString=k_file_label_text;
        };
        controls {
           XmPushButton m_print_button;
           XmPushButton m_quit_button;
        };
        callbacks {
           MrmNcreateCallback=procedure
              create_proc (k_file_menu);
        };
    };
```

Note that the objects and values in this example have meaningful names (for example, *file_menu* and *k_file_label_text*). Using meaningful names helps you recall the purpose of the object or value in the user interface. (See Section 22.1.8 for a summary of recommended coding techniques.) As shown in this example, a widget declaration generally consists of three parts: an arguments list, a controls list, and a callbacks list. These parts are explained in the following sections.

22.1.6.1 Specifying Arguments in an Object Declaration

Use an arguments list to specify the arguments (attributes) for an object. An arguments list defines the arguments to be specified in the *override_arglist* argument when the creation function for a particular object is called at run time. An arguments list also specifies the values that these arguments are to have. You identify an arguments list to the UIL compiler by using the keyword **ARGUMENTS**.

Each entry in the list consists of the argument name and the argument value. In the previous example, the XmNlabelString argument for the *file_menu* pull-down menu is defined as *k_file_label_text*. The value *k_file_label_text* is a compound string defined in a value section at the beginning of the module.

If you use the same argument name more than once in an arguments list, the last entry supersedes all previous entries, and the compiler issues a message.

22.1.6.2 Specifying Children in an Object Declaration

You use a controls list to define which widgets are children of, or controlled by, a particular widget. The controls lists for all the widgets in a UIL module define the widget tree for an interface. If you specify that a child is to be managed (the default), at run time the widget is created and managed; if you specify that the child is to be unmanaged at creation (by including the keyword **UNMANAGED** in the controls list entry), the widget is only created. You identify a controls list to the UIL compiler by using the keyword **CONTROLS**.

In the previous example, the objects *m_print_button* and *m_quit_button* are children of the *file_menu* widget, which is a pull-down menu. The objects *m_print_button* and *m_quit_button* are defined as push buttons, which are valid children of the object type XmPulldownMenu.

In the following example, the bulletin board dialog called *control_box* is a top-level composite widget, having a variety of widgets as children. Some of these children are also composite widgets, having children of their own. For example, the *button_box* and *burger_doneness_box* widgets are declared later on in the module, and each of these has its own controls list.

```
object            ! The control panel.  All order entry
                  ! is done through this dialog box.
  control_box : XmBulletinBoardDialog {
    arguments {
        XmNdialogTitle = k_motifburger_title;
        XmNdialogStyle = XmDIALOG_MODELESS;
        XmNx = 600;
        XmNy = 200;
        XmNmarginWidth = 20;
        XmNbackground = lightblue;
    };
    controls { ! Some labels and decoration.
        XmLabel        burger_label;
        XmLabel        fries_label;
        XmLabel        drink_label;
        XmSeparator    {arguments {
                       XmNx = 220;
                       XmNy = 20;
                       XmNunitType = XmPIXELS;
                       XmNorientation = XmVERTICAL;
                       XmNheight = 180; };};
        XmSeparator    {arguments {
                       XmNx = 410;
                       XmNy = 20;
                       XmNunitType = XmPIXELS;
                       XmNorientation = XmVERTICAL;
                       XmNheight = 180; };};
        XmRowColumn button_box;
        ! Command push buttons inside a menu
        ! across the bottom.  For the hamburger,
        ! fries, and drink entry we use a
        ! different mechanism ! to demonstrate
        ! various widgets and techniques.  Hamburger
        ! 'doneness' uses a radio box because
        ! although it is a '1 of N' type of entry,
        ! one (and only one) entry is allowed.
        XmRadioBox        burger_doneness_box;
```

22–18

Notice that the separators are defined locally in the controls list for *control_box*, rather than in object sections of their own. As a result, the separators do not have names and cannot be referenced by other objects in this UIL module. However, the local definitions make it easier for someone reading the UIL specification file to tell that the separators are used only by the *control_box* widget. When you define an object locally, you do not need to create an artificial name for that object.

Unlike the arguments list (and the callbacks list, described in the next section), when you specify the same widget in a controls list more than once, MRM creates multiple instances of the widget at run time when it creates the parent widget.

22.1.6.3 Specifying Callbacks in an Object Declaration

Use a callbacks list to define which callback reasons are to be processed by a particular widget at application run time. As shown in the example in Section 22.1.7, each entry in a callbacks list has a reason name (in this example, XmNactivateCallback) and the name of a callback function (*activate_proc*).

For Motif Toolkit widgets, the reason names are already built into UIL. For a user-defined widget, you can refer to a user-defined reason name that you previously specified by using the **REASON** function (see Section 18.5.14). If you use a built-in reason name in a widget definition, the UIL compiler ensures that the reason name is supported by the type of widget you are defining.

If you use the same reason name more than once in a callbacks list, the last entry that uses that reason name supersedes all others, and the UIL compiler issues a message.

The callback procedure names you use in a callbacks list must be declared in a procedure section. In this example, the procedure *activate_proc* was declared in the beginning of the UIL module.

Because the UIL compiler produces a UID file rather than an object module, the binding of the UIL name to the address of the function entry point is not done by the linker. Instead, the binding is established at run time with the MRM function **MrmRegisterNames**. You call this function before fetching any widgets, giving it both the UIL names and the function addresses of each callback. The name you register with MRM in the application program must match the name you specified in the UIL module. Section 22.2 explains how the Motifburger callback function names are registered with MRM.

Each callback function receives three arguments. The first two arguments have the same form for each callback. The form of the third argument varies from widget to widget.

The first argument is the address of the data structure maintained by the Motif Toolkit for this widget instance. This address is called the widget ID for this widget.

The second argument is the address of the value you specified in the callbacks list for this function. If you do not specify an argument, the address is NULL. This is called the **tag_value** argument. If you specify a value type for the **tag_value** argument, this type must match the value type of the parameter in the corresponding procedure declaration (see Table 22-2).

The third argument is a data structure specific to the widget. The reason name you specified in the UIL module is the first field of this data structure.

22.1.7 Using an Icon as a Widget Label

Figure 22-1 highlights the drink quantity selector. This widget in the user interface for the Motifburger application uses icons for the labels on its push buttons. When the user clicks on the up-arrow icon, the drink quantity increases. When the user clicks on the down-arrow icon, the drink quantity decreases.

Figure 22-1. Using an Icon in the Motifburger Application Interface

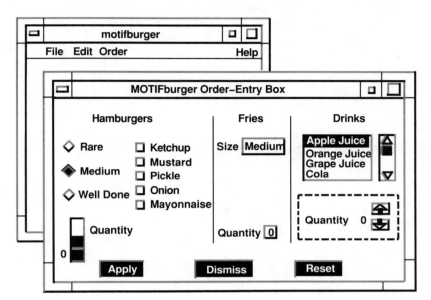

The icon named *drink_up_icon* was defined in the example in Section 22.1.5.6. The following example shows how to specify this icon as a push-button label in a widget declaration. In the Motifburger UIL module, the icon named *drink_up_icon* is a pixmap label argument to the *up_value* push-button widget. In turn, the *up_value* widget is controlled by the *drink_quantity* form widget.

```
object
  drink_quantity : XmForm {
    arguments {
        XmNx = 460;
        XmNy = 170;
        XmNunitType = XmPIXELS;
        };
```

```
        controls {
            XmLabel          quantity_label;
            XmLabel          value_label;
            XmPushButton     up_value;
            XmPushButton     down_value;
            };
        };
    .
    .
    .

object
  up_value : XmPushButton widget {
    arguments {
        XmNy = 00 ;
        XmNleftAttachment = XmATTACH_WIDGET;
        XmNleftOffset = 20 ;
        XmNleftWidget = XmLabel value_label ;
        XmNlabelType = XmPIXMAP;
        XmNlabelPixmap = drink_up_icon;
        };
    callbacks {
        XmNactivateCallback =
            procedure
                activate_proc (k_drink_add);
        };
    };
```

22.1.8 Recommended Coding Techniques

The Motifburger UIL module shows recommended coding practices
that should improve your productivity and increase the flexibility of
your programs. This section explains how these practices can help
you write better UIL modules. The language elements and
semantics of UIL are similar to those in other high-level
programming languages.

22.1.8.1 Naming Values and Objects Meaningfully

The names of constants, labels, colors, icons, and widgets in the Motifburger UIL module indicate their purpose in the application. For example, the name for the constant having integer value 12 is *k_burger_rare*. From its name, you can tell that this constant represents the choice Rare on the Hamburgers menu. Similarly, the names for objects (widgets and gadgets) indicate their purpose in the application. Object names should, in addition, reflect the object type. For example, you can tell by its name that *m_copy_button* is a button of some kind on a menu and is associated with the Copy option.

22.1.8.2 Grouping Value, Identifier, and Procedure Declarations

You should group value declarations according to purpose and list them near the beginning of the module. Although you could have a value section to declare a value immediately preceding an object section in which the value is used, you can look up the definition of a particular value more easily if all declarations are in one place in the module. In the Motifburger UIL module, separate value sections are used to group values as follows:

- Constants for positioning within forms
- Constants for callback functions
- Labels
- Fonts
- Colors
- Color tables
- Icons

Constants for callback procedures must be defined in the program as well as in the UIL module. Therefore, if these constants are in a single value section, it is easier to cut the section from the module and paste it into the application program.

By setting up all labels as compound string values, rather than hardcoding them in the object declarations, you can more easily change the labels from one language to another. Specify a string as a compound string by using the UIL built-in function **COMPOUND_STRING**. (Some arguments for the simple text widget and the command window widget accept only null-terminated strings. Labels for these widgets must be declared as null-terminated (ASCIZ) strings, delimited with single quotation marks.)

The same technique applies to procedure declarations. In the Motifburger UIL module, all procedure declarations are listed in a single procedure section at the beginning of the module, immediately following the module declaration and include directive. The Motifburger application does not use identifiers (which function like global variables). Treat identifier sections as you treat value sections. Identifiers are described in Section 19.7.

22.1.8.3 Ordering Object Declarations to Reflect the Widget Tree

Once all your values, identifiers, and procedures are declared, the rest of the UIL module consists of object declarations. You should structure your module to reflect the widget tree of the application interface. For example, in the Motifburger UIL module, the choices for how the hamburger should be cooked are presented in a radio box having three children, which are toggle buttons. The following figure shows how this radio box looks in the Motifburger application interface.

Figure 22-2. Radio Box with Toggle Buttons in the Motifburger Application

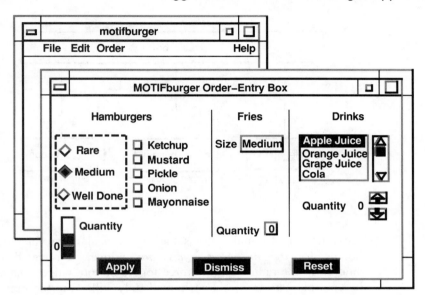

The following figure shows how these widgets are arranged in a hierarchy, which is defined by the controls list for the radio box named *burger_doneness_box*.

Figure 22-3. Widget Tree for the Motifburger Radio Box

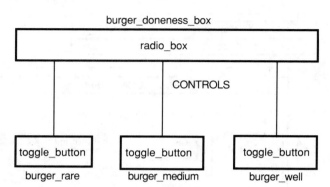

The following example shows the object declaration in the UIL
module for the *burger_doneness_box* widget. Notice that the
children of the radio box (the three toggle button widgets named in
the controls list) are declared immediately following the radio box
declaration. By ordering your object declarations in this way, you
can get an idea of the overall widget tree for your interface by
scanning the UIL module.

```
object
  burger_doneness_box : XmRadioBox {
      arguments {
      .
      .
      .
          };
      controls {
          XmToggleButton    burger_rare;
          XmToggleButton    burger_medium;
          XmToggleButton    burger_well;
          };
      };
```

```
object
  burger_rare : XmToggleButton {
    .
    .
    .
      };

object
  burger_medium : XmToggleButton {
    .
    .
    .
      };

object
  burger_well : XmToggleButton {
    .
    .
    .
      };
```

22.1.8.4 Using Local Definitions for Certain Objects

If you need to define an object that is used as a child of a single parent and is not be referred to by any other object in the UIL module, define the object in the controls list for its parent rather than in an object section of its own. This simplifies the UIL module and saves you from having to create an artificial name for that object. The example in Section 22.1.6.2 shows a separator defined locally.

22.2 Creating a User Interface at Run Time with MRM

MRM creates interface objects based on definitions in UID files, which are the compiled form of UIL specification files. You call MRM functions in your application to initialize MRM, to provide information required by MRM to interpret information in UID files, and to create objects using UID file definitions.

MRM allows you to defer fetching top-level objects until the application needs to display them. By deferring fetching, you can improve the start-up performance of your application. Section 22.2.2 explains how to defer fetching.

MRM also has functions that allow an application to read literal definitions from UID files. You create these literal definitions when you declare a literal value to be exported in UIL. You can use these literals in your application program for any purpose. Section 22.2.3 explains how to read literals from UID files.

You can use an MRM function to override values you specified for widget attributes. In effect, a single object definition can be used like a template to create multiple widget instances from a single UIL definition. Section 22.2.4 describes this function. All definitions required to use MRM are contained in the **MrmAppl.h** file.

MRM does not replace the X Resource Manager, but complements it. The X Resource Database (an in-memory database, stored in the **.Xdefaults** file) supplies default values. When you use UIL to specify a user interface, you do not need to specify all argument values (resources); you need only specify an argument when you want to override the default value stored in the X Resource Database. The MRM generates the *override_arglist* argument for the appropriate widget creation functions at run time.

Figure 22-4 shows how widget argument values are applied inside the MRM fetch operation.

Figure 22-4. Widget Creation in an MRM Fetch Operation

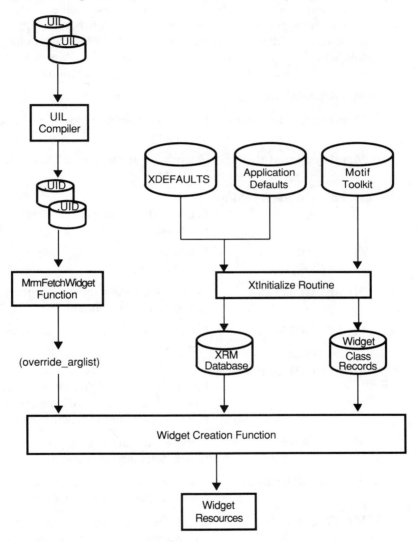

The examples in this section are based on the C program for the Motifburger application. The Motifburger application is part of the Motif software kit. Section 22.1 explains how you can access the source files for this application. The Motifburger application demonstrates the most commonly used MRM functions. The following list briefly describes the available MRM functions. See Chapter 21 for a complete description of these functions.

MrmCloseHierarchy   Closes a UID hierarchy

MrmFetchColorLiteral   Fetches a named color literal from a UID hierarchy

MrmFetchIconLiteral   Fetches a named icon from a UID hierarchy

MrmFetchInterfaceModule
Fetches all the objects defined in some interface module in the UID hierarchy

MrmFetchLiteral   Fetches a named string literal from a UID hierarchy

MrmFetchSetValues   Fetches the values to be set from literals stored in a UID hierarchy

MrmFetchWidget   Fetches any named widget in a UID hierarchy

MrmFetchWidgetOverride
Fetches any named widget and overrides values stored in the UID hierarchy with those supplied in the function call

MrmInitialize   Prepares an application to use MRM widget fetching facilities

MrmOpenHierarchy   Allocates a hierarchy descriptor and opens all the files in the UID hierarchy

MrmRegisterClass   Saves the information needed to access the widget creation function using the information in a UID hierarchy and to perform type conversion of arguments lists

MrmRegisterNames   Registers a vector of names and associated values for access by MRM in the global namespace

MrmRegisterNamesInHierarchy

Registers a vector of names and associated values for access by MRM in a namespace attached to a particular UIL hierarchy

22.2.1 Accessing the UID File at Run Time

As Figure 22-5 shows, setting up an interface specified with UIL requires the following steps:

1. **Initialization**

   In the initialization step, the application program must make calls to the MRM and Motif Toolkit intrinsics functions in the following sequence:

   - Initialize MRM.

   The MRM function **MrmInitialize** prepares your application to use MRM widget-fetching facilities. This call must come before the call to initialize the Motif Toolkit.

   - Initialize the Motif Toolkit.

   The intrinsics function **XtAppInitialize** parses the command line used to invoke the application, opens the display, and initializes the Motif Toolkit.

   - Open the UID hierarchy.

   The UID hierarchy is the set of UID files containing the widget definitions for the user interface. The MRM function **MrmOpenHierarchy** opens these UID files.

   - Register names for MRM.

   The MRM functions **MrmRegisterNames** and **MrmRegisterNamesInHierarchy** register names and associated values for access by the MRM. The values may be callback functions, pointers to user-defined data, or any other

22–31

values. MRM uses this information to resolve symbolic references in UID files to their run-time values.

2. **Creation**

In the creation step, you call the MRM function **MrmFetchWidget** to fetch the user interface. Fetching is a combination of widget creation and child management. The MRM function **MrmFetchWidget** performs the following tasks:

- Locates a widget description in the UID hierarchy

- Creates the widget and recursively creates the widget's children

- Manages all children as specified in the UID hierarchy

- Returns the widget identifier

You specify the top-level widget of the application (usually the main window) and its parent (the widget identifier returned by the call to **XtAppInitialize**) in the call to **MrmFetchWidget**. As a result of this single call, MRM fetches all widgets in the widget tree below the top-level widget. You can defer fetching portions of an application interface until they are requested by the end user. For example, you can defer fetching a pull-down menu until the user activates the corresponding cascade button. Consider deferring fetching of some portions of your interface if you need to improve the start-up performance of your application. Deferred fetching is explained in Section 22.2.2.

3. **Realization**

The steps to manage and realize a user interface created using UIL and MRM are the same as those for an interface created with Motif Toolkit functions:

- Manage the top-level widget.

The intrinsics function **XtManageChild** adds a child to the top-level widget returned by the call to **XtAppInitialize**. The entire widget tree below the top-level widget in the interface (usually the main window) is automatically managed as a result of this call to **XtManageChild**.

- Realize the top-level widget.

The intrinsics function **XtRealizeWidget** displays the entire interface (the widget tree below the top-level widget) on the screen.

Figure 22-5. Setting Up a User Interface Specified with UIL

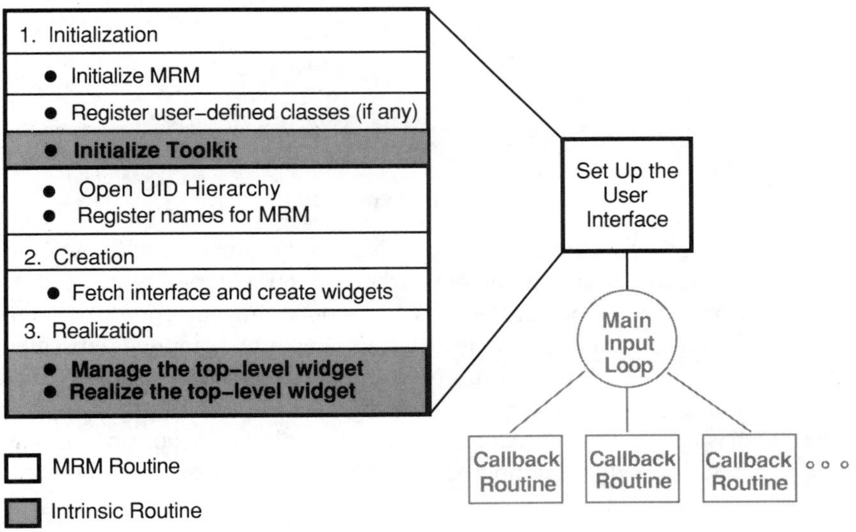

The role of MRM in a Motif application is limited primarily to widget creation. MRM makes run-time calls that create widgets from essentially invariant information (information that does not change from one invocation of the application to the next). After MRM fetches a widget (creates it and manages its children), it provides no further services. All subsequent operations on the widget, such as realization, managing and unmanaging children after initialization, and getting and setting resource values, must be done by run-time calls. After widget creation, you modify widgets during application execution by using widget manipulation functions.

The call to the **MrmInitialize** function must come before the call to the **XtAppInitialize** function. The following example shows the initialization of MRM and the Motif Toolkit in the Motifburger application.

```
unsigned int main(argc, argv)
  unsigned int argc;
  char *argv[];
{
  Widget toplevel_widget;
  XtAppContext app_context;
  MrmInitialize();

  toplevel_widget = XtAppInitialize(
        &app_context, "example", NULL,
        0, &argc, argv, NULL, NULL, 0);
```

The compiled interface, described in one or more UIL modules, is connected to the application when the UID hierarchy is set up at run time. The names of the UID files containing the compiled interface definitions are stored in an array. Because compiled UIL files are not object files, this run-time connection is necessary to bind an interface with an application program. The Motifburger application has a single UIL module, so the MRM hierarchy consists of one file. The following example shows the declaration of the UID hierarchy for Motifburger.

```
static MrmHierarchy s_MrmHierarchy;
static MrmType *dummy_class;
static char *db_filename_vec[] =
  {"motifburger.uid"
  };
```

The name of the UID hierarchy is *s_MrmHierarchy*. The array containing the names of the UID files in the UID hierarchy is *db_filename_vec*. In the following example, the application opens this UID hierarchy. At this point in the application's execution, MRM has access to the Motifburger interface definition and can fetch widgets.

```
if (MrmOpenHierarchy(db_filename_num,
  db_filename_vec,
  NULL,
  &s_MrmHierarchy)
  !=MrmSUCCESS)
  s_error("can't open hierarchy");
```

The final step in preparing to use MRM to fetch widgets is to register a vector of names and associated values. These values can be the names of callback functions, pointers to user-defined data, or any other values. MRM uses the information provided in this vector to resolve symbolic references that occur in UID files to their run-time values. For callback procedures, the vector provides procedure addresses required by the Motif Toolkit. For names used as variables in UIL (identifiers), this information provides whatever mapping the application requires. The use of identifiers is explained in Section 19.7. The following example shows the declaration of the names vector in the Motifburger C program. In the Motifburger application, the names vector contains only names of callback procedures and their addresses.

```
static MRMRegisterArg reglist[] = {
    {"activate_proc",
        (caddr_t) activate_proc},
    {"create_proc",
        (caddr_t) create_proc},
    {"list_proc", (caddr_t) list_proc},
    {"pull_proc", (caddr_t) pull_proc},
    {"quit_proc", (caddr_t) quit_proc},
    {"scale_proc", (caddr_t) scale_proc},
    {"show_hide_proc",
        (caddr_t) show_hide_proc},
    {"show_label_proc",
        (caddr_t) show_label_proc},
    {"toggle_proc", (caddr_t) toggle_proc}
};
```

```
static int reglist_num =
    (sizeof reglist / sizeof reglist [0]);
```

The names are registered in a call to the **MrmRegisterNames** function, as shown in the following example:

```
MrmRegisterNames(reglist, reglist_num);
```

22.2.2 Deferring Fetching

MRM allows you to defer fetching off-screen widgets until the application needs to display these widgets. There are two types of off-screen widgets: pull-down menus and dialogs. Whenever MRM fetches an off-screen widget, it also fetches the entire widget tree below that widget. By deferring the fetching of off-screen widgets, you can reduce the time taken to start up your application.

The Motifburger application makes use of deferred fetching. The pull-down menus for the File, Edit, and Order options are not fetched when the main window is fetched. Instead, these menus are fetched and created by individual calls to the **MrmFetchWidget** function when the corresponding cascade button is activated (selected by the end user). You can use the **MrmFetchWidget** function at any time to fetch a widget that was not fetched at application startup.

The UIL module for the Motifburger application is set up to allow either deferred fetching or a single fetch to create the entire widget tree. To fetch the entire interface at once, remove the comment character (!) from the controls list for the *file_menu_entry*, *edit_menu_entry*, and *order_menu_entry* widgets. As long as the comment characters remain on the controls list for the pull-down menu entries, their associated pull-down menus are no longer children; they are top-level widgets and can be fetched individually.

The following example shows the object declaration for the XmCascadeButton named *file_menu_entry*.

```
object
  file_menu_entry : XmCascadeButton {

    arguments {
      XmNlabelString = k_file_label_text;
    };
    controls {
      XmPulldownMenu file_menu;
     };
    callbacks {
      XmNcascadingCallback =
        procedure pull_proc (k_file_pdme);
      MrmNcreateCallback =
        procedure create_proc (k_file_pdme);
    };
  };
```

When you remove the comment characters, the controls list on each XmCascadeButton specifies the pull-down menu as a child. The pull-down menus are no longer top-level widgets; instead, they are loaded when the XmCascadeButton is created.

22.2.3 Getting Literal Values from UID Files

Using the literal fetching functions (**MrmFetchColorLiteral**, **MrmFetchIconLiteral**, and **MrmFetchLiteral**), you can retrieve any named, exported UIL value from a UID file at run time. This is useful when you want to use a literal value in a context other than fetching an object. These functions allow you to treat the UID file as a repository for all the programming variables you need to specify your application interface.

The MRM literal fetching functions have a wide variety of uses. For example, you can store the following as named, exported literals in a UIL module for run-time retrieval:

- All the error messages to be displayed in a message box (stored in a string table)

- All string tables used to query the operating system

- Language-dependent strings

In the C program for the Motifburger application, the text string displayed in the title bar of the main window is supplied directly to the **XtAppInitialize** function, as shown in the following example:

```
toplevel_widget = XtAppInitialize(
    &app_context, "example", NULL,
    0, &argc, argv, NULL, NULL, 0);
```

Alternatively, this string could be specified in a UIL module as a named, exported compound string, and retrieved from the UID file at run time with the **MrmFetchLiteral** function. Since this string appears in the interface, you should declare it as a compound string. Compound strings can be displayed in a variety of character sets, as required by the language of the interface.

22.2.4 Setting Values at Run Time Using UID Resources

The MRM function **MrmFetchSetValues** allows you to modify at run time an object that has already been created. The **MrmFetchSetValues** function works like the **XtSetValues** function except that MRM fetches the values to be set from named, exported values (literals) in the UID file. The fetched values are converted to the correct data type, if necessary, and placed in the *args* argument for a call to the function **XtSetValues**. Since the **MrmFetchSetValues** function looks for the literal values in a UID file, the argument names you provide to the **MrmFetchSetValues** function must be UIL argument names (not Motif Toolkit attribute names).

You can think of **MrmFetchSetValues** as a convenience function that packages the functions provided by **MrmFetchLiteral** and **XtSetValues**.

The value member of the name and value pairs passed to **MrmFetchSetValues** is the UIL name of the value, not an explicit value. When the application calls **MrmFetchSetValues**, MRM looks up the names in the UID file, then uses the values corresponding to those names to override the original values in the object declaration. Therefore, the **MrmFetchSetValues** function allows you to keep all values used in an application in the UIL module and not in the application program. (The values you pass to the **MrmFetchSetValues** function must be named, exported literals in the UIL module.)

The **MrmFetchSetValues** function offers the following advantages:

- It performs all the necessary UIL resource manipulation to make the fetched UIL values usable by the Motif Toolkit. (For example, the **MrmFetchSetValues** function performs address recomputation for tables of strings and enables a UIL icon to act as a pixmap.)

- It lets you isolate a greater amount of interface information from the application program, to achieve further separation of form and function.

There are some limitations to the **MrmFetchSetValues** function:

- All values in the *args* argument must be names of exported resources listed in a UIL module (UID hierarchy); therefore, the application cannot provide computed values from within the program itself as part of the argument list.

- It uses the **XtSetValues** function, ignoring the possibility of the less costly high-level function that the widget itself may provide.

The examples in this section are based on a simple application that displays text in two list widgets. The text displayed in the second list widget depends on what the user selected in the first. Figure 22-6 shows the interface for this application.

Figure 22-6. Sample Application Using the MrmFetchSetValues Function

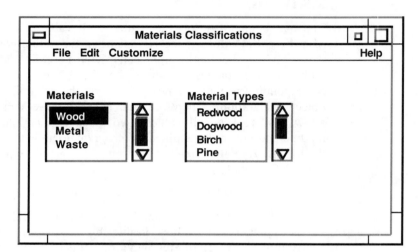

This application is well-suited to using the MRM function **MrmFetchSetValues** for the following reasons:

- The data (list widget contents) are all known in advance; the values themselves do not need to be computed at run time.

- The data consists of tables of compound strings that appear in the user interface and, therefore, must be translated for international markets. (Strings that must be translated should be stored in a UID file.)

- The structure of compound string tables, if retrieved from the UID file using the **MrmFetchLiteral** function, must be modified by the application program due to the nature of MRM storage methods. (Since string tables are stored in contiguous blocks, indexes to string-table values are offsets, not true addresses, and must be added together to compute the actual address at run time.) The **MrmFetchSetValues** function performs this address computation automatically and deallocates memory used to store the fetched tables. Since the program does not use the fetched string table directly, but intends only to modify the visual appearance of a widget based on items in the table, the **MrmFetchLiteral** function is less convenient to use.

The following examples show the UIL module for this application and excerpts from the C program. The segment of the UIL module shown assumes that the module header, procedure declarations, include files, and value declarations for each of the names used in the example are in place.

```
value
(1)  cs_wood       : compound_string("Wood");
     cst_materials_selected :
          string_table(cs_wood);
(2)  cst_materials : exported string_table(
               cs_wood,       ! material type 1
               "Metal",       ! material type 2
               "Waste");      ! material type 3
(3)   cst_type_1   : exported string_table(
             ! Materials for type 1 (wood)
             "Redwood","Dogwood","Birch",
             "Pine","Cherry");
     l_count_type_1 : exported 5;
     cst_type_2 : exported string_table(
             ! Materials for type 2 (metal)
             "Aluminum","Steel","Titanium",
             "Iron","Linoleum");
     l_count_type_2 : exported 5;
     cst_type_3 : exported string_table(
             ! Materials for type 3 (waste)
             "Toxic","Solid","Biodegradable",
             "Party Platforms");
     l_count_type_3 : exported 4;
     k_zero : exported 0;
  object
     materials_ListBox   : XmList
     {
         arguments
         {
             XmNx = k_tst_materials_ListBox_x;
             XmNy = k_tst_materials_ListBox_y;
             XmNwidth =
```

```
                k_tst_materials_ListBox_wid;
            XmNvisibleItemCount = 4;
            XmNitems = cst_materials;
            XmNselectedItems =
                cst_materials_selected;
        };
        callbacks
        {
            MrmNcreateCallback =
              procedure tst_create_proc(
                k_tst_materials_ListBox);
            XmNsingleSelectionCallback =
              procedure tst_single_proc(
                k_tst_materials_ListBox);
        };
    };
    types_ListBox       : XmList
    {
        arguments
        {
            XmNx = k_tst_types_ListBox_x;
            XmNy = k_tst_types_ListBox_y;
            XmNwidth =
                k_tst_types_ListBox_wid;
            XmNvisibleItemCount = 4;
            XmNitems = cst_type_1;
        };
        callbacks
        {
            MrmNcreateCallback =
              procedure tst_create_proc(
                k_tst_types_ListBox);
            XmNsingleSelectionCallback =
              procedure tst_single_proc(
                k_tst_types_ListBox);
        };
    };
```

NOTES:

1. Prefixes on value names indicate the type of value. For example, *cs_* means compound string, *cst_* means compound string table, and *l_* means long integer.

2. This string table provides the contents for the Materials list box widget (on the left in Figure 22-6). This string table does not need to follow the naming scheme for the string table in the Material Types list widget (that is, *cst_type_n*) because the contents of the Materials list does not change once the application is realized. (The numbering of the string tables (3)) is vital to the proper functioning of the Material Types list widget. The string table for the Materials list box widget could have been named anything.)

3. These string tables provide the contents for the various versions of the Materials Types list box widget (on the right in Figure 22-6). Each one of these lists of strings corresponds (in order) to the string names in the first list widget (Materials). These tables are numbered to facilitate programming. When the user selects an item in the Materials list widget, the index of the selected item is concatenated with the string *cst_type_* to form the name of one of these tables. This named table is retrieved with the **MrmFetchSetValues** function and placed in the Materials Type list widget.

   Note that in addition to the string table, a count of the number of items in the table is declared as an exported value. This is done because using the **XtSetValues** function on a list widget requires that three arguments be set: **XmNitems**, **XmNitemCount**, and **XmNselectedItemsCount** (which must be set to 0).

In the following C program segment, note the activation function named *tst_single_proc*, where the user's selection causes the program to act.

```
#define k_zero_name    "k_zero"
#define k_table_name_prefix    "cst_type_"
#define k_table_count_name_prefix    "l_count_type_"
```

```
(1)   void tst_single_proc(w,object_index,callbackdata)
      Widget       w;
      int          *object_index;
      XmListCallbackStruct     *callbackdata;
  {
(2)   char *t_number;
(3)   char t_table_name[32] = k_table_name_prefix;
      char t_table_count_name[32] =
          k_table_count_name_prefix;
(4)   Arg r_override_arguments[3] =
      {{XmNitems,NULL},{XmNitemsCount,NULL},
          {XmNselectedItemsCount,k_zero_name} };
      switch (*object_index)
      {
(5)      case     k_tst_materials_ListBox:
        {
(6)         sprintf(&t_number,"%d",callbackdata->
               item_number);
(7)         strcpy(&t_table_name[sizeof(
               k_table_name_prefix)-1],&t_number);
            XtSetArg(r_override_arguments[0],XmNitems,
               &t_table_name);
(8)         strcpy(&t_table_count_name[sizeof(
               k_table_count_name_prefix)-1],
               &t_number);
            XtSetArg(r_override_arguments[1],
               XmNitemsCount,&t_table_count_name);
(9)         MrmFetchSetValues(ar_MRMHierarchy,
               object_ids[k_tst_types_ListBox],
               r_override_arguments,3);
            break;
        };
(10)     case     k_tst_types_ListBox:
        {
     .
     .
     .

            break;
        };
   };
  };
```

NOTES:

1. Function that handles the XmNsingleSelectionCallback callback functions for any object. When the user selects an item in a list widget, the contents of the neighboring list widget are replaced. This function uses the list widget callback structure named **XmListCallbackStruct**. This structure contains the following fields: reason, event, item, item_length, and item_number.

2. Used to form the string version of the item number.

3. Local character storage.

4. Override argument list for the **MrmFetchSetValues** function.

5. User has selected an item from the Materials list widget. The application needs to place a new items list in the Types list widget. The string tables stored in the UID file are named *cst_type_"index number"* and their count names are *l_count_type_"index number"* (where *index number* corresponds to the item's position in the list widget). Using the index of the selected item from this list, the application forms the name of the appropriate compound string table.

   Using the item number instead of the text value of the selection separates the function of the application from the form (in this case, the contents of the list widgets) and reduces complexity. If the program used the text value of the selected item as the means to determine what to display, it must deal with possible invalid characters for a UIL name in the text and convert the text value (a compound string) to a null-terminated string so that the string could be passed to the function **XtSetValues**.

6. Used to form the string version of the item number.

7. Used to form the name of the string table.

8. Used to form the name of the string table count.

9. Used to fill the types list widget with a new list of items.

10. Similar selection recording code goes here.

22.2.5 Using an Object Definition as a Template

The **MrmFetchWidgetOverride** function is useful if you have to create several similar widgets. Consider an application interface that has a lot of push buttons contained in a bulletin board. The push buttons are the same except for their **XmNy** position and label. Instead of declaring each push button individually, you can declare one push button and use the MRM function **MrmFetchWidgetOverride** to use that declaration as a template, modifying the **XmNy** position and label at run time.

By calling the **MrmFetchWidgetOverride** function instead of the **MrmFetchWidget** function, the application program creates the widget and overrides the original values in the declaration with the values specified in the **MrmFetchWidgetOverride** call. The argument list you supply to the **MrmFetchWidgetOverride** function must contain Motif Toolkit attribute names; therefore, it is also possible to override the callbacks for an object using the **MrmFetchWidgetOverride** function, since callbacks are Motif Toolkit attributes.

To use the **MrmFetchWidgetOverride** function in an application, you should use UIL identifiers to specify the tag value for each callback procedure. The tag is specified in the callback structure and cannot be changed unless the callback is deleted and replaced. The callback structure is not stored in the widget data, but by the X Toolkit intrinsics.

If you do not use identifiers for tag values, your callback procedures must contain a check for the parent of the calling widget or some other field of the widget (as opposed to checking only the tag value) because it is not possible to override the tag value with the **MrmFetchWidgetOverride** function. If you do not use an identifier for the tag value, all instances of the fetched object return identical tag values for all callbacks. If the callback function checks only the tag value, the callback function could not distinguish which instance made the call. Section 19.7 explains how to use UIL identifiers.

Another practical use of the **MrmFetchWidgetOverride** function is to create objects with arguments whose values can only be determined at run time (that is, are not known at UIL compilation time).

The MRM function **MrmFetchSetValues** works like the **MrmFetchWidgetOverride** function. The **MrmFetchSetValues** function, like the **MrmFetchWidgetOverride** function, accepts a vector of name and value pairs. This vector is passed as the *override_args* argument for the **MrmFetchWidgetOverride** function and as the *args* argument for the **MrmFetchSetValues** function. For the **MrmFetchWidgetOverride** function, the name and value pairs consist of the Motif Toolkit attributes name and an explicit value for that attribute.

The value member of the name and value pairs passed to **MrmFetchSetValues** is the UIL name of the value, not an explicit value. When the application calls **MrmFetchSetValues**, MRM looks up the names in the UID file, then uses the values corresponding to those names to override the original values in the object declaration. The **MrmFetchSetValues** function, therefore, allows you to keep all values used in an application in the UIL module, and not in the application program. (The values you pass to the **MrmFetchSetValues** function must be named, exported literals in the UIL module.)

The **MrmFetchSetValues** function is a convenience function that packages the functions provided by the **MrmFetchLiteral** and **MrmFetchWidgetOverride** functions.

22.3 Customizing a Motif Interface Using UIL and MRM

UIL offers the advantage of separating the form an interface takes from the functions of the application. The form of the interface can change, while the functions the application performs remain the same. By specifying these varying forms of the interface in separate UIL modules, you can change the interface by changing the definition of the UID hierarchy (the set of UID files) in the application program, and recompiling and relinking the application.

Consider the UIL module in the following example, which shows the compound string literals for the Motifburger interface translated into French. This is a separate UIL module, not an edited version of the original Motifburger UIL module.

```
module french_literals
       version = 'v1.0'
       names = case_sensitive
value
   k_motifburger_title    :
       exported "Motifburger - Commandes";
   k_nyi_label_text       :
       exported "Fonction non disponible";
   k_file_label_text      : exported "Fichier";
   k_quit_label_text      : exported "Quitter";
   k_edit_label_text      : exported "Edition";
   k_cut_dot_label_text      : exported "Couper";
   k_copy_dot_label_text     : exported "Copier";
   k_paste_dot_label_text    : exported "Coller";
   k_clear_dot_label_text    :
       exported "Effacer tout";
   k_select_all_label_text   :
       exported "Sélectionner tout";
   k_order_label_text           : exported "Commande";
   k_show_controls_label_text   :
       exported "Voir codes...";
   k_cancel_order_label_text    :
       exported "Annuler commande";
   k_submit_order_label_text    :
       exported "Transmettre commande";
   k_hamburgers_label_text   : exported "Hamburgers";
   k_rare_label_text         : exported "Saignant";
   k_medium_label_text       : exported "A point";
   k_well_done_label_text    : exported "Très cuit";
   k_ketchup_label_text      : exported "Ketchup";
   k_mustard_label_text      : exported "Moutarde";
   k_onion_label_text        : exported "Oignons";
   k_mayonnaise_label_text   : exported "Mayonnaise";
   k_pickle_label_text       : exported "Cornichons";
   k_quantity_label_text     : exported "Quantité";
   k_fries_label_text        : exported "Frites";
   k_size_label_text         : exported "Taille";
   k_tiny_label_text         : exported "Minuscule";
   k_small_label_text        : exported "Petit";
   k_large_label_text        : exported "Gros";
   k_huge_label_text         : exported "Enorme";
```

```
k_drinks_label_text        : exported "Boissons";
k_0_label_text             : exported '0';
k_drink_list_text          : exported
    string_table ('Jus de pomme', 'Jus d'orange',
    'Jus de raisin', 'Cola', 'Punch',
    'Root beer', 'Eau', 'Ginger Ale',
    'Lait', 'Café', 'Thé');
k_drink_list_select        :
    exported string_table("Jus de pomme");
k_u_label_text             : exported "U";
k_d_label_text             : exported "D";
k_apply_label_text         : exported "Appliquer";
k_reset_label_text         : exported "Remise à 0";
k_cancel_label_text        : exported "Annulation";
k_dismiss_label_text       : exported "Terminé";
```

```
end module;
```

In order to generate a French version of the Motifburger application, perform the following steps:

1. Change all string literal declarations in the original Motifburger UIL module to be imported compound strings. For example, change the value declaration for the Fries label as follows:

```
k_fries_label_text      :
        imported compound_string;
```

As shown in the previous example, the French UIL module specifies the corresponding values as exported and gives their definitions.

2. In the original C program for the Motifburger application, specify the name of the UID file containing the compiled French UIL module as the first element of the UID hierarchy array. Assume the name of the UIL specification file containing the French strings is french_literals.uil. Change the UID hierarchy array definition as follows:

```
static char *db_filename_vec[] =
    {"french_literals.uid",
     "motifburger.uid"
    };
```

3. Add a line to the script that compiles the French UIL module, and execute the script.

22.4 Using UIL on Large Projects

When several programmers are working together to specify the interface for a Motif application, contention for access to the UIL module can develop. The UIL module can be broken up into several small files, each containing a segment of the total interface specification, to allow several people to work on it at one time.

One approach is to construct a main UIL file containing the following information; once you create a main UIL file, you should rarely need to change its contents:

- Comments describing copyright information, module history, project information, and other relevant information.

- Global declarations, such as case sensitivity, objects clause, and procedure declarations.

- A series of include directives. Each include directive points to a UIL specification file containing some portion of the interface specification.

The UIL specification for an application interface might be divided into four files, as follows:

- Shared literals

  This file defines all literals shared between the UIL module and the application source code. These are the constants used as tags to the callback procedures.

- Main window

  This file defines the main window for the application. This might include a menu bar with associated cascade buttons, the work region, and other relevant pieces.

- Bulletin board dialogs

  This file defines all the bulletin board dialogs used in the application.

- Other interface objects

  This file defines all the other objects that do not fit into the first three categories. This file might include display windows with their menu bars and work regions, pop-up menus, and the command dialog box.

The purpose of using multiple UIL files is simply to make it easier for large programming project teams to work concurrently on the same application interface. It is a matter of style whether the included files themselves contain include directives.

Some programmers prefer to work with a single main UIL file, and know that this file names all of the remaining files needed to complete the interface specification. Having a list of all needed files visible in the main UIL file can be helpful, for example, to someone translating the user interface into another language. All files can be accounted for easily and included in the translation.

22.5 Working with User-Defined Widgets in UIL

You can extend the Motif Toolkit by building your own widgets. In UIL, such a user-defined widget is identified by the UIL object type **user_defined**. A user-defined widget can accept any UIL built-in argument or callback reason. If needed, you can use UIL to define your own arguments and callback reasons for a user-defined widget. You can specify any object as a child of a user-defined widget.

To use a user-defined widget in an application interface, follow these steps in the UIL module:

1. Define the arguments and callback reasons for the user-defined widget that are not UIL built-ins. This can be done inline when declaring an instance of the user-defined widget or in one or more value sections.

2. Declare the creation function for the user-defined widget.

3. Declare an instance of the user-defined widget. Use **user_defined** as the object type and include the name of the widget creation function in the declaration.

In the application program, you must register the class of the user-defined widget using the MRM function **MrmRegisterClass**. Part of the information you provide to the **MrmRegisterClass** function is the name of the widget creation function. By registering the class (and creation function), you allow MRM to create a user-defined widget using the same mechanisms used to create Motif Toolkit objects. You can specify the widget using UIL and fetch the widget with MRM.

The examples in this section are based on a previously built user-defined widget called the XYZ widget. The following sections explain how to include the XYZ widget in an application interface using UIL and how to create the widget at run time using MRM.

22.5.1 Defining Arguments and Reasons for a User-Defined Widget

The UIL compiler has built-in arguments and callback reasons that are supported by objects in the Motif Toolkit. A user-defined widget can be built having only standard Motif Toolkit arguments and reasons as its resources. If your application interface uses a user-defined widget of this type, you can use the UIL built-in argument names and callback reasons directly when you declare an instance of the user-defined widget. If the user-defined widget supports arguments and reasons that are not built into the UIL compiler, you need to define these arguments and reasons using the **ARGUMENT** and **REASON** functions, respectively, before specifying them.

The following example shows a UIL specification file that defines arguments and callback reasons and declares the creation function for the XYZ widget. This UIL specification file should be included in any UIL module in which you declare an instance of the XYZ widget.

```
(1)   value
      xyz_font_level_0 : argument ('fontLevel0', font);
      xyz_font_level_1 : argument ('fontLevel1', font);
      xyz_font_level_2 : argument ('fontLevel2', font);
      xyz_font_level_3 : argument ('fontLevel3', font);
      xyz_font_level_4 : argument ('fontLevel4', font);
      xyz_indent_margin :
          argument ('indentMargin', integer);
      xyz_unit_level :
          argument ('unitLevel', integer);
      xyz_page_level :
          argument ('pageLevel', integer);
      xyz_root_widget :
          argument ('rootWidget', integer );
      xyz_root_entry :
          argument ('rootEntry', integer);
      xyz_display_mode :
          argument ('displayMode', integer);
      xyz_fixed_width_entries :
          argument ('fixedWidthEntries', Boolean);
(2)   value
      xyz_select_and_confirm :
          reason ('selectAndConfirmCallback');
      xyz_extend_confirm :
          reason ('extendConfirmCallback');
      xyz_entry_selected :
          reason ('entrySelectedCallback');
      xyz_entry_unselected :
          reason ('entryUnselectedCallback');
      xyz_help_requested: reason ('helpCallback');
      xyz_attach_to_source :
          reason ('attachToSourceCallback');
      xyz_detach_from_source :
          reason ('detachFromSourceCallback');
      xyz_alter_root : reason ('alterRootCallback');
      xyz_selections_dragged :
          reason ('selectionsDraggedCallback');
      xyz_get_entry : reason ('getEntryCallback');
      xyz_dragging : reason ('draggingCallback');
```

```
        xyz_dragging_end : reason ('draggingEndCallback');
        xyz_dragging_cancel :
            reason ('draggingCancelCallback');
(3)     value
        XyzPositionTop :        1;
        XyzPositionMiddle :     2;
        XyzPositionBottom :     3;
        XyzDisplayOutline :     1;
        XyzDisplayTopTree :     2;
(4)     procedure XyzCreate();
```

NOTES:

1. Defines UIL argument names for the XYZ widget that are not built-in Toolkit arguments. The strings you pass to the **ARGUMENT** function must match the names listed in the resource list structure in the widget class record for the XYZ widget. In addition to the string, specify the data type of the argument. Just as for built-in arguments, when you declare an instance of the XYZ widget in a UIL module, the UIL compiler checks the data type of the values you specify for these arguments. For example, the UIL compiler checks that the value you specify for the *xyz_indent_margin* argument is an integer.

2. Defines the XYZ widget's callback reason names that are not UIL built-in reasons. The strings you pass to the **REASON** function must match the names listed in the resource list structure in the widget class record for the XYZ widget. (Callback reasons, like UIL arguments, are considered to be widget-specific attributes in the Motif Toolkit and are defined as resources.)

3. Defines some integer literals for specifying arguments of the XYZ widget.

4. Declares the widget creation function for the XYZ widget. This creation function is registered with MRM through the **MrmRegisterClass** function (see the example in Section 22.5.3).

22.5.2 Using a User-Defined Widget in an Interface Specification

The following example shows how to specify the XYZ widget in a UIL module. This UIL module includes the UIL specification file shown in the previous example as **xyz_widget.uil**.

```
        module xyz_example
            names = case_sensitive
        include file 'XmAppl.uil';
(1)     include file 'xyz_widget.uil';
(2)         procedure
              XyzAttach          ();
              XyzDetach          ();
              XyzExtended        ();
              XyzConfirmed       ();
              XyzGetEntry        ();
              XyzSelected        ();
              XyzUnselected      ();
              XyzDragged         ();
              XyzDragging        ();
              XyzDraggingEnd     ();
              create_proc        ();
              MenuQuit           ();
              MenuExpandAll      ();
              MenuCollapseAll    ();
(3)         object
            main : XmMainWindow
                { arguments
                    {
                        XmNx = 0;
                        XmNy = 0;
                        XmNheight = 0;
                        XmNwidth = 0;
                    };
                controls
                    { XmMenuBar main_menu;
                      user_defined xyz_widget;
                    };
                };
```

```
(4)          xyz_widget :
                 user_defined procedure XyzCreate
                 { arguments
                     {
                         XmNx = 0;
                         XmNy = 0;
                         XmNheight = 600;
                         XmNwidth = 400;
(5)                      xyz_display_mode =
                             XyzDisplayOutline;
                     };
                 callbacks
                     {   xyz_attach_to_source =
                             procedure XyzAttach();
                         xyz_detach_from_source =
                             procedure XyzDetach();
                         xyz_get_entry =
                             procedure XyzGetEntry();
                         xyz_select_and_confirm =
                             procedure XyzConfirmed();
                         xyz_extend_confirm =
                             procedure XyzExtended();
                         xyz_entry_selected =
                             procedure XyzSelected();
                         xyz_entry_unselected =
                             procedure XyzUnselected();
                         xyz_selections_dragged =
                             procedure XyzDragged();
                         xyz_dragging =
                             procedure XyzDragging();
                         xyz_dragging_end =
                             procedure XyzDraggingEnd();
(6)                      MrmNcreateCallback =
                             procedure create_proc();
                     };
                 };
```

```
(7)              main_menu: XmMenuBar
                   { arguments
                       { XmNorientation = XmHORIZONTAL;
                       };
                     controls
                       { XmCascadeButton file_menu;
                       };
                   };
              file_menu: XmCascadeButton
                   { arguments
                       { XmNlabelString = 'File';
                       };
                     controls
                       { XmPulldownMenu
                          { controls
                              { XmPushButton
                                   expand_all_button;
                                XmPushButton
                                   collapse_all_button;
                                XmPushButton
                                   quit_button;
                              };
                          };
                       };
                   };
              expand_all_button: XmPushButton
                   { arguments
                       { XmNlabelString = "Expand All";
                       };
                     callbacks
                       { XmNactivateCallback = procedure
                            MenuExpandAll();
                       };
                   };
              collapse_all_button: XmPushButton
                   { arguments
                       { XmNlabelString = "Collapse All";
                       };
```

```
            callbacks
                {  XmNactivateCallback = procedure
                        MenuCollapseAll();
                };
            };
        quit_button: XmPushButton
            {  arguments
                {  XmNlabelString = "Quit";
                };
            callbacks
                {  XmNactivateCallback = procedure
                        MenuQuit();
                };
            };
end module;
```

NOTES:

1. Includes a directive to include the definition of the XYZ widget shown in the example in Section 22.5.1.

2. Declarations for the callback functions defined in the application program.

3. Declaration for the main window widget. The main window widget has two children: a menu bar widget and the XYZ widget.

4. Declaration for the XYZ widget. Note that the object type is **user_defined** and that the creation function, *XyzCreate*, is included in the declaration.

5. The *xyz_display_mode* argument, defined with the **ARGUMENT** function in the example in Section 22.5.1, is specified using one of the integer literals also defined in that example.

6. All widgets support the **MrmNcreateCallback** reason.

7. The remaining objects declarations comprise the menu bar widget and its pull-down menu widgets.

22.5.3 Accessing a User-Defined Widget at Run Time

The following example shows a C application program that displays the XYZ widget (defined in the example in Section 22.5.1 and declared in the example in Section 22.5.2).

```
        #include <Mrm/MrmAppl.h>
(1)     #include <XmWsXyz.h>
(2)     globalref int xyzwidgetclassrec;
(3)     extern void XyzAttach        ();
        extern void XyzDetach        ();
        extern void XyzGetEntry      ();
        extern void XyzConfirmed     ();
        extern void XyzExtended      ();
        extern void XyzSelected      ();
        extern void XyzUnselected    ();
        extern void XyzHelpRoutine   ();
        extern void XyzDragged       ();
        extern void XyzDragging      ();
        extern void XyzDraggingEnd   ();
        extern void create_proc      ();
        extern void MenuQuit         ();
        extern void MenuExpandAll    ();
        extern void MenuCollapseAll  ();
(4)     static MrmRegisterArglist    register_vector[] =
        {
            {"XyzAttach", (caddr_t) XyzAttach},
            {"XyzDetach", (caddr_t) XyzDetach},
            {"XyzGetEntry", (caddr_t) XyzGetEntry},
            {"XyzConfirmed", (caddr_t) XyzConfirmed},
            {"XyzExtended", (caddr_t) XyzExtended},
            {"XyzSelected", (caddr_t) XyzSelected},
            {"XyzUnselected", (caddr_t) XyzUnselected},
            {"XyzHelpRoutine", (caddr_t) XyzHelpRoutine},
            {"XyzDragged", (caddr_t) XyzDragged},
            {"XyzDragging", (caddr_t) XyzDragging},
            {"XyzDraggingEnd", (caddr_t) XyzDraggingEnd},
            {"create_proc, (caddr_t) create_proc},
            {"MenuQuit", (caddr_t) MenuQuit},
```

```
                {"MenuExpandAll",  (caddr_t) MenuExpandAll},
                {"MenuCollapseAll", (caddr_t) MenuCollapseAll}
            };
      #define register_vector_length
                ( (sizeof register_vector) /  \
                (sizeof register_vector[0]) )
(5)   static MrmHierarchy  hierarchy_id ;
      static char          *vec[]={"xyz_example.uid"};
      static MrmCode        class ;
        Widget toplevel;
        XtAppContext app_context;
        Widget mainwindow;
(6)     int main (argc, argv)
        unsigned int argc;
        char **argv;
  {
(7)       Arg arguments[1];
(8)       MrmInitialize();
(9)       toplevel = XtAppInitialize (&app_context,
                        "xyz", NULL, 0, &argc, argv,
                        NULL, NULL, 0);
(10)      if( MrmRegisterClass
                ( MRMwcUnknown,
                  XyzClassName,
                  "XyzCreate",
                  XyzCreate,
                  &xyzwidgetclassrec )
            != MrmSUCCESS )
        {
          printf ("Can't register XYZ widget");
        }
(11)      if( MrmOpenHierarchy
                ( 1,
                  vec,
                  NULL,
                  &hierarchy_id )
            != MrmSUCCESS )
        {
          printf ("Can't open hierarchy");
        }
```

```
(12)      MrmRegisterNames( register_vector,
              register_vector_length );
          XtSetArg (arguments[0], XmNallowShellResize,
              TRUE);
          XtSetValues (toplevel, arguments, 1);
(13)      if( MrmFetchWidget
                ( hierarchy_id,
                  "main",
                  toplevel,
                  &mainwindow,
                  &class )
              != MrmSUCCESS )
      {
          printf ("Can't fetch interface ");
      }
      XtManageChild (mainwindow);
      XtRealizeWidget (toplevel);
      XtAppMainLoop(app_context);
      return (0);
  }
```

.
.
.

NOTES:

1. Includes XYZ declarations.

2. Provides a reference to the widget class record for the XYZ widget (named *xyzwidgetclassrec*).

3. Declares callback routines defined (but not shown) later in the program.

4. Defines the mapping between UIL procedure names and their addresses.

5. Specifies the UID hierarchy list. The UID hierarchy for this application consists of a single UID file, the compiled version of **xyz_example.uil**. (Assume the UIL specification file has the same name as the UIL module; see the module header. The file named **xyz_example.uil** includes the file **xyz_widget.uil**, shown in Section 22.5.1.)

6. Main routine.

7. Arguments for the widgets.

8. Initializes MRM.

9. Initializes the Motif Toolkit.

10. Registers the XYZ widget class with MRM. This allows MRM to use standard creation mechanisms to create the XYZ widget (see (13)). The arguments passed to the **MrmRegisterClass** routine are as follows:

    • MRMwcUnknown -- Indicates that the class is user defined

    • XyzClassName -- Class name of XYZ widget, defined in **XmWsXyz.h**.

    • "XyzCreate" -- Name of the creation routine

    • *XyzCreate* -- Address of the creation routine

    • &xyzwidgetclassrec -- Pointer to the widget class record

11. Defines the UID hierarchy.

12. Registers callback routine names with MRM.

13. Fetches the interface (the main window widget with a menu bar widget and the XYZ widget in the work area). Note that the XYZ widget is treated like any Motif Toolkit widget. MRM calls the XYZ widget's creation routine (*XyzCreate*) and passes this routine the values for the XmNx, XmNy, XmNwidth, XmNheight, and *xyz_display_mode*) arguments as specified in the UID file, using the standard creation routine format.

Chapter 23

The Widget Meta-Language Facility

The widget meta-language facility (WML) is used to generate the components of the user interface language (UIL) compiler that can change depending on the widget set. Using WML you can add support in UIL for new widgets to the OSF/Motif widget set or for a totally new widget set.

UIL is made up of:

- Static syntax

- Dynamic syntax

- Data types

The static syntax elements are the basic syntax and keywords of UIL. The static elements do not change as you modify the widget set. The static syntax elements of UIL are defined in the file **Uil.y**.

The dynamic syntax elements are the parts of UIL that change with the widget set. The dynamic syntax elements describe the widget and gadget classes supported by UIL including their resources and hierarchy. The dynamic elements of UIL are defined in WML files. The dynamic elements of the OSF/Motif widget set are defined in the file **motif.wml**.

The data type elements describe the allowable data types for each widget and gadget resource. Although the data types do not change, the resources that they are assigned to change with the widget set. The data types are provided in UIL for better error checking. The allowable data types for each resource are defined in the same file as the dynamic syntax elements.

The WML facility combines the static syntax, dynamic syntax, and data type elements to produce new source code for UIL. This allows you to modify the dynamic elements of your version of UIL; giving you the ability to add resources, widgets, gadgets, or even new widget sets.

Once you have modified your WML file, run the WML facility with that file as input and compile the new UIL compiler. A number of useful reports are also created by the WML facility to help you analyze, debug, and document your changes.

23.1 Using WML

Every time Motif is built, UIL is built from the **motif.wml** file using the WML facility. You can create your own WML file in the directory **tools/wml** to use in place of **motif.wml**. By convention, WML files have a suffix of **.wml**. Section 23.2 describes how to modify WML files. After you have created your new WML file, building a new UIL is a four step process:

1. Build WML.

2. Run WML with your WML file.

3. Install the UIL source files.

4. Build UIL.

All four steps are done as needed each time Motif is built. You should follow your standard Motif build instructions to rebuild UIL. In most cases you will simply move to the top of your build tree and enter **make**. By default, UIL is built using the **motif.wml** file from the **tools/wml** directory. You can specify a different WML file in the **tools/wml** directory with the command line make variable **TABLE** as follows:

```
make TABLE=anyfile.wml
```

Where *anyfile.wml* is the name of a WML file in the tools/wml directory of your Motif build tree.

You should refer to the *OSF/Motif Release Notes* for more information about building Motif.

The following sections describe how to do each of the four steps independently.

23.1.1 Building WML

WML is built by default when you build Motif. You should only need to build WML if you want to use it without building Motif. The WML source is located in the subdirectory **tools/wml**. Before WML is built, the directory should contain the files:

Imakefile	wml.c	wmlparse.y
Makefile	wml.h	wmlresolve.c
Makefile.hp	wmllex.l	wmlsynbld.c
README	wmlouth.c	wmluiltok.l
Uil.y	wmloutkey.c	wmlutils.c
UilDBDef.h	wmloutmm.c	
motif.wml	wmloutp1.c	

The files **Imakefile**, **Makefile**, and **Makefile.hp** are used to build and run the WML facility. The **README** file contains this technical bulletin. The files **Uil.y** and **motif.wml** are the data files for the static syntax, dynamic syntax and data type elements of UIL. The files with the **wml** prefix are the source files for the WML facility.

To build WML, change to the directory **tools/wml**, build the make file for your machine, and build WML using the following commands:

```
cd tools/wml
make Makefile
make depend
make wmltools
```

The make file is built from the Imake facility using the **make Makefile** and **make depend** commands. The **make Makefile** command produces a machine dependent **Makefile** for your machine. The **make depend** command adds include file dependencies to the new make file.

After you have built the WML facility the **tools/wml** directory should contain the following additional files:

lex.yy.c	wmloutkey.o	wmlresolve.o
libwml.a	wmloutmm.o	wmlsynbld.o
wml	wmloutp1.o	wmluiltok
wml.o	wmlparse.c	wmlutils.o
wmllex.c	wmlparse.h	
wmlouth.o	wmlparse.o	

23.1.2 Running WML

You need to run WML separately only if you do not want to install and build the new version of UIL. Running WML automatically builds the WML source files if necessary.

The **make runwml** command from the **tools/wml** directory runs the WML facility. You can specify the WML file to use with the make variable **TABLE**.

```
make runwml TABLE=anyfile.wml
```

Where *anyfile.wml* is a WML file in the **tools/wml** directory. If you do not set the **TABLE** make variable, the **motif.wml** file is used by default.

Running WML produces the following files:

UIL source files   **make copy** copies these files to the **clients/uil** directory to be used in building UIL. The UIL source files are **UilConst.h**, **UilDBDef.h**, **UilKeyTab.h**, **UilLexPars.c**, **UilLexPars.h**, **UilSymArTa.h**, **UilSymArTy.h**, **UilSymCSet.h**, **UilSymCtl.h**, **UilSymEnum.h**, **UilSymGen.h**, **UilSymNam.h**, **UilSymRArg.h**, **UilSymReas.h**, **UilTokName.h**, and **UilUrmClas.h**.

wml.report   This report describes the widget set supported by the newly created UIL sources. You can use it to help validate your WML source file. It is organized so you can easily compare it to reference documentation as follows:

- Class names are ordered alphabetically by name.

- Resources are ordered by ancestor(top down).

- Resources are listed alphabetically, with datatype and default.

- Reasons are ordered by ancestor then alphabetically.

- Controls are ordered alphabetically.

wml-uil.mm   This file contains the **Appendix B** of this manual. You can process this file using tbl, troff and the mm macro package to produce two tables for each supported widget class. The first table lists the controls and reasons supported by the class. The second table lists the resources for the class, their types and default values.

These files overwrite any existing WML output files in the **tools/wml** directory. If you do not want to lose the existing files, save them somewhere else.

23.1.3 Installing UIL

You need to install the UIL source files separately only if you do not want to build the new version of UIL. Installing the UIL source files automatically builds the WML source files and runs WML if necessary.

The **make** command from the **tools/wml** directory installs the UIL source files in the **clients/uil** directory. The **make all** and **make copy** commands are synonyms for the **make** command. This overwrites the existing source files in the **clients/uil** directory. If you do not want to lose your existing source files, save them somewhere else.

You can specify the WML file on the **make** command line using the make variable **TABLE.**

```
make TABLE=anyfile.wml
```

Where *anyfile.wml* is the name of a WML file. If you do not specify **TABLE, motif.wml** is used by default.

23.1.4 Building UIL

You only need to build UIL separately if you do not want the new UIL to reflect the current WML tables. To build UIL separately, move to the **clients/uil** directory and enter **make**.

```
cd clients/uil
make
```

You should refer to the *OSF/Motif Release Notes* for more information about building UIL.

23.2 Modifying WML files

WML files are ASCII files that you can modify with any standard text editor. They are accessed in the **tools/wml** directory by WML. By convention WML files have the suffix **.wml**. The Motif widget set is described in the **motif.wml** file. This is also the default WML file when using the WML facility.

When adding new widgets or changing widget characteristics, you should start with a copy of the **motif.wml** file. If you are creating a new widget set for use with UIL, you should start from scratch. In either case the **motif.wml** file is a good example of WML syntax, and you should familiarize yourself with it before writing your own WML file.

23.2.1 WML Syntax

WML files have a simple syntax, similar in structure to UIL. It is made up of seven elements:

- Comments
- Data Type Definitions
- Character Set Definitions
- Enumeration Set Definitions
- Control List Definitions
- Class Definitions
- Resource Definitions

You can use space, tabs, or newlines anywhere in the syntax, as long as you do not split up keywords or strings, except that comments end at a newline. The order of elements is not important to the syntax.

This section uses the following additional conventions to describe the syntax of the widget meta-language:

[ ]   Indicates optional elements.

...   Indicates where an element of syntax can be repeated.

| Indicates a choice among multiple items.

For example:

ExactlyTyped [{**ONE** | **TWO** | *anything.else* [...]}];

indicates that **ExactlyTyped** must be typed exactly as shown, and that any number of optional arguments of **ONE**, **TWO**, or *anything.else* must be inclosed in braces if used. Any of the following lines would fit this sample syntax:

```
ExactlyTyped;
ExactlyTyped {ONE};
ExactlyTyped {  variable } ;
ExactlyTyped {ONE TWO variable};
```

23.2.1.1 Comments

You can include comments in the WML file. Comments have the following syntax:

[*any.element*]!*any.comment*

Comments begin with an exclamation point and extend to the end of the line. A comment can begin on a line by itself or follow any part of another element. A comment does not change the meaning of any other element. For example:

```
!This is a comment
!  that spans two lines.
DataType     !This is a comment following code.
```

23.2.1.2 Data Type Definitions

Data type definitions register all the resource data types used in the file. You must register all the data types used in your WML file. Data type definitions have the following syntax:

DataType
  any.datatype [{ **InternalLiteral** = *internal.name* |
      DocName = "*string*"; [...]}];
  [...]

A data type definition begins with the keyword **DataType**. Following the **DataType** keyword is a list of data types that can be further modified with:

InternalLiteral
  This forces the value of the internal symbol table literal definition of the data type name. This modifier is only used to get around symbol table definitions hard coded into the UIL compiler. It should rarely be used.

DocName which gives an arbitrary string for use in the documentation. This string is meant to supply a different name for the data type for use in the documentation, or a single name for the data type if the data type has aliases.

For example:

```
DataType OddNumber {DocName="OddNumber";};
         NewString;
```

23.2.1.3 Character Set Definitions

Character set definitions register the Motif Toolkit name and other information for the character set names used in UIL. Character set definitions have the following syntax:

CharacterSet
    any.character.set
        { **XmStringCharsetName** = "*string*" ;
        [**Alias** = "*string*" ... ; |
          Direction = [**LeftToRight** | **RightToLeft**] ; |
          ParseDirection = [**LeftToRight** | **RightToLeft**] ; |
          CharacterSize = [**OneByte** | **TwoByte**] ;]
        [...] } ;
    [...]

A character set definition begins with the keyword **CharacterSet**. Following the **CharacterSet** keyword is a list of character sets that can be further modified with:

XmStringCharsetName
        Specifies the name of the character set, which will become the character set component of a compound string segment created using this character set. This modifier is required.

Alias
        Specifies one or more aliases for the character set name. Each alias can be used within UIL to refer to the same character set.

Direction
        Specifies the direction of a compound string segment created using this character set. The default is **LeftToRight**.

ParseDirection   Specifies the direction in which an input string is parsed when a compound string segment is created using this character set. The default is whatever **Direction** is specified.

CharacterSize   Specifies the number of bytes in each character of a compound string segment created using this character set. The default is **OneByte**.

For example:

```
CharacterSet
  iso_latin1
    { XmStringCharsetName = "ISO8859-1";
      Alias = "ISOLatin1"; };
  iso_hebrew_lr
    { XmStringCharsetName = "ISO8859-8";
      Alias = "iso_latin8_lr";
      Direction = RightToLeft;
      ParseDirection = LeftToRight; };
  ksc_korean
    { XmStringCharsetName = "KSC5601.1987-0";
      CharacterSize = TwoByte; };
```

23.2.1.4 Enumeration Set Definitions

Enumeration set definitions register the named constants used in the Motif Toolkit to specify some resource values. Enumeration set definitions have the following syntax:

EnumerationSet
   resource.name **:** *resource.type*
      { *enum.value.name* **;** [...] **}** **;**

An enumeration set definition begins with the keyword **EnumerationSet**. For each enumeration set defined, the name and type of the resource are listed. The resource name is the Motif Toolkit resource name, with the beginning **XmN** removed and with the initial letter capitalized. For example, the name of the Motif Toolkit resource **XmNrowColumnType** is **RowColumnType**. The resource type is the data type for the resource; for most resources, this is **integer**. Following the resource name and type is a list of names of enumeration values that can be used as settings for the resource. These names are the same as those in the Motif Toolkit.

For example:

```
EnumerationSet
   RowColumnType: integer
      { XmWORK_AREA; XmMENU_BAR; XmMENU_POPUP;
        XmMENU_PULLDOWN; XmMENU_OPTION; };
```

23.2.1.5 Control List Definitions

Control list definitions assign a name to groups of controls. You can use these control lists later in class definitions to simplify the structure of your WML file. Control list definitions have the following syntax:

ControlList
  any.control.list [{ *any.control*; [...]}];

A control list definition starts with the **ControlList** keyword. Following the **ControlList** keyword are any number of control list definitions. Control list definitions are made up of a control list name followed by the set of controls it represents. For example:

```
ControlList
        Buttons {PushButton;
                 RadioButton;
                 CascadeButton;
                 NewCascadebutton;};
```

Each control specified in the control list must be defined as a class in the file.

23.2.1.6 Class Definitions

Class definitions describe a particular widget class including its position in the class hierarchy, toolkit convenience function, resources, and controls. There should be one class definition for each widget or gadget in the widget set you want to support in UIL. Class definitions have the following syntax:

Class *class.name* **: MetaClass I Widget I Gadget**
  [{[**SuperClass** = *class.name*; I
    InternalLiteral = *internal.name*; I
    Alias = *alias*; I
    ConvenienceFunction = *convenience.function*; I
    WidgetClass = *widget.class*; I
    DocName = "*string*"; I
    DialogClass = **True I False**; I
    Resources { *any.resource.name* [{**Default** = *new.default.value*; I
                     Exclude = **True I False**;
                    [...]}
                 ];
        [...]}; I
    Controls { *any.control.name*; [...]};
    [...]
  }}];

Class definitions start with the **Class** keyword. For each class defined, the name of the class and whether the class is a metaclass, widget, or gadget is listed. Each class definition can be further modified with the following keywords:

SuperClass   This indicates the name of the parent class. Only the root of the hierarchy does not specify a SuperClass.

InternalLiteral
             which forces the value of the internal symbol table literal definition of the class name. This modifier is only used to get around symbol table definitions hard coded into the UIL compiler. It should rarely be used.

Alias   This indicates alternate names for the class for use in a UIL specification.

ConvenienceFunction
This indicates the name of the creation convenience function for this class. All widget and gadget classes must have a **ConvenienceFunction**.

WidgetClass This indicates the associated widget class of gadget type classes. Presently, nothing is done with this value.

DocName This defines an arbitrary string for use in the documentation. Presently, nothing is done with this value.

DialogClass This indicates whether the class is a dialog class. Presently, nothing is done with this value.

Resources This lists the resources of the widget class. This keyword can be further modified with:

    Default This specifies a new default value for this resource. Resource default values are usually set in the resource definition. If an inherited resource's default value is changed by the class, the new default value should be noted here.

    Exclude This specifies whether an inherited resource should be excluded from the resource list of the class. Exclude is **False** by default.

Controls This lists the controls that the widget class allows. The controls can be other classes or a control list from the control list definition.

The example below uses the examples from the data type definitions and control list definitions above.

```
Class
     TopLevelWidget : MetaClass
            {
            Resources
                 {
                 XtbNfirstResource;
                 XtbNsecondResource;
                 };
            };
     NewWidget : Widget
            {
            SuperClass = TopLevelWidget;
            ConvenienceFunction =
                 XtbCreateNewWidget;
            Resources
                 {
                 XtbNnewResource;
                 XtbNfirstResource
                     {Default="XtbNEW_VALUE";};
                 XtbNsecondResource
                     {Exclude=True;};
                 };
            Controls
                 {
                 NewWidget;
                 Buttons;
                 };
            };
```

23.2.1.7 Resource Definitions

Resource definitions describe a particular resource including its type, and default value. There should be a resource definition for each new resource referenced in the class definitions. Resource definitions have the following syntax:

Resource
   resource.name **: Argument I Reason I Constraint I**
      SubResource
      [{[**Type** = *type* ; I
         ResourceLiteral = *resource.literal* ; I
         InternalLiteral = *internal.name*; I
         Alias = *alias* ; I
         Related = *related* ; I
         Default = *default* ; I
         DocName = *doc.name* ;]
         [...]}]
      [...]

Resource definitions start with the **Resource** keyword. For each resource definition, the name of the resource and whether the resource is an argument, reason, constraint or subresource is listed.

Argument   Indicates a standard resource.

Reason   Indicates a callback resource.

Constraint   Indicates a constraint resource.

SubResource   Presently, nothing is done with this value.

The resource definition can be further modified with the following keywords:

Type   This indicates the data type of the resource. It must be listed in the data type definition.

ResourceLiteral This indicates the keyword used in the UIL file to reference the resource. In Motif, the resource name is the same as the **ResourceLiteral**.

InternalLiteral which forces the value of the internal symbol table literal definition of the resource name. This modifier is only used to get around symbol table definitions hard coded into the UIL compiler. It should rarely be used.

Alias This indicates alternate names for the resource for use in a UIL specification.

Related This lists other related resources. It is for documentation purposes only. Presently, nothing is done with this value.

Default This indicates the default value of the resource.

DocName This defines an arbitrary string for use in the documentation. Presently, nothing is done with this value.

The example below uses the examples from the data type definitions, control list definitions and class definitions above.

```
Resource
    XtbNfirstResource : Argument
        { Type = OddNumber;
          Default = "XtbOLD_VALUE";};
    XtbNsecondResource : Argument
        { Type = NewString;
          Default = "XtbNEW_STRING"; };
    XtbNnewResource : Argument
        { Type = OddNumber;
          Default = "XtbODD_NUMBER"; };
```

Appendix A

Constraint Arguments

You can specify the following constraint arguments for children of the XmForm widget and the XmFormDialog widget:

Constraint Arguments	
XmNbottomAttachment	XmNrightAttachment
XmNbottomOffset	XmNrightOffset
XmNbottomPosition	XmNrightPosition
XmNbottomWidget	XmNrightWidget
XmNleftAttachment	XmNtopAttachment
XmNleftOffset	XmNtopOffset
XmNleftPosition	XmNtopPosition
XmNleftWidget	XmNtopWidget
XmNresizable	

You can specify the following constraint arguments for children of the XmPanedWindow widget:

Constraint Arguments	
XmNallowResize	XmNpaneMinimum
XmNpaneMaximum	XmNskipAdjust

For a complete description of constraint arguments, see Chapter 19.

Appendix B

UIL Built-In Tables

This appendix contains a listing of part of the UIL built-in tables used during compilation to check that your UIL specification is consistent with the Motif Toolkit.

For each object in the Motif Toolkit, this appendix contains a table that lists the reasons and controls (children) supported by UIL for that object. The arguments supported by UIL for each object are the same as the Motif Toolkit resources for that object. Appendix C lists the name and UIL data type of each UIL argument. For information on which arguments are supported for which objects and for the default values of arguments, see the widget manual pages in the *OSF/Motif Programmer's Reference* .

ArrowButton

Controls	Reasons
No children are supported	MrmNcreateCallback
	XmNactivateCallback
	XmNarmCallback
	XmNdestroyCallback
	XmNdisarmCallback
	XmNhelpCallback

XmArrowButtonGadget

Controls	Reasons
No children are supported	MrmNcreateCallback
	XmNactivateCallback
	XmNarmCallback
	XmNdestroyCallback
	XmNdisarmCallback
	XmNhelpCallback

BulletinBoard

Controls	Reasons
XmArrowButton	MrmNcreateCallback
XmArrowButtonGadget	XmNdestroyCallback
XmBulletinBoard	XmNfocusCallback
XmBulletinBoardDialog	XmNhelpCallback
XmCascadeButton	XmNmapCallback
XmCascadeButtonGadget	XmNunmapCallback
XmCommand	
XmDrawingArea	
XmDrawnButton	
XmErrorDialog	
XmFileSelectionBox	
XmFileSelectionDialog	

BulletinBoard (Continued)

Controls	Reasons
XmForm	
XmFormDialog	
XmFrame	
XmInformationDialog	
XmLabel	
XmLabelGadget	
XmList	
XmMenuBar	
XmMessageBox	
XmMessageDialog	
XmOptionMenu	
XmPanedWindow	
XmPopupMenu	
XmPromptDialog	
XmPulldownMenu	
XmPushButton	
XmPushButtonGadget	
XmQuestionDialog	
XmRadioBox	
XmRowColumn	
XmScale	
XmScrollBar	
XmScrolledList	
XmScrolledText	
XmScrolledWindow	
XmSelectionBox	
XmSelectionDialog	
XmSeparator	
XmSeparatorGadget	
XmText	
XmTextField	
XmToggleButton	
XmToggleButtonGadget	
XmWarningDialog	

BulletinBoard (Continued)

Controls	Reasons
XmWorkArea	
XmWorkingDialog	
user_defined	

XmBulletinBoardDialog

Controls	Reasons
XmArrowButton	MrmNcreateCallback
XmArrowButtonGadget	XmNdestroyCallback
XmBulletinBoard	XmNfocusCallback
XmBulletinBoardDialog	XmNhelpCallback
XmCascadeButton	XmNmapCallback
XmCascadeButtonGadget	XmNunmapCallback
XmCommand	
XmDrawingArea	
XmDrawnButton	
XmErrorDialog	
XmFileSelectionBox	
XmFileSelectionDialog	
XmForm	
XmFormDialog	
XmFrame	
XmInformationDialog	
XmLabel	
XmLabelGadget	
XmList	
XmMenuBar	
XmMessageBox	
XmMessageDialog	
XmOptionMenu	
XmPanedWindow	
XmPopupMenu	
XmPromptDialog	

XmBulletinBoardDialog (Continued)

Controls	Reasons
XmPulldownMenu	
XmPushButton	
XmPushButtonGadget	
XmQuestionDialog	
XmRadioBox	
XmRowColumn	
XmScale	
XmScrollBar	
XmScrolledList	
XmScrolledText	
XmScrolledWindow	
XmSelectionBox	
XmSelectionDialog	
XmSeparator	
XmSeparatorGadget	
XmText	
XmTextField	
XmToggleButton	
XmToggleButtonGadget	
XmWarningDialog	
XmWorkArea	
XmWorkingDialog	
user_defined	

XmCascadeButton

Controls	Reasons
XmPulldownMenu	MrmNcreateCallback
	XmNactivateCallback
	XmNcascadingCallback
	XmNdestroyCallback
	XmNhelpCallback

XmCascadeButtonGadget

Controls	Reasons
XmPulldownMenu	MrmNcreateCallback
	XmNactivateCallback
	XmNcascadingCallback
	XmNdestroyCallback
	XmNhelpCallback

XmCommand

Controls	Reasons
No children are supported	MrmNcreateCallback
	XmNcommandChangedCallback
	XmNcommandEnteredCallback
	XmNdestroyCallback
	XmNfocusCallback
	XmNhelpCallback
	XmNmapCallback
	XmNunmapCallback

XmDrawingArea

Controls	Reasons
XmArrowButton	MrmNcreateCallback
XmArrowButtonGadget	XmNdestroyCallback
XmBulletinBoard	XmNexposeCallback
XmBulletinBoardDialog	XmNhelpCallback
XmCascadeButton	XmNinputCallback
XmCascadeButtonGadget	XmNresizeCallback
XmCommand	
XmDrawingArea	
XmDrawnButton	
XmErrorDialog	
XmFileSelectionBox	

XmDrawingArea (Continued)

Controls	Reasons
XmFileSelectionDialog	
XmForm	
XmFormDialog	
XmFrame	
XmInformationDialog	
XmLabel	
XmLabelGadget	
XmList	
XmMenuBar	
XmMessageBox	
XmMessageDialog	
XmOptionMenu	
XmPanedWindow	
XmPopupMenu	
XmPromptDialog	
XmPulldownMenu	
XmPushButton	
XmPushButtonGadget	
XmQuestionDialog	
XmRadioBox	
XmRowColumn	
XmScale	
XmScrollBar	
XmScrolledList	
XmScrolledText	
XmScrolledWindow	
XmSelectionBox	
XmSelectionDialog	
XmSeparator	
XmSeparatorGadget	
XmText	
XmTextField	
XmToggleButton	
XmToggleButtonGadget	

XmDrawingArea (Continued)

Controls	Reasons
XmWarningDialog XmWorkArea XmWorkingDialog user_defined	

XmDrawnButton

Controls	Reasons
No children are supported	MrmNcreateCallback XmNactivateCallback XmNarmCallback XmNdestroyCallback XmNdisarmCallback XmNexposeCallback XmNhelpCallback XmNresizeCallback

XmErrorDialog

Controls	Reasons
XmMessageBox	MrmNcreateCallback XmNcancelCallback XmNdestroyCallback XmNfocusCallback XmNhelpCallback XmNmapCallback XmNokCallback XmNunmapCallback

XmFileSelectionBox

Controls	Reasons
XmArrowButton	MrmNcreateCallback
XmBulletinBoard	XmNapplyCallback
XmBulletinBoardDialog	XmNcancelCallback
XmCascadeButton	XmNdestroyCallback
XmCommand	XmNfocusCallback
XmDrawingArea	XmNhelpCallback
XmDrawnButton	XmNmapCallback
XmErrorDialog	XmNnoMatchCallback
XmFileSelectionBox	XmNokCallback
XmFileSelectionDialog	XmNunmapCallback
XmForm	
XmFormDialog	
XmFrame	
XmInformationDialog	
XmLabel	
XmList	
XmMenuBar	
XmMessageBox	
XmMessageDialog	
XmOptionMenu	
XmPanedWindow	
XmPopupMenu	
XmPromptDialog	
XmPulldownMenu	
XmPushButton	
XmQuestionDialog	
XmRadioBox	
XmRowColumn	
XmScale	
XmScrollBar	
XmScrolledList	
XmScrolledText	
XmScrolledWindow	
XmSelectionBox	

XmFileSelectionBox (Continued)

Controls	Reasons
XmSelectionDialog	
XmSeparator	
XmText	
XmTextField	
XmToggleButton	
XmWarningDialog	
XmWorkArea	
XmWorkingDialog	
user_defined	

XmFileSelectionDialog

Controls	Reasons
XmArrowButton	MrmNcreateCallback
XmBulletinBoard	XmNapplyCallback
XmBulletinBoardDialog	XmNcancelCallback
XmCascadeButton	XmNdestroyCallback
XmCommand	XmNfocusCallback
XmDrawingArea	XmNhelpCallback
XmDrawnButton	XmNmapCallback
XmErrorDialog	XmNnoMatchCallback
XmFileSelectionBox	XmNokCallback
XmFileSelectionDialog	XmNunmapCallback
XmForm	
XmFormDialog	
XmFrame	
XmInformationDialog	
XmLabel	
XmList	
XmMenuBar	
XmMessageBox	
XmMessageDialog	
XmOptionMenu	

XmFileSelectionDialog (Continued)

Controls	Reasons
XmPanedWindow	
XmPopupMenu	
XmPromptDialog	
XmPulldownMenu	
XmPushButton	
XmQuestionDialog	
XmRadioBox	
XmRowColumn	
XmScale	
XmScrollBar	
XmScrolledList	
XmScrolledText	
XmScrolledWindow	
XmSelectionBox	
XmSelectionDialog	
XmSeparator	
XmText	
XmTextField	
XmToggleButton	
XmWarningDialog	
XmWorkArea	
XmWorkingDialog	
user_defined	

XmForm

Controls	Reasons
XmArrowButton	MrmNcreateCallback
XmArrowButtonGadget	XmNdestroyCallback
XmBulletinBoard	XmNfocusCallback
XmBulletinBoardDialog	XmNhelpCallback
XmCascadeButton	XmNmapCallback
XmCascadeButtonGadget	XmNunmapCallback

XmForm (Continued)

Controls	Reasons
XmCommand	
XmDrawingArea	
XmDrawnButton	
XmErrorDialog	
XmFileSelectionBox	
XmFileSelectionDialog	
XmForm	
XmFormDialog	
XmFrame	
XmInformationDialog	
XmLabel	
XmLabelGadget	
XmList	
XmMenuBar	
XmMessageBox	
XmMessageDialog	
XmOptionMenu	
XmPanedWindow	
XmPopupMenu	
XmPromptDialog	
XmPulldownMenu	
XmPushButton	
XmPushButtonGadget	
XmQuestionDialog	
XmRadioBox	
XmRowColumn	
XmScale	
XmScrollBar	
XmScrolledList	
XmScrolledText	
XmScrolledWindow	
XmSelectionBox	
XmSelectionDialog	
XmSeparator	

XmForm (Continued)

Controls	Reasons
XmSeparatorGadget	
XmText	
XmTextField	
XmToggleButton	
XmToggleButtonGadget	
XmWarningDialog	
XmWorkArea	
XmWorkingDialog	
user_defined	

XmFormDialog

Controls	Reasons
XmArrowButton	MrmNcreateCallback
XmArrowButtonGadget	XmNdestroyCallback
XmBulletinBoard	XmNfocusCallback
XmBulletinBoardDialog	XmNhelpCallback
XmCascadeButton	XmNmapCallback
XmCascadeButtonGadget	XmNunmapCallback
XmCommand	
XmDrawingArea	
XmDrawnButton	
XmErrorDialog	
XmFileSelectionBox	
XmFileSelectionDialog	
XmForm	
XmFormDialog	
XmFrame	
XmInformationDialog	
XmLabel	
XmLabelGadget	
XmList	
XmMenuBar	

XmFormDialog (Continued)

Controls	Reasons
XmMessageBox	
XmMessageDialog	
XmOptionMenu	
XmPanedWindow	
XmPopupMenu	
XmPromptDialog	
XmPulldownMenu	
XmPushButton	
XmPushButtonGadget	
XmQuestionDialog	
XmRadioBox	
XmRowColumn	
XmScale	
XmScrollBar	
XmScrolledList	
XmScrolledText	
XmScrolledWindow	
XmSelectionBox	
XmSelectionDialog	
XmSeparator	
XmSeparatorGadget	
XmText	
XmTextField	
XmToggleButton	
XmToggleButtonGadget	
XmWarningDialog	
XmWorkArea	
XmWorkingDialog	
user_defined	

XmFrame

Controls	Reasons
XmArrowButton	MrmNcreateCallback
XmArrowButtonGadget	XmNdestroyCallback
XmBulletinBoard	XmNhelpCallback
XmBulletinBoardDialog	
XmCascadeButton	
XmCascadeButtonGadget	
XmCommand	
XmDrawingArea	
XmDrawnButton	
XmErrorDialog	
XmFileSelectionBox	
XmFileSelectionDialog	
XmForm	
XmFormDialog	
XmFrame	
XmInformationDialog	
XmLabel	
XmLabelGadget	
XmList	
XmMenuBar	
XmMessageBox	
XmMessageDialog	
XmOptionMenu	
XmPanedWindow	
XmPopupMenu	
XmPromptDialog	
XmPulldownMenu	
XmPushButton	
XmPushButtonGadget	
XmQuestionDialog	
XmRadioBox	
XmRowColumn	
XmScale	
XmScrollBar	

XmFrame (Continued)

Controls	Reasons
XmScrolledList	
XmScrolledText	
XmScrolledWindow	
XmSelectionBox	
XmSelectionDialog	
XmSeparator	
XmSeparatorGadget	
XmText	
XmTextField	
XmToggleButton	
XmToggleButtonGadget	
XmWarningDialog	
XmWorkArea	
XmWorkingDialog	
user_defined	

XmInformationDialog

Controls	Reasons
XmMessageBox	MrmNcreateCallback
XmPushButton	XmNcancelCallback
user_defined	XmNdestroyCallback
	XmNfocusCallback
	XmNhelpCallback
	XmNmapCallback
	XmNokCallback
	XmNunmapCallback

XmLabel

Controls	Reasons
No children are supported	MrmNcreateCallback XmNdestroyCallback XmNhelpCallback

XmLabelGadget

Controls	Reasons
No children are supported	MrmNcreateCallback XmNdestroyCallback XmNhelpCallback

XmList

Controls	Reasons
No children are supported	MrmNcreateCallback XmNbrowseSelectionCallback XmNdefaultActionCallback XmNdestroyCallback XmNextendedSelectionCallback XmNhelpCallback XmNmultipleSelectionCallback XmNsingleSelectionCallback

XmMainWindow

Controls	Reasons
XmArrowButton XmArrowButtonGadget XmBulletinBoard XmBulletinBoardDialog XmCascadeButton XmCascadeButtonGadget	MrmNcreateCallback XmNdestroyCallback XmNhelpCallback

XmMainWindow (Continued)

Controls	Reasons
XmCommand	
XmDrawingArea	
XmDrawnButton	
XmErrorDialog	
XmFileSelectionBox	
XmFileSelectionDialog	
XmForm	
XmFormDialog	
XmFrame	
XmInformationDialog	
XmLabel	
XmLabelGadget	
XmList	
XmMenuBar	
XmMessageBox	
XmMessageDialog	
XmOptionMenu	
XmPanedWindow	
XmPopupMenu	
XmPromptDialog	
XmPulldownMenu	
XmPushButton	
XmPushButtonGadget	
XmQuestionDialog	
XmRadioBox	
XmRowColumn	
XmScale	
XmScrollBar	
XmScrolledList	
XmScrolledText	
XmScrolledWindow	
XmSelectionBox	
XmSelectionDialog	
XmSeparator	

XmMainWindow (Continued)

Controls	Reasons
XmSeparatorGadget	
XmText	
XmTextField	
XmToggleButton	
XmToggleButtonGadget	
XmWarningDialog	
XmWorkArea	
XmWorkingDialog	
user_defined	

XmMenuBar

Controls	Reasons
XmArrowButton	MrmNcreateCallback
XmArrowButtonGadget	XmNdestroyCallback
XmBulletinBoard	XmNentryCallback
XmBulletinBoardDialog	XmNhelpCallback
XmCascadeButton	XmNmapCallback
XmCascadeButtonGadget	XmNunmapCallback
XmCommand	
XmDrawingArea	
XmDrawnButton	
XmErrorDialog	
XmFileSelectionBox	
XmFileSelectionDialog	
XmForm	
XmFormDialog	
XmFrame	
XmInformationDialog	
XmLabel	
XmLabelGadget	
XmList	
XmMenuBar	

XmMenuBar (Continued)

Controls	Reasons
XmMessageBox	
XmMessageDialog	
XmOptionMenu	
XmPanedWindow	
XmPopupMenu	
XmPromptDialog	
XmPulldownMenu	
XmPushButton	
XmPushButtonGadget	
XmQuestionDialog	
XmRadioBox	
XmRowColumn	
XmScale	
XmScrollBar	
XmScrolledList	
XmScrolledText	
XmScrolledWindow	
XmSelectionBox	
XmSelectionDialog	
XmSeparator	
XmSeparatorGadget	
XmText	
XmTextField	
XmToggleButton	
XmToggleButtonGadget	
XmWarningDialog	
XmWorkArea	
XmWorkingDialog	
user_defined	

XmMessageBox

Controls	Reasons
No children are supported	MrmNcreateCallback XmNcancelCallback XmNdestroyCallback XmNfocusCallback XmNhelpCallback XmNmapCallback XmNokCallback XmNunmapCallback

XmMessageDialog

Controls	Reasons
No children are supported	MrmNcreateCallback XmNcancelCallback XmNdestroyCallback XmNfocusCallback XmNhelpCallback XmNmapCallback XmNokCallback XmNunmapCallback

XmOptionMenu

Controls	Reasons
XmPulldownMenu	MrmNcreateCallback XmNdestroyCallback XmNentryCallback XmNhelpCallback XmNmapCallback XmNunmapCallback

XmPanedWindow

Controls	Reasons
XmArrowButton	MrmNcreateCallback
XmArrowButtonGadget	XmNdestroyCallback
XmBulletinBoard	XmNhelpCallback
XmBulletinBoardDialog	
XmCascadeButton	
XmCascadeButtonGadget	
XmCommand	
XmDrawingArea	
XmDrawnButton	
XmErrorDialog	
XmFileSelectionBox	
XmFileSelectionDialog	
XmForm	
XmFormDialog	
XmFrame	
XmInformationDialog	
XmLabel	
XmLabelGadget	
XmList	
XmMenuBar	
XmMessageBox	
XmMessageDialog	
XmOptionMenu	
XmPanedWindow	
XmPopupMenu	
XmPromptDialog	
XmPulldownMenu	
XmPushButton	
XmPushButtonGadget	
XmQuestionDialog	
XmRadioBox	
XmRowColumn	
XmScale	
XmScrollBar	

XmPanedWindow (Continued)

Controls	Reasons
XmScrolledList	
XmScrolledText	
XmScrolledWindow	
XmSelectionBox	
XmSelectionDialog	
XmSeparator	
XmSeparatorGadget	
XmText	
XmTextField	
XmToggleButton	
XmToggleButtonGadget	
XmWarningDialog	
XmWorkArea	
XmWorkingDialog	
user_defined	

XmPopupMenu

Controls	Reasons
XmArrowButton	MrmNcreateCallback
XmArrowButtonGadget	XmNdestroyCallback
XmBulletinBoard	XmNentryCallback
XmBulletinBoardDialog	XmNhelpCallback
XmCascadeButton	XmNmapCallback
XmCascadeButtonGadget	XmNunmapCallback
XmCommand	
XmDrawingArea	
XmDrawnButton	
XmErrorDialog	
XmFileSelectionBox	
XmFileSelectionDialog	
XmForm	
XmFormDialog	

XmPopupMenu (Continued)

Controls	Reasons
XmFrame	
XmInformationDialog	
XmLabel	
XmLabelGadget	
XmList	
XmMenuBar	
XmMessageBox	
XmMessageDialog	
XmOptionMenu	
XmPanedWindow	
XmPopupMenu	
XmPromptDialog	
XmPulldownMenu	
XmPushButton	
XmPushButtonGadget	
XmQuestionDialog	
XmRadioBox	
XmRowColumn	
XmScale	
XmScrollBar	
XmScrolledList	
XmScrolledText	
XmScrolledWindow	
XmSelectionBox	
XmSelectionDialog	
XmSeparator	
XmSeparatorGadget	
XmText	
XmTextField	
XmToggleButton	
XmToggleButtonGadget	
XmWarningDialog	
XmWorkArea	
XmWorkingDialog	

XmPopupMenu (Continued)

Controls	Reasons
user_defined	

XmPromptDialog

Controls	Reasons
XmPushButton	MrmNcreateCallback
user_defined	XmNapplyCallback
	XmNcancelCallback
	XmNdestroyCallback
	XmNfocusCallback
	XmNhelpCallback
	XmNmapCallback
	XmNnoMatchCallback
	XmNokCallback
	XmNunmapCallback

XmPulldownMenu

Controls	Reasons
XmArrowButton	MrmNcreateCallback
XmArrowButtonGadget	XmNdestroyCallback
XmBulletinBoard	XmNentryCallback
XmBulletinBoardDialog	XmNhelpCallback
XmCascadeButton	XmNmapCallback
XmCascadeButtonGadget	XmNunmapCallback
XmCommand	
XmDrawingArea	
XmDrawnButton	
XmErrorDialog	
XmFileSelectionBox	
XmFileSelectionDialog	
XmForm	

XmPulldownMenu (Continued)

Controls	Reasons
XmFormDialog	
XmFrame	
XmInformationDialog	
XmLabel	
XmLabelGadget	
XmList	
XmMenuBar	
XmMessageBox	
XmMessageDialog	
XmOptionMenu	
XmPanedWindow	
XmPopupMenu	
XmPromptDialog	
XmPulldownMenu	
XmPushButton	
XmPushButtonGadget	
XmQuestionDialog	
XmRadioBox	
XmRowColumn	
XmScale	
XmScrollBar	
XmScrolledList	
XmScrolledText	
XmScrolledWindow	
XmSelectionBox	
XmSelectionDialog	
XmSeparator	
XmSeparatorGadget	
XmText	
XmTextField	
XmToggleButton	
XmToggleButtonGadget	
XmWarningDialog	
XmWorkArea	

XmPulldownMenu (Continued)

Controls	Reasons
XmWorkingDialog user_defined	

XmPushButton

Controls	Reasons
No children are supported	MrmNcreateCallback XmNactivateCallback XmNarmCallback XmNdestroyCallback XmNdisarmCallback XmNhelpCallback

XmPushButtonGadget

Controls	Reasons
No children are supported	MrmNcreateCallback XmNactivateCallback XmNarmCallback XmNdestroyCallback XmNdisarmCallback XmNhelpCallback

XmQuestionDialog

Controls	Reasons
XmMessageBox	MrmNcreateCallback XmNcancelCallback XmNdestroyCallback XmNfocusCallback XmNhelpCallback XmNmapCallback

XmQuestionDialog (Continued)

Controls	Reasons
	XmNokCallback
	XmNunmapCallback

XmRadioBox

Controls	Reasons
XmArrowButton	MrmNcreateCallback
XmArrowButtonGadget	XmNdestroyCallback
XmBulletinBoard	XmNentryCallback
XmBulletinBoardDialog	XmNhelpCallback
XmCascadeButton	XmNmapCallback
XmCascadeButtonGadget	XmNunmapCallback
XmCommand	
XmDrawingArea	
XmDrawnButton	
XmErrorDialog	
XmFileSelectionBox	
XmFileSelectionDialog	
XmForm	
XmFormDialog	
XmFrame	
XmInformationDialog	
XmLabel	
XmLabelGadget	
XmList	
XmMenuBar	
XmMessageBox	
XmMessageDialog	
XmOptionMenu	
XmPanedWindow	
XmPopupMenu	
XmPromptDialog	
XmPulldownMenu	

XmRadioBox (Continued)

Controls	Reasons
XmPushButton	
XmPushButtonGadget	
XmQuestionDialog	
XmRadioBox	
XmRowColumn	
XmScale	
XmScrollBar	
XmScrolledList	
XmScrolledText	
XmScrolledWindow	
XmSelectionBox	
XmSelectionDialog	
XmSeparator	
XmSeparatorGadget	
XmText	
XmTextField	
XmToggleButton	
XmToggleButtonGadget	
XmWarningDialog	
XmWorkArea	
XmWorkingDialog	
user_defined	

XmRowColumn

Controls	Reasons
XmArrowButton	MrmNcreateCallback
XmArrowButtonGadget	XmNdestroyCallback
XmBulletinBoard	XmNentryCallback
XmBulletinBoardDialog	XmNhelpCallback
XmCascadeButton	XmNmapCallback
XmCascadeButtonGadget	XmNunmapCallback
XmCommand	

XmRowColumn (Continued)

Controls	Reasons
XmDrawingArea	
XmDrawnButton	
XmErrorDialog	
XmFileSelectionBox	
XmFileSelectionDialog	
XmForm	
XmFormDialog	
XmFrame	
XmInformationDialog	
XmLabel	
XmLabelGadget	
XmList	
XmMenuBar	
XmMessageBox	
XmMessageDialog	
XmOptionMenu	
XmPanedWindow	
XmPopupMenu	
XmPromptDialog	
XmPulldownMenu	
XmPushButton	
XmPushButtonGadget	
XmQuestionDialog	
XmRadioBox	
XmRowColumn	
XmScale	
XmScrollBar	
XmScrolledList	
XmScrolledText	
XmScrolledWindow	
XmSelectionBox	
XmSelectionDialog	
XmSeparator	
XmSeparatorGadget	

XmRowColumn (Continued)

Controls	Reasons
XmText	
XmTextField	
XmToggleButton	
XmToggleButtonGadget	
XmWarningDialog	
XmWorkArea	
XmWorkingDialog	
user_defined	

XmScale

Controls	Reasons
XmArrowButton	MrmNcreateCallback
XmArrowButtonGadget	XmNdestroyCallback
XmBulletinBoard	XmNdragCallback
XmBulletinBoardDialog	XmNhelpCallback
XmCascadeButton	XmNvalueChangedCallback
XmCascadeButtonGadget	
XmCommand	
XmDrawingArea	
XmDrawnButton	
XmErrorDialog	
XmFileSelectionBox	
XmFileSelectionDialog	
XmForm	
XmFormDialog	
XmFrame	
XmInformationDialog	
XmLabel	
XmLabelGadget	
XmList	
XmMenuBar	
XmMessageBox	

XmScale (Continued)

Controls	Reasons
XmMessageDialog	
XmOptionMenu	
XmPanedWindow	
XmPopupMenu	
XmPromptDialog	
XmPulldownMenu	
XmPushButton	
XmPushButtonGadget	
XmQuestionDialog	
XmRadioBox	
XmRowColumn	
XmScale	
XmScrollBar	
XmScrolledList	
XmScrolledText	
XmScrolledWindow	
XmSelectionBox	
XmSelectionDialog	
XmSeparator	
XmSeparatorGadget	
XmText	
XmTextField	
XmToggleButton	
XmToggleButtonGadget	
XmWarningDialog	
XmWorkArea	
XmWorkingDialog	
user_defined	

XmScrollBar

Controls	Reasons
No children are supported	MrmNcreateCallback
	XmNdecrementCallback
	XmNdestroyCallback
	XmNdragCallback
	XmNhelpCallback
	XmNincrementCallback
	XmNpageDecrementCallback
	XmNpageIncrementCallback
	XmNtoBottomCallback
	XmNtoTopCallback
	XmNvalueChangedCallback

XmScrolledList

Controls	Reasons
No children are supported	MrmNcreateCallback
	XmNbrowseSelectionCallback
	XmNdefaultActionCallback
	XmNdestroyCallback
	XmNextendedSelectionCallback
	XmNhelpCallback
	XmNmultipleSelectionCallback
	XmNsingleSelectionCallback

XmScrolledText

Controls	Reasons
No children are supported	MrmNcreateCallback
	XmNactivateCallback
	XmNdestroyCallback
	XmNfocusCallback
	XmNgainPrimaryCallback

XmScrolledText (Continued)

Controls	Reasons
	XmNhelpCallback
	XmNlosePrimaryCallback
	XmNlosingFocusCallback
	XmNmodifyVerifyCallback
	XmNmotionVerifyCallback
	XmNvalueChangedCallback

XmScrolledWindow

Controls	Reasons
XmArrowButton	MrmNcreateCallback
XmArrowButtonGadget	XmNdestroyCallback
XmBulletinBoard	XmNhelpCallback
XmBulletinBoardDialog	
XmCascadeButton	
XmCascadeButtonGadget	
XmCommand	
XmDrawingArea	
XmDrawnButton	
XmErrorDialog	
XmFileSelectionBox	
XmFileSelectionDialog	
XmForm	
XmFormDialog	
XmFrame	
XmInformationDialog	
XmLabel	
XmLabelGadget	
XmList	
XmMenuBar	
XmMessageBox	
XmMessageDialog	
XmOptionMenu	

XmScrolledWindow (Continued)

Controls	Reasons
XmPanedWindow	
XmPopupMenu	
XmPromptDialog	
XmPulldownMenu	
XmPushButton	
XmPushButtonGadget	
XmQuestionDialog	
XmRadioBox	
XmRowColumn	
XmScale	
XmScrollBar	
XmScrolledList	
XmScrolledText	
XmScrolledWindow	
XmSelectionBox	
XmSelectionDialog	
XmSeparator	
XmSeparatorGadget	
XmText	
XmTextField	
XmToggleButton	
XmToggleButtonGadget	
XmWarningDialog	
XmWorkArea	
XmWorkingDialog	
user_defined	

XmSelectionBox

Controls	Reasons
XmPushButton	MrmNcreateCallback
user_defined	XmNapplyCallback
	XmNcancelCallback

XmSelectionBox (Continued)

Controls	Reasons
	XmNdestroyCallback
	XmNfocusCallback
	XmNhelpCallback
	XmNmapCallback
	XmNnoMatchCallback
	XmNokCallback
	XmNunmapCallback

XmSelectionDialog

Controls	Reasons
XmPushButton	MrmNcreateCallback
user_defined	XmNapplyCallback
	XmNcancelCallback
	XmNdestroyCallback
	XmNfocusCallback
	XmNhelpCallback
	XmNmapCallback
	XmNnoMatchCallback
	XmNokCallback
	XmNunmapCallback

XmSeparator

Controls	Reasons
No children are supported	MrmNcreateCallback
	XmNdestroyCallback
	XmNhelpCallback

XmSeparatorGadget

Controls	Reasons
No children are supported	MrmNcreateCallback XmNdestroyCallback XmNhelpCallback

XmText

Controls	Reasons
No children are supported	MrmNcreateCallback XmNactivateCallback XmNdestroyCallback XmNfocusCallback XmNgainPrimaryCallback XmNhelpCallback XmNlosePrimaryCallback XmNlosingFocusCallback XmNmodifyVerifyCallback XmNmotionVerifyCallback XmNvalueChangedCallback

XmTextField

Controls	Reasons
No children are supported	MrmNcreateCallback XmNactivateCallback XmNdestroyCallback XmNgainPrimaryCallback XmNhelpCallback XmNlosePrimaryCallback XmNlosingFocusCallback XmNmodifyVerifyCallback XmNmotionVerifyCallback XmNvalueChangedCallback

XmToggleButton

Controls	Reasons
No children are supported	MrmNcreateCallback
	XmNarmCallback
	XmNdestroyCallback
	XmNdisarmCallback
	XmNhelpCallback
	XmNvalueChangedCallback

XmToggleButtonGadget

Controls	Reasons
No children are supported	MrmNcreateCallback
	XmNarmCallback
	XmNdestroyCallback
	XmNdisarmCallback
	XmNhelpCallback
	XmNvalueChangedCallback

XmWarningDialog

Controls	Reasons
No children are supported	MrmNcreateCallback
	XmNcancelCallback
	XmNdestroyCallback
	XmNfocusCallback
	XmNhelpCallback
	XmNmapCallback
	XmNokCallback
	XmNunmapCallback

XmWorkArea

Controls	Reasons
XmArrowButton	MrmNcreateCallback
XmArrowButtonGadget	XmNdestroyCallback
XmBulletinBoard	XmNentryCallback
XmBulletinBoardDialog	XmNhelpCallback
XmCascadeButton	XmNmapCallback
XmCascadeButtonGadget	XmNunmapCallback
XmCommand	
XmDrawingArea	
XmDrawnButton	
XmErrorDialog	
XmFileSelectionBox	
XmFileSelectionDialog	
XmForm	
XmFormDialog	
XmFrame	
XmInformationDialog	
XmLabel	
XmLabelGadget	
XmList	
XmMenuBar	
XmMessageBox	
XmMessageDialog	
XmOptionMenu	
XmPanedWindow	
XmPopupMenu	
XmPromptDialog	
XmPulldownMenu	
XmPushButton	
XmPushButtonGadget	
XmQuestionDialog	
XmRadioBox	
XmRowColumn	
XmScale	
XmScrollBar	

XmWorkArea (Continued)

Controls	Reasons
XmScrolledList	
XmScrolledText	
XmScrolledWindow	
XmSelectionBox	
XmSelectionDialog	
XmSeparator	
XmSeparatorGadget	
XmText	
XmTextField	
XmToggleButton	
XmToggleButtonGadget	
XmWarningDialog	
XmWorkArea	
XmWorkingDialog	
user_defined	

XmWorkingDialog

Controls	Reasons
XmPushButton	MrmNcreateCallback
user_defined	XmNcancelCallback
	XmNdestroyCallback
	XmNfocusCallback
	XmNhelpCallback
	XmNmapCallback
	XmNokCallback
	XmNunmapCallback

user_defined

Controls	Reasons
XmArrowButton	
XmBulletinBoard	
XmBulletinBoardDialog	
XmCascadeButton	
XmCommand	
XmDrawingArea	
XmDrawnButton	
XmErrorDialog	
XmFileSelectionBox	
XmFileSelectionDialog	
XmForm	
XmFormDialog	
XmFrame	
XmInformationDialog	
XmLabel	
XmList	
XmMenuBar	
XmMessageBox	
XmMessageDialog	
XmOptionMenu	
XmPanedWindow	
XmPopupMenu	
XmPromptDialog	
XmPulldownMenu	
XmPushButton	
XmQuestionDialog	
XmRadioBox	
XmRowColumn	
XmScale	
XmScrollBar	
XmScrolledList	
XmScrolledText	
XmScrolledWindow	
XmSelectionBox	

user_defined (Continued)

Controls	Reasons
XmSelectionDialog	
XmSeparator	
XmText	
XmTextField	
XmToggleButton	
XmWarningDialog	
XmWorkArea	
XmWorkingDialog	
user_defined	

Appendix C

UIL Arguments

This appendix provides an alphabetical listing of the UIL arguments and their data types. Each argument name is the same as the corresponding Motif Toolkit resource name. For information on which arguments are supported for which objects and for the default values of arguments, see the widget manual pages in the *OSF/Motif Programmer's Reference* .

UIL Argument Name	Argument Type
XmNaccelerator	string
XmNacceleratorText	compound_string
XmNaccelerators	translation_table
XmNadjustLast	boolean
XmNadjustMargin	boolean
XmNalignment	integer
XmNallowOverlap	boolean
XmNallowResize	boolean
XmNancestorSensitive	boolean

UIL Argument Name	Argument Type
XmNapplyLabelString	compound_string
XmNarmColor	color
XmNarmPixmap	pixmap
XmNarrowDirection	integer
XmNautoShowCursorPosition	boolean
XmNautoUnmanage	boolean
XmNautomaticSelection	boolean
XmNbackground	color
XmNbackgroundPixmap	pixmap
XmNblinkRate	integer
XmNborderColor	color
XmNborderPixmap	pixmap
XmNborderWidth	integer
XmNbottomAttachment	integer
XmNbottomOffset	integer
XmNbottomPosition	integer
XmNbottomShadowColor	color
XmNbottomShadowPixmap	pixmap
XmNbottomWidget	widget_ref
XmNbuttonFontList	font_table
XmNcancelButton	widget_ref
XmNcancelLabelString	compound_string
XmNcascadePixmap	pixmap
XmNcolormap	identifier
XmNcolumns	integer
XmNcommand	compound_string
XmNcommandWindow	widget_ref
XmNcommandWindowLocation	integer
XmNcursorPosition	integer
XmNcursorPositionVisible	boolean
XmNdecimalPoints	integer
XmNdefaultButton	widget_ref
XmNdefaultButtonShadowThickness	integer
XmNdefaultButtonType	integer
XmNdefaultPosition	boolean

UIL Argument Name	Argument Type
XmNdepth	identifier
XmNdialogStyle	integer
XmNdialogTitle	compound_string
XmNdialogType	integer
XmNdirListItemCount	integer
XmNdirListItems	string_table
XmNdirListLabelString	compound_string
XmNdirMask	compound_string
XmNdirSearchProc	any
XmNdirSpec	compound_string
XmNdirectory	compound_string
XmNdoubleClickInterval	integer
XmNeditMode	integer
XmNeditable	boolean
XmNentryAlignment	integer
XmNentryBorder	integer
XmNentryClass	class_rec_name
XmNfileListItemCount	integer
XmNfileListItems	string_table
XmNfileListLabelString	compound_string
XmNfileSearchProc	any
XmNfileTypeMask	integer
XmNfillOnArm	boolean
XmNfillOnSelect	boolean
XmNfilterLabelString	compound_string
XmNfontList	font_table
XmNforeground	color
XmNfractionBase	integer
XmNheight	integer
XmNhelpLabelString	compound_string
XmNhighlightColor	color
XmNhighlightOnEnter	boolean
XmNhighlightPixmap	pixmap
XmNhighlightThickness	integer
XmNhistoryItemCount	integer

UIL Argument Name	Argument Type
XmNhistoryItems	string_table
XmNhistoryMaxItems	integer
XmNhistoryVisibleItemCount	integer
XmNhorizontalScrollBar	widget_ref
XmNhorizontalSpacing	integer
XmNincrement	integer
XmNindicatorOn	boolean
XmNindicatorSize	integer
XmNindicatorType	integer
XmNinitialDelay	integer
XmNinitialResourcesPersistent	boolean
XmNinsertPosition	identifier
XmNisAligned	boolean
XmNisHomogeneous	boolean
XmNitemCount	integer
XmNitems	string_table
XmNlabelFontList	font_table
XmNlabelInsensitivePixmap	pixmap
XmNlabelPixmap	pixmap
XmNlabelString	compound_string
XmNlabelType	integer
XmNleftAttachment	integer
XmNleftOffset	integer
XmNleftPosition	integer
XmNleftWidget	widget_ref
XmNlistItemCount	integer
XmNlistItems	string_table
XmNlistLabelString	compound_string
XmNlistMarginHeight	integer
XmNlistMarginWidth	integer
XmNlistSizePolicy	integer
XmNlistSpacing	integer
XmNlistUpdated	boolean
XmNlistVisibleItemCount	integer
XmNmainWindowMarginHeight	integer

UIL Argument Name	Argument Type
XmNmainWindowMarginWidth	integer
XmNmappedWhenManaged	boolean
XmNmappingDelay	integer
XmNmargin	integer
XmNmarginBottom	integer
XmNmarginHeight	integer
XmNmarginLeft	integer
XmNmarginRight	integer
XmNmarginTop	integer
XmNmarginWidth	integer
XmNmaxLength	integer
XmNmaximum	integer
XmNmenuAccelerator	string
XmNmenuBar	widget_ref
XmNmenuHelpWidget	widget_ref
XmNmenuHistory	widget_ref
XmNmenuPost	compound_string
XmNmessageAlignment	integer
XmNmessageString	compound_string
XmNmessageWindow	widget_ref
XmNminimizeButtons	boolean
XmNminimum	integer
XmNmnemonic	keysym
XmNmnemonicCharSet	string
XmNmultiClick	integer
XmNmustMatch	boolean
XmNnavigationType	integer
XmNnoMatchString	compound_string
XmNnoResize	boolean
XmNnumColumns	integer
XmNokLabelString	compound_string
XmNorientation	integer
XmNpacking	integer
XmNpageIncrement	integer
XmNpaneMaximum	integer

UIL Argument Name	Argument Type
XmNpaneMinimum	integer
XmNpattern	compound_string
XmNpendingDelete	boolean
XmNpopupEnabled	boolean
XmNprocessingDirection	integer
XmNpromptString	compound_string
XmNpushButtonEnabled	boolean
XmNqualifySearchDataProc	any
XmNradioAlwaysOne	boolean
XmNradioBehavior	boolean
XmNrecomputeSize	boolean
XmNrefigureMode	boolean
XmNrepeatDelay	integer
XmNresizable	boolean
XmNresizeHeight	boolean
XmNresizePolicy	integer
XmNresizeWidth	boolean
XmNrightAttachment	integer
XmNrightOffset	integer
XmNrightPosition	integer
XmNrightWidget	widget_ref
XmNrowColumnType	integer
XmNrows	integer
XmNrubberPositioning	boolean
XmNsashHeight	integer
XmNsashIndent	integer
XmNsashShadowThickness	integer
XmNsashWidth	integer
XmNscaleHeight	integer
XmNscaleMultiple	integer
XmNscaleWidth	integer
XmNscreen	identifier
XmNscrollBarDisplayPolicy	integer
XmNscrollBarPlacement	integer
XmNscrollHorizontal	boolean

UIL Argument Name	Argument Type
XmNscrollLeftSide	boolean
XmNscrollTopSide	boolean
XmNscrollVertical	boolean
XmNscrolledWindowMarginHeight	integer
XmNscrolledWindowMarginWidth	integer
XmNscrollingPolicy	integer
XmNselectColor	color
XmNselectInsensitivePixmap	pixmap
XmNselectPixmap	pixmap
XmNselectThreshold	integer
XmNselectedItemCount	integer
XmNselectedItems	string_table
XmNselectionArray	any
XmNselectionArrayCount	integer
XmNselectionLabelString	compound_string
XmNselectionPolicy	integer
XmNsensitive	boolean
XmNseparatorOn	boolean
XmNseparatorType	integer
XmNset	boolean
XmNshadowThickness	integer
XmNshadowType	integer
XmNshowArrows	boolean
XmNshowAsDefault	integer
XmNshowSeparator	boolean
XmNshowValue	boolean
XmNskipAdjust	boolean
XmNsliderSize	integer
XmNspacing	integer
XmNstringDirection	integer
XmNsubMenuId	widget_ref
XmNsymbolPixmap	pixmap
XmNtextAccelerators	translation_table
XmNtextColumns	integer
XmNtextFontList	font_table

UIL Argument Name	Argument Type
XmNtextString	compound_string
XmNtextTranslations	translation_table
XmNtitleString	compound_string
XmNtopAttachment	integer
XmNtopCharacter	integer
XmNtopItemPosition	integer
XmNtopOffset	integer
XmNtopPosition	integer
XmNtopShadowColor	color
XmNtopShadowPixmap	pixmap
XmNtopWidget	widget_ref
XmNtranslations	translation_table
XmNtraversalOn	boolean
XmNtroughColor	color
XmNunitType	integer
XmNuserData	any
XmNvalue	any
XmNverifyBell	boolean
XmNverticalScrollBar	widget_ref
XmNverticalSpacing	integer
XmNvisibleItemCount	integer
XmNvisibleWhenOff	boolean
XmNvisualPolicy	integer
XmNwhichButton	integer
XmNwidth	integer
XmNwordWrap	boolean
XmNworkWindow	widget_ref
XmNx	integer
XmNy	integer

Appendix D

UIL Diagnostic Messages

This appendix lists the diagnostic messages produced by the UIL compiler. The severity, a description of the message, and a suggestion for correcting the problem are listed for each message. The following strings are used to represent data that varies in the actual message you receive from the UIL compiler:

String	Data Represented
%c	Character
%d	Decimal number
%s	String

Messages are listed alphabetically by IDENT code.

arg_count   procedure %s was previously declared with %d arguments

Severity: Error
The declaration of the marked procedure specified a different number of arguments than are present in this procedure reference.

User Action:
Check that you are calling the correct function. If you intend to call the procedure with a varying number of arguments, omit the argument list in the procedure declaration.

arg_type

found %s value - procedure %s argument must be %s value

Severity: Error
The declaration of the marked procedure specified a different type of argument than is present in this procedure reference.

User Action:
Check that you are passing the correct argument to the correct function. If you intend to call the procedure with varying argument types, declare the procedure specifying **any** for the type of the argument.

backslash_ignored

unknown escape sequence "\%c" - ignored

Severity: Error
A backslash was followed by an unknown escape character. The \ (backslash) is the escape character in UIL. A selected set of single characters can follow a backslash such as \n for newline or \\ to insert a backslash. The character following the backslash was not one of the selected set.

User Action:
If you want to add a backslash, use \\. See Section 18.4.1 for a description of the supported escape sequences.

bug_check

internal error: %s

Severity: Severe
The compiler diagnosed an internal error.

User Action:
Submit a software problem report.

circular_def
widget %s is part of a circular definition

Severity: Error
The indicated object is referenced as a descendant of itself, either within its own definition or within the definition of one of the objects in the widget tree it controls.

User Action:
Change the definition of the indicated object so that it is not a descendant of itself.

control_char
unprintable character \%d\ ignored

Severity: Error
The compiler encountered an illegal control character in the UIL specification file. The decimal value of the character is given between the \ (backslash) characters.

User Action:
Replace the character with the sequence specified in the message (for example, \3 if the control character's internal value is 3). UIL provides several built-in control characters such as \n and \r for newline and carriage return. See Section 18.4.1 for a complete list of supported escape sequences.

create_proc
creation procedure is not supported by the %s widget

Severity: Error
You specified a creation procedure for a Motif Toolkit widget. You can specify a creation procedure only for a user-defined widget.

User Action:
Remove the procedure clause following the object type.

create_proc_inv
creation procedure is not allowed in a %s widget reference

Severity: Error

You specified a creation procedure when referencing an object. You can specify a creation procedure only when you declare the object.

User Action:

Remove the procedure clause following the object type.

create_proc_req

creation procedure is required in a %s widget declaration

Severity: Error

When defining a user-defined widget, you must specify the name of the creation function for creating an instance of this widget.

User Action:

Insert a procedure clause following the widget type in the widget declaration. You also need to declare the creation procedure using a procedure declaration. For example:

```
procedure my_creation_proc();
object list_box:
   user_defined procedure
       my_creation_proc()
          { arguments ... };
```

ctx_req

context requires a %s - %s was specified

Severity: Error

At the point marked in the specification, one type of object (such as a widget) is required and your specification supplied a different type of object (such as value).

User Action:

Check for misspelling or that you have referred to the intended object.

d_add_source

additional UIL source file: %s was ignored

Severity: Error
More than one source file was specified. Only the first source file will be compiled.

User Action:
Compile additional source files using separate invocations of the compiler.

d_dupl_opt   duplicate option \ "%s" \ was ignored

Severity: Warning
The same command line option has been repeated more than once (for example, the "-o" option or the "-v" option)

User Action:
Remove duplicate command line option.

d_miss_opt_arg   %s missing following \ "%s" \ option

Severity: Error
You used a command line option that requires an argument and you did not provide that argument.

User Action:
Omit the option or provide the argument.

d_no_source   no source file specified

Severity: Severe
No source file was specified to compile.

User Action:
Specify the name of a UIL specification file to compile.

d_unknown_opt   unknown option \ "%s" \ was ignored

Severity: Warning
An unknown option has been used in the compiler command line.

User Action:
Check what you typed on the command line.

dup_letter   color letter used for prior color in this table

Severity: Error

Each of the letters used to represent a color in a color table must be unique. If not, that letter in an icon would represent more than one color; each pixel can have only one color associated with it at a time. The letter marked has been assigned to more than one color.

User Action:

Choose which color the letter is to represent and remove any duplicates or assign them a new character.

dup_list   %s %s already specified for this %s %s

Severity: Error

A widget or gadget declaration can have at most one arguments list, one callbacks list, and one controls list.

User Action:

If you want to specify multiple lists of arguments, controls, and callbacks, you can do so within one list. For example:

```
arguments { arguments_list1;
    arguments_list2; };
```

gadget_not_sup   %s gadget is not supported - %s widget will be used instead

Severity: Warning

The indicated object type does not support a gadget variant; only a widget variant is supported for this object type. The UIL compiler ignores the gadget indication, and creates widgets of this object type.

User Action:

Specify that this object type is a widget instead of a gadget.

icon_letter   row %d, column %d: letter \"%c"\ not in color table

Severity: Error
You have specified a color to be used in an icon that is not in that icon's color table. The invalid color is identified in the message by displaying the letter used to represent that color between the \ (backslashes). This letter was not defined in the specified color table.

User Action:
Either add the color to the icon's color table or use a character representing a color in the color table. The default color table defines " " (double quotation marks) as background and * (asterisk) as foreground.

icon_width   row %d must have same width as row 1

Severity: Error
The icons supported by UIL are rectangular (that is, x pixels wide by y pixels high). As a result, each of the strings used to represent a row of pixels in an icon must have the same length. The specified row does not have the same length as the first row.

User Action:
Make all the strings in the icon function the same length.

inv_module   invalid module structure - check UIL module syntax

Severity: Error
The structure of the UIL module is incorrect.

User Action:
If there are any syntax errors reported, fix them and recompile. For example, if the error occurs before the first object declaration (that is, before your value and object declarations), check the syntax of the module header for unwanted ; (semicolons) after the module clauses. If the error occurs at the end of the module, check that the module concludes with the keywords "end module;".

D–7

list_item   %s item not allowed in %s %s

Severity: Error
The indicated list item is not of the type required by the list. Arguments lists must contain argument entries, callbacks lists must contain callback entries, controls lists must contain control entries, and procedures lists must contain callback entries.

User Action:
Check the syntax for the type of list entry that is required in this context and change the indicated list item.

listing_open   error opening listing file: %s

Severity: Severe
The compiler could not create the listing file noted in the message.

User Action:
Check that you have write access to the directory you specified to hold the listing file.

listing_write   error writing to listing file: %s

Severity: Severe
The compiler could not write a line into the listing file noted in the message.

User Action:
Check to see that there is adequate space on the disk specified to hold the listing file.

name_too_long   name exceeds 31 characters - truncated to: %s

Severity: Error
The UIL compiler encountered a name longer than 31 characters. The compiler truncated the name to the leftmost 31 characters.

User Action:
Shorten the name in the UIL module source.

names   place names clause before other module clauses

Severity: Error
The case-sensitivity clause, if specified, must be the first clause following the module's name. You have inserted another module clause before this clause.

User Action:
Reorder the module clauses so that the case-sensitivity clause is first. (It is acceptable to place the version clause ahead of the case-sensitivity clause; this is the only exception.)

never_def %s %s was never defined

Severity: Error
Certain UIL objects such as gadgets and widgets can be referred to before they are defined. The marked object is such an object. However, the compiler never found the object's declaration.

User Action:
Check for misspelling. If the module is case sensitive, the spellings of names in declarations and in references must match exactly.

no_uid no UID file was produced

Severity: Informational
If the compiler reported error or severe diagnostics (that is, any of the diagnostic abbreviations starting with %UIL-E or %UIL-F), a UID file is not created. This diagnostic informs you that the compiler did not produce a UID file.

User Action:
Fix the problems reported by the compiler.

non_pvt value used in this context must be private

Severity: Error
A private value is one that is not imported or exported. In the context marked by the message, only a private value is legal. Situations where this message is issued include

D–9

defining one value in terms of another, and arguments to functions. In general, a value must be private when the compiler must know the value at compilation time. Exported values are disallowed in these contexts, even though a value is present, because that value could be overridden at run time.

User Action:
Change the value to be private.

not_impl   %s is not implemented yet

Severity: Error
You are using a feature of UIL that has not been implemented.

User Action:
Try an alternate technique.

null   a null character in a string is not supported

Severity: Warning
You have created a string that has an embedded null character. Strings are represented in a UID file and in many Motif Toolkit data structures as null terminated strings. So, although the embedded nulls will be placed in the UID file, Motif Toolkit functions may interpret an embedded null as the terminator for the string.

User Action:
Be very careful using embedded nulls.

obj_type   found %s %s when expecting %s %s

Severity: Error
Most arguments take values of a specific type. The value specified is not correct for this argument.

User Action:
The message indicates the expected type of argument. Check that you have specified the intended value and that you specified the correct argument.

operand_type   %s type is not valid for %s

Severity: Error
The indicated operand is not of a type that is supported by this operator.

User Action:
Check the definition of the operator and make sure the type of the operand you specify is supported by the operator.

out_of_memory   compiler ran out of virtual memory

Severity: Severe
The compiler ran out of virtual memory.

User Action:
Reduce the size of your application.

out_range   value of %s is out of range %s

Severity: Error
The value specified is outside the legal range of its type.

User Action:
Change the UIL module source.

prev_error   compilation terminated - fix previous errors

Severity: Severe
Errors encountered during the compilation have caused the compiler to abort.

User Action:
Fix the errors already diagnosed by the compiler and recompile.

previous_def   name %s previously defined as %s

Severity: Error
The name marked by the message was used in a previous declaration. UIL requires that the names of all objects declared within a module be unique.

User Action:
Check for a misspelling. If the module is case sensitive, the spellings of names in declarations and in references must match exactly.

single_letter   color letter string must be a single character

Severity: Error
The string associated with each color in a color table must hold exactly one character. You have specified a string with either fewer or more characters.

User Action:
Use a single character to represent each color in a color table.

single_occur   %s %s supports only a single %s %s

Severity: Warning
You have specified a particular clause more than once in a context where that clause can occur only once. For example, the version clause in the module can only occur once.

User Action:
Choose the correct clause and delete the others.

src_limit   too many source files open: %s

Severity: Severe
The compiler has a fixed limit for the number of source and include files that it can process. This number is reported in the message.

User Action:
Use fewer include files.

src_null_char   source line contains a null character

Severity: Error
The specified source line contains a null character. The compiler ignores any text following the null character.

User Action:
Replace each null character with the escape sequence \ (backslash).

src_open
error opening source file: %s

Severity: Severe
The compiler could not open the UIL specification file listed in the message.

User Action:
Check that the file listed in the message is the one you want to compile, that it exists, and that you have read access to the file. If you are using a large number of include files, you may have exceeded your quota for open files.

src_read
error reading next line of source file: %s

Severity: Severe
The compiler could not read a line of the UIL specification file listed in the message.

User Action:
In the listing file, this message should appear following the last line the compiler read successfully. First check that the file you are compiling is a UIL specification file. If it is, the file mostly likely contains corrupted records.

src_truncate
line truncated at %d characters

Severity: Error
The compiler encountered a source line greater than 132 characters. Characters beyond the 132 character limit were ignored.

User Action:
Break each source line longer than 132 characters into several source lines. Long string literals can be created using the concatenation operator.

submit_spr
internal error - submit an SPR

Severity: Severe
The compiler diagnosed an internal error.

User Action:
Get a listing and look where the error is being issued. Try fixing any faulty syntax in this area. If you are unable to prevent this error, submit a software problem report.

summary   errors: %d warnings: %d informationals: %d

Severity: Informational
This message lists a summary of the diagnostics issued by the compiler, and appears only when diagnostics have been issued.

User Action:
Fix the problems reported. You can use the -I option qualifier to suppress informational and warning diagnostics that you have determined to be harmless.

supersede   this %s %s supersedes a previous definition in this %s %s

Severity: Informational
An argument or callback list has either a duplicate argument or duplicate reason.

User Action:
This is not necessarily an error. The compiler is alerting you to make sure that you intended to override a prior argument's value. This informational message can be suppressed using the -I option qualifier.

syntax   unexpected %s token seen - parsing resumes after \"%c"\

Severity: Error
At the point marked in the module, the compiler found a construct such as a punctuation mark, name, or keyword when it was expecting a different construct. The

compiler continued analyzing the module at the next occurrence of the construct stated in the message.

User Action:
Check the syntax of your UIL module at the point marked by the compiler. If the module specifies case-sensitive names, check that your keywords are in lowercase characters.

too_many
too many %ss in %s, limit is %d

Severity: Error
You exceeded a compiler limit such as the number of fonts in a font table or the number of strings in a translation table. The message indicates the limit imposed by the compiler.

User Action:
Restructure your UIL module.

uid_open
error opening UID file: %s

Severity: Severe
The compiler could not create the UID file noted in the message. A UID file holds the compiled user-interface specification.

User Action:
Check that you have write access to the directory you specified to hold the UID file. If you have a large number of source and include files, check that you have not exceeded your open file quota.

undefined
%s %s must be defined before this reference

Severity: Error
The object pointed to in the message was either never defined or not defined prior to this point in the module. The compiler requires the object to be defined before you refer to the object.

User Action:
Check for a misspelling of the object's name, a missing declaration for the object, or declaring the object after its first reference. If names in the module are case sensitive, the spellings of the name in the declaration and in the reference must match exactly.

unknown_charset   unknown character set

Severity: Error
The message is pointing to a context where a character set name is required. You have not specified the name of a character set in that context.

User Action:
Check for misspelling. A list of the supported character sets is given in Section 18.1. If you specified case-sensitive names in the module, check that the character set name is in lowercase characters.

unknown_seq   unknown sequence \"%s"\ ignored

Severity: Error
The compiler detected a sequence of printable characters it did not understand. The compiler omitted the sequence of characters listed between the " " (double quotation marks).

User Action:
Fix the UIL module source.

unsupported   the %s %s is not supported for the %s %s

Severity: Warning
Each widget or gadget supports a specific set of arguments, reasons, and children. The particular argument, reason, or child you specified is not supported for this widget or gadget.

User Action:
See the UIL built-in tables in Appendix B for the arguments, reasons, and children supported for each object. If a widget creation function accepts an argument that UIL rejects, this does not necessarily indicate that the UIL compiler is in error. Widget creation functions ignore arguments that they do not support, without notifying you that the argument is being ignored.

unterm_seq

%s not terminated %s

Severity: Error
The compiler detected a sequence that was not properly terminated, such as a string literal without the closing quotation mark.

User Action:
Insert the proper termination characters.

wrong_type

found %s value when expecting %s value

Severity: Error
The indicated value is not of the specific type required by UIL in this context.

User Action:
Check the definition of the function or clause.

Glossary

accelerator A keyboard key or keys used to cause some action to occur. For example, the **<Shift><Menu>** keys could be used to post a menu instead of a mouse button action.

active window The terminal window where what you type appears. If there is no active window, what you type is lost. Only one terminal window can be active at a time.

ampersand (&) Placed at the end of a command, an ampersand specifies that the client started by the command should be started as a background process.

application program A computer program that performs some useful function, such as word processing, computer-aided design, or data base management.

application server	A computer used solely to provide processing power for application programs.
atom	A 32-bit number that represents a string value.
background process	A process that does not require the total attention of the computer for operation. Background processing enables the operating system to execute more than one program or command at a time.
bitmap	An array of data bits used for graphic images. Strictly speaking, a pixmap of depth one (capable of two-color images).
bitmap device	An output device, such as a Cathode Ray Tube (CRT), that displays bitmaps.
button (mouse)	A button on a mouse pointing device; mouse buttons can be mapped to the keyboard.
button (window frame)	A graphical control that simulates a real-life pushbutton. The pointer and the mouse are used to ''push'' the button and perform some action.
button binding	Association of a mouse button operation with a window manager or application function.
callback	A procedure that is called if and when certain specified conditions are met. This is accomplished by specifying the procedure in a callback list. Individual widgets can define callback lists as required.
cancel	A label given to a push button in some dialog boxes that performs the action of closing the dialog box without implementing any changes.

cascading menu	A submenu that provides selections that amplify the parent selection on a pull-down or pop-up menu.
child widget	A child widget is a subwidget of a composite widget. The composite widget is referred to as the *parent* of the child widget. The parent controls where the child is placed and when it is mapped. If the parent is destroyed, the child is automatically destroyed.
child window	A window that is not a primary window, but rather is an offspring of a primary or secondary window.
class	The general group that a widget belongs to.
click	To press *and release* a mouse button. The term comes from the fact that pressing and releasing the buttons of most mice makes a clicking sound.
client	An application program written specifically for the X Window System. Some clients make their own windows. Other clients are utility programs.
client area	The area within the borders of a primary window's frame that is controlled by an application.
close	A label given to a push button in some dialog boxes that performs the action of closing the dialog box. Close is also used as a selection in menus to close the window associated with the menu.
colormap	A display resource that controls the set of colors appearing on the display.
composite manager	A composite manager is a manager widget with special knowledge about the handling of one or more particular widgets. For example, a TitleBar and

ScrollBar can be registered with a Panel widget, and the Panel widget will position the TitleBar and ScrollBar widgets correctly. Normally, a manager widget has no knowledge about its children.

Composite

This class provides the resources and functionality that allows subclass widgets to manage the layout and children.

constraint

Resources that certain manager widgets can impose on their children are called *Constraint* resources. For example, if a PanedWindow widget wants its children to be a certain size, it can specify the size by using the resources **XtNmin** and **XtNmax**. The manpages will specify those manager widgets that have Constraint resources.

control key

The keyboard key usually labeled <Ctrl> and used as a modifier key.

convenience dialog

A widget or collection of widgets created by a Dialog convenience function.

convenience function

A convenience function is a function that creates certain combinations of widgets, including the necessary Shell widget.

Core

Core is the basic class from which all widgets are built. It acts as a superclass for other widget classes and provides resources that are required by all widgets.

cursor	A graphical image, usually an I-beam or rectangle, that shows the location where text will appear on the screen when keys on the keyboard are typed or where a selection will be made using the Select mouse button or the <**Select**> key.
default (selection)	An object or action that is specified for selection if no other selection is specified.
dialog	A collection of widgets, including a DialogShell, a BulletinBoard (or a subclass of BulletinBoard or some other container widget), plus various children of BulletinBoard such as Label, PushButton, and Text widgets. Dialogs are used as an interface between the application and its user.
dialog box	A secondary window that the user can display and that contains application controls.
display	Strictly speaking, the combination of a keyboard, mouse, and one or more screens that provide input and output services to a system. While ''display'' is sometimes used to mean just the CRT screen, a display, as defined here, can actually include more than one physical screen.
double-click	To press *and release* a mouse button twice in rapid succession.
drag	To press *and hold down* a mouse button while moving the mouse.
grab	A procedure by which a window will act upon a key or button event that occurs for it or any of its descendents. This precludes the necessity of setting up translations for all windows.

graphical user interface	A form of communication between people and computers that uses graphics-oriented software such as windows, menus, and icons to ease the burden of the interaction.
grayed selection	A menu selection that is not currently available and so has been dimmed.
highlight	A graphic technique used to provide a visual cue to the current selection or to the current location of the input focus. Highlighting is frequently accomplished by reversing the video image of the selection.
icon	A small graphic image used to represent a window. Windows can be turned into icons (minimized) to save room or unclutter the workspace.
inactive	A window that does not have the input focus.
insertion cursor	The graphical symbol that provides the visual cue to the location of the insertion point.
instantiate	To represent an abstraction by a concrete instance. To instantiate a widget means that a widget class creates an instance of that class.
intern	The procedure used to define an atom.
keyboard	One of many input devices; the traditional method of entering text into an application.
label	The text part of an icon.

location cursor	A graphic symbol that marks the current location of the keyboard input focus for selection. Typically, this symbol is a box that surrounds the current object. The location cursor is sometimes known as the selection cursor.
lower	To move a window to the bottom of the window stack on the workspace.
manager class	A class that provides the resources and functionality to implement certain features, such as keyboard interface and traversal mechanism. It is built from core, composite, and constraint classes.
matte	An optional decorative border between the client area and the window frame, similar to a matte used in framing real-life pictures.
maximize	To enlarge a window to its maximum size.
maximize button	A control button placed on the MWM window frame and used to initiate the maximize function.
menu	A list of available selections from which a user chooses.
menu bar	A rectangular area at the top of the client area of a window that contains the titles of the standard pull-down menus for that application.
message box	The generic name for any dialog box that provides information, gives the current state of a work in progress, asks a question, issues a warning, or draws attention to an error.

meta class	A meta class is a set of structures and functionality that a widget uses to export that functionality to subclass widgets. Each instance of a widget subclass will have the features common to that widget class and will export these features to child widgets of that class. Included in this class are Core, Composite, Constraint, Primitive, Button, Manager, MenuMgr, and MenuPane. A meta class widget is never instantiated.
minimize	To turn a window into an icon. The term "iconify" is sometimes used instead of minimize.
minimize button	A control button placed on the MWM window frame and used to initiate the minimize function.
mnemonic	A single character (frequently the initial character) of a menu selection, which when the menu is displayed and the character is typed on the keyboard, initiates the selection.
modal dialog	A Dialog that interrupts the work session to solicit input from the user.
modeless dialog	A Dialog that solicits input from the user but does *not* interrupt the work session.
modifier key	A key that, when pressed with another key, changes the meaning of the other key. <Ctrl>, <Alt>, and <Shift> are modifier keys.
mouse	A pointing device commonly used in conjunction with a keyboard in point-and-click, object-oriented user interfaces.

mouse button	One of the buttons on a mouse pointing device. Mouse buttons can be pressed, released, dragged, clicked, and double-clicked.
normalize	To change an icon back into its normal (original) client window appearance. The opposite of iconify.
open	To start an action or begin working with a text, data, or graphics file.
persistence	Persistence means that a specified character set is used for all subsequent text segments in a compound string until a new character set is encountered.
pixel	Short for picture element. The individual dots, or components, of a display screen. They are arranged in rows and columns and form the images that are displayed on the screen.
pixmap	An array of data bits used for graphics images. Each pixel (picture element) in the map can be several bits deep, resulting in multicolor graphics images.
point	To position the pointer or location cursor.
pointer	The graphical image that appears on the workspace and represents the current location of a mouse or other pointing device.
pointing device	A device such as a mouse, trackball, or graphics tablet that allows users to move a pointer about on the workspace and point to graphical objects.
pop-up	A type of widget that appears as the result of some user action (usually clicking a mouse button) and then disappears when the action is completed.

pop-up menu

A menu that provides no visual cue to its presence, but simply pops up when users perform a particular action. Pop-up menus area associated with a particular area of the workspace, such as the client area of an application, and users must memorize where these areas are.

post

The action required to make a pop-up or pull-down menu appear. This action is normally a click or button press on one of the mouse buttons.

press

To hold down a mouse button or a key. Note that to hold down a mouse button *and move* the mouse is called "dragging."

primary window

A top-level window of an application. Primary windows can be minimized.

Primitive

The primitive class provides the resources and functionality for the low-level widgets that are managed by the manager class. Primitive class widgets cannot have normal child widgets, but they can have pop-up child widgets.

property

Public information (that is, information that is available to any client) associated with a window.

protocol

A mutually agreed upon mechanism for communicating between clients to accomplish certain actions.

pull-down menu

A menu that is pulled down from a client application's title bar.

push button

A graphic control that simulates a real-life push button. The pointer and mouse are used to push the button and start some action.

release	To let up on a mouse button or key that has been pressed. Sometimes it is the press that initiates the action; sometimes it is the release.
resize	To change the height or width of a window.
resize border	See **resize frame handles**.
resize frame handles	The MWM frame part that surrounds the client area of an application and that is used to change the height or width of the window.
resource	A program parameter that controls an element of appearance or behavior. Resources are usually named for the elements they control.
restart	To start again; generally referring to starting the window manager again.
restore	To return an icon or maximized window to its normal size.
root menu	See **workspace menu**.
root window	See **workspace**.
save	To write changes in a data file to a storage device for safekeeping.
screen	The physical CRT that displays information from the computer. In the OSF/Motif environment, in most cases "screen" and "workspace" are synonymous.
scroll bar	A graphic device used to change a user's view of a list or data file. A scroll bar consists of a slider, scroll area, and scroll arrows. The user changes the view by sliding the slider up or down in the scroll area or by pressing one of the

scroll arrows. This causes the view to scroll up or down in the window adjacent to the scroll bar.

scroll region
The rectangular portion of a ScrollBar that contains the two arrows and the slider.

select
To choose an object to be acted upon or an action to be performed.

selection
The object or action that is selected. Menus are composed of selection items. Dialog boxes contain controls, each of which represents a selection.

selection cursor
See **location cursor**.

select button
The mouse button used to make a selection.

<Select> key
The special-purpose keyboard key used to make a selection. Keyboards without a Select key use a substitute to provide the select functionality.

set or setting
Usually refers to specifying a value for a resource or a property.

<Shift> key
One of the modifier keys on the keyboard.

size
Used as a verb to describe changing the size of a window on the workspace.

slider
One of graphical components of a scroll bar or scale. The slider is the object that is dragged along the scroll area to cause a change.

state
A generic term used to describe the condition or mode of an object or action.

subclass
A class of widgets that inherits resources from a higher class.

submenu	A cascading menu.
text cursor	See **insertion cursor**.
title area	An area at the top of the window frame immediately beneath the resize border. The title bar has two functions: it contains a title or name that identifies the window and it can be grabbed and dragged to relocate the window.
title bar	The bar at the top of the window frame immediately beneath the resize frame handle. The title bar may contain the title area and window buttons.
transient window	A window of short duration such as a dialog box. The window is displayed for only a short time, usually just long enough to convey some information or get some operational directions.
translations	Action procedures that are invoked for an event or sequence of events.
type	As a verb, to press and release a keyboard key.
underlined letter	A letter used as a mnemonic. The underline provides the visual cue to the mnemonic function.
widget	A widget is a graphic device capable of receiving input from the keyboard and the mouse and communicating with an application or another widget by means of a callback. Every widget is a member of only one class and always has a window associated with it.
widget instance	The creation of a widget so that it is seen on the display. Note that some widgets (meta class, for example) cannot be instantiated.

widget tree

A widget tree is a hierarchy of widgets within a specific program. Examples of widget trees can be found in Chapter 3. The shell widget is the root of the widget tree. Widgets with no children of any kind are leaves of the tree.

window

A data structure that represents all or part of the CRT display screen. Visually, a window is represented as a rectangular subset of the display screen.

window decoration

The frame and window control buttons that surround windows managed by the a window manager such as the OSF/Motif Window Manager.

window frame

The area surrounding a window. A window frame can consist of resize frame handles, a window menu button, a title bar, and window control buttons.

window manager

A program that controls the size, placement, and operation of windows on the workspace. The window manager includes the functional window frames that surround each window object and may include a separate menu for the workspace.

window menu

The menu that appears when the window menu button is pressed. The window menu typically contains selections for restoring, moving, sizing, minimizing, maximizing, and closing the window.

window menu button

The graphic control button that appears at the left side of the title bar in the window frame.

workspace

The CRT screen. The area on which the windows of a user's environment display. The workspace is sometimes called the "desk," "desktop," or "root window."

workspace menu

An optional pop-up menu associated with the workspace.

Index

B

C

D

Data type conversion, 18-47, 18-48

Data type
conversions, 18-46

Declaring objects in UIL
using as template, 22-46

decoration
icons, 15-8

decorations field
WM_HINTS, 12-14

default behavior
modifying, 11-4

default window menu
configuration file, 14-4

default
keyboard bindings, 14-24
mouse button bindings, 14-18

Default, dynamic, 8-49

Defaulting, dynamic, 8-1

Defaults file
example, 3-22
XMdemos, 3-6

Defaults files, 3-19
.Xdefaults, 3-20
application, 3-20
app-defaults, 3-20
create, 3-2
localization, 8-2, 8-49
user, 3-21
Xdefaults, 3-21

deiconifyKeyFocus resource, 13-10,
16-8

Diagnostic messages, D-1

Dialog convenience functions, 5-3

Dialog convenience functions, using,
5-5

Dialog functions, 5-1

Dialog widgets, 1-7, 2-21, 5-1

dialog, GL-5

Dialog
widgets, 2-3

Dialog, definition, 2-22

Dialogs, using, 5-5

DialogShell, 2-5, 4-3

Direction, compound string, 8-3, 8-5

display option, 13-2

Display widgets, 2-3, 2-6

Double click, 7-7

doubleClickTime resource, 14-24,
16-9

DrawingArea, 2-13

DrawnButton, 2-7

Dynamic resource defaulting, 8-1,
8-49

E

Efficient operation, 3-20

enableWarp resource, 13-32

enforceKeyFocus resource, 13-10,
16-8

M

N

O

P

Q

R

S

V

X

OPEN SOFTWARE FOUNDATION

INFORMATION REQUEST FORM

Please send me the following:

( )   OSF Membership Information

( )   OSF/Motif™ License Materials

( )   OSF/Motif™ Training Information

Contact Name   _____

Company Name   _____

Street Address   _____

Mail Stop   _____

City   _____ State _____ Zip _____

Phone   _____ FAX _____

Electronic Mail   _____

MAIL TO:

Open Software Foundation
11 Cambridge Center
Cambridge, MA 02142

Attn: OSF/Motif™

For more information about OSF/Motif™, call 617-621-8755.